The Meaning of Life Great Philosophers

The Meaning of Life and the Great Philosophers reveals how great philosophers of the past sought to answer the question of the meaning of life. This edited collection includes thirty-five chapters which each focus on a major philosophical figure, from Confucius to Rorty, and that imaginatively engage with the topic from their perspective. This volume also contains a Postscript on the historical origins and original significance of the phrase 'the meaning of life'.

Written by leading experts in the field, such as A.C. Grayling, Thaddeus Metz and John Cottingham, this unique and engaging book explores the relevance of the history of philosophy to contemporary debates. It will prove essential reading for students and scholars studying the history of philosophy, philosophy of religion, ethics, metaphysics or comparative philosophy.

Stephen Leach is Honorary Senior Fellow at Keele University, UK. He is the author of *The Foundations of History: Collingwood's Analysis of Historical Explanation* (2009).

James Tartaglia is Professor of Metaphysical Philosophy at Keele University, UK. He is the author of *Philosophy in a Meaningless Life* (2016).

The Meaning of Life and the Great Philosophers

Edited by Stephen Leach and James Tartaglia

Routledge
Taylor & Francis Group

LONDON AND NEW YORK

First published 2018
by Routledge
2 Park Square, Milton Park, Abingdon, Oxon OX14 4RN

and by Routledge
711 Third Avenue, New York, NY 10017

Routledge is an imprint of the Taylor & Francis Group, an informa business

British Library Cataloguing in Publication Data
A catalogue record for this book is available from the British Library

Library of Congress Cataloging in Publication Data
Names: Leach, Stephen D., editor.
Title: The meaning of life and the great philosophers / edited by Stephen Leach and James Tartaglia.
Description: 1 [edition]. | New York : Routledge, 2018. | Includes bibliographical references and index.
Identifiers: LCCN 2017060531 | ISBN 9781138220935 (hardback : alk. paper) | ISBN 9781138220959 (pbk. : alk. paper) | ISBN 9781315385945 (ebook)
Subjects: LCSH: Life. | Meaning (Philosophy) | Philosophers.
Classification: LCC BD431 .M46884 2018 | DDC 128--dc23
LC record available at https://lccn.loc.gov/2017060531

ISBN: 978-1-138-22093-5 (hbk)
ISBN: 978-1-138-22095-9 (pbk)
ISBN: 978-1-315-38594-5 (ebk)

Typeset in Times New Roman
by Taylor & Francis Books

Contents

Contributors

Raymond Angelo Belliotti, Distinguished Teaching Professor at the State University of New York at Fredonia, USA

Mark Bernier, Visiting Assistant Professor at Azusa Pacific University, Research Fellow at the University of Notre Dame, USA

Joseph S. Catalano, Professor Emeritus, Kean University of New Jersey, USA

Arindam Chakrabarti, Lenney Distinguished Professor, University of Hawai'i at Manoa, USA

Bridget Clarke, Professor of Philosophy, University of Montana, USA

David E. Cooper, Emeritus Professor of Philosophy, Durham University, UK

John Cottingham, Professor Emeritus of Philosophy, University of Reading, UK, Professorial Research Fellow, Heythrop College, University of London, UK, Honorary Fellow, St John's College, University of Oxford, UK

Will Desmond, Lecturer, Department of Ancient Classics, Maynooth University, Ireland

Nader El-Bizri, Associate Professor of Philosophy and Director of the Civilization Studies Program, American University of Beirut, Lebanon

Edward Feser, Associate Professor of Philosophy, Pasadena City College, USA

Terry F. Godlove, Professor of Philosophy, Hofstra University, New York, USA

Pedro Blas González, Professor of Philosophy, Barry University, USA

A.C. Grayling, Master of New College of the Humanities, London, UK, Supernumerary Fellow of St Anne's College, University of Oxford, UK

Reza Hosseini, Research Fellow at Stellenbosch University, South Africa

Samuel Imbo, Professor of Philosophy, Hamline University, USA

Alfred L. Ivry, Professor Emeritus of Jewish and Islamic Philosophy, New York University, USA

Monte Ransome Johnson, Associate Professor of Philosophy, University of California, San Diego, USA

Richard Kim, Postdoctoral Fellow, Saint Louis University, USA

Stephen Leach, Honorary Senior Fellow, Keele University, UK

Genevieve Lloyd, Emeritus Professor of Philosophy, University of New South Wales, Australia

A.A. Long, Professor of Classics, Professor Emeritus of Literature, Affiliated Professor of Philosophy and Rhetoric, University of California, Berkeley, USA

William McBride, Arthur G. Hansen Distinguished Professor of Philosophy, Purdue University, USA

Lissa McCullough, Adjunct Professor of Philosophy, California State University, Dominguez Hills, USA

Alan Malachowski, Research Fellow of the Centre of Applied Ethics, Stellenbosch University, South Africa

Thaddeus Metz, Distinguished Professor of Philosophy, University of Johannesburg, South Africa

Wendell O'Brien, Emeritus Professor of Philosophy, Moreland State University, USA

Joshua W. Seachris, Adjunct Professor of Philosophy, University of Notre Dame, USA

Mark Siderits, Emeritus Professor of Philosophy, Illinois State University, USA

David Skrbina, Lecturer in Philosophy, University of Michigan-Dearborn, USA

Svavar Hrafn Svavarsson, Associate Professor, University of Iceland

Frans Svensson, Senior Lecturer, Umeå University, Sweden

James Tartaglia, Professor of Metaphysical Philosophy, Keele University, UK

Jonathan Webber, Professor of Philosophy, Cardiff University, UK, Visiting Fellow at the University of Bristol, UK

Amy E. Wendling, Professor of Philosophy, Creighton University, USA

Robert Wicks, Associate Professor of Philosophy, University of Auckland, New Zealand

Catherine Wilson, Anniversary Professor of Philosophy, University of York, UK

Preface

What is the meaning of life? A great many people ask that question at some point during their lives. By visiting the website ExcellenceReporter.com, you can discover what over 800 thoughtful individuals, from all walks of contemporary life, think the meaning of life is. But although many different kinds of people are interested, and may bring valuable insights to the matter, if there is one particular walk of life from which you would expect to hear some especially strong answers, it is philosophy. It is a philosophical question, after all, so if there is any point to having philosophical traditions in our world, it is surely to shed light on questions like this.

There are some people, however, who are suspicious both of the question, and of philosophy's ability to address it. There are hard-core scientific rationalists who think the best answers always have to be scientific, and there are hard-line religious thinkers who want faith to override this kind of philosophical questioning. But they must realize that in expressing such views, they are entering into core philosophical territory. To persuade us that the question is not legitimate, they would have to engage in philosophical reasoning more compelling than all the reasoning which has been invested in the question throughout the history of philosophy; reasoning which makes it seem very much as if the question is a perfectly reasonable one to ask – a question to which many sensible answers can be provided, even if they are sometimes rather speculative. With it being the most iconic of all philosophical questions, and with so many of the acknowledged greats having said ingenious things about it, it would be surprising indeed if it were not a genuine question, indicative of genuine issues. And with so many people still asking the question, and philosophy the obvious place to turn for answers, those answers must surely be a great source of potential for developing interest in philosophy.

There is still a job to be done, however, in isolating the answers the great philosophers gave, given that very few of them told us anything remotely in the ballpark of: 'I think the meaning of life is so and so.' The actual phrase 'the meaning of life' – the origin of which is the topic of our Postscript, 'The Blue Flower' – only acquired widespread currency during the nineteenth century. Long before it caught on, however, the issues 'meaning of life' now readily indicates to us were most certainly being discussed. What is problematic in trying to encapsulate the highlights of this discussion is that even after the standard label was culturally embedded, the issues it indicates were typically discussed amid so many other concerns, and under such a wide range of different terminologies, that it can sometimes be far from obvious what a particular philosopher's views in the area amount to. Even Heidegger, who arguably did more than anyone else to place the topic firmly on the map of twentieth-century philosophy, chose to address 'the meaning of Being' rather than 'the meaning of life'; and he certainly made no clear and succinct statements about what he thought the meaning of Being was.

The task of compiling and consolidating the history of philosophy's wealth of opinion on the meaning of life was delayed in the twentieth century by the rise of hard-core scientific rationalism within Anglophone philosophy. Since the topic seemed paradigmatically unscientific to the logical positivists, as well to those who fell under their widespread influence, it began to be shunned. But as seems to be known to everyone else apart from hard-core scientific rationalists, science cannot answer every question that interests us. There are questions we can ask about our existence – such as about the meaning of life – which science is simply ill-equipped to address. The same could be said about innumerable other questions that may concern us throughout our lives, such as those about our personal relationships or careers; about how the next waves of technological innovation will affect us; about the status of science within human understanding; or about the fact that there is a reality at all.

Anyone can ask philosophical questions, of course, and some may be able to bring scientific knowledge usefully to bear on them; but they are still philo-sophical questions whoever is asking or trying to address them – 'philosophical' is just the label that has been given to questions such as that of the meaning of life. Hard-core scientific rationalism might lead you to think the questions must be spurious if they cannot be addressed by science; or that if any legitimate issues are indicated by such questions, then they must be ones which science can indeed address. But since hard-core scientific rationalism itself rests on contentious philosophy, we need not allow it to deflect us from taking an interest in the meaning of life. Concerns about the legitimacy of the question need only be addressed if the philosophy behind the concerns is good enough. So unless it obviously is good enough – which is not how it seems to us – these concerns need not be a priority. The fact that there is scepticism about climate science does not mean that those interested in what the science has to say must first address the scepticism. For we might be prepared to assume that the science is good; and likewise, in the case of the meaning of life, we might be prepared to assume that the philosophy is good.

As the twentieth century wore on, and the heyday of positivism became an increasingly distant memory, a growing trickle of Anglophone philosophers became prepared to work on the assumption that there are, at the very least, good philosophical questions in the area. In time, the meaning of life started to look prime for a comeback; which only actually occurred during the last two decades, thanks primarily to the pioneering work of Susan Wolf and Thaddeus Metz – by actively embracing the phrase, 'the meaning of life', they ensured that their intentions could not be missed. What the new analytic debate about life's meaning has hitherto lacked, however, is some guiding history; it thereby runs the risk of imposing upon itself multiple tasks akin to reinventing the wheel. An accessible contribution to the task of historicizing the question of the meaning of life for a new generation was Julian Young's *The Death of God and the Meaning of Life*, a book which highlights how many poignant and distinctive views on the meaning of life can be found within, primarily, nineteenth- and twentieth-century Continental philosophy. This present volume follows a similar path but spreads the net wider. It contains Metz's article on Koheleth, for instance, which concerns one of the world's most influential reflections on the meaning of life: the book of Ecclesiastes in the Bible.

So our task was to find out more about what the great philosophers said on the meaning of life and to produce a book which makes it easier for others who share our interest to find out. The book is also designed to provide a platform for our authors to reveal views in the area which have been covered over or overlooked, and to scrutinize old arguments which still hold sway. To do this, we needed to choose a selection of great philosophers to be included, of course, and for practical and entirely sensible reasons, we were limited to thirty-five articles. Our selection – which was no doubt contentious enough already when we first drew up our wish list – was further limited and randomized by the fact that, almost inevitably, not everybody we invited to write an article was going to accept. Most did, but there are still many great philosophers we wish we could have included; Boethius, Pascal, Fichte, Russell, Stein and Nozick are examples that spring to mind. Nevertheless, we are pleased with the selection on offer, and – what is more significant – delighted with its quality: it seems our contributors have all enthusiastically risen to the challenge. The result, we think, is a rich and novel resource of clear and accessible statements about the views on the meaning of life held by a targeted cross-section of planet Earth's great, dead philosophers. At the very least, it is the book we wanted to read. We hope it is what you were looking for too.

1 Confucius and the meaning of life

RICHARD KIM AND JOSHUA W. SEACHRIS

Confucius

While ancient Greek philosophers were often engaged in highly theoretical and abstract pursuits such as understanding the nature of being or the metaphysical foundation of goodness, Confucius was preoccupied with the ethical transformation of people, and restoring the values that he believed were the linchpins of a healthy and well-ordered society; his teachings bear a deeply *practical orientation.*

Confucius was alarmed by what he perceived to be the moral and spiritual decline of his society. The remedy, Confucius believed, was to turn both the ruler and people back to the forgotten cultural values of the past such as filial piety and ritual propriety, and develop certain character traits such as benevolence and empathic understanding that would enable people to live well. Only once society had become recharged with these basic values would peace and good order return.

But how should we classify these concerns of Confucius? Are they prudential? Moral? Spiritual? Or, might they be better captured by the category of *meaning*? Contemporary moral philosophers often make sharp distinctions between altruistic reasons and egoistic reasons: between reasons and motives of self-interest or personal well-being, and reasons and motives of morality or other-regard. While Confucius does distinguish material goods or narrow self-interest, and moral goods that center on following the Way, nowhere in the text does he explicitly distinguish between self-interest and morality, in the sense that one's own flourishing is pitted against moral goodness. Since Confucius's discussions do not neatly proceed through these familiar categories of altruism, egoism, well-being, and morality, it might be helpful to think of Confucius as providing a picture, and a general curriculum, of how to live a meaningful life. There are a number of reasons that support this way of think about Confucius's project. First, Confucius says much about how one's life should be ordered around particular ends, and how there are priorities among them. (*Analects* 4.5)[1] Second, Confucius often discusses how certain activities and goods are more or less noble or base, and seeks to push his students toward the kind of life that is worthy of admiration and esteem. He discusses the kind of life that would not produce regret: "The Master said, 'Having in the morning heard that the Way was being put into practice, I could die that evening without regret'" (*Analects* 4.8). And finally, Confucius's ideals, at the substantive level, are almost always aimed at deepening one's connection to others, and embracing a wider circle of concerns that are directed outside of oneself – toward communal ritual practice or the Way.

Meaning: a prolegomenon

In order to connect core Confucian teachings to meaning, we must first briefly survey the conceptual space associated with this tricky yet important concept. It was not too long ago that analytic philosophers were suspicious of talk of life's meaning.[2] Words and other semantic constructions are the proper bearers of meaning, not objects, events, or states of affairs, and certainly not *life* itself. To ask what the meaning of life is might then be akin to asking "What does the color red taste like?" or "What is smaller than the smallest of all objects?"[3] Such worries were largely misguided. "Meaning" has important semantic shades that include and yet move well beyond narrowly linguistic contexts. Though the numerous connotations of "meaning" can seem a bit unwieldy, collectively they provide important clues as to the kinds of issues we have in mind when life's meaning is in view. We can group ordinary uses of "meaning" relevant to life's meaning into a triad of general categories: Intelligibility-Meaning, Purpose-Meaning, and Significance-Meaning.

Intelligibility-Meaning.

- What you said didn't *mean* a thing.
- What did you *mean* by that statement?
- What did you *mean* by that face?
- What is the *meaning* of this? (For example, when asked upon coming home to find one's house plundered.)

Purpose-Meaning.

- What did you *mean* by that face?[4]
- The tantrum is *meant* to catch his dad's attention.
- I really *mean* it!
- I didn't *mean* to do it. I didn't do it on purpose, I promise![5]

Significance-Meaning.

- That was such a *meaningful* conversation.
- This watch really *means* something to me.
- You *mean* nothing to me.
- That is a *meaningful* finding.

Using "meaning" in the above ways is natural. There is nothing infelicitous about using "meaning" to communicate any of the above ideas, many of which are distinct from (or have applications outside of) asking for the meanings of words and other semantic constructions. Our concerns over meaning *in* life (anthropocentrically focused) or the meaning *of* life (cosmically focused) largely center on this triad of *intelligibility, purpose,* and *significance.* We want to make sense of life, especially its existentially weighty aspects, we want purpose (s) around which to orient our lives, and we want our lives to be significant, to truly matter. Meaningful life makes sense; it fits together properly. Meaningful life is sufficiently ordered around goals; it is lived on purpose. Meaningful life is significant; it matters and makes a difference from some relevant perspective and set of norms. The various normative theories of meaning in life that we discuss immediately below are in conflict about how best to make sense of our lives, about the kinds of purposes there are and around which we should order our lives, and what gives significance to our lives. Despite this disagreement, however, such theories of meaning are *about* this triad of ideas.

In focusing on the more anthropocentric notion of meaning – meaning *in* life – it is generally thought that meaning or meaningfulness is a good-making feature that one's life can possess in addition to, for example, moral goodness and subjective well-being. Perhaps being moral and happy are not sufficient for the good life; maybe we need to lead lives of meaning too. Theories of meaning aim to understand this feature, and fall within a now fairly well-developed taxonomy of objectivist naturalist, subjectivist naturalist, hybrid naturalist, and supernaturalist theories.

Objectivist naturalism claims that neither God nor any supernatural entity nor some overarching meaning *of* life is necessary for meaningful life. On this view, meaning results from appropriately connecting to objectively valuable or worthwhile sources whose value is independent of what one thinks and feels. One can be wrong about whether one is leading a meaningful life on objectivist views. Watching re-runs of your favorite sitcom for most of your waking hours, no matter how enjoyable, does not count as meaningful on this view. Furthermore, one need not enjoy what she is doing in order to accrue meaning. As long as one is appropriately related to objective value (for example, causally responsible for good impacts in the world), one has led a meaningful life.

Like objectivist naturalism, subjectivist naturalism claims that meaningful life is possible in a world devoid of the supernatural or any overarching meaning *of* life. However, subjectivism views meaningful life in terms of getting what one strongly wants, achieving self-established goals, or accomplishing what one believes to be important. Meaningful life, for the subjectivist, primarily is about how *you feel* about and respond to your life.

Hybrid naturalism is, to put it simply, something of a cross between objectivist and subjectivist views. As memorably put by Susan Wolf: "Meaning arises when subjective attraction meets objective attractiveness" (Wolf 1997a: 211). In order to lead a meaningful life, one has to successfully participate in *and* be satisfied by the right sorts of activities. One cannot lead a meaningful life if one largely cares about worthless projects and pursuits. Nor can one lead a meaningful life if one does not care about worthwhile, objectively valuable projects and pursuits. Neither the satisfied couch potato nor the unfulfilled philanthropist leads a meaningful life – one is fulfilled by the wrong stuff, the other is not fulfilled by the right stuff even though he or she does the right stuff.

In contrast to all naturalistic theories of meaning, supernaturalism sees God's existence, along with appropriately orienting one's life around God, as necessary and sufficient for meaningful life. Supernaturalism's meaning requirements are generally threefold: God must exist (metaphysical), one must believe in God in some relevant sense (epistemic), and, finally, one must properly orient one's life around God (ethical/practical). Much debate, of course, exists over the precise details, as it does with any of these general theories of meaning. For some objective naturalists, for example, the kinds of objective value that are emphasized are creative accomplishments of great worth, for others, family relationships are more important.

How might Confucius's views fit within the meaning triad (intelligibility, purpose, significance) and within the various theories of meaning? Attempting to answer this question raises the danger of anachronistically attributing ideas to an ancient Chinese philosopher that would have been alien to him. Nowhere in the *Analects* do we find Confucius attempting to offer anything like a *theory* of meaning (or happiness and morality for that matter). As we clarify below, what Confucius offers is a picture of human lives going well or badly, and substantive discussions about what matters in life.

In terms of theories of meaning, a case could be made that Confucius's discussion has relevant points of connection with objectivist and, especially, hybrid naturalist views. He clearly distinguishes between *petty* and *noble* lives, while at the same time constructing a picture of the ideal life as one that is internally fulfilling: "What a worthy man was Yan Hui! Living in a narrow alley, subsisting on a basket of grain and gourd full of water – other people could not have borne hardship, yet it never spoiled Hui's joy" (*Analects* 6.11). His views on family and ritual that we explore below reveal important points of contact between his thought and contemporary theories about what makes life meaningful (see e.g. Levy 2005; Metz 2012: esp. ch. 12; Thomas 2005; Velleman 2005).

The core teachings of Confucius

Confucius's teachings can contribute to the discussion about meaningful lives, especially with regard to the kinds of practices and values that can contribute to life's meaning. Though not a theoretician, he was a wise and keen observer of human life, seeking after what really matters and understanding that not all ends carry the same value: "The gentleman cherishes virtue, whereas the petty person cherishes physical possessions" (*Analects* 4.11). Accordingly, we will focus on the substantive proposals, those practices and values that Confucius sees as critical for meaningful lives, more specifically ritual and family. Neither ritual nor family are objects of intense scrutiny within contemporary Western analytic philosophy, and for this reason alone, Confucius – whether one ultimately agrees with him or not – has a contribution to make to our understanding of meaning in life, directing us toward neglected values that deserve more careful study. It is worth noting how contemporary philosophical discussions on meaning in life often focus on either highly intellectual pursuits (mathematical, scientific, musical, artistic) or grand projects (curing cancer, eradicating famine). There is a tendency to focus on figures that exemplify such values to a high degree: Mozart, Michaelangelo, Schweitzer, or Mother Teresa. But most people do not have lives that center on such extraordinary accomplishments. Most human lives are built around relatively mundane experiences and activities such as simple enjoyments, connections to their neighbors, and the raising of children. Discussion of topics such as life's meaning should draw on values and experiences that touch the lives of people in the broadest way possible. Here reflecting on Confucius's thoughts, which exerted an enormous influence on the cultures of Eastern civilization for over two millennia, can help us stay grounded in matters that lie close to the heart of most people.

Rituals

Benjamin Schwartz defines ritual as, "all those 'objective' prescriptions of behavior, whether involving rite, ceremony, manners, or general deportment, that bind human beings and spirits together in networks of interacting roles within the family, within human society, and with the numinous realm beyond" (Schwartz 1985: 67). As a fundamental aspect of Confucius's teachings, rituals provide, to use Chengyang Li's phrase, the "cultural grammar" for navigating the social world. Just as a presupposed grammatical structure allows English speakers to make sense of one another's speech, rituals provide basic structure and patterns of behavior and response. Consider a world without any norms about how far apart one should stand with strangers in a line, the kinds of bodily gestures that are appropriate, or words that are considered offensive. Without such norms and protocols, social life would disintegrate. Given that the expression and development of our sociality and our shared life in the public square are significant sources of meaning for our lives, rituals play an important role in establishing the conditions for obtaining meaning through social intercourse.

Relatedly, rituals can contribute to meaning by transforming fundamental human experiences in ways that bind members of a community. Think about ceremonial rituals, such as the college graduation ceremony. Graduation ceremonies mark out an important event in one's life, drawing attention to the hard work, dedication, and sacrifice of students, parents, and families. It also helps us to gratefully acknowledge the support one has received from others, and allots a proper time and place to express such affections through joyful celebration. When the ceremonial ritual goes well, it provides a deeply enriching experience that strengthens close relationships and provides an impetus for students to move forward with their lives.

Another example, much attended to by Confucians, is the funeral ritual. Like the graduation ceremony, which helps find proper expression of certain basic emotions such as gratitude and pride, the funeral ritual enables the proper expression of the powerful and fundamental human emotion of grief. Xunzi (one of the earliest and most prominent followers of Confucius), explains the role and significance of funerals:

> What is the reason for the three-year mourning period? I say: it takes measure of people's dispositions and establishes a proper form for them. It accordingly ornaments the various groups of people, distinguishing different regulations for close and distant relatives and for the noble and the lowly, such that one can neither add to nor subtract from it. Thus I say: It is a method that is to be neither adapted nor changed. When a wound is great, it lasts for many days. When hurt is deep, the recovery is slow. The three-year mourning period takes measure of people's dispositions and establishes a proper form for them. It is the means by which one sets a limit for the utmost hurt.
>
> (Xunzi third century BCE: 213)

Through the powers of tradition and culture, rituals help give shape to, and express, certain basic dispositions such as joy and sorrow, transforming them into profound human experiences. These powerful experiences stretch our emotional capacities and help us to feel deeply human, often reminding ourselves what matters most to us. While we should not discount the way that small events and interactions also contribute to meaningful lives, we should also acknowledge how special occasions such as graduations, funerals, or weddings occupy a unique place in our hearts, often constituting the richest experiences we obtain in the course of our lives.

Family

The focus on the value of family, with a spotlight on the virtue of filial piety (*xiao*), is one of the core elements of Confucianism. Not all, however, see this in a positive light. Bertrand Russell remarks, "Filial piety, and the strength of the family generally, are perhaps the weakest points in Confucian ethics, the only point where the system departs seriously from common sense" (Russell 1922: 40). On the other hand, the concept of family is one of those rare ideas that transcend culture and time, and studies in empirical psychology in the past century have only vindicated the enormous impact that parents and caretakers have on children.[6] Anybody who has taken care of infants and young children can testify to how much care and attention is needed to ensure not just their basic survival but also their social and emotional growth. Within the Confucian tradition, the emphasis has been on the filial duties of children toward parents captured by the virtue of filial piety (*xiao*) that determines certain standards of thought and behavior. (Mengzi fourth–third centuries BCE: 4A 19.1) For Confucius, the values and character that initially arise within the context of family through the teachings of parents play a foundational role in our development as moral agents. The development and exercise of one's natural love for parents is, Confucius believed, the basis for other moral virtues: "The gentleman applies himself to the roots. 'Once the roots are firmly established, the Way will grow.' Might we not say that filial piety and respect for elders constitute the root of Goodness?" (*Analects* 1.2) These reflections suggest that families play a crucial role in how we come to think of meaningfulness in life – the kinds of activities, commitments, and goods that matter to us.

But besides the epistemological effects on how we come to think of meaning, can family itself also serve as a significant source of meaning? For most people, family ties stand as the most intimate and enduring of all human relationships. How one conceives of the value of family will of course also depend on the particular perspective one brings as a member. The way that parents, children, siblings, grandparents, aunts, and uncles think of each other, their unique role and purpose within that family, will all vary quite widely and in significant ways. Here let us focus on just one perspective to get a sense of how one's connection to a family might contribute to the meaningfulness of her or his life – that of parents. Seeing the birth of one's child, hearing their first cry, and seeing their first steps, are undoubtedly sources of profound joy and meaning. Parents are also deeply invested in the raising of their children, working hard to ensure that they become healthy, productive, and morally good adults who can lead rich and happy lives. The project of parenting itself, upon which human civilization and culture hinges, is an important source of meaning and purpose.

Another concept we might draw on, discussed among contemporary philosophers, is narrativity. One difficulty we grapple with in our lives is our mortality. Giving birth to and rearing children offer a way of "continuing on" in some sense, of seeing one's heritage and values extend beyond one's own life.[7] Children provide parents with a link to the future, even though it will be a future in which one is non-existent, and in this way they both lengthen and thicken the parent's narrative arc. They thicken it by becoming a witness to new human life, sharing in the children's discoveries, joys, and pain. Think of all the stories parents tell about their children at every stage (sometimes to the annoyance of others). Such stories reveal the way that the lives of the children become entangled with the parents' own lives in deep and intimate ways. And by becoming intertwined, the life stories of parents are extended through the lives of the children. In the stories adult children tell about their parents, and the culture and traditions they carry forward in their lives, they help sustain a bridge between the past and present.

Returning briefly to the three broad categories of meaning (intelligibility, purpose, significance) it appears that both ritual and family provide different ways of expressing all three kinds of meaning. Rituals, for example, help our behaviors and speech make sense to others (Intelligibility-Meaning), allowing us to intentionally express certain basic emotions such as gratitude and grief (Purpose-Meaning), and help mark out certain events such as death as carrying special importance (Significance-Meaning). Families seem especially hospitable for generating purpose and significance in our lives. Recent empirical studies indicate that while parents have less pleasure and subjective happiness than those without children, they do gain a greater sense of purpose (see White and Dolan 2009). Moreover, parenting gives rise to certain events that are inherently profound or significant, such as the birth of one's child.

What both rituals and families have in common when reflecting on them from the perspective of meaningfulness in human life is the way that they help build, strengthen, and sustain human relationships and communities. The fact that human beings are hyper-social beings, while seemingly obvious, is deeply important. The idea that we build meaning into our lives by "moving outside of ourselves" and sharing our lives with others expresses this fundamental point. Jonathan Haidt comments:

> One of the great challenges of modernity is that we must now find hives for ourselves. We can't create them on our own any more than we can create a language on our own. But the view from positive psychology is that we can find meaning in life if we take advantage of our capacity for vital engagement and bind ourselves to projects and people. We can co-create, or join into, something larger than ourselves. We can join others in pursuit of common goals, nested in shared traditions and common values.
>
> (Haidt 2010: 100–1)

The Confucian framework of ritual and family can be understood as a way of creating a healthy hive for ultra-social creatures like ourselves. First, we must form healthy families that are anchored in mutual affection and care between children and parents. Second, we must participate in rituals that allow us to collectively express those deep-seated emotions of joy and grief, as well as establish social norms that regulate our behaviors. Whatever one thinks of the particular ideas about rituals and family Confucius advocates, there is much truth in the general Confucian attitude that meaningful lives do not arise in a vacuum. Rather, they are cultivated in families, culture, and tradition, all of which allow us to develop and express basic inclinations and emotions that are central to our humanity. Familial relationships are plausible candidates for adding meaning in life in subjective, objective, and especially hybrid senses given Confucius's claim that ideal lives should be internally fulfilling. For Confucius and his followers, rituals also carried spiritual significance, revealing the sacredness of reality, especially within human relationships. In this way, rituals may also add religious meaning to one's life. Though Confucius did not make explicit use of categories like objective, subjective, hybrid, and supernaturalist meaning, his teachings on family and ritual can point to neglected sources of meaningfulness that may have important implications for each of these contemporary theories.[8]

Notes

1 Sixth to fifth centuries BCE.
2 The relative silence of the analytic tradition has not been as characteristic of the continental tradition.
3 Suspicion is also the result of debatable metaphysical assumptions that often accompany questions about life's meaning insofar as a meaning of life would likely require the existence of God or some sort of transcendent realm.
4 Some instances of meaning can fall into more than one category.
5 One might draw a further distinction within the Purpose-Meaning category to include something like Intention-Meaning. A life with Intention-Meaning is one in which the agent sufficiently intends salient portions of her life as opposed to being forced against her will or living life haphazardly. She really *means* to do the things she does.
6 For example, John Bowlby's highly influential 'attachment theory' – which enjoys great empirical support – demonstrates the significance of caretakers for the proper development of children.
7 This is not to say that there aren't other ways of "continuing on," for example, through teaching or building organizations that will endure beyond one's life.
8 We thank Anne Baril and Micah Lott for their helpful feedback.

2 The Buddha and the meaning of life

MARK SIDERITS

As far as we can tell from the available sources, the Buddha (flourished fifth century BCE) never explicitly addressed the question of the meaning of life, so what follows must be somewhat speculative. There is, however, ample evidence in his discourses that his teachings are meant to address the problem of existential suffering – the fact that realization of our mortality can induce feelings of alienation and despair, or the sense that life is somehow 'absurd'. If this is indeed what the Buddha's proposed path to the cessation of suffering (*nirvāna*) is intended to resolve, then a case can be made that his teachings do respond to this question. Other readings of his project are, of course, possible. Here I try to make a case for the reading that privileges existential suffering as his intended target. Such an interpretation leads to the interesting result that the Buddha's response to the question of the meaning of life is to dissolve its presupposition: one overcomes the problem of suffering by realizing that there is no 'I' for whom the question of the meaning of life can arise.

Mortality, meaning and rebirth

If the question of the meaning of life were no more than a question about what one's chief aim in life should be, then the Buddha could be said to propose an answer to the question. Nor was he the only classical Indian philosopher to do so. Most of the major Indian systems are built around the claim that what one should aim at in life is liberation from the round of rebirth. At about the same time that the karma–rebirth ideological complex gained acceptance in Indian thought, this ideal of liberation was added to an existing list of three more prosaic aims or goals (*artha*) in life: sensual pleasure, wealth and power, and virtue and repute. While there seems to have been no ranking in the original list, those who propounded the new goal of liberation held it to be the only goal worth striving for. Their thinking was grounded in an understanding of how karma is thought to work. The basic idea of karma is that every intentional action causes the later occurrence of a pleasant, painful or neutral result for the agent, the valence of this result being determined by the ethical character of the intention. Since karmic results have not all come to fruition at death, one will be reborn – in circumstances that assure the hedonic character appropriate for that agent. As for why one should want to bring this cycle of rebirth (*saṃsāra*) to an end, the usual answer is that actions fueled by mistaken views about one's true nature – such as that one is the sort of thing that will be made better off by states of sensual pleasure, or by having wealth and power – cannot bring about genuine well-being. Here the echoes of Aristotle's views on *eudaimonia* are obvious: one achieves true well-being by having as one's aim only those actions that manifest and develop one's true nature. For these Indian theorists, bondage to the cycle of rebirth is a sign that one has not yet realized who one really is.

The Buddha does not subscribe to this account of the value of liberation: it is not compatible with the key Buddhist doctrine of non-self (*anātman*). Indeed the term *ātman* can mean 'self' or, more broadly, 'essence'; the doctrine of non-self is precisely the claim that there is no such thing as the essence of the person. There is, then, no scope in the Buddhist project for the *eudaimonistic* package at work in other Indian liberation soteriologies. Why, then, would the Buddha hold that escape from *saṃsāra* is the ideal state? The answer, in a word, is suffering. The Buddha claims that sentient existence as ordinarily lived (i.e. under conditions of ignorance concerning the nature of reality) is predominantly suffering. If we also believe that there is rebirth, then since the beginning of the series of lives leading up to this life cannot be discerned, one has already undergone an unimaginably vast amount of suffering, and unless steps are taken, this series might continue indefinitely.

Now even if one were to accept the rebirth hypothesis, it still seems possible that happiness might outweigh suffering in a given series. Particularly if one knew the karmic causal laws, it seems that one might arrange things so that suffering did not predominate in particular lives in the series. Later in the Buddhist tradition we find attempts to respond to this question by arguing that all experiences – including those we would ordinarily classify as pleasant – are inevitably marked by suffering. But these attempts come later. In the Buddha's discourses themselves we find something else: a focus on mortality as a source of suffering. This is clearly evident in the tale of a former buddha, Vipassī, at whose birth a soothsayer predicts that he will become either a universal monarch or else an ascetic who discovers and teaches the path to the cessation of suffering (*Dīgha Nikāya*, trans. Walshe 1995: 14). Vipassī's father installs him in luxurious surroundings in order to assure the first outcome. But on four successive days the young prince sees, for the first time, an old person, a sick person, a corpse, and then a renunciant. He abandons the life of a householder and begins the search for the end of suffering. The trio of old age, sickness and death then becomes emblematic of the suffering that the Buddha's teachings are meant to cure.[1]

That mortality plays a prominent role in the suffering targeted by the Buddha also comes out in a discourse where the Buddha singles out the experience of observing great pain and death of others as the goad that reliably initiates renunciation of the householder's life (*Aṅguttara Nikāya*, trans.

Bodhi and Nyanaponika Thera 2000: 4.113). There is likewise much on cultivating mindfulness of death as a crucial part of the path to the cessation of suffering (e.g. ibid.: 6.19–20). The Buddha's core teaching of the Four Noble Truths is also said to inspire fear in the gods who hear it (ibid.: 4.33). Their anxiety apparently stems from its making them realize that they are not, after all, immortal.[2] And we find a rather plaintive hint as to why this might be in the *Raṭṭhapāla Sutta*. There a king explains why he might renounce his station in order to seek *nirvāna*: "These five superior pleasures that I presently enjoy will, once I go where my karma dictates, be taken for enjoyment by others" (*Majjhima Nikāya*, trans. Ñānamoli and Bodhi 1995: 82). This realization of the consequences of mortality – that what one now sees as having significance for one's life will continue to be available to others when one is no longer there to enjoy it – often fuels the desire for immortality. If, however, one (like the king) believes in rebirth, the series of lives may be extended indefinitely – provided one does not attain *nirvāna*. So there must be more going on here than just the sense that the party will go on without me. Since I shall be able to attend other parties elsewhere, what is special about death when rebirth is part of the picture?

Narrativity and suffering

I would suggest that what is missing from our account so far is the fact that the life of a person is thought of as a happiness-seeking project. Persons have the capacities of self-monitoring, self-control and self-revision. Given the cognitive limitations of the sorts of systems persons are, it turns out that these capacities are best exercised when the system comes to see itself as the owner and controller of a body and brain, and of the life that it lives. And for such a system to see itself as the owner of a life is to see that life as a self-authored narrative. To see a life in this way is to see the events that make it up as contributing to a narrative arc. Happiness is to be distinguished from mere pleasure precisely on the grounds that it always involves an element of assessment: one is made happy by events that are seen to say good things about who one is and where one is going. To see one's life as a self-authored narrative is to adopt a stance according to which a life "can only ever be fully understood and evaluated retrospectively, reflecting on what has happened before; in light of a prospective outlook of what is yet to happen; and by constantly juggling the parts to ensure that all this aligns with what is happening now" (Wagner forthcoming: 3). Now given the way that rebirth is thought to work, the prospect of a future life does not mitigate the sting of death. For while the succeeding life represents the working out of the karmic consequences of things done in this life, it cannot be seen as the continuation of the narrative one takes oneself to be authoring in living this life. Not only is there no guarantee that one will be reborn as a human, there is ordinarily no continuity of memory.[3] While the circumstances of the future life are determined in part by actions performed in this life, there will in that life be no capacity to see those actions as meaningful by virtue of their having set the stage for one's present situation. The possibility of rebirth does not change the way that our mortality undermines the happiness-seeking project.

Indeed this project might be seen as a sort of hedonic Ponzi scheme. Financial Ponzi schemes are built on the assumption that the pool of potential investors is infinite. They inevitably collapse because that assumption is false. The happiness-seeking project is similarly built on the assumption that the story that is my life may be prolonged indefinitely. Even if my death were followed by rebirth and not merely annihilation, the fact that I can foresee a time when none of the events in my life to date can be invested with meaning, by way of their contribution to the story of the living of this life, casts doubt on the meaning-investing project as a whole. So the Buddhist who accepts rebirth can join Steven Luper-Foy in saying that in order to achieve a life that is immune from existential suffering, we should have to "give up all desires that give us reason to live" (Luper-Foy 1989: 252).

Now Luper-Foy is arguing against the Epicurean project, which he understands as aiming at removing the sting of death by shedding any and all desires that are not conditional on one's being alive at their fulfillment. The Buddhist could agree in rejecting such a project; this seems to be what lies behind the Buddha's rejection of the view known as 'annihilationism'.[4] Still the Buddhist holds that the existential suffering caused by the happiness-seeking project may be overcome. This is because Buddhists deny the existence of that for which events in a life may be said to have meaning. While it may be better, all things considered, that this life continue, they claim that there is no such thing as a 'me' for whom this fact could supply a "reason to live."

The Buddha describes his position as a 'middle path' between the two extremes of eternalism and annihilationism. Eternalism is the view that persons are eternal. It is usually understood to involve the existence of an eternal self that can exist apart from the psychophysical complex; on this view, liberation consists in stopping the karma-rebirth cycle so that the self may enjoy its true nature. The second view, annihilationism, holds that death is annihilation of the person. And it is difficult to see how there could be a third, 'middle' view intermediate between these two positions; even if one were to say that persons live multiple lives but then cease to exist at some particular death, this should count as just a variant on the annihilationist view. But the Buddha's middle path involves rejection of the assumption common to the two views: that there is such a thing as a person, the owner of a life that either continues or ceases at death. The purport of the doctrine of non-self is precisely that while there are those entities and events that comprise a life, there is nothing that can count as the owner of that life. There then being no 'me', the question of the meaning of my life simply cannot arise.

Persons as fictions

It is, of course, no easy task to explain how it might be true that lives are ownerless. The Buddhist strategy is two-pronged: argue that there is no such thing as the simple self demanded by eternalists; and argue that the person – understood as the whole constituted by suitably arranged psychophysical elements – is a mere conceptual construction. The standard argument for the non-existence of the self is that none of the empirically given psychophysical elements endures as long as a single lifetime,[5] and that such continuities as are commonly thought to require the positing of a self (e.g. continuity of episodic memory and of character, cross-modal synthesis of perception, and the like) can instead be explained in terms of causal connections among the psychophysical elements. The more difficult task is to defend the claim that the person is a construction and so not strictly speaking real. This is approached by supporting a general stance of mereological nihilism, which is then applied to the case of the person as a particular composite. The argument against composition is that if composite and constituents were equally real, then either the composite would be identical with its suitably arranged constituents or else it would be distinct. Identity is ruled out on the grounds that the composite has properties – such as that of being one in number – not had by the constituents. Distinctness would mean that the composite must then inhere either wholly or else only partly in each of its constituents. The first option leads to co-residence of conflicting properties, while the second leads to an infinite regress of *partly*'s. It is then said to follow that strictly speaking there is no composition.[6] Buddhists would thus agree with Parfit (1984: 223) that the person is a mere *façon de parler*.

The Buddha was well aware that the non-self view is highly counter-intuitive. The path he taught to those seeking the cessation of suffering involves a laborious practice consisting of equal parts meditation and philosophical reflection: meditation in order to uproot those mental habits that reinforce the sense of an 'I'; philosophical reflection in order to analyze mental processes observed in meditation into their ultimately impersonal constituents. When addressing lay followers unwilling to take up the strenuous practices of this path, however, his teachings are largely confined to discussions of karma and rebirth, and the moral rules thought to follow from them. Later exegetes explained this disparity as an instance of the Buddha's pedagogical skill: by inducing his lay followers to obey the moral precepts, he was helping them advance toward renunciation of the householder's life, a key step in attaining the cessation of suffering. This distinction between types of teachings led to a further distinction drawn by Buddhist philosophers between conventional truth – how things may be said to be when we use our conventional designators for composites – and ultimate truth – how things mind-independently are when described in a way that makes no concessions to our interests and cognitive limitations. This distinction allows the Buddhist to explain the strong intuitive pull of the personhood convention. While 'person' is merely an enumerative term (like 'pair', 'gross' and 'heap'), its usefulness for cognitive systems like ours has led to its playing a central role in our conceptual economy. But to point this out is to acknowledge that while our use of the personhood concept may set the stage for existential suffering, it must have its benefits as well. Persons are to be reduced, not eliminated.

This point is quite clearly made in an early post-canonical text (*Milindapañho*, trans. Rhys Davids 1965: 40) that examines what might happen if we simply stopped employing our personhood concept to conveniently designate a causal series of psychophysical elements. In that case a pregnant woman would not identify with the woman who gives birth, a young student would not identify with the educated adult they might become, a convicted criminal would not identify with the person who committed the crime. What these examples are meant to bring out is the benefits conferred – the suffering prevented – by the personhood convention. While there is, strictly speaking, no such thing as the person who first becomes pregnant and then gives birth, there is ultimately such a thing as the suffering that results from neglect of maternal and fetal health during pregnancy. Identification – the practice of seeing earlier and later stretches of a causal series of psychophysical elements as temporal parts of the present system – is a useful way to prevent such suffering. The newly pregnant woman who sees the future mother as herself is more likely to do those things that promote the welfare of future mother and infant. Likewise the young student who can see the educated and successful adult as their future self is more likely to persevere in their studies. And the convicted criminal is more likely to see their punishment as justified, and resolve to avoid future crime, if they identify with the earlier criminal act. So while our use of the personhood convention sets the stage for existential suffering, it has its plus side as well.

We clearly need some shorthand device for denoting a system of psychophysical elements if we are to deal with the vicissitudes of daily life in real time. The question whether we are to be reductionist or eliminativist about persons is the question whether or not we can improve on the performance of our personhood concept by replacing it with some other way of bundling psychophysical elements. One popular replacement proposal is that we use the personal pronouns and similar devices to refer to just those connected psychophysical elements that exist simultaneously. The point would be that then I could not identify with past and future stages of the causal series of which the present set of connected elements is one stage. This would make me immune from existential suffering. When people say that the point of the Buddha's teaching of non-self is that we should 'live in the moment', they seem to think that this sort of eliminativism is what he had in mind. The examples of the pregnant woman, the student and the convict show this interpretation is mistaken. What, though, does it mean to be instead a reductionist about persons?

To be a reductionist about things of kind K is to hold that an entity of that kind *just is* an entity or entities of some more particular kind arranged in a certain way. There is a load of mischief lurking in that *just is*: 'is' suggests identity, but 'just' suggests the lesser status of an ontological backbencher. The Buddhist doctrine of two truths suggests a way around this difficulty: relegate the reduced entity to the realm of useful conceptual constructions. In that case, since the reduced entity is something that is thought of as real only by virtue of our pretense of so treating it, the question whether it is identical with or distinct from its ultimately real reduction base does not arise. To see the person as a useful fiction is, though, to invite inquiry into the ultimate source of its usefulness. The three examples point us in the right direction. While such enduring persons as the mother-to-be, the student, and the criminal are not themselves ultimately real, the future suffering that their present actions could either cause or prevent would be ultimately real. The person-hood concept is an algorithm deployed in the interest of preventing suffering. Like all algorithms, though, it sometimes misfires where a more fine-grained analysis would not. The misfiring here is existential suffering.

Nirvāṇa and the meaning of life

It is sometimes claimed that *nirvāṇa*, the goal of Buddhist practice, is a state that transcends any possible description. This claim is based on a misreading of something the Buddha said – or rather, did not say. Buddhists distinguish between two kinds of *nirvāna* or cessation of suffering: cessation with remainder and without remainder. The 'remainder' in question is of the karmic seeds that fuel the continuation of a life. Completion of the Buddha's path means that one will not be reborn at the end of this life, but there may still be karmic residue from past actions remaining to be exhausted during this life. People were naturally curious to know about cessation without remainder: What is it like for the liberated person after they die? This question the Buddha refused to answer. His refusal is taken by some as evidence that *nirvāna* is ineffable. But his silence comes instead from the fact that the question has a false presupposition: that there is such a thing as the liberated person. Once we dispense with all talk of persons and stick to the ultimate truth, we can give a perfectly clear account of what happens at cessation without remainder: there is no successor set of psychophysical elements arranged in the way that would count as the continuation of the causal series. It would be a mistake to take this as the annihilation of the liberated person. But this is what happens.

What we should be looking at, though, is cessation *with* remainder, for this is what life without existential suffering should be like.[7] Now that we better understand the (implicit) rationale behind the personhood convention, we can see why the liberated person's life might seem deeply meaningful. Having achieved liberation, they will seek to help others attain this goal. They will thus be doing what many say we should do to take the sting out of our own mortality: embark on a project that transcends us (see e.g. Nozick 1981: 73). And the liberated person might see their own life through the lens of some such story. But if so, this would be tempered by the knowledge that any story told about the meaning of one's life is just an efficient tool for organizing action to end suffering. There being no 'I' to serve as subject of suffering, what matters is just that suffering be prevented, regardless of where and when it occurs. The fact that I cannot be around to appreciate how this story ends is neither here nor there.

Notes

1 See e.g. the formulation of dependent origination found at Paṭiccasamuppāda Sutta, *Saṃyutta Nikāya*, trans. Davids 1950–56: 12.1–2.

2 Buddhism's renowned atheism stems from its denial of an eternal creator; it does, though, acknowledge the standard Indian pantheon of powerful but still mortal deities.

3 Memory of past lives is said to be one of the special powers acquired through yogic practice.

4 *Ucchedavāda*. For discussion see *Alagaddūpmasutta* (*Milindapaṇho*, trans. Rhys Davids 1965: 22).

5 Indeed later Buddhists argue that nothing exists longer than a moment.

6 The argument is a post-canonical development. It is, however, foreshadowed by what was reportedly said by the nun Vajirā in the Buddha's presence (and so presumably with his approval). See *Milindapaṇho*, trans. Rhys Davids 1965: 28.

7 For more on how extirpating the 'I'-sense might dispel existential suffering, and what that might be like, see Strawson 2017: 81.

3   Vyāsa and the meaning of life

ARINDAM CHAKRABARTI

How we hang in there, lusting for life in the midst of meaningless suffering

Once upon a time, a certain *brāhmaṇa* (learned high-born man) lost his way in an enormous jungle teeming with wild ferocious roaring beasts. Running about in that scary wilderness, the panic-stricken person could not get away from those fierce creatures as the forest was surrounded by a net cast by a horrifying hag, and guarded by several dreadful five-hooded sky-high snakes hissing at him. Wandering, the *brāhmaṇa* fell into a hole in the ground concealed by a mesh of tough creepers and shrubs. His feet tangled in those creepers, the man hung like a jackfruit head downwards. At the bottom of the pit was a mighty serpent, and at the mouth of the pit a gigantic black elephant with six faces and twelve feet. The pachyderm gradually approached that pit covered with creepers around which buzzed swarms of virulent bees drinking honey collected in a huge hive. Repeatedly, the dangling fellow tried to lick the few drops of honey that he could get. Never satiated, he thirsted for more. Even then, he did not become indifferent to life. A number of black and white rats were eating away the roots of that tree. In spite of his mortal fear of the beasts, the fierce woman guarding the forest, that snake at the bottom of the well, that elephant near the rim of the pit, his chance of falling off the creeper being gnawed at by those rats, the threat of those venomous bees vying with him for the honey, this miserable man never lost the hope to prolong his life.

Towards the end of the *Mahābhārata* (Vyāsa, *MBh* XI.5),[1] Vyāsa narrates and unpacks this allegorical tale revealing, for example, that days and nights are the white and black rats gnawing at the creeper of life, when he makes Vidura tell the blind king Dhṛtarāṣṭra that it is not just he who is in such senseless plight, since meaningless suffering is the destiny of us all. As an author of this epic saga of a royal family feud spreading into mass slaughter, virile Vyāsa inserted himself also as the sperm-donor father, both of Dhṛtarāṣṭra and Vidura. For all the apparent endorsement of the official Vedic Karma doctrine which 'explains' human suffering as a deserved consequence of past sin, Vyāsa's *Mahābhārata* reverberates, at crucial junctures, with King Lear-like

"Howl, howl, howl, howl!" – lament at the deaths and miseries of sons and lovers who did no wrong. In the face of such absurd agonies of embodiment, Vyāsa insists that one must understand suffering, because bodily and mental sufferings make up the beginning, middle and end of life. Such suffering increases as our possessions and our illusory ego-investment in them increase. Entrenchment of a sense of "mine" (the two letters '*ma-ma*' in Sanskrit) spell death, whereas giving up possessiveness and recognizing "not-mine" (*na-ma-ma*) makes us transcend death (*MBh* XII.213.18/19).

But for such slackening of the grip of a possessive ego to take place, we first need to go through an "aesthetic of suffering" (see Hudson 2013) – a disinterestedly relishable taste of the truth of human vulnerability to ageing, impossible moral conundrums, deaths of beloved persons and so on. After this ethical transformation, our worldly active life itself can become non-cruel, non-greedy, and positively caring for others.

For Vyāsa, the *meaninglessness* of this ubiquitous suffering *means* the human folly of egoism, attachment and the error of blaming destiny, God, or other external sources for self-inflicted injuries. And yet, a wise swan, in the encyclopedic Book XII, tells us that only humans are able to resist the immoral drive to avenge violence by violence; and when they can so forgive and forbear, "there is nothing loftier than humanity"!

Is *life* even the right sort of thing to have a (single) meaning?

In a straightforward sense, only a word or a sentence can have meaning ("*S* means that *p*"). Some events or natural signs can have causal meaning ("Those rashes mean measles" or "Those clouds mean an imminent cyclone"). Some human acts or conventional signs can have a purposive meaning. (By raising her hand she meant to speak.) But how can life as a whole, or human life in general, have such semantic, causal or gestural-semiotic meaning? Vyāsa never asks the question: "What is the meaning of life?" Most probably he would agree with Terry Eagleton that that question is as senseless as the question "What is the taste of Geometry?" (Eagleton 2007: 1).

Yet, once we notice that the ancient Sanskrit word for "meaning" – *artha* – is also the word for "purpose" (what is wanted, hence also 'money') we can imagine that Vyāsa would have offered all 100,000 verses of his epic *Mahābhārata* as an answer to the profoundly important question: "What is the *artha* of life"?

Indeed, Vyāsa was the first to systematize the four ends of man (*puruṣārtha*-s): Pleasure (desire), Power (interest / prosperity), Order (virtue or piety), and Freedom (ultimate liberation) (see Malamoud 1996: ch. 6). These are what men live for. Vyāsa does have a lot to say about alternative meanings, that is, *points* of life, in this sense.

Mahābhārata, the epic poem from which the *Bhagavadgītā* – the central Hindu text of practical ethics, theology and metaphysics – is extracted, is attributed by the Indian literary tradition to a historical-mythical individual: Krishna Dvaipāyana (dark and island-born) Vyāsa. The influence of this epic on the Indic civilization is unparalleled. Through a complex narrative of numerous stories within stories, it teaches us a complex and situation-relative morality, albeit in a self-questioning way (see Chakrabarti and Bandyopadhyaya 2014: ch. 9). Vyāsa's "take" on the human condition is systematically two-sided and warns us repeatedly against any one-sided take. In this essay we shall attempt the nearly impossible task of synthesizing the *Mahābhārata's* (hence its author Vyāsa's) views on the *meaning, purpose or point* of human life.

After telling us the tragic tale of total ruin of an entire civilization, ensuing from a fratricidal war between two factions of a royal family which ruled over Bhārata (India), Vyāsa ends the epic ruefully with an appeal to his future readers: "Raising my hand I say but no one listens to me: from a life following the moral order come prosperity and happiness, so why not live a righteous life?" (*MBh* XVIII.5.62).

One of the most important lessons of the section "ethics at the time of crisis" in *Mahābhārata's* encyclopedic "XIIth Book of Peace," is that you cannot determine the meaning of life by thinking in a one-sided manner or practicing a single-branched *dharma*. Moral insight is generated only by two-sided reflection, which need not mean vacillation. One is reminded of a remark by R.G. Collingwood (in *Speculum Mentis*) here: "In each case an error as to the true nature and meaning of life ... produces not indeed a reality corresponding to the error ... but *a reality of a one-sided kind* resulting from the error" (Collingwood 1924: 173, emphasis mine).

Death-bound humanity's undying thirst for life is awe-inspiring. "What is amazing?" a mysterious crane asks Yudhisthira, the eldest of the virtuous five brothers, and he answers: "Every day creatures enter the house of death, yet the remaining ones still wish to live forever. What is more amazing than this?" (*MBh* III.311)

Vyāsa often switches to a beast's-eye view of human life which, though full of suffering and ruptures of relationships, remains worth living. The meaning of life lies literally within the reach of our human *hands*. Kāśyapa was a high-caste scholarly fellow. On the street, one day, he got knocked over by the speeding chariot of an arrogant rich merchant. Fallen and outraged, Kāśyapa "gave up his sense of self," cursed the life of a poor intellectual and decided that it was better to die, since life without money (*artha*) is life without meaning (*artha*). As he lay there on the road, half-dead and half-conscious, Indra – the king of gods – assumed the form of a jackal and whispered to the frustrated scholar: "Get up lucky fellow! Not only are you in the most enviable species of humans, you have attained rare erudition. Above all – *you have got a pair of hands – no other achievement is greater than having hands.* Just as you are craving the wealth of that merchant, other beasts like us are craving your hands and your human intelligence. Lacking those limbs, we cannot even reach all parts of our own bodies to take out thorns or worms or biting bugs from our skin. Those who have hands, with God-given ten fingers, can build homes to protect themselves from rain, snow, and the sun, weave fine clothing, cook food, make a bed, and can enjoy life in so many artful ways. At least thank your destiny that you do not have the body of a jackal or a frog or a rat or a worm" (*MBh* XII.180). In this life-celebrating story, it is not thought, reasoning, creative imagination, moral virtues, or the cognitive linguistic superiority of man, but rather the special structure of his hands, that is deemed to be what makes humans special.

Incidentally, in his *De Anima*, Aristotle underlines the centrality of this same body part by comparing the soul to the hand. Thomas Aquinas, in his commentary, elaborates: "The hand is the most perfect of organs, for man can provide all these needs for himself with his hands. In the same way the soul in man takes the place of all the forms of being, so that his intellect can assimilate intelligible forms and his senses sensible forms" (*De Anima*, 431b20–432a14). It is worth investigating why the hand is so important to such dissimilar philosophers as Vyāsa and Aristotle? (See also Kant 1785a: §323.)

Meaning of life to be found out by dialogical reasoning and discourse

If life is to be understood as a "sacrifice," as Vyāsa recommends, our public communicative actions must turn into a sacrifice of our ego-centric biases, which is possible only through dialogue and debate. Life is made up of actions. Actions bear fruits to which we get attached. Attachments lead to desire, and desires – insatiable as they are – when frustrated lead to anger, which befuddles our intellect. And befuddlement brings the ruin of our recollection of who we are.

Like Hannah Arendt in *The Human Condition* (Arendt 1958), Vyāsa teaches us that the paradigm example of human action is speaking to each other. Conversation, thus, is central also to the two-sided moral thinking of the *Mahābhārata*. It is through the sieve of kind, accurate, reasoned, sincere and candid conversation – discussing together (*sam-vāda*) – that reflective human beings sift out good from bad, correct from incorrect, virtuous from vicious conduct.[2] Vedic culture's normative preoccupation with open debate continues to be expressed in the *Mahābhārata*, where it is both exemplified and self-critically theorized about. The epic is itself a complex narrative of many conversations within conversations; and of course, at the center of this array of interdiscursive metanarratives of conversation shines the awesome conversation between Krishna and Arjuna, which is the *Bhagavadgītā*. Mercilessly derisive about bigots and knowledge-merchants, Vyāsa relates the story of a bitter war of words between a self-proclaimed wise philosopher, King Janaka, and a young beautiful nun, Sulabhā, in chapter 142 of Book XII. Here we are taught a full scale "Ethic of Speech."

To speak wrongly is to speak out of small-mindedness, undignified egotism, shame, pity for the interlocutor, or conceit of class or rank. Good sentences should be complete, unequivocal, logically well-constructed, not too long-winded, gracefully flowing and nuanced, free from doubt or vagueness. In a public setting, one's speech ought to show: acuteness or subtlety, proper division and enumeration of pros and cons, a well-planned sequence of what is to be discussed after what, it should begin with a clear statement of the thesis to be proved and end with a QED, and contain an articulate open statement of the discourse-driving purpose (desire or aversion). Finally, Sulabhā formulates, in a couple of terse verses, her central general norm for good communication – "just talk" as we have called it – as her normative philosophy of language:

> When the speaker, the listener, and the sentence take *equal* shares, without losing any part, into what is intended to be said, only then, O King, does that *meaning* come to light.
>
> (*MBh* XII.320.91)

This emphasis on equality in making sense of talk, I submit, has a deeper connection to *Mahābhārata*'s general valuation of equality, which is reflected in *Bhagavadgītā*'s definition of Yoga as practice of "equality," and to Bhī ṣma's unusual definition of cruelty in terms of gloating over flaunted inequality. In XII.164.6, Bhīṣma defines a cruel person as one who is mean, controlling, harsh, over-anxious, pompous, a user of foul words, a proud advertiser of his own acts of making gifts, a praiser of his own clan or class, and – most importantly – not ready to share and distribute power and wealth equally (*a-samvibhāgī*). Bhīṣma equates cruelty with shameless over-consumption of edible, drinkable, and lickable delicacies, in front of the starving poor (*MBh* XII.164.11). There is a connection between linguistic conversational justice, economic distributive justice and truthfulness as practice of equality, which Vyāsa, Bhīṣma and Sulabhā are drawing our attention to.[3]

The point of life is *dharma*

The normative meaning of life is *dharma*: but what is *dharma*? "Do not inflict on others that which is intolerably abhorrent to yourself. Briefly, this practical principle is said to be *dharma* which naturally goes against the flow of desire" (*MBh* XIII.113.8). It is tested by three criteria: it must promote flourishing of all living beings; it must hold them together by commitment to truth and promise-keeping; and it must avoid violence and cruelty (shameless inequality). But *dharma* is also *double bind*. Vyāsa tells story after story relating moral dilemmas which resonate with individual and collective life-situations; even in our own times. A pigeon chased by a hawk comes to the generous King Śibi seeking refuge. Śibi is then accosted by the hawk who needs to eat up the pigeon as his necessary nourishment. The pious king can neither deprive the hawk of his natural victuals, nor cause the death of the innocent pigeon, whose life he has vowed to protect. This and similar stories of insoluble double bind are told in great and subtle detail. Meaning of life dawns gradually on us as we ask, but cannot answer, the question: what should be done under such conflicting moral demands? In another story, an irate father suspecting his wife of adultery leaves home, commanding his obedient son to kill his mother. Notorious for his slow, hesitant character, the son waits, sword in hand, and weighs both sides of the conundrum. His deliberative delay eventually earns him his father's loving praise when the father returns home repentant. The moral dilemma is not resolved for the unhurried son, but the woman's life is saved. In every case, Vyāsa suggests that two-sided moral thinking gives us better (albeit still fallible) insight into the meaning of life.

Another pervasive feature of the *Mahābhārata* is the use of taxonomies and enumerated typologies to interpret nature, people and people's actions. Life's meaning is explained in terms of four human goals: pleasure, power, right-eousness and salvific liberation; three affective strands or temperaments: serene delight, striving dynamicity, and delusive inertia; five sense organs; five material elements; four stages of life: celibate studentship, married home-dwelling, retirement in the forest, and monastic renunciation. The basic variety of affective constitutions of people can help us understand our own stages and phases of life, as well as the nature of people around us. This morally value-laden typology of people is done according to the threefold scheme of ancient Samkhya: the highly rated, contemplative and cognitive clarity of the delightful type; the aggressive and anguished "business" of the striving, restless type; the turgid, lethargic, bored, depressed nature of the lowest, torpid type.

Life need not mean only human life. The talkative and magnanimous birds, beasts, reptiles and insects of Vyāsa's grand narrative open up a trans-species point of view: one which judges humans as a simultaneously noble and ignoble, intelligent but cruel, heroic yet heinous species. In an ecologically imaginative attempt to make a *them* out of *us*, Vyāsa tells us the story of an insect (*kīṭa*), which whispers: "I am rushing to cross the road before that scary bullock-cart comes and crushes me because I love to live." Vyāsa asks: "Would it not be better if you die rather than live in this crawling insect's body?" and the insect answers, "Everywhere the same life-force is at work; I think, therefore I wish to live" (*MBh* XIII.117.17).

Vyāsa's early Sāmkhya views on the five senses matched up with their objects: the five material elements also remain at the foundation of his "theory of meaning of life." In spite of the famous solution offered in the *Bhagavadgītā* – in terms of the stillness of a non-attached, contemplative mind in the midst of tireless performance of duties and socially engaged actions – the tussle between *vita activa* and *vita contemplativa* continues to haunt Yudhisthira, the moral, tragic hero of the epic.

Omnivorous Time as the existential, naturalistic meaning of life

At a different level of making sense of life, time is compared to a mysterious steed, a cosmic cook, and again, as the divine devourer of all:

> Its nature is inscrutable, its intangible body made of fragments of hours,/ moment by minute moment/ Seconds are the fine body-hair of this mysterious sacrificial horse./ Its eyes (twin fortnights) one black, one white, are of equal power./ Months make up its limbs, dawns and dusks its mighty shoulders/ Humans are saddled to this unstoppably speedy steed called "Ageing" (vayo-hayah).
>
> (*MBh* XII.321.25)

Time had been talked about in Book III, "Of Wilderness," during that life-saving interview given by Yudhisthira – by the side of a lethal lake, where all four of his brothers, one after the other, had lost their lives showing their human hubris against natural ecological justice. An awe-inspiring crane guarding the waters asks prince Yudhisthira a mysterious question, among hundreds of other tough riddles:

> "What is the news?" asked the bird. Yudhisthira [whose name meant: firm in all battles] replied calmly: "In this cauldron filled with the grease of great delusion, with the fire of the sun, the fuel of day and night, stirring with the ladles of months and seasons, Time the great cook is cooking all of us living beings. That, verily, is the news."
>
> (*MBh* III.311)

The universe is an enormous kitchen. We are Time's food. Arjuna, the middle brother who had the divine incarnation Krishna as his friend and charioteer, had a glimpse of this truth, when at the start of the battle, in an ecstatic cosmic vision recorded in the eleventh chapter of *Bhagavadgītā*, he saw Krishna (the Supreme Lord) as Time incarnate, chewing away the heads of all past, present and future kings and soldiers. All "paths of glory" he saw as leading to that blazing fiery mouth of Krishna, like rivers rushing towards the ocean. In wise amazement, Arjuna, stunned by this cosmic vision, had said, "You are All because you consume all."

Primacy of Desire: how there is no getting away from desire

The *Bhagavadgītā* is known for its recommendation of *desireless* performance of duty for duty's sake. One way of making that consistent with Vyāsa's urging us to *desire* the beatitude of emancipation (*moksa*) is to treat Vyāsa's ethics as act-deontological but rule-consequentialist.

After propounding the ethic of desireless action in the VIth Book, in the fourteenth of the eighteenth chapters of his epic, Vyāsa comes up with the following Song of Desire (*Kāma-gītā*): "No living being can defeat me without an appropriate method," sings Desire. "Some try hard to kill me with a weapon they know to be powerful. For them, I re-emerge anew in that very weapon. When for example, some people try to destroy me by means of sacrificial rituals, giving away various kinds of precious gifts (trying to cultivate non-attachment), I – Desire – appear in their minds again, in the form of desire for heaven or reputation, like a pious soul reborn as a living moving sentient creature. When people try to destroy me by constant contemplation of Veda and Vedanta, I reappear in their philosophical egos, imperceptibly as the elemental soul is present in a subtle form even in immobile plants. The learned one exerts himself to get rid of me by attaining liberation – an esoteric freedom from all cravings. I dance and laugh at him, because he sits right in the middle of his burning *desire* for freedom! Thus, am I one perennial force, never to be killed by any embodied being" (*MBh* XIV.13.12–18).

So, how are we to live an active life of desire and yet control our desires? Are we doomed to perpetual hypocrisy in the name of the ethical overcoming of our cravings? Vyāsa – recognized by the tradition as the first divider of the massive Vedic corpus – goes back to a solution hinted at by the *Isa Upanishad* of *Yajur Veda*: desire to live we must. Rather than starving our senses or withdrawing from active life, simply changing the style of consumption can make us desire but not drool, grasp but not grab, eat but not hog. This is called enjoyment through renunciation.

Even if absence of suffering is preferred as a description of the final state, aversion to the ills of human bondage is also a negative affect which would stand in the way of liberation. The only cognitive emotive attitude which is appropriate to the final goal of liberation is perhaps the one that is intended to be brought about in the reader of the *Mahābhārata*. It is a tranquil recognition of the fragility of our pains and pleasures and the futility of our individual material existences. It is this state which is supposed to flow from a true awareness of the exact nature of things. It does not consist in any hatred towards this world, or any yearning for a heavenly or beatific hereafter. It is a state beyond hatred and yearning, a state of "colourlessness" – loss of concern – for everything transitory.

Transcendence of transcendence: life is meaningful when one gives up giving up

So, in different situations, the meaning of life is *dharma* (as feeling the double bind of morality), the inexorable passage of time, the impetus of desire, and normative liberation through complete detachment and transcendence of desire remaining the regulative ideal. Liberation consists in victory over death by giving up the sense of "mine" and eventually, giving up even that pride of renunciation. Life is best lived with moral vigilance against egotism and cruelty; without lust or hate for life. The heart of Vyāsa's life-affirming message is: "Live to give." Life should mean sacrifice. The ultimate cognitive sacrifice is renunciation of all dualities and binary oppositions, including the duality of meaningful (merited) suffering versus meaningless (unmerited, random) suffering. Final freedom means: the giving up of giving up. After leading a good life according to *dharma*, give up the duality of good and bad, truth and falsehood; but give up also that by which you gave up these opposites (*MBh* XII.239).

Notes

1   All of the translations are by the author.
2   "Here, as the wise ones filter out good from bad speech, as barley is sifted with a sieve, friends recognize the nature of real friendship and an auspicious sign is impressed upon their conversation" – *Rig Veda* (ed. Doniger 1200–900 BCE) X.71.2.
3   An imaginative way to reinterpret this connection between semantic justice and equality can be found in the work of Rancière (1995).

4 Socrates and the meaning of life

A.C. GRAYLING

Because Socrates wrote nothing, or at least nothing that has survived, our knowledge of him and his teachings comes to us by report: chiefly in the writings of Plato and Xenophon, but also in references by Aristotle and in a few other places. The picture we get of Socrates the individual is not a consistent one in these sources. The Socrates of Xenophon lacks the brilliance and edge of the Socrates of Plato, and whereas the Socrates of Plato is an urbanite who did not like to leave Athens unless he was obliged to (as when he did his military service), Xenophon the country gentleman has Socrates extolling the rural life and its charms.

These and other contrasts tell us that Socrates comes to us filtered through the interpretations, predilections and biases of those who wrote about him, which doubtless say as much about them as about him. But one thing emerges with important clarity: his method and its aim. He asked questions, through them seeking clarifications of the concepts that others employed in their pronouncements on questions of ethics – concepts such as courage, continence, piety, 'the good' itself. We learn from the *Meno* that he believed that showing his interlocutors their failure fully to understand what they were talking about when they talked about these things was a first and vital step to making better sense of how to live. His method fed directly into the one positive thing we are sure is his own great insight into the question of the good and worthwhile life, to be discussed below.

'The one positive thing we are sure is his own great insight': this has to be said because the question of the distinction between Socrates' philosophical views and those of Plato is problematic. To what extent are the earlier dialogues of Plato, in which questions of ethics are most fully addressed – *Laches, Charmides, Euthyphro, Crito, Apology, Protagoras, Meno, Gorgias* – accurate reflections of Socrates' teachings, and to what extent is the Socrates of these dialogues a mouthpiece for Plato himself, as in the later dialogues?[1] One would think that as a pupil and admirer of Socrates, Plato would have been reasonably faithful in recording the spirit, at least, of his teacher's views, at least in those earlier dialogues, even though in the later dialogues the figure of Socrates unequivocally serves the form of Plato's enquiries without supplying their content. But even if the account of the ethical discussions in

Plato's earlier dialogues, and such positive views as can be drawn from them, cleave more closely to the tendency of Socrates' outlook than is the case in later dialogues, there is still no determinate way in which one can say 'this is Socrates and this is Plato'. What I shall do, therefore, is to outline these views, and then draw out, in a slightly different direction, what I think can be fruitfully regarded as the quintessential Socratic inspiration in ethics, as later philosophers profited from it and as one might profit from it now.

Socrates famously said that the one thing he knew was that he knew nothing. He had been told that the oracle at Delphi, when asked who was the wisest man living, had nominated him; and the only way he could solve the puzzle this presented, given his certainty that he was neither knowledgeable nor wise – as people standardly thought of wisdom – was by disclaiming wisdom. This of course sets up a different puzzle, which is that in questioning people about ethical concepts and revealing their lack of understanding of them, Socrates at least appeared to know what the *wrong* answers were, even if – as so often in the early dialogues – no definite right answer is found.

One way to resolve the puzzle is to note the tactic Socrates employs. A good example is given in the *Gorgias* where he debates with two opponents the question whether it is better or worse to do wrong than to suffer wrong. The opponents argue that it is better to be an agent than a patient in such cases; Socrates demonstrates to them that the contrary is true – 'true', as shown by what he describes as the irresistible 'iron' force of the arguments he uses. But he then says that he does not know why the arguments are irresistible, it is just that he has never found anyone who could deny them without contradiction (*Gorgias* 509a).

That might not seem as satisfactory a justification as it might be, but it could be defended by saying that even if one cannot arrive at watertight definitions of the central concepts of ethics, explorations of them are nevertheless illuminating, and seeing what they do not mean, or how given positions cannot be supported, is a gain nevertheless. This is the power of the 'aporia', the end point of a debate that does not arrive at a conclusion but which anyway sheds much light on the way to trying to reach that conclusion.

It is in the *Gorgias* that Socrates outlines the idea of a craft or technique he calls *politike*, dealing with 'the good of the soul', rather as exercise deals with the health of the body. Commentators regard this dialogue as transitional between the earlier dialogues, where aporia is more apparent, and later dialogues, where more positive doctrines begin to emerge, doubtless from Plato's own thinking. The transition can be seen as one from asking questions of the form 'What is such-and-such?' – 'What is continence? What is fineness?', where what is desired is a definition, a specification of the essence of the idea – to the provision of answers.

Critics of Socrates' approach claim that his method involves a fallacy, for in seeking a definition of the essence of a given virtue, he appears to be committing himself to the view that it would otherwise be impossible to recognize an instance of the virtue in a given case. In the *Charmides* Socrates tells the eponymous youth that to cultivate self-restraint requires understanding what continence itself is; in the *Laches* the point at issue is how one can learn to be courageous and that this, similarly, requires knowing what courage is. In the *Euthyphro* the argument is that to be genuinely pious one must grasp the nature of piety. In the *Protagoras* and *Meno* attention is turned to the wholly general matter of which any question about a particular virtue is part, namely, what *goodness itself* is. The quest in each case is for a definition of the essence; and hence the problem.

But is this a problem, or is Socrates' point different? Perhaps it is not that one cannot know whether something is courageous unless one can define the essence of courage, but rather that recognizing instances of a virtue shows that there is something that the virtue is in itself, and that reflection on what this might be will, even if it does not yield the precise specification sought, lead to two things: the practical ability to acquire the virtue, and a form of expertise in acting according to it and in guiding others to its acquisition also. Both *these* points were of great significance to Socrates, and their being so is a clue to his method and the resolution of its apparently paradoxical nature.

Indeed, this perspective on Socrates' method fits well with a thesis that becomes clear in the two dialogues which deal with the general question of the nature of the good itself, the *Protagoras* and the *Meno*, and especially the latter. Here Socrates argues for a positive thesis, that *virtue is knowledge*. The claim results from his response to a question asked by Meno, that of whether virtue is teachable. If virtue is knowledge, then the answer is yes; and to Socrates (according to Plato) the affirmative answer matters greatly. The idea is that a good life is one lived according to one's best interests, so that one achieves the best life by properly identifying or recognizing what will bring about what is best for oneself, that is, what is good. No one (or perhaps one should say, no one normal) would willingly harm himself; if one does what is not in one's interests, it will be because of ignorance. Therefore to know what is good is to do it or be it: one only does bad or is bad through failure to understand what is good; hence the identification of knowledge and virtue. In the *Protagoras* Socrates says that it is against human nature to prefer what is known to be bad to what is good; if anyone acts in a way contrary to the best, it is because he or she is in error about the matter.

This is controversial. Aristotle pointed out the refutation of this view, namely that it is a commonplace of human nature 'to know the better but to do the worse' as a result of *akrasia*, 'weakness of will'. The psychological truth of this is enough to call the Socratic identification of knowledge and virtue into question; but there is the added difficulty that by the time of the *Meno* Plato had himself come to think that the fallibility of human perceptual capacities and powers of reason meant that *knowledge* could not be acquired from experience – at best one can only form fallible *opinions* about things from sensory experience and reasoning – and that therefore knowledge must be explained by a more dramatic thesis. This thesis is that we have immortal souls, that our souls were in contact with the eternal, perfect and unchanging Forms of things ('Forms' or 'Ideas' being the exemplars or paradigms of the imperfect copies of them we meet with in the world), that we forgot everything about the Forms when our souls were embodied, and that education is the process of being partially reminded of them – literally, of 'unforgetting' them, as the term *anamnesis* shows.

This elaborate metaphysical doctrine is almost certainly Platonic rather than Socratic, so it leaves unanswered the question of what Socrates thought about the nature of knowledge and how the virtue which is knowledge is to be learned. Certainly the Platonic doctrine of *anamnesis* is not a theory about the teachability of virtue – the topic about which Meno asked – in anything like a normal sense of the notion. In the *Meno* we are given a demonstration (in which Socrates allegedly draws a geometrical proof out of an ignorant slave boy by artfully 'reminding' him of what his immortal soul once knew) of how virtue can be 'taught', i.e. by the prompting of memory. Later, in the *Symposium*, we see how this might work: love of another's beauty can be a royal road to love of beauty itself and thence to intellectual love of the highest beauty, which is The Good: this is pure Plato and no antecedent for it is discernible in the earlier dialogues, so it cannot be attributed to Socrates even as an embryonic view. But recourse to this more florid metaphysics shows that such of Socrates' views as are captured in the earlier dialogues did not provide a ready basis for the 'virtues as knowledge' thesis.

It is an immediate consequence of this thesis that all the virtues are therefore the same thing. Socrates says as much explicitly in the *Protagoras*. 'Justice, continence and courage', he says, 'are names of one and the same thing … [they are all] knowledge.' This is because knowledge of the good – of what is good for the individual, and brings him or her the success of a flourishing life – integrates all the aspects of what is good into one whole. This has the inconsistent result of identifying virtue as the knowledge of what is good for the individual, and at the same time as that individual's good. The means and the end are made to be the same thing. It might be and arguably is plausible to argue that virtues and values should be consistent (however there are views, such as Isaiah Berlin's, that certain values are inconsistent: for example, liberty and equality); but to say that they are all literally the same thing (that courage is piety, that continence is courage) is a good deal less intuitive.

Plato was not unaware that he had left Socrates with a less than consistent thesis, dependent on his own addition of a substantive metaphysical theory to underpin the requisite epistemology. In the *Euthydemus* he revisits the difficulty, there providing Socrates with the view that knowledge – or better, wisdom; the terms are used interchangeably – is the only unconditional good, to which all other goods are instrumental. But he now adds that it is in the skilful deployment of these subordinate goods that the achievement of wisdom consists, making wisdom 'the kingly art' – of making one wise! And then

Socrates adds that he recognizes that this is circular, and indeed unhelpful, since we do not know what 'the kingly art' itself is (*Euthydemus* 291b–292e).

At this point, discussion of Socrates' views has to segue into discussion of the further developments of Plato's own thought, where some of the unsatisfactory compromises thus far reached are given a rather different handling elsewhere, not least in the *Republic*. But we can see something of the struggle and intention of Socrates' approach, and the principle lessons to be derived from it, which have less to do with the content of the view than with two identifiable and impressive wellsprings of it – or one might call them inspirations, for so they were treated by later schools of ethical reflection, and they still have a live interest in thinking about the ethical life.

The inspirations Socrates offers derive from two things we can be very confident come from him: his idea that the life genuinely worth living is the *examined* life – his whole practice of questioning and forcing people to think illustrates this fundamental conviction of his – and his determined adherence to principle, as evidenced by his refusal to disobey the law once he had been condemned to death. The idea of the examined life as the life truly worth living is a simple-seeming one, but it is in fact exceedingly deep and consequential. I return to this point shortly. The other point, about cleaving to principle, is more summarily describable.

The *Crito* is Plato's account of Socrates' conversations with friends in his cell in the days before his death. Crito attempted to persuade Socrates to escape from Athens, given that it appeared that the city did not really wish him to die, but was making it clear by hints and apparent laxity in prison security that he could make off if he wished. But Socrates refused, on the grounds that he refused to listen to any argument but that which was best, and that the best argument said that wrong must not be returned for wrong, nor injury for injury, and that he would be inflicting a wrong on Athens if he unlawfully escaped into exile. He would, he said, be confirming the trial's accusations against him if he made himself an outlaw. 'Do not think of Socrates, but of the truth; agree with me if I speak the truth, but if I do not, argue back!' he urged Crito. Thus he espoused the idea of life lived according to principle, by the strict adherence to truth or the soundest argument; to do otherwise was to do harm, and because one knew that to do harm is wrong, one could not do it.

The point about the examined life is not so explicitly textually based, but as an implication of Socrates' insistent and utterly central practice, and accordingly as the task he saw himself as bound to – namely, to be a gadfly, goading people into thinking about what they meant by the ideas they lived by, and what therefore they should do and be – it is the quintessential Socratic legacy to ethics. The point is usually put in the negative, as having Socrates say, 'The unexamined life is not worth living', meaning that a life not thought about, not chosen by the person living it, is a life lived according to others' conceptions of what a worthwhile life should be; one becomes a ball in someone else's game, thrown or kicked in directions chosen by others. Unpacking the implications of the assertion yields a rich view: that the worthwhile life is a chosen life, based on one's self-understanding (obeying the Delphic oracle's injunction to 'know thyself') so that one can see what talents and capacities might direct one's choices; and that of fundamental importance is the autonomy involved: one must think for oneself, one must reflect, and take responsibility.

What this means, in turn, is something that many who subscribe to one or another major ideology, whether religious or political, would find subversive: that there is not a one-size-fits-all answer to the question of what kind of life is worth living, but instead that there are as many answers as there are people to seek them. For if each individual must choose and take responsibility on the basis of his or her own self-knowledge, then, given the diversity of human nature, abilities and interests, there will be many kinds of lives that will be good for the people living them. This indeed is why in the early dialogues there is no hint of a detailed and comprehensive prescription of A Good Life, like the individual recipes of a magazine diet, but instead a description at a high level of generality of the characteristics that mark the space of the good: the characteristic of seeking by reflection to grasp the nature of the virtues and to *know* the good that can be realized in them.

The later schools of ethics – the Epicureans and Stoics – can be characterized as offering both theoretical and practical responses to the question which is, one might say, the distinctively Socratic question, namely: How shall I live? What sort of person shall I be? For these are the questions that the adjuration to autonomy and responsibility make us focus upon. And even more directly in the tradition of this Socratic question is the first major unified treatise of ethics, Aristotle's *Nichomachean Ethics,* which I find it irresistible to see as anything other than a worked-out response to it. It might be that the thinkers who saw the ethical challenge as first and foremost answering the 'how to live' question did not name Socrates as this questioner; but the fact that in broadly humanistic (non-Divine Command) ethics this is indeed the approach to how the question of the meaning of life must be answered, is vastly to the credit of the man whose adjuration to the examined life is the starting point of our entire ethical tradition.

Note

1   For the Socratic dialogues referenced in this chapter, see Plato fifth–fourth century BCE.

5   Plato and the meaning of life

DAVID SKRBINA

'The meaning of life' is one of those perennially imponderable philosophical questions. As old as philosophy itself, it has been confronted in many ways and with many different interpretations over the centuries. Like all such questions, even understanding the meaning of the phrase 'meaning of life' poses many challenges and yields little agreement. I won't debate all the nuances here, but will simply take it in the ordinary sense, as something inquiring about the significance, value, or purpose of human existence. Thus understood, it's clear that the Greeks had much to say about the meaning of life.

Plato in particular had many thoughts about this matter, certainly far beyond that which was offered up by his pre-Socratic predecessors, most of whom concentrated on purely metaphysical issues. Plato took a more comprehensive and balanced view of philosophy, covering in detail the three traditional areas of metaphysics, epistemology, and ethics.[1] The three areas were furthermore deeply interrelated, and a philosopher could scarcely discuss one without touching on major issues in the others. Human meaning, therefore, was necessarily a question not only of morality but also of knowledge and of the nature of ultimate reality.

Goals and purposes of human existence, for Plato, were rooted in the broader teleological structure of the cosmos itself. The universe is neither arbitrary nor pointless; it exists for a reason, and all things that happen in it also occur for a reason. The Demiurge, as we recall, constructed the cosmos with an end in view – namely, to produce the best and most beautiful cosmos possible, one that embodied the virtue and wisdom of the creator himself. "[The Demiurge] was good, and ... he wanted everything to become as much like himself as was possible... . The god wanted everything to be good ..." (*Timaeus* 29e–30a). In *Phaedo*, Plato sympathetically discusses a variant of Anaxagoras' theory in which mind (*nous*) is the goal-oriented efficient cause of all events: "the directing Mind would direct everything and arrange each thing in the way that was best" (97c). Plato goes on to remark that a striving toward the best is the "real cause" (99b) of events, and that everything has a "capacity for being in the best place"; indeed, it is "the truly good and 'binding'" that organizes the cosmic whole.[2] The universe, in short, strives for the best.

If the Demiurge and the cosmos aim for the best, then clearly that is our mission in life as well. In fact, there is a sense in which we serve, or at least ought to serve, at the behest of the cosmos and the gods. We are not autonomous actors, on Plato's view. Right livelihood involves serving the broader teleological aims of the whole. Every individual action matters to the cosmos, as Plato explains in his late work *Laws*:

> The supervisor of the universe has arranged everything with an eye to its preservation and excellence, and its individual parts play appropriate active or passive roles according to their various capacities .... [We] are one such part – a mere speck that nevertheless constantly contributes to the good of the whole ... [N]othing is created except to provide the entire universe with a life of prosperity. You forget that creation is not for your benefit; you exist for the sake of the universe.
>
> (903b–c)

Our lives acquire meaning, then, by our becoming the best persons that we can be, and by working towards the glory of the larger whole of which we are a part. But what, specifically, does this entail? Plato seems to identify two main components of a meaningful life. The first is to lead a life of virtue, and thus to become a truly good person. The second is a politically oriented objective: to be the best possible citizen. Let me explore each of these in some detail.

The virtuous life

In order to live a virtuous and hence meaningful life, one must first know what virtue is. Next we must examine the specific forms that it takes. Finally we need to understand how to acquire the virtues and build them into our souls, thus becoming virtuous people. Each step is fraught with difficulties.

Plato provides his first enumeration of the core virtues in the early dialogue *Protagoras*, where he lists five by name: knowledge (*epistêmê*), justice (*dikaiosunê*), courage (*andreia*), temperance (*sôphrosunê*), and piety (*hosiotês*).[3] The subsequent discussion shows, however, that these are not easy to define, and furthermore that their interrelationship is complex. Are they individual virtues in themselves, or are they parts of a single entity called virtue? Is there a hierarchy or rank order among them? Can a person be partly virtuous and partly vice-ridden at the same time – by, for example, possessing an abundance of one but a complete lack of another? These become highly important issues for Plato.

Then we have the nagging question of how one ought to go about acquiring virtue. If virtue is a form of knowledge, then it must be teachable, and therefore we need only seek out teachers of ethics in order to become virtuous. Unfortunately, throughout several dialogues Plato emphasizes the difficulty of understanding the true nature of virtue. In the early work *Laches*, for example, he defers tackling virtue as a whole; that would be "too great a task" (190c). In *Protagoras*, Socrates seems to argue that all virtue is a form of knowledge, thus apparently making that the chief virtue. Furthermore, since all knowledge is teachable, this implies that all virtue is teachable. Specifically, Socrates argues that the individual virtues all involve questions of "excess" and "deficiency." Good and bad, pleasure and pain, happiness and sadness, all involve an ability to make quantitative and comparative judgments about things. One must therefore cultivate an "art of measurement" (*metrêtikê technê*; 356d) in order to obtain the truth about virtue, and thus to achieve "salvation in life." And yet at the same time, Socrates' antagonist Protagoras gives a strong argument that virtue is in fact not a form of knowledge, and hence not teachable at all. The dialogue ends in something of a stand-off.

Later, in his middle-period work *Meno*, Plato seems to side with Protagoras. It opens with a pessimistic statement, one that has dire implications for a meaningful life. Socrates now disavows any knowledge of what virtue actually is: "I blame myself," he says, "for my complete ignorance about virtue" (71b). And it gets worse: "Not only that, my friend, … I have never yet met anyone else who did know." An ominous sign.

Later in the dialogue Plato seems to adopt the pragmatic and empirical argument that virtue *cannot* in fact be taught; otherwise, the great and virtuous men of the past would have taught their children, but that evidently did not happen – as he explains with several examples. Virtue undeniably seems to be a kind of "true belief" about ethics, and yet it is not a *justified* or rational true belief; if it were, it would be teachable.

So how, in the end, does one acquire virtue, and thus obtain a life of meaning? Plato's surprising answer: as a kind of divine dispensation, a "gift from the gods." As Socrates says, "virtue [is] neither an inborn quality nor taught, but comes to those who possess it as a gift from the gods" (99e). A difficult prospect indeed; we neither know what virtue is, nor have we any direct means of obtaining it.

In the roughly contemporaneous *Republic*, however, Plato seems to offer us a somewhat more hopeful prospect of attaining a meaningful life. The prime virtues are now down to four: wisdom, courage, temperance, and justice (427e). Of these, justice now takes a dominant role, rather than knowledge or wisdom. Justice is, in fact, a kind of meta-virtue: an organizing principle of the psyche. The other three virtues reside in parts of the soul: wisdom in the rational part, courage in the spirited, and temperance equally in all three parts (rational, spirited, and appetitive). Justice, however, is different; a person is just when each part of the soul performs its own dedicated task   the rational part rules, the spirited part serves the rational in order to overcome difficulties and hardship, and the appetitive keeps the body healthy and sound. Consequently the just person has an inner harmony, is psychologically balanced, and at peace. He is fully self-realized and the master of himself.

"Virtue then," says Plato, "seems to be a kind of health, fine condition, and well-being of the soul" (444d). Armed with the four leading virtues, a person is wise, temperate, brave, and just; he is thereby happy and leads the best possible life. As Plato states concisely in *Laws*, "[a man's] highest good is to become as virtuous as possible" (707d) – thus achieving a life of meaning in the truest sense of the word.

Living well is vitally important, but the ultimate reward for a just and meaningful life comes after death. Two of Plato's most important dialogues, *Gorgias* and *Republic*, end with so-called eschatological myths that describe the soul's reward or punishment in the afterlife. In one of the earliest depictions of something like heaven and hell in Western history,[4] Plato describes his "true" stories about how the just and pious man "goes to the Isles of the Blessed, to make his abode in complete happiness," whereas the unjust and godless man "goes to the prison of payment and retribution, the one they call Tartarus" (*Gorgias* 523a–b). *Republic* concludes with the Myth of Er, an account of the afterlife in which the just go upwards into the heavens, and the unjust downward under the Earth (614b–c). After a thousand years, both groups assemble to choose their future lives.[5] The wise and just inevitably choose well, and the ignorant and unjust choose poorly. Plato's overall moral: by "practicing justice with reason in every way ... we'll receive our rewards. Hence, both in this life and on the thousand-year journey we've described, we'll do well and be happy" (621c–d).

In the service of the state

As important as it is, the virtuous life is unattainable and even inconceivable outside of society. The above stipulations, therefore, are meaningless apart from the social and political context in which they reside. "Man is the political animal," said Aristotle (*Politics* 1253a), and Plato surely would have agreed. A meaningful and virtuous life is only relevant in the setting of a well-organized and well-run political system; hence the need to elaborate on the nature of the ideal state.

Plato makes two such attempts – in the middle-period *Republic* and in his final work *Laws*. The similarities and contrasts between these two are fascinating and enlightening, but here I will examine only those aspects of each system that relate most directly to the meaning of life.

Just as we are citizens of the cosmo-polis – and hence 'cosmopolitans' – and therefore rightly serve to benefit it, so too do we find meaning as citizens of the man-made polis or state. But this does not entail blind patriotism or slavish obedience to one's government. Unlike the cosmopolis, human states can easily become corrupt, thereby forfeiting our allegiance. Therefore, to live meaningful lives, it's of highest importance that we construct and sustain the proper kind of state. This is why Plato places such emphasis on right politics. It is central to our quest for meaning.

What, then, is his ideal state like? The first depiction comes in Book II of *Republic*, where Socrates constructs an ideal state in order to locate justice and injustice in it. Such a state meets all the basic human needs, as well as all the reasonable and necessary functions of a civil society. It provides all the goods and services needed for a satisfying life while avoiding wasteful and corrupting luxury. The ideal state is self-sufficient but does engage in trade. It has enough land to meet its own needs. It controls its population by encouraging its citizens "to bear no more children than their resources allow, lest they fall into either poverty or war" (372b). The people eat well – healthy local produce without excess 'junk food'.[6] In general, the citizens "will live in peace and good health, and when they die at a ripe old age, they'll bequeath a similar life to their children." The ideal polis is peaceful, healthy, and happy.

It is also *small*. In *Republic* Plato gives us only clues to its ideal size. The polis should be allowed to grow only to a point that is "consistent with unity"; it should be "one and self-sufficing" (423b–c). In the same passage he provides some indication of the proper size by suggesting that a polis with 1,000 defenders or warriors might serve as a kind of upper limit for a well-governed society. By inference, this implies a total population of something like 25,000 citizens, though the total figure would be somewhat higher depending on the presence of foreigners and slaves.[7]

By present-day standards, of course, a state with only some 25,000 citizens would be extremely small. Modern countries in that range would include Lichtenstein, Monaco, San Marino, and tiny Pacific island nations like Palau and Nauru. Lest we think Plato is deceiving us here, or speaking merely metaphorically, we need only consult *Laws*. There he is exact: the ideal number is 5,040 households, a figure that apparently derives from being roughly the right size but also mathematically divisible by the numbers 1 through 10, which makes for ease of apportioning resources and tasks (*Laws* 737e–738a). If we assume an average of five members per household, we again arrive at a figure of about 25,000 citizens.

Size is crucial not only for effective management of civil society, but even more because it allows each citizen to be intimately connected to his fellow man, which in turn is important for a meaningful and virtuous life. Plato is emphatic:

> There can be no greater benefit for a state than that the citizens should be well-known one to another. Where they have no insight into each other's characters and are kept in the dark about them, no one will ever enjoy the respect he merits or fill the office he deserves or obtain the legal verdict to which he is entitled.
>
> (*Laws* 738e)

On Plato's view, a polis of 25,000 would yield perhaps 10,000 adult males, of whom a few thousand would be actively involved in civic life. Such a number may be knowable, each to all – though not many more. Any larger and we risk being unable to evaluate one another's character, thus opening the way to deception, fraud, and criminality.

As noted above, a life of meaning must be consistent with the divine and eternal rules of the cosmos. Civic laws guiding the ideal state are therefore not really due to humans, or even wise humans; rather, they are products of the gods themselves: "to whom do you give credit for establishing your codes of law? Is it a god, or a man? A god, sir, a god" (*Laws* 624a). Reason, justice, and goodness are eternal qualities like the Forms themselves, and are not subject to human whim. Human nature is likewise fixed. All this implies a relatively fixed legal code. Proper laws are not subject to governmental or ruler dictat; rather, the opposite is true: "if law is the master of the government, and the government is its slave, then the situation is full of promise" (715d). Wise rulers must understand the eternal and divine laws of nature, and follow them accordingly.

Among these unchanging laws are ones that stipulate both a social homogeneity and a rank-ordering among men: homogeneity in the sense that the state should be ethnically uniform, to the greatest extent possible; and rank-ordered because men, even of the same ethnic group, fall into a natural hierarchy of the better and the worse. These somewhat contentious aspects require elaboration. They will round out our investigation of a meaningful life.

Given that there is "no greater benefit" than knowing our fellow citizens, they clearly must be as much like us as possible, reasons Plato. Those from different backgrounds, different races, or different cultures are intrinsically harder to know, and thus harder to judge, he thinks. Plato is unambiguous and clear. In describing the potentially disastrous outcome of the Persian war, he remarks that "if it hadn't been for the joint determination of the Athenians and the Spartans ... we should have by now virtually a complete mixture of the races" (693a), meaning Greek with non-Greek. Persian lands are "horribly jumbled together" by their mixed ethnicities, which presents a deep and intractable problem.

Any new or expanding state is tempted to import people, but immigrants "haven't the unity of a swarm of bees; they are not a single people" (708b). This is important because "a single people speaks the same language and observes the same laws," yielding "a certain feeling of community." Any potential newcomers must undergo something like 'extreme vetting'; we must "screen the bad candidates [and] refuse their application to enter and become citizens of the state" (736c). There can be little worse, according to Plato, than to accept someone with a contrary or poor upbringing: "we ought not to import citizens who have been brought up by a bastard education" (741a).

Even more controversially, according to Plato, the ideal state must periodically "purge" its worst elements in order to maintain a high-quality citizenry. Like a wise breeder of animals, the wise government must "weed out the unhealthy and inferior stock" (735b) by sending them off to colonies or other states. "To purge a whole state" is a difficult task, to be sure, and "like drastic medicines, the best purge is a painful business." Still, it must be done. After all, "the water" of the state ought to be "as pure as possible" in order to be well-run.

On the other point of contention, Plato emphasizes the necessity of acknowledging the stark inequality of human beings. Early in *Laws* he cites seven varieties of relationships in which the naturally better rule over the naturally worse, the most important being that "the ignorant man should follow the leadership of the wise" (690b). Uneducated and unphilosophical types ought not to take it upon themselves to judge such things as art, music, or culture; where this happens, we have little better than a "theatrocracy" (701a) in which the lesser pass judgment on the better, inevitably leading to cultural and moral decay.

Then we have a lengthy passage (757a–e) in which Plato decries those who would proclaim equal status between master and slave; under such a condition, "friendship between them is inherently impossible" because the nominal equality supervenes on natural law. In fact, "indiscriminate equality for all amounts to inequality, and both fill a state with quarrels between its citizens."

Equality, according to Plato, is of two forms. The first is a purely legalistic and technical sense in which all are equally citizens of the state and possess equal needs. This poses little problem. Far more difficult is the other form in which people are seen as intrinsically or qualitatively equal. Bluntly stated, on Plato's view, there are better people and there are worse; the better deserve more, and the worse deserve less. This is a key aspect of social justice, hence of social virtue, hence of living a good life. This whole notion lay behind Plato's critique of democracy in *Republic*, where he issues a scathing attack on the system that "grants a sort of equality to equals and unequals alike" (*Republic* 558c).

The ideal state, then, is a small, self-sufficient, ethnically homogenous community of people who know each other well, and can adequately judge each others' characters. The system is run as an aristocracy – the best and wisest rule, and the rest willingly consent, without anger or resentment. They know that each person has natural, inborn skills, and that it is best if each plays the part in society for which they are best suited. There is neither talk nor expectation of 'equality' or 'equal rights'. All know that the best among them will rightly reap greater benefits than most, but this is seen as fair and just. An important corollary to all this – which I have not discussed here – is that excess wealth must be limited, or the state risks lapsing into an oligarchy or plutocracy; indeed, "virtue and great wealth are quite incompatible ... [T]he very rich are not good" (*Laws* 742e, 743c). In such an ideal state, then, citizens achieve full self-realization and are encouraged in multiple ways to become as virtuous as possible.

Any real-life state, of course – especially in the present day – is very far from this Platonic ideal. The implications of trying to implement it would be significant: to live a life of meaning today, one would not only strive for virtue, for 'the best', but also seek to move one's social order in the direction of the ideal. For most of us, this would mean decentralizing and downsizing the federal government, perhaps even to the point of secession; limiting immigration and moving toward ethnic uniformity; and transitioning away from democracy and more towards a system, however imperfect, in which the wisest and best will rule. That such things are counter to popular mainstream opinion scarcely needs mention.

Towards the divine

In the final analysis, human meaning is connected to the nature of the gods. The realm of the divine was never far from Plato's mind. His dialogues are replete with references to the Demiurge, the gods, and various spiritual entities. The gods serve as our role models and inspiration. They embody our highest and noblest aims. They reflect the very real and very mysterious powers present in the cosmos. The gods are immortal, and so is the human race. A bit of the divine resides in each of us, and it should rightly serve as an ongoing impulse. "We should run our public and our private life, our homes and our states, in obedience to what little spark of immortality lies in us" (*Laws* 714a).

As the embodiment of virtue and wisdom, the gods represent a kind of ultimate truth about the world. This is important because "truth heads the list of all things good, for gods and men alike" (*Laws* 730c). He who hopes for happiness and meaning should "live as much of his life as possible a man of truth." Though it may be difficult at times, "we should never shrink from speaking the truth as we see it" (779e). In doing so, we approach, ever so slightly, the realm of the divine.

"For gods there are," wrote Epicurus, some hundred years after Plato's time. Perhaps, on this matter, Epicurus and Plato were right. Perhaps there are certain divine cosmic powers out there, urging us onward, impelling us upward, toward the higher, the better. If so, then perhaps we owe them some respect, and a small debt of gratitude. This, perhaps, is the first step on the road to a life of value and meaning.

Notes

1 The fourth major branch, logic, would come to fruition in Aristotle.
2 This broadly teleological standpoint is again further developed along the same lines by Aristotle. See especially Book II of *Physics*.
3 In later works Plato would employ the word *eusebeia* for 'piety'; see for example *Republic* 615c.
4 Biblical depictions in the gospels of the New Testament date to 70–100 CE. Notably, there are no clear references to a heaven or a hell in the Old Testament.
5 Plato was a firm believer in reincarnation.
6 Notably, among the extensive list of specific foods there is no meat. Meat in fact is later discussed as an aspect of the feverish luxury polis, and as something that introduces sickness into the populace: "we'll also need many more cattle, won't we, if people are going to eat meat? Of course. And if we live like that, we'll have a far greater need for doctors than we did before? Much greater" (373c).
7 I use the term 'citizen' in the modern sense, inclusive of women and children. For the Greeks, citizenship was restricted to adult males.

6 Diogenes and the meaning of life

WILL DESMOND

The images are famous: Diogenes spurning Alexander's gifts, Diogenes in the marketplace searching for an honest man, Diogenes living in a barrel with only a cloak and a staff as possessions, Diogenes throwing away his cup to drink with his bare hands. Such images of "the Dog," celebrating his shameless antics, his scorn of convention, defiance of authority, simplicity of life, and radical freedom, proliferated across the ancient Mediterranean world to give it one model for a meaningful life. Our own pluralistic times tend to honour a multiplicity of world-views, but Diogenes' ancient admirers believed that their hero had discovered *the* meaningful life: he had shown the way by abandoning home and possessions to wander city streets, to harden himself to the simple pleasures of the moment, and to "bark" at others for their slavery to convention.[1] Of the many heroes and sages of antiquity, did Diogenes indeed discover – or create, or serve as the revelatory conduit for – the, or a, meaning of life? If so, how might he now be revived as a guide to a significant life? If he cannot, what can his shortcomings teach us? To evaluate Diogenes fully, one really has to live his Cynic outlook. But failing immediate experience, sympathetic imagination can help, and to this end, conceptual study – involving comparison with other outlooks, and analysis of fundamental ideas. As one of antiquity's sages, and an outlier in Jaspers' Axial Age, Diogenes has invited comparisons with Socrates, Plato, Zeno, Isaiah, Hindu ascetics. As a figure for the ages, he has been compared with Jesus, Epictetus, St Francis, Rousseau, Thoreau, Nietzsche, Tao and Zen masters, as well as hobos, beatniks, hippies, punks – hermits, contemplatives, and rebels of all types. "Every age and ours in particular needs its Diogenes" (D'Alembert 1759: I, 380) and to this end may project its own more familiar order onto the heap of ancient images. But to get at "the thing itself," one may, I think, fasten on a few major concepts which probably did structure Diogenes' outlook, and which help one to appreciate and appropriate it *today*.

Four formulae are important for the Cynics' conceptualization of their lifestyle: rejecting inherited custom (*nomos*), living according to nature (*physis*), cultivating self-sufficiency (*autarkeia*), and speaking with uncompromising honesty (*parrhēsia*). Each of these facets of the Cynic life illuminates the others, and points towards what may be the highest Cynic goal:

momentary freedom, or the ability to live in the present moment with unconditional acceptance of oneself and one's circumstances. Such radical freedom is one response to the necessary exigencies of human life, as they range the spectrum between simplicity and complexity, needs and desires, solitude and community, self-sufficiency and inter-connectedness, nakedness and technological prowess, freedom and responsibility, self-regard and self-emptying, skepticism and dogmatism, sensuous immediacy and intellectual abstraction, immanence and transcendence. In veering toward the former element in each of these dichotomies, Diogenes presents a simple, rather unnuanced, articulation of life's meaning: easy to dismiss, it yet remains a challenge and limiting case that cannot in the end be avoided.

Absolute freedom in the moment is a peak experience barred from most people most of the time, according to a Cynic like Diogenes. Human beings begin bound by city and society, whose mass of conventions tacitly bind desire, conception, and action. Conservative thinkers may wisely view shared customs as a necessary asylum sheltering the majority from the terrifying infinity of life's possibilities; as a cocoon woven from innumerable strands of experience and tested wisdom; as a nest accommodating all abilities and ages, out of which well-grounded, colourful individuals can launch forth; as the matrix of a living culture, and more resonantly still, as that which constitutes a meaningful *home*.[2] If custom is the "principal magistrate of man's life" (Bacon 1625: 471), then rootless cosmopolitans suffer from a lack of communal customs, and the gradual loss of traditional ways can only deepen the unhappiness and *anomie* of modern populations – now ever more dependent for direction on market whims, and the technology that serves them. In Diogenes' Greece, custom was indeed "king" (as Pindar said (fifth century BCE: 40)), but lacking a theoretical defence was somewhat vulnerable to Sophistic and Cynic attacks. Diogenes led the most uncompromising assault on custom, as if it were the citadel of tyranny. For him, custom represents no repository of wisdom or meaning, and the *polis* does not educate individuals to virtuous activity or well-being. Rather, the bonds of *nomos* are unnatural fetters that must be burst asunder: Give away possessions that tie one to one spot of earth; give up even the desire to possess, for what does one possess except what one physically holds? Refuse the customs of work, marriage, religion, citizenship – for what are these but so many chains? Reject the city and all its vanity – its idle gossip, its trumpet calls to war. Go into voluntary exile, and if one feels generous in one's poverty, then bark at passers-by, to sting them into trading everything for the riches of simplicity.

Separated from the comforts that communal custom makes possible, a Diogenes seeks to recover their true meaning in the simple necessities of ascetic, natural living: eating, drinking, sleeping only according to bodily need; consuming only what nature directly produces, avoiding anything tainted by technology; avoiding too all the "smoke" (*typhos*) of abstract conceptions like *wealth, honour, family*, or *fatherland* woven into the net of social desire.

And so, beans, lentils, figs, and other wild, free fare are Diogenes' favourite sustenance; a single cloak and staff; no house or shoes. It remained controversial whether fire, cooking, and meat-eating were natural to man or not – and the Cynics seemed little worried whether their practice of begging might be an unnatural form of parasitism. In any case, "the natural" becomes the Cynic norm, buzzword, and "God-term": "nature" is primary, universal, and provides for all needs abundantly and freely – no miserly stepmother she, for it is rather her wayward human children who often fail to adapt themselves to her beneficence. Contemporary nature-lovers, Darwinian and otherwise, may not place such deep trust in the cosmos' generosity; certainly our own more degraded environment, and huge populations, hardly allow for a revival of Diogenes' exact ideals here. Nevertheless he remains an ally for contemporary advocates of simple living, and his critique of *pleonexia* is revived in diagnoses of the *affluenza, luxury fever,* and the *growth fetish* that infect whole populations with the assumption that the sheer accumulation of things and experiences is deeply meaningful. Such accumulation has its price, and in the face of overwork, over-consumption, debt, pollution, and obesity, a contemporary Diogenes would repeat the old wisdom: simplify, simplify! The distinction between necessary needs and superfluous desires is of course difficult to specify definitively. Yet it articulates an important fact of conscious experience: mindful attention to present goods is often more satisfying than distracted over-consumption. A popular formula for happiness (accepted by William James, among others) can be taken as Cynic in spirit: $H = C/D$. Here H (= happiness) increases proportionally to C (= capacity to satisfy desire), and inversely proportional to D (= desire). Thus, H increases *either* as one's power increases, *or* as one's desires decrease, or both: our will-to-power focuses on the numerator, Diogenes on the denominator. Here, in the limit, as it were, no desire implies infinite happiness, and Cynics did indeed speculate that God is that being which needs nothing beyond itself.

Such a regulative ideal suggests that other Cynic watchword and candidate for human meaning – self-sufficiency. Not to need others, economically, psychologically, or spiritually: to be able to produce all one's energy, food, clothes, bodily goods, and entertainment; to be self-content and not "needy," not beholden to fashions, others' opinions, societal honours; even to attain a sense of oneself as absolute, unconditioned by anything or anyone – such ideals may each be impossible, or too high for attainment, and yet they can beckon nonetheless as ideals that regulate the ambitions and actions of individuals and nations. The present-day need for more sustainable living inspires such handbooks as *Self Sufficiency for the 21st Century* (Strawbridge and Strawbridge 2017) and even if only a few return to the land as homesteaders, or head for the wilderness as survivalists, nevertheless projects for promoting autonomous buildings, local agriculture, and off-the-grid energy production may well, in coming years, give more people a greater sense of meaningful autonomy. Installing solar panels was far from Diogenes' mind when he told

Alexander to get out of his sun, but his recommendation of self-reliance has, again, a rough, perennial wisdom. Without some measure of self-sufficiency, one cannot become a mature, *substantial* individual; with it, Thoreau (and perhaps Diogenes in his tub) felt the exhilaration of a sublime freedom. Of course Diogenes' tub, and Thoreau's axe and iron nails, amply illustrate that only an animal or god can be utterly self-sufficient (Aristotle fourth century BCE: *Politics* I, 1253a), that "no man is an island," but all are "part of the main" (Donne 1624: 108). The interrelatedness of being has pushed much modern thought in monistic directions, and is perhaps not adequately articulated in the Diogenes tradition: his debts to the Greek city, the inherent sociability of the human animal, are jettisoned for a gruff and jealous solitude. A challenge for coming generations may be to reconcile an ever deeper awareness of inter-connectedness and interdependence, with Diogenes' assertion of individual difference and liberty – even in all its potentially rude anarchy.

Experience may elude full articulation, and perhaps wisdom cannot be taught. Certainly not all the wise have tried or even wished to communicate their wisdom. Diogenes for his part was not a silent sage. He heckled passers-by, shocked onlookers with his shameless cavorting, and the sheer variety of his quips, jokes, insults, vignettes, maxims and syllogisms, punctuated or crowned with lewd capers, has impressed some as a kind of performance art: in Diogenes' own words, *parrhēsia* is "the most beautiful human thing" (Diogenes Laertius third century CE: 6.69). His famed *parrhēsia* – freedom of speech exercised at *all* times, on *all* occasions, without fear of offending hearers or suffering their anger – has been admired as both a kind of playful self-affirmation, and a serious social service. According to variations of the latter, Diogenes serves as the "scout of God" who spies out human vices and with a missionary love of mankind preaches the good news of natural simplicity (Epictetus); or, as the neo-Enlightenment champion of the "courage of truth," whose radical self-disciplining presages a radical reshaping of social power-relations (Foucault).[3] Since Foucault, the courage to "speak truth to power" has become a cliché, and one might doubt how easily anyone can rightly claim "*the* truth" and the moral superiority it confers. In any case, bearing witness to the truth may be indispensable for a fully meaningful life. As he critiques custom and praises nature, Diogenes' defiant *parrhēsia* fits one way of attaining or creating meaning: having a cause, or an entity *for* or *against* which to strive, is necessary for a sense of self-worth, and even self-consciousness. If so, then Diogenes' shameless *parrhēsia* illustrates in its own way great insights of Fichte and William James. On the other hand, Diogenes' ridiculous capers are often quite funny, and admirers like Nietzsche and Sloterdijk (1983) have praised the glee and good-natured cheekiness, the sheer exuberance and zest that he represents. Nothing is ultimately serious, and a Diogenes looks out on the fantastical happenings of the world as if on a universal carnival. Life is a festival, a party, and each moment brings some-thing good, if only one has the high spirits to roll with it. Here Diogenes the jester may affirm himself with a joy beyond the cynical denigration of others. Does this exuberance imply something more? A self-emptying perhaps, or an expansion of the self to embrace the Stoics' cosmos or Spinoza's intellectual love of God/Nature? Behind the rough exterior, was Diogenes a deeply spiritual man, "born of Zeus" as puns on his name suggest? By contrast, Nietzsche would speak for godless moderns when he makes the joyful wisdom of *his* Diogenes "the highest thing one can reach on earth":[4] a heroism that embraces ascetic suffering as a needful part of its earthy self. A transcendent God or self-sufficient Will: what deeper consciousness rings through Diogenes' laughter? We leave this question as an exercise for the reader, and his or her honest intuitions. But the main point should not be missed: the meaning of life for Diogenes is carefree laughter.

Before asking about the wisdom or foolishness of this, permit me a rushed, semi-personal analysis of the phrase, "the meaning of life."[5] Most obviously, a word, sentence, proposition, has "meaning" for those who understand its reference; by contrast, chance syllables, ungrammatical sentences, or random strings of words are gibberish. An old metaphor is that all objective entities are "words," signs, or symbols of something else more real than the tangible thing itself. One may (with Diogenes) reject this Platonic outlook, and yet waver before the thought that objects can have "meaning": an artwork, piece of music, memento, or monument all have meaning for those who can understand them, and seem to point "beyond" their surface physicality to a deeper intelligibility and value. So for some, the universe itself has meaning – not only physically intelligible and structured by objective patterns ("laws of nature"), but also beautiful, good, and charged with a grandeur – of God, or of itself.[6] Given this sense of *objective* meaning, can a human life be "meaningful"? It would be so if it were itself not merely coherent and intelligible, but valuable – either in its own self-sufficiency, or because grounded in a "greater" reality of which it is a part, moment, image, or imitation. Many religious and philosophical schemes stress objective meaning in the latter mode, at least rhetorically: life is meaningful to the degree that it subsists in the shadow of a group, hero, cause, or God – entities that often exist *in illo tempore* (see esp. Eliade 1963). In such schemes, lives may be meaningful, no matter how hard or miserable: suffering does not preclude, and may be a necessary moment in personal salvation or historical providence. Our shock before world history, or our consumerist prejudices, can make us balk at such formulations, and in the waning of the "ascetic imperative" (Harpham 1987), we may be more attracted to *subjective* schemes for meaning. Here a life becomes meaningful to the degree that it is or seems so to *me*: in my decisions, goals, chosen character, and even chosen nature, I am free and self-justifying. Nobody, let alone any "experience machine" (Nozick 1974: 42–45), can live my life for me. Images of Diogenes mocking Plato's forms have led many after Nietzsche to take him as a model of subjective self-fashioning: in a world decentered by the "death of God" and uncoupled from objective grand narratives and Platonic Goods, Diogenes' laughing self-sufficiency is the model for a meaningful existence.

A purely subjective understanding of meaning justifies all life-schemes, no matter how petty, selfish, or sadistic: when "God" is dead, everything is justifiable and anything goes.[7] But Diogenes' practice of *parrhēsia* damns many life-choices as false, and so despite Nietzschean projections, Diogenes was no relativist – Sophistic, postmodern, or otherwise. Before the dichotomy of a created subjective meaning and a discovered objective one, he veers clearly towards the latter. Certainly it is in the immediacy of subjective experience that Diogenes would find true freedom, but it is the freedom of adapting to the constraints of nature – one's shifting objective circumstances, and one's own objective natural needs. Namely, one must return to one's given nature – as an animal that needs no external objects or goals. Paradoxically then, Diogenes' goal is not to have any goals, but to live in the fullness of the present, the only objective reality. More radically timeless than Parfit's "Timeless" (Parfit 1984: 174), Diogenes' momentary freedom would upset all my categories, pointing towards a subjective objectivity, as it were, a natural law that is often broken, though wholly immanent to its subjects: old and young, men and women, Greek and barbarian, each can leave behind their cultural differences to return to the simplicity of natural living and there become the "thing itself," equal "citizens of the cosmos" (*cosmopolitai*).

Would such a status confer meaning on life that is both objectively true, and subjectively felt? The shortcomings of Cynicism are legion: the anecdotes of Diogenes do not help much to clarify words, analyze basic concepts, or coordinate ideas and theories. Some Cynic talk of *virtue* and *happiness* can be translated into the related language of *worth, significance, importance*, and *meaning*. But to divine the deeper significance or possible varieties of Cynic "nature" or "self-sufficiency," to ask about the relation of natural determination to subjective freedom, of finitude to meaning, or of world history to individual worth – such questions demand creative interpretations and extrapolations going much beyond the ancient images. This anti-intellectual philosophy would thus seem radically insufficient for a society dependent on abstract ideas. Would a contemporary Diogenes go about half-naked, unkempt, lewd, and obscene? Would he in his ignorance loudly mock the arts and sciences as mere "smoke"? Would he reject community, even while dependent on its handouts? Would he be cruel and cynical towards the "common things that crave"? These aspects of Cynicism strike me as undesirable, not least in our own time. How could a sensualist, whose nominalism is insistent to the point of stinking, make others' lives more meaningful? Would it itself be meaningful? Certainly Cynic laughter is painful medicine for our all-too-human illusions of grandeur. Yet beyond the pride taken in debunking vanity, could Diogenes' laughter inspire the subjective confidence that one's life is objectively significant? Could it bring the conscious certainty that what I am and what I do are important – no matter how short or inglorious my life, no matter how vast and silent the universe? Diogenes ensconces himself in his tub and his naturalism: is this enough?[8] Debunking the debunker, a skeptic might compose some Mennippean lines to sum up Diogenes' little life:

> He snubbed the world and all its ways
> With wit and shameless glee –
> Whistling in his kingdom-tub,
> None was so fiercely free.

Is that all? – Plato's skeptical ghost might ask. Unless Diogenes' ascetic naturalism is the seed for some deeper spiritual consciousness, one may well doubt that it is enough.

And yet one should not shirk from a final, challenging thought. The Greeks marvelled to see Diogenes in their midst; medieval Italians marvelled at Francis and his fellow *joculatores Dei*; Hindus have marvelled at their "gymnosophists" and *avadhuta* sages. So it is with all peoples, who have wondered at ascetics in their midst, so simple, sometimes so startlingly joyful. Such affirmation comes at a price. Shakespeare's Lear marvels at the sight of Edgar naked on the heath, and addresses him as this *Athenian*, this *Theban* – a Cynic philosopher.

> Is man no more than this? Consider him well. – Thou owest the worm no silk, the beast no hide, the sheep no wool, the cat no perfume. Ha! Here's three on 's are sophisticated. Thou art the thing itself. Unaccommodated man is no more but such a poor, bare, forked animal as thou art. – Off, off, you lendings! Come. Unbutton here.
>
> (Shakespeare 1606: III.iv.103–11)

Unaccommodated Diogenes remains a challenge and a limiting case. The naked Cynic is "the thing itself" – a human being unprotected and unhindered by clothes, technology, society, everything. Lear's nakedness is symbolic of how each of us, for all our present wealth and pride, will be unbuttoned at some point, and left alone under some battering storm. What experiences or objective accomplishments can hold their meaning, can offer shelter – before that final nakedness? In Shakespeare's tragedy, it is through suffering that Lear learns the wisdom of humility, love, and joy in simple things. The self-imposed asceticism of a Diogenes would also teach some wisdom – one with less Christian love, and less humility, but perhaps greater joy in simple sensation, and great optimism that when freed of false ideas, each individual can enjoy each moment as a festive thing. In plumbing extremes of pain and pleasure, asceticism, and joy, Diogenes presents a challenge for all. For his admirers he represents *the* image of a meaningful life: laughing, mocking, honest, simple, free in the moment, and strong enough to take the sun – image of the Good, life's constant companion.

Notes

1 See Navia 1998: 1–44 for an attempted "Biographical Sketch" of Diogenes.
2 For one philosophical defence of custom and tradition, see Kekes 1985: 252–68; cf. 1998.
3 Epictetus, *Discourses* 3.22 (with Billerbeck 1996) On Foucault's last lecture series, see Shea 2010: 169–91.
4 "... das Höchste, was auf Erden erreicht werden kann, den Cynismus": *Ecce Homo* (Nietzsche 1908: "Why I Write Such Good Books," §3); cf. Branham 2004 and Desmond 2008: 229–34. Directly modelled on Diogenes with his lamp, Nietzsche's image of the "Madman" is (as he so willed) a starting point for very many modern thinkers, e.g. Young 2014; Cottingham 2003: 12–15.
5 My remarks take some inspiration from Metz's distinction between subjective and objective naturalism (Metz 2012: 163–248); cf. Cottingham's distinction of exogamous and endogamous meaning (Cottingham 2003: 11–12).
6 "The world is charged with the grandeur of God./ It will flame out ...": G.M. Hopkins 1877: 128. "Thus, from the war of nature, from famine and death, the most exalted object which we are capable of conceiving, namely, the production of the higher animals, directly follows. There is *grandeur* in this view of life ...": C. Darwin, *On the Origin of Species, ad fin.* (italics added) (Darwin 1859: 211). One should not immediately conflate this sense of an objective grandeur, sublimity, or beauty with an explicit teleology: so too the Cynics' naturalism is fairly stripped of determinate purposes.
7 See Desmond 2008: 112, for the anecdote of Diogenes playing Sisyphus – to show the absurdity of human customs of war. "One must imagine Sisyphus happy" – Camus' prescription for modern man (Camus 1942a: 123) – is taken by Taylor to the subjectivist conclusion that "the point of his [a person's] living is simply to be living, in the manner that it is his nature to be living" (Taylor 1970: 334) – wording somewhat redolent of Diogenes' ideal of momentary freedom.
8 Cf. the question motivating Haught (2006).

7 Zhuangzi and the meaning of life

DAVID E. COOPER

Zhuang Zhou (*c.* 369–286 BCE) – or Zhuangzi (Master Zhuang) – was probably a minor official in the Chinese state of Song who, if legend is to be believed, turned down an offer of high office, preferring to be like a turtle 'alive and dragging his backside through mud' than one ossified inside a royal palace (*Z* 17).[1] He was the author, most scholars think, of the first seven or 'inner' chapters of the text that goes by his name. Like the *Daodejing*, the other great text of classical or 'philosophical' Daoism, the *Zhuangzi* is the work of many hands over many years. The resulting inconsistencies, as well as the book's use of irony, allegory and other rhetorical devices, make interpretation challenging. But this has not prevented what Oscar Wilde praised as a 'very dangerous' work, full of 'destructive criticisms' of received ideas,[2] being recognized as anticipating important themes in Nietzsche, Heidegger, postmodernist thought, virtue epistemology and 'godless' philosophy of religion.

The Period of the Warring States, during which the Daoist texts were assembled, was one of intense philosophical activity in response, as one authority puts it, to a growing and 'profound metaphysical doubt, as to whether Heaven is after all on the side of human morality' (Graham 1995: 107). By the time of Confucius (sixth–fifth century BCE) the notion of heaven had largely lost the religious meaning it had earlier possessed and had become virtually equivalent to that of nature. The problem for later thinkers was whether Confucius was justified in assuming as he did, and without argument, that human morality was in harmony with nature. Among the responses to this problem was that of Zhuangzi's Confucian contemporary, Mencius, who presented arguments for holding that human beings are naturally predisposed to be moral, and that of followers of Mozi (fifth century BCE) who maintained that morality could anyway be justified, without any appeal to heaven or nature, on utilitarian grounds.

The response in the two Daoist classics was more radical. The right way for human beings must indeed, as the Ancients rightly saw, be in accord with heaven – or, better, with the Way (the *dao*) that 'generates' and 'sustains' heaven, earth and all beings (*Z* 6) – but this is not the way of morality. As the *Daodejing* explains (ch. 38), preoccupation with righteousness, benevolence, rites and principles is a sure sign that the Way has been lost.[3] Moral principles and precepts, Zhuangzi observes, are merely 'customs of the time', contrived human inventions that actually obstruct the capacity to 'draw on heaven' and to 'cultivate [one's] own person [and] what is genuine' (Z 31).

As those words suggest, the *Zhuangzi* certainly advances a conception of the good life, of what it is to be a 'fine' or 'consummate' person, a sage, who manifests what is authentically human in accordance with the Way that gives human beings, like everything else, their 'inborn nature' (Z 8). Would the life of such a person thereby have meaning? Talk of life's meaning is not a Daoist idiom, and the *Zhuangzi* roundly rejects the thought that a life should be a progression towards some end-state or goal. The Way or heaven is not some purposive being that sets goals, and dedication to 'any particular goal' – rather like commitment to moral rules – is incompatible with the 'flow' and 'stability' of lives that are 'in the Way' (Z 6). While, for example, the authors of the classic texts encourage care of the body, they would not endorse the later idea, popular in organized Daoist religious sects, that the sole 'goal' of 'our whole existence' is a 'wonderful old age' and 'a good death' (Schipper 1993: 214).

There are, however, other senses in which a life may be said to have meaning that are consonant with, indeed implied by, remarks in the *Zhuangzi*. If, to have meaning, a life must be appropriately related to something larger than or beyond itself, then, to begin with, it can have meaning by exemplifying this, by being a salient exemplar or 'cipher' of it. Secondly, it may have meaning in and through being guided and shaped by a sense of what is larger than or beyond itself. In the *Zhuangzi*, we find these two combined. Because the sage's life is guided by a sense of the *dao* – of what 'maintains ... and ties all things together' – it in effect emulates the *dao* (Z 6), and for this reason exemplifies it. This is how the life of the sage or consummate person acquires meaning or significance. (To take a favourite analogy from the *Daodejing* (ch. 8), water emulates the *dao* in various respects and for that reason has deep significance.)

But how can people emulate or 'model themselves' on the Way? The short answer given in the *Daodejing* (ch. 25) is that, since the Way itself is 'natural', a person must live 'naturally'. As much was suggested, of course, by the Daoist critique of morality as contrived and artificial – a critique that is just part of a more general one of the artificiality of everyday human life. Targets of the *Zhuangzi*'s critique are the imposition of human goals on nature, the use of 'tricky' technology to achieve such goals, a 'lust after knowledge' of a calculating kind (Z 10), and the artificial distinctions that our languages and conceptual schemes introduce into the world (Z 2 and 5). The text is full of admiring references to butchers, fishermen, carpenters and others who not only dispense with technical gadgets, but whose skill manifests implicit, wordless understanding – know-how that is 'in the hands' rather than 'in the head'.

Despite the Luddite and anti-intellectual tone of these remarks – and of the so-called 'primitivist chapters' (8–10) of the *Zhuangzi*[4] – the main message of the text is not that human beings should 'go back to nature', to wildness, and live like animals uncorrupted by civilization. Zhuangzi's heroes are not wild men or noble savages, but craftsmen and sages, and far from recommending surrender to uncultivated instincts and basic 'likes and dislikes', it is precisely these that we must be freed from if we are to be 'moved by heaven' (Z 15).

The 'primitivist', rather like some modern-day 'naturalists', fails to recognize respects in which human beings essentially differ from animals and anything else in nature. The *dao*-given *de* ('potency' or what makes anything what it essentially is) of people is radically unlike that of all other beings. One difference is that human beings alone can 'lose the Way' and so 'lose touch with their inborn nature'. Indeed, it is because most of them have done so through the artificial lives they lead that the world is brought into 'disorder', with the consequence that the integrity of all creatures is threatened by crass human interference (Z 13). The crucial difference, however, is that only human beings are able to 'understand the Way' and 'see through to the way that things fit together' (Z 17).

This capacity implies some further philosophically significant and distinctively human capacities. First, whereas 'fish come together in water', in the river or lake to which their movement and awareness is confined, 'human beings come together in the Way': they are able to conceive of the world as a whole, so that their attention is not restricted to their immediate environments and can roam freely. Second, since fish have no inkling of the Way, they have no sense of behaving in or out of harmony with it. 'Human beings', by contrast, 'can become aware that they are moved by the Way, and this awareness *is* [a] freedom' belonging to no other beings (Møllgaard 2011: 124; see also Perkins 2010). And since they are able to be moved by the Way, they are therefore able to redress the 'disorder' they may have created, and instead to 'nourish things' and restore harmony and order (Z 33).

To grasp how these capacities enable people to emulate and exemplify the *dao*, we need to explore a close cluster of notions that figure in the *Zhuangzi*: wandering or roaming (*you*), fasting of the heart-mind (*xinzhai*), and illumination (*ming*). It is helpful to think of these as a set of spiritual exercises, or perhaps exercises of epistemic virtues, that sages practise in cultivating the spontaneity or naturalness (*ziran*) that makes them exemplars of the Way.

Wandering is Zhuangzi's metaphor for 'soaring above the restricted viewpoints of the worldly'.[5] When wandering, sages not only transcend their own limited perspectives, but survey the equally limited perspectives of other people and creatures, inducing a sense of a 'vastness' that exceeds whatever can be captured in these perspectives. The sage's mind, in effect, 'wanders in the heavenly' (Z 26). Fasting of the heart-mind is a meditative practice that continues the wanderer's liberation from parochial perspectives. The fasting sage achieves a 'stillness' in which all everyday 'tallies', judgements and preconceptions are set aside, and is thereby ready to encounter 'the presence of beings' undistorted by any limiting perspective (Z 4). Illumination is the non-conceptual, non-verbal form of understanding of things available to the sage once preconceptions, perspectives and schemes of knowledge have been put in abeyance – 'bracketed', as Husserl would say. The sage's mind is now a like a mirror, lit up only by what is present before it (Z 7).

The *Daodejing* encourages us to 'reside in non-action (*wu wei*)', a gentle, non-assertive, non-interfering comportment towards people and things (e.g. chs. 1 and 10). So does the *Zhuangzi*, where one is urged, for example, to help things grow but not to 'control' them (Z 19). The main emphasis, however, is on non-action as the abstinence from imposing one's own preconceptions, 'likes and dislikes,' on things, which has been prepared for by wandering, fasting and illumination. What replaces the assertive action and imposition from which the sage abstains is *ziran*, spontaneity. The Chinese term literally means 'self-so' and certainly does not refer to spontaneity in the sense of a tendency to sudden capricious behaviour. Rather, the spontaneous person 'follows along with the way each thing is of itself … without trying to add anything' (Z 5). Spontaneity is mindful, flexible responsiveness to how things show themselves to be to someone whose vision and awareness is not obstructed by prejudices, preconceptions, artificial distinctions and conventional *idées fixes*. The concept is comparable to Heidegger's notion of *Gelassenheit*, a comportment towards things that 'lets them be' or 'releases' them into being what they are (see Heidegger 1966). In a sense, the spontaneous person has 'lost the self', recognizing that the self simply intrudes on and distorts what is engendered by the *dao* and heaven.

Spontaneity, then, is the paramount virtue that the *Zhuangzi* invites men and women to cultivate, the primary aspect of an authentic human life that accords with the *de* 'given' to human beings by the *dao*. But it is not simply a virtue, for it is its quality of spontaneity that, above all else, provides a human life with meaning. This is because a spontaneous life emulates and exemplifies the *dao* which itself, as we saw above, is 'self-so' or spontaneous. This rather bare statement may be elaborated by identifying some dimensions of the *dao*'s spontaneity and their analogues in the life of a sage or consummate person.

To begin with, the *dao* is not like a god that stands outside the world upon which it then imposes its will, purposes and moral demands. There is nothing outside of the *dao* for it to contend with, impose upon, or demand from: it meets with no resistance. Rather, it is the source of and what sustains the world, a continuous 'giving forth' of things and their 'transformations' (Z 17). It is the 'opening out and arraying of *de*' and a harmonizing of these into a cohesive whole (Z 24). Likewise, the sage does not contend with or impose on the world: mirroring how things are, mindful of their own *de* and potentials, and appreciating how they 'fit together' in a harmonious whole, the consummate person 'lets them be' and indeed 'nourishes' them. He or she will, for example, praise the horse-whisperer who respects the 'true inborn nature of horses' and not the domineering trainer who 'brands, shaves, clips, bridles and fetters them' (Z 9). In this respect sages continue the work of the *dao*. Sages, in effect, aspire to become as purpose-less and self-less as the *dao* itself.

Precisely because the world is a harmonious, cohesive whole – one of a 'reciprocal overflowing of things' into one another – nothing can be objectively deemed more valuable than anything else. Everything is dependent on everything else. From the point of view of the Way, nothing is 'worthy or unworthy' (Z 17). The *dao* is entirely impartial, unconstrained by anything that could bias its 'allotment of things'. In everyday life, by contrast, men and women are, without realizing it, constantly judging and assessing things on the basis of conventions or their own interests, ambitions, likes and dislikes. The wandering, fasting, illuminating sage, however, emulates the *dao* in 'sorting out but not assessing' (Z 2). This is not a matter, simply, of suspending the norms of conventional morality, for the partiality of everyday judgements is quite general. All the claims people make about the world – and not just overtly evaluative ones – are made from particular, limited perspectives. It is these that the sage succeeds – in meditative moments and times of wandering, at least – to transcend and, in doing so, to be in accord with the impartiality of the Way.

A critic might argue that the *dao* cannot, as a person can, be literally described as non-contending, giving, harmonizing or impartial. Zhuangzi would respond that this is hardly surprising given the ineffability of the *dao*: that which 'forms all forms is not itself a form', it 'cannot be spoken' (Z 22). Any attempt to speak of it, therefore, can only gesture at it in figurative, poetic or analogical terms. But he would then question why the non-literal character of the descriptions should constitute a criticism. Christian theologians, for example, who compare human beings in certain respects with God, are generally happy to allow that it is only analogically that God can be described as wise, forgiving or just. This is not taken to destroy the idea that, in these respects, people can and should aspire to be like their God. A person's emulation of something can be genuine without what is emulated having literally the same qualities as the emulator's.

If the *Zhuangzi*'s conception of the sage as emulating the Way (if only analogically) is cogent, then the sage's life is not only a good one that realizes the human *de*. It is also one with a significance beyond itself. For it is a life that is a cipher, a living symbol of the Way of things, of the wellspring of the world and the beings that occupy it. It is, perhaps, less in virtue of the recognition of living well than of living in consonance with the *dao* that the sage is said not only to be 'still and calm', but someone whom 'nothing can harm' (Z 17). This conception of the sage, moreover, is grounded in philosophical reflections and proposals that still resonate in the present and with which many recent philosophers might sympathize.

Central to the *Zhuangzi* is a critique of knowledge, including moral knowledge. Commentators disagree as to whether the book is defending relativism, radical scepticism or, more mildly, a fallibilist attitude towards all statements and beliefs (see Coutinho 2004: ch. 4). Remarks like 'Things are so only by being called so' and each thing must 'have some place from which it can be affirmed as thus and so' (Z 2) surely suggest that, in some chapters at least, the book advances a form of 'perspectivalism', a theory particularly associated in modern times with Nietzsche. According to this view, no statements, true or false, can be made about things except from a perspective and it is invidious to privilege any particular perspective above any other. The resonance with Nietzsche is confirmed when we appreciate that, for both philosophers, the case for perspectivalism is primarily the inseparability of perspectives, and hence of judgements, from needs, interests, ambitions and purposes. There is no description of the world that is free from such constraints, and hence no description of it that can pretend to be an 'absolute' or objective one.

Like Nietzsche and Richard Rorty, Zhuangzi at times seems to advocate an ironic stance towards perspectives, including one's own – a laconic recognition that, while for practical purposes it is necessary to assess things from a certain point of view, there is nothing that objectively warrants this point of view. Elsewhere, however, the text seems, rather, to be advocating the cultivation of epistemic virtues. In order to achieve an illuminated, wordless awareness of things, the sage must exercise humility, become open, tolerant and flexible, and in other ways control the intrusion of self into what ought to be a passive mirroring of the world. These may not be the virtues that are most emphasized by contemporary virtue epistemologists, focused as they tend to be on scientific knowledge and respect for evidence, but they would recognize in Zhuangzi a pioneer of the kind of enquiry they pursue.

That the *Zhuangzi* calls for humility and passivity rather than irony is indicative of a decisive difference from Nietzschean and Rortyan critiques of knowledge, one with an important bearing on the issue of the meaning of life. While Zhuangzi is a perspectivalist, he thinks – unlike these other philosophers – that all perspectives and the world itself have a source in a reality that cannot be articulated, the *dao*. Whereas the Nietzschean hero, the Overman, imposes his individual stamp on the world, creating his own 'table of values', the Daoist hero surrenders individuality in order to be receptive to the *dao*-given world as it comes to presence. The difference also entails that, whereas for Nietzsche and his postmodernist admirers there can be no meaning in life other than that conferred by an individual, for Zhuangzi meaning accrues to a life that emulates and exemplifies what is larger than and beyond it, the *dao*.

It is surely Heidegger's 'shepherd of Being', not Nietzsche's Overman, that is the heir in modern times to the Daoist sage. Given the obvious echoes of the classic Daoist texts in Heidegger's writing, it comes as no surprise to learn that he once began a translation of the *Daodejing*. We have already heard some of those echoes – in, for example, the 'letting-be' of things that recalls the *Zhuangzi*'s talk of nourishing what is 'self-so'. More generally, there is a striking correspondence between the Heideggerian idea of ineffable Being that is the source or wellspring of beings and the Daoist idea of a *dao* that is 'the mother of the 10,000 things'. Heidegger, of course, recognized this correspondence, invoking the name of the *dao* to characterize his own conception of a mysterious source of things, a 'great hidden stream which moves all things along and makes way for everything' (Heidegger 1971a: 92). Heidegger would not resist, I think, the suggestion that the life of his shepherd of Being has meaning in the same kind of way that the life of the Daoist sage has. The shepherd and the sage, after all, both 'make a way for everything' – letting things be – just as the 'great hidden stream' and the *dao* do.

Notes

1 References are to chapters of the *Zhuangzi*. I have drawn on several translations, especially Zhuangzi fourth–third century BCE-a and fourth–third century BCE-b. Most scholars today use the Pinyin romanization, *Zhuangzi*, in preference to the older Wade-Giles one, *Chuang-Tzu*.
2 Quoted in J. Cooper 2010: 42.
3 Among the good translations of *Daodejing* (*Tao Te Ching* in Wades-Giles' spelling) are Lao Tzu sixth century BCE-a and sixth century BCE-b.
4 See Zhuangzi fourth–third century BCE-b: pt 4.
5 Zhuangzi fourth–third century BCE-b: 43.

8   Aristotle on the meaning of life

MONTE RANSOME JOHNSON

Aristotle is the first philosopher on record to subject the meaning of life to systematic philosophical examination: he approaches the issue from logical, psychological, biological, and anthropological perspectives in some of the central passages in the *Corpus Aristotelicum*[1] and, it turns out, in some fragments from his (lost) early popular work the *Protrepticus* (*Exhortation to Philosophy*).[2] In the present context I can do little more than call attention to these texts and attempt to offer a coherent interpretation of them, without being able to enter into the usual controversies, many of them centuries and some millennia old.

From an Aristotelian perspective, in asking about life's "meaning," we may be asking either a theoretical question about the *definition* of the term life (and this either generically or with specific reference to human life), or a practical question about the final *end* or *purpose* of life (or human life). Aristotle carefully considered both questions, and in his view answering the theoretical question is the key to answering the practical question. Thus my plan is as follows. After examining a network of texts that show Aristotle's theoretical definition of life, I will discuss the practical implication he draws from his answer in the ethical works and the *Protrepticus*. A single continuous fragment of the *Protrepticus* begins with the premise "the word 'life' appears to have a double meaning" and concludes: "therefore, *living* with pleasure and enjoyment belong truly, either only or most of all, to the philosophers."[3] This view, as extreme and rebarbative as it may seem at first glance, is maintained in Aristotle's ethical works.

In Aristotle's naturalistic view, all living things, including plants, animals, human beings, and even gods, may be rank-ordered according to their *erga* or functions, which are determined by a consideration of the generic features of their form of life and specific features of their way of life. Human beings can reflect on the meaning of their own lives in an Aristotelian way by reflecting on the capabilities that all living things possess, on the unique capabilities of their own species, and on the specific way that those capabilities may be employed in their own lives. These reflections aim to determine not just the theoretical meaning of "life" but also the practical means of "living well" and finding "the good life." To state Aristotle's position as briefly as possible:

living means actively engaging one or more vital capabilities (nutrition, sensation, movement, intellect), and living as a human specifically means engaging
in intellectual activity. Thus the ultimate meaning of life, for humans, is
engagement in intellectual activity.

Aristotle uses a pair of Greek terms that are commonly translated into
English as "life": *zôê* and *bios*, from which we get the terms "zoology" and
"biology." Although he frequently uses them interchangeably, we may distinguish Aristotle's technical uses of them. *Zôê*, "life, or living," is defined by the
capabilities that any living natural kind possesses by definition, the activities
that are sufficient for a thing's survival as a thing of that kind: nutrition and
reproduction (for plants), sensation and self-movement (for animals), and
reason and intellect (for humans and gods). *Bios*, which is often better translated as "way of life," refers to the mode of existence employed by a living
kind within its ecological niche: e.g. the solitary or gregarious ways of life
possible for land-animals, or the banausic or philosophical ways of life possible for human beings. The "meaning of life" can accordingly be determined
relative to both a generic natural kind and to an individual specimen, that is,
both by generic vital capabilities, and by the specific ways that an individual
exercises its vital capacities.

Let us begin with *zôê*. In the *Topics,* a treatise on the logic and strategy of
dialectical reasoning, Aristotle discusses the meaning of the term in order to
illustrate a potential problem in the construction of definitions: things which
have the same name and definition are named "synonymously," while things
which have the same name but different definitions are named "homonomously." If then there are things homonomously named "living," a given
definition of *zôê* would fail to apply to one of the things called by that name.
As an example, Aristotle cites Dionysius' definition of life.

> This happened also in the case of Dionysius' definition of the term living
> (*zôê*): "movement sustaining a kind of congenital nutrition." For this definition
> applies not more to the animals (*zôiois*) than it does to the plants. But the
> term living (*zôê*) seems to be said not in accordance with a single form, rather
> one exists for the animals (*zôiois*) and another for the plants. At the same
> time, it is possible also to deliberately frame the definition in this way and to
> speak in accordance with a single form of every living thing (*zôês*).
> (VI.10.148a23–33)

The problem with Dionysius' definition of *zôê* is the following. The cognate
term *zôion* means both "living being" and "animal." It can be used to refer to
any living thing, including a plant (and also to a figure or image of a living
thing[4]), but is commonly used in a narrower sense with reference only to
"animals," for example, horses, apes, or humans. Now if one were to accept
Dionysius' definition of *zôê*, but intend to speak about *zôion* in the usual
restricted sense, then one could be led into a problem, for example if one were

to argue that "every *zôion* has an organ of sensation"; the problem is that plants fit Dionysius' definition of *zôê*, since they use nutrition, but they do not have any sense organs, no plant being a *zôion* in the narrow sense of "animal." The ambiguity in the term *zôion* is reflected in the fact that at the time Aristotle was writing and for a long time afterwards there was a debate about whether plants are alive and have a *psychê*. For this reason, Aristotle remarks, the term *zôê seems* to be applied homonymously to both plants and animals: plants on the basis of their capability for nutrition, animals on the basis of their capability for sensation. In that case there would be no single definition of *zôê* that applies to every *zôion* in the wider sense that includes plants.

But in the final sentence of the *Topics* passage, Aristotle changes perspectives and suggests that one might deliberately frame a definition of *zôê* so that it synonymously applies a single form to every *zôion* in the wider sense. Aristotle does not explain this suggestion in the *Topics*, but it becomes clear what he means in *On the Soul*, when he discusses a parallel problem with respect to the definition of the term *psychê* (usually translated *anima* or soul). He complains that all of his predecessors' research on the *psychê* was restricted to the human one, but he exhorts us to take seriously and not neglect the question "whether the account of *psychê* is a single one, as in the case of 'living thing' (*zôiou*), or whether each one has a different account, for example "horse," "dog," "human," "god," in which case the universal is either nothing or posterior" (I.1.402b3–9). If the terms *zôion* and *psychê* are applied to things that necessarily have different definitions, then attempting to frame a single definition of these terms will occasion the problem with homonymy that Aristotle warned about in the *Topics*. For example, if one were to define the *psychê* as a sensing thing or a thinking thing, then, since the term *psychê* is also applied to cows and other animals that cannot think, these things, since they have different definitions, will be homonymously referred to by the same term.

Aristotle's solution to this problem is to frame a disjunctive definition of *psychê* which explicitly recognizes that there are different kinds of *psychê* (or different souls), and this definition will reflect the fact that the term *zôê* has several senses.

> Taking up the inquiry from the beginning, one may say that the animate (*empsuchon*) is distinguished from the inanimate by reference to the living (*toi zên*). But the term "living" (*tou zên*) is said in many ways, and any one of these alone being present, we say this thing is living, for example intellect, sensation, motion and rest with respect to place, and even motion in accordance with nutrition and decay and growth.
>
> (*On the Soul* I.1.413a20–25)

Thus there will be as many kinds of soul (or souls) as there are ways of being a living thing, and the term "living" is rightly applied to anything that shows any one or more of the capabilities on the above list. It immediately follows that all plants, since they possess the capability for nutrition and decay and growth, are living things (413a25–26). But it is not merely by disjunction that the term "living" is applied synonymously to both plants and animals because, it turns out, both plants and animals possess the vegetative capability: "It is possible to separate this capability from the others, but it is not possible to separate the others from this in the case of the mortals" (413a31–32). It may be possible in the case of the gods to separate their activities (e.g. intellection) from the vegetative capability, assuming they do not use nutrition and the stories about ambrosia and nectar are myths. But in mortal living things, including plants, animals, and humans, the vegetative capability is a necessary condition for the presence of any other capability. So Aristotle says that "because of this principle the term 'living' (*to zên*) applies to the animals (*tois zôsi*), even though the term 'animal' (*to zôion*) is primarily used because of sensation. For even those things that do not move, not even with respect to place, but yet have sensation, we say are 'animals' (*zôion*) and not merely 'living' (*zên*) (413a20–b4; cf. 412a13–16).

We thus have a definitive answer to the theoretical question of the generic "meaning of life" for Aristotle: setting aside immortal life, living *means* having an ability to use nutrition, and perhaps also sensation, or locomotion, or intellection. But as Aristotle points out, although it is possible to attribute life to animals on the basis of their vegetative capability, in a sense this does not seem to reflect what makes them specifically "animals," since we say that they live as animals primarily because of their capability for sensation. A sign of this is that even sea creatures that remain motionless, like a rooted plant, but are nevertheless capable of even minimal sensation, we call "animals," not merely "living things." Thus we can call something "living" because of nutrition, but we can only call it an "animal" if it has sensation.

Aristotle's reference to a species that resembles a plant in being motionless but an animal in having sensation reflects his metaphysical doctrine that there is a continuous series of natural kinds that proceeds from lifeless things, like the elements, through inanimate compounds, plants, animals, humans, and gods. There are natural kinds that "dualize" between inanimate things and plants; plants themselves dualize between inanimate things and animals; some kinds "dualize" between plants and animals (as we have just seen); and some other kinds dualize between animals and humans. And since Aristotle holds that a human may become like a god, there is even a human kind that dualizes between human and god, namely, the philosopher. Each kind is actually discrete and in theory has its own definition, but the exact differences between them are often difficult to perceive, especially at the lower levels, and in some cases require further research – this is the reason Aristotle calls the series continuous: "and so from the lifeless things nature makes a transition little by little into the living things, such that the border between them, and which side the intermediate thing is on, escapes our notice. For beyond the kind of lifeless things is, first, the kind of plants" (*History of Animals* VIII.1.588b4–7).

The continuous series can be rank-ordered according to a number of different criteria, including degree of vital heat, mode of locomotion, ecological niche, and mode of reproduction. But a single rank-ordering of natural kinds corresponds to relative degrees of vitality or "participation in life": "among plants one kind differs from another kind with respect to seeming to participate more in life, but as a whole the kind of plants seems animate relative to the other bodies, but relative to animals inanimate" (588b7–10). The fact that plants resemble both inanimate things and animals is why there was a controversy about whether they were alive and thus had souls. Animals, in turn, resemble on the one hand plants, and on the other humans. And the transition between animal kinds with respect to degrees of vitality and activity, as with plant kinds, is continuous (*History of Animals* VIII.1.588b10–21; cf. *On the Parts of Animals* IV.5.681a10–29). So there is a continuous series with respect to living and moving (588b21–23), and with respect to modes of sensation. Some animals, for example, are capable only of tactile sensation, while others are capable of other kinds of sensation in addition to this, including smelling, tasting, hearing, and seeing. Some animals, including humans, possess capabilities for all these modes of sensation. On the basis of these different degrees of sensation, Aristotle is willing to allow that some things actually "live more": "inasmuch as more sensation is a property of the thing living more, so less sensation will be a property of the thing living less, and the most sensation of the most living and the least sensation of the least, and sensation without qualification of life without qualification" (*Topics* VIII.1.137b23–27).

Most consequentially, there is for all living things a continuous variation with respect to "the activities of their way of life" (*History of Animals* 588b23) and thus their *erga* or functions. Even spontaneously generated organisms show differences in activities that make their lives "more or less valuable or honorable" (762a24–25), depending on the "degree to which they embrace the principle of animation" (762a25–26). In general, "the *ergon* of the soul is to produce living" (*Eudemian Ethics* II.1.1219a24). Plants clearly have an *ergon*, but it is mere reproduction: "among the plants that come about through seeds there is no other *ergon* apparent except to make another again like itself" (*History of Animals* 588b24–26). And some animals have virtually no *ergon* beyond that of a plant (588b26–27). But animals show immense variation in degree of vitality and activity: "Some animals, like plants, achieve procreation simply according to the seasons, but others also labor at nurturing the offspring, and when they have achieved this, separate and never make anything in common with them. But others, being more sagacious and taking part in memory do so for longer and get along with their descendants on a more political basis" (588b21–589a2). By attributing a degree of sociality and even intelligence to some animals, Aristotle holds that some natural things dualize between animals and humans, that is, in their way of life they resemble both animals and humans.

Humans, then, can be said to live not only on the basis of their vegetative capabilities, but also their animal capabilities for sensation and locomotion. But it seems obvious that the distinctive activity and goal of a human life is not based on such capabilities but rather: "obviously it is sensing and knowing ... For each person, the most choiceworthy thing is to sense oneself and know oneself, and that is why everyone has an innate desire to live. For we should specify that living is a kind of knowing" (*Eudemian Ethics* VII.12.1244b23–29). When he says that we should "specify that living is a kind of knowing" Aristotle here means that living *for a human being* is a kind of knowing. Just as living *for an animal* means sensing and not just vegetating, so living *for a human* means knowing and not just sensing.

In the biological works and the *Politics*, Aristotle raises the possibility that a human could metamorphose from being the most perfect and divine specimen on earth into a four-footed animal, or a many-footed insect, or even a plant.[5] Aristotle seems best interpreted in all these passages not as describing a process of evolution (or devolution) of species, but instead a transformation of an individual person, with results that can be correlated to the rank-ordering of the continuous series of living things. The idea of becoming like a brute animal or plant, I would suggest, is the flip side to the hortatory rhetoric of "becoming like a god." Thus, in the *Protrepticus* both possibilities are mentioned together in order to make a moral point: "when sensation and intellect are taken away, a human becomes roughly the same as a plant; when intellect alone is taken away, he turns into a beast; when irrationality is taken away but he remains in his intellect, a human becomes similar to a god" (*Protrepticus, apud* Iamblichus, *Protrepticus* V.35.14–18). So, an individual human may devolve into a beast (thus the pleasures that cause intemperance are *bestial; Nicomachean Ethics* III.10.1118b5), or even a plant (thus we still describe some patients as being in a persistent *vegetative* state). This is not metaphorical: eating, drinking and sex are the pleasures we have in common with animals, and when we cannot move or sense we literally have the capabilities of a plant.

On the other hand, by exercising their intellect, a human may also meta-morphose into something like a god. It seems this is the reason that only humans among animals can be *eudaimon*, as Aristotle stipulates in the *Eudemian Ethics*.[6] The conventional term for "happiness," "flourishing" or "success," *eudaimonia* indicates the final end of human life, and Aristotle holds that it requires participation in a special kind of intellectual activity, one available uniquely to humans. We see this line of reasoning at work in all versions of the *ergon* argument in the ethical works, beginning with the *Protrepticus*, where "contemplating truth" is said to be the ultimate *ergon*, whether a human is conceived as an animal with a single *ergon* or with several *erga*.

So if a human is a simple animal whose substance is ordered according to reason and intellect, there is no other function for him than only the most precise truth, i.e. to tell the truth about existing things; but if more capabilities are ingrown in him, it is clear that, of the larger number of things he can naturally bring to perfection, the best of them is always a function, e.g. of a medical man health, and of a navigator safety. And we can name no function of thought or of the contemplating part of our soul that is better than truth. Truth therefore is the function in the strictest sense of this portion of the soul.

(*Protrepticus, apud* Iamblichus, *Protrepticus* VII.42.13–23)

We have already discussed what is meant by saying that humans might have multiple *erga*: as mortal animals, humans have as *erga* nutrition, reproduction, growth, sensation, movement, and intellect. The vegetative capabilities can be eliminated on the grounds that they are not unique to humans (*Eudemian Ethics* II.1.1219b20–1220a1). The animal capabilities can be eliminated on similar grounds: "Living seems to be common even to plants, but we are seeking what is unique to a human. Let us exclude, therefore, the life of nutrition and growth. Next would be a life of sensation, but it also seems to be common even to the horse, the ox, and every animal. There remains, then, an active life of the part having reason" (*Nicomachean Ethics* I.7.1097b33–1098a4). These arguments, when read in light of Aristotle's claims about the continuous series of *erga* among living things, cohere with the extreme intellectualist account of *eudaimonia* at the end of *Nicomachean Ethics*. After all, we need to find a kind of activity that, despite the continuity of vital activities between humans, animals, and plants, does not overlap with any other, lower capability. Although some of the animals have, more or less, "sagacity," a kind of "political" existence, and even a kind of "intelligence," they do not have intellects and cannot think or attain theoretical wisdom.[7] And for this reason, while other forms of animal life and ways of human life can be pleasant and good, without participating in this *divine* activity, they cannot be *eudaimon* (*Nicomachean Ethics* X.8.1178b21–30).

Aristotle goes so far as to claim that even the cultivation of the moral virtues, which certainly requires intellectual activity, is not our ultimate end, but when we take into account the criteria of self-sufficiency, finality, leisureliness, and uniqueness, only theoretical contemplation corresponds to the "complete *eudaimonia* for a human, assuming he has a complete term of life (*biou*)" (*Nicomachean Ethics* X.7.1177b24–25). The result is that, somewhat paradoxically, the ultimate end of human life is to transcend human life and become like a god – this would be to act on what is at once the most human and the most divine part in us, the overlap being due to the continuity of all living things.

But such a life would be too high for a human; for it is not in so far as he is a human that he will live so, but in so far as something divine is present in him; and by so much as this is superior to our composite nature is its activity superior to that which is the exercise of the other kind of virtue. If reason is divine, then, in comparison, the life according to it is divine in comparison with human life. But we must not follow those who advise us, being human, to think of human things, and, being mortal, of mortal things, but must, so far as we can, make ourselves immortal, and strain in every way to live in accordance with the best thing in us; for even if it be small in bulk, much more does it in power and worth surpass everything. This would seem, too, to be each human itself, since it is the authoritative and better part. It would be strange, then, if one were to choose not the life of oneself but that of something else. And what we said before will apply now; that which is proper to each thing is by nature best and most pleasant for each thing; for a human, therefore, the life according to reason is best and pleasantest, since reason more than anything else is human. This life therefore is also the happiest.

(*Nicomachean Ethics* X.7.1177b27–1178a8)

Thus we have both the theoretical and practical answer, to both the general and specific questions about the meaning of life. In general, the meaning of life is the exercise of the best and most unique capability that makes a living thing a being of a certain kind. Specifically, the meaning and end of human life is to engage in intellectual activity, both because intellect is not shared with any lower living things (with whom we share so much else), and because it is shared with the gods (with whom we share so little else). Although scholars frequently recoil from intensely intellectualist and arguably elitist conclusions about the final human end, you, the reader, should take comfort in the fact that you are, even right now, engaging in the very activity that Aristotle thinks gives human life its meaning.

Notes

1 All translations of the *Corpus Aristotelicum* are adapted from those included in the Revised Oxford Translation, edited by J. Barnes.

2 On the authenticity of the fragments of the *Protrepticus* see Düring 1961 and Hutchinson and Johnson 2005.

3 Aristotle, *Protrepticus, apud* Iamblichus, *Protrepticus* XI.56.15–59.11–13.

4 This happens to be the very first example in the whole *Corpus Aristotelicum*: as an example of homonymy, Aristotle points out that both a human and a sketching are called *zôion*, and as an example of synonymy, both a human and a cow are (*Categories* I.1a1–8).

5 "The bodies of animals grow smaller and many-footed, and finally become footless and stretched out on the earth. Proceeding in this way a little, even their origin is below, and the part corresponding to the head is in the end unable to move and sense, and a plant comes to be, having its above below and its below above" (*On the Parts of Animals* IV.10.686b29–34; cf. *On the Generation of Animals* I.23.731a25-b8; V.1.778b29–779a4; *Politics* V.3.1302b34–1303a3).

6 "Perhaps there could be *eudaimonia* of some other, better thing, among the things that exist, e.g. of a god. Surely, among the other animals, who are in their nature worse than the humans, none participates in this; for the predicate *eudaimon* applies to neither a horse, nor a bird, nor a fish, nor any of the other things that exist which, in accordance with the general name of their kind, do not in their nature participate in a certain divine thing. But in accordance with participation in some other of the good things, some of them live better and others live worse than others" (*Eudemian Ethics* I.7.1217a22–29).

7 *On the Parts of Animals* I.1.641b8. In the *Protrepticus*, Aristotle makes it even more clear how humans differ from other animals: "for what makes us different from the other animals shines through in this life alone, a life in which what happens cannot fail to have great worth. For animals too have little glimmers of reason and intelligence, but they have absolutely no share of theoretical wisdom, and this is shared only with the gods, just as humans are actually left behind by many animals in the precision and strength of their senses and their drives" (Aristotle, *Protrepticus, apud* Iamblichus, *Protrepticus* V.36.6–13).

9   Epicurus and the meaning of life

CATHERINE WILSON

Epicureanism is the natural and moral philosophy taught by the ancient Greek philosopher Epicurus (341–270 BCE), and by his Roman follower Titus Carus Lucretius (99–55 BCE), who set his admired forerunner's doctrines to verse in his *On the Nature of Things*.

The master notoriously defended pleasure as the starting point for reflection on the good life and the goal of rational activity. He says:

> Pleasure is our first and kindred good. It is the starting point of every choice and of every aversion, and to it we always come back, inasmuch as we make feeling the rule by which to judge of every good thing.
>
> (In Diogenes Laertius third century CE: X, 129)

Many readers are apt to feel strongly from the outset that there is a distinction between a *pleasant* life and a *meaningful* life. A meaningful life is one with a number of meaningful experiences and meaningful actions. It seems to be compatible with endurance and hardship, and even to require them. Rather than setting out the conditions for a meaningful life, Epicurus seems to saying that we needn't be concerned with meaningfulness at all and should aim instead for the maximum of enjoyment.

For many centuries, two main conceptions of the meaningful life have been available in cultures with literary philosophical traditions. Neither one mentions pleasure. On one conception, worldly achievement makes an individual's life meaningful, and on the other, it is only moral or spiritual achievement that can do so.

On the worldly view, the best sort of life involves *doing* something or *being* something that earns admiration and respect and that can leave a mark on history, and keep one's memory alive. The great artists, writers, conquerors, scientists and philosophers have achieved this status. Thus Michelangelo, Shakespeare, Alexander the Great, Einstein, Socrates and a number of others have all had meaningful lives according to this criterion, but very few women. Altogether, however, only a small percentage of past humans have had *very* meaningful lives, while a somewhat larger percentage have had somewhat meaningful lives, as they didn't accomplish as much and are not as widely recognized and remembered.

On the moral-spiritual view, the purpose of life is to love God, to do good works, and to pass moral tests, acquitting oneself well in the moral struggle against the temptations of the world to earn eternal life or resurrection in a new body. Anybody, male or female, slave or free, peasant or aristocrat, can achieve this kind of life. This perspective was strongly associated with Christian doctrine and with Kant's moral philosophy.

The Epicurean perspective on what Epicurus called the 'blessed' life does not urge a life dedicated to achievement and fame. The Epicureans rejected political and military activity, the main routes to glory and fame, seeing them as causes of painful vexation and corrupting ambition. Nor did they believe that service to a divinity made life meaningful. If a god or gods actually existed outside the human imagination, they were entirely removed from any concern with human affairs, enjoying a life free of care in some remote part of the universe.[1] The ideals of devotion to a family and sacrifices made on their behalf were equally irrelevant in the eyes of the Epicureans. The wise man will marry and raise children but only if circumstances are just right, and family life will never be the centre of his concerns (Diogenes Laertius third century CE: X, 119). The best sort of life is one free of deprivations – especially those of hunger, thirst and cold – and free of fears and anxieties for the future. On the positive side, it requires two things: friends, for '[f]riendship dances around the world, announcing to all of us that we must wake up to blessedness', and the serious study of the empirical world.[2]

This third conception of the good life is not absent from the Christian Bible. Ecclesiastes 8.15 says, 'Then I commended mirth, because a man hath no better thing under the sun, than to eat, and to drink, and to be merry', and Isaiah 22.13 says 'Let us eat and drink; for to morrow we shall die.' Later, Spinoza describes human virtue in his *Ethics* as simply 'acting, living, preserving our being' in a manner guided by reason (Spinoza 1677: pt IV, prop. 24).[3] But this third conception has never achieved the philosophical respectability of the other two. To their contemporary critics, especially the ancient Stoics, the Epicureans seemed selfish, irresponsible and self-indulgent.[4] Their inclusion of women in the philosophical and social activities of the Garden – the Epicurean school's location outside the city boundaries of Athens – was unique in the Greek philosophical world and gave rise to much pejorative commentary.[5]

By way of defending Epicureanism as offering a credible vision of a meaningful life, as opposed to rejecting the identification of a good life with a meaningful life, it is helpful to step back and query the critical term. What is it to call an experience, or an action, as opposed to some words and phrases – for example, an utterance in one's native language or a particular poem – 'meaningful' or 'meaningless?' What is implied, I take it, is a sense of 'ownership', recognition, and acceptance. I recognize *my* native language, in which words and sentences have meaning, as the one in which I express myself, guide others, and am guided. The meaningful poem has a similar feature – it uses the images and phrasing that resonate with me; I feel known and guided by it, and try in some way to claim it as belonging to me. By analogy, a meaningful life is one that I can identify with, or can wish to make my own. The depiction of it can guide or inspire me. Meaningfulness thus involves a sense of belonging to a system greater than oneself; meaningful words and experiences provide what feels like an opening onto a wider reality; meaningful actions link my agency to that wider reality.

This way of thinking about meaningfulness helps to pull the third conception in closer as an alternative to the worldly-achievement and moral-spiritual conceptions, both of which put the individual into a relationship with something greater than his or her self. Yet it still seems insufficient. Pleasure in food, drink, warmth and companionship is available to any gregarious animal, but we don't usually think of sparrows, dogs and horses or chimpanzees as having meaningful lives.

The quotation on pleasure does not, however, capture the Epicurean view on what makes a life worthwhile. The members of the ancient school and their later philosophical followers would have considered the Scriptural remarks quoted above somewhat misleading, superficial and incomplete. After explaining briefly their natural philosophy and the role of pleasure, pain, fear and anxiety, I'll explore the role of self-development and cultivation of the understanding in Epicurean philosophy to try to bring out the way the ideal life commended by that sect could satisfy the conditions of meaningfulness.[6]

Epicurean natural philosophy

A central claim of the Epicurean philosophy is that the universe and all that exists within it was not created by God or the gods for any purpose or according to any model; it simply emerged from a chaotic soup of particles: the atoms. They, unlike the objects they compose, are indivisible and indestructible. Life arose through the concourse of individual atoms that over long intervals assembled into planets, stars, geological features, and even functional plants and animals.[7] Lucretius's text hints at a kind of process of natural selection, according to which forms that were not adapted to life and reproduction failed to survive and perpetuate their type.[8] Hence the question 'for what purpose were humans *created?*' as well as 'To what purpose was non-living and living nature created?' are senseless: no agent with intentions, plans or demands has created anything.

Living things instinctively engage in activities that feel rewarding and avoid, or try to escape from, or remedy pain-inducing objects and situations. If they weren't equipped with these instincts, they would not survive. In this respect, animal life is ruled by pleasure and pain. But survival is limited by time. No conglomerate of atoms can survive dissolution, and eventually the atoms of the soul (for the soul too is a collection of especially small and lively atoms) disperse and the individual dies. Her soul atoms drift about, eventually being taken in elsewhere and animating some other being. Because death is final and permanent, a condition from which no one returns, a meaningful life takes place within the boundaries of our biological lifespan and cannot involve any state of preparation for an afterlife in which we continue to exist or are restored to life.

Neither death nor the process of dying are to be feared because without the soul there can be no experiences, and the approach of death means the diminution of all pains and pleasures (see Rosenbaum 1986). No one need fear hell and no one can hope for heaven, as these places do not exist. But seeking death is wrong. Unlike the Stoics, who maintained that certain kinds of worldly deprivations such as incurable illness, loss of fortune, oppression by a tyrant, or simply being tired of life, made suicide a rational and acceptable choice,[9] Epicurus insisted that mitigation of pain, not the curtailment of life, should be the aim. One should avoid exposure to worldly disappointment in the first place. But if things go badly, one can live even with what seems to others an intolerable condition, such as blindness (Diogenes Laertius third century CE: X, 119).

Living pleasantly

The avoidance of pain and death rather than the all-out pursuit of pleasure governs Epicurean ethics. As Epicurus points out, there is no pleasure greater than that we experience in being spared some disaster (see DeWitt 1950). So the answer to the question 'How should I live?' is simple and straightforward: prudently and harmlessly.

First, we realize that some forms of pleasure-seeking produce pain in the long term, and that some pains must be endured for the sake of future happiness. The good life therefore does not consist in excess. Too much drink, too much food, too much sexual promiscuity, result in poor health, poverty and the ruination of strength and beauty.

> When we say pleasure is the goal we do not mean the pleasures of the profligate or the pleasures of consumption, as some believe, either from ignorance and disagreement or from deliberate misinterpretation, but rather the lack of pain in the body and disturbance in the soul. For it is not drinking bouts and continuous partying and enjoying boys and women, or consuming fish and the other dainties of an extravagant table, which produces a pleasant life, but sober calculation ... [P]rudence is the source of all the other virtues, teaching that it is impossible to live pleasantly without living prudently, honourably and justly ...
>
> (Letter to Menoeceus, in Diogenes Laertius third century CE: X, 131–32)

Second, we realise that some goods are natural to want but not strictly necessary (ibid.: X, 148–50). It is possible to do without them. If nature determines that I cannot have children, or it turns out that I have no talent for the occupation I desperately wished to pursue, or if I cannot win the heart of the one I love, my life is not thereby ruined. It was natural to want what I wanted; it would have been good had I obtained what I desired, but the Epicurean maintains that life has enough to offer without the satisfaction of every desire, even every strong desire. Killing oneself for unrequited love, or on account of some business failure, is absurd. We can console ourselves in a difficult time by remembering past happiness and by anticipating its possible return.

Third, we realize that some forms of pleasure-seeking and pain-avoidance create pains for others. Doing harm to others by aggression, deceit, or manipulation can result in temporary gratification for the perpetrator, but the enlightened person refrains from this and obeys the conventions of morality. 'Natural justice is a symbol or expression of expedience, to prevent one man from harming or being harmed by another' (ibid.: 150). Morality is thus a kind of prudence, aimed at not offending other people, who tend to retaliate in unpleasant ways against violators. The perpetrator must always live with a painfully bad conscience, fearing discovery.

Meaningfulness in the Epicurean way of living

A life can, then, be good and enjoyable, on the Epicurean view, even if it is bounded by death and involves serious deprivations, and even if it does not involve struggles against worldly temptations or achievements validated and rewarded by society. It can still be felt to be meaningful, to provide a sense of belonging to something greater than oneself. For nearly every human being is able to philosophize, to reflect on the past and the future, and life as it is now, in a way that the other animals, as far as we know, cannot.

The fact of belonging to the human species in the biological sense – being born, growing up, interacting cheerfully with others, loving some of them, producing offspring, and dying to make way for the next generation – is a source of meaningfulness. The Epicurean understands that each living individual is part of system that is ancient and perpetual and that will continue for a long time into the future, though not forever, since everything is reduced ultimately to its constituents, the atoms.

So living things participate in cycles of renewal and destruction. We hand on the 'torch of life', as Lucretius calls it, to the next generation (see Lucretius *c.* 55 BCE: 37; bk II, ll. 75–79), and the beauty of living nature – the fading away of winter, and the reappearance of plant life and the birth of young animals in springtime – testifies to nature's permanence as well as its impermanence. We can feel and know that we are part of a vast system of worlds, all made from the same stuff, that is constantly evolving and changing and inventing new forms as well as preserving the old ones. The knowledge that death is inevitable and irreversible gives meaning to this life as the only life. The knowledge that other people's lives are their only lives makes us other than indifferent to the harms they suffer and desirous of not adding to their burdens.

To experience oneself as part of this system is too feel at once diminished – since our petty concerns about being liked and disliked, successful or ignored, rich or strapped for money to fulfil consumer ambitions, can come to feel trivial – and at the same time enlarged. The very fact of having been produced by mindless atoms and yet having a mind; of having been produced by blind forces and yet having direction and purpose, can seem miraculous. We become aware of our good fortune in existing in a vast, and, for all we know, largely lifeless universe.[10]

So there is a difference between the eating, drinking and mirthfulness of any social animal and that of the Epicurean philosopher who puts human vitality into the wider context of life and beauty. Beauty has come into the world as evolution developed the nervous systems of animals so that they respond to and favour certain adornments. Although the gods did not make the world beautiful to gratify human beings, the scents and colours of flowers, the feathers of birds, and the faces and limbs of members of our own species, have been shaped by the tastes and behaviour of other living things.

That is one way in which a philosophical perspective on the role of time and chance can confer meaning on ordinary life. In addition, the Epicurean philosopher seeks an understanding of the natural and social phenomena around him or her.

For Epicurus, knowledge of nature was not to be sought for profit but because it countered superstition, especially superstitious fear; the fear of being the target of the same wrath that could produce thunder, lightning, earthquakes and volcanoes. The enquirer understands that all phenomena depend on invisible, but purely material causes which cannot be apprehended directly because the atoms are too small ever to be seen. Thus the true explanations can rarely be known and there is no possibility of controlling nature by understanding it. It is important nevertheless, and satisfying, to conjecture possible explanations for what we observe around us.

The situation for us modern persons has changed dramatically. We have optical and other scientific instruments at our disposal for seeing or visualizing the elements of the subvisible world and their interactions, and the theoretical knowledge that enables us to alter atomic configurations to transmute substances into other substances, for example, oil into plastics. We are no longer helpless in the face of the living particles that cause disease.

At the same time, even if we no longer fear the wrath of the gods, we have much reason to fear the products we have made. Our ingenuity led us to manufacture ever more lethal weapons that are capable of wiping out entire cities through the exploitation of atomic power, and we have polluted air, water and earth with our transmutations of raw materials through the knowledge of chemistry. Here the Epicurean disdain for politics and indifference to finding out the correct explanation of particular phenomena looks dismaying in the face of these evils.

But if the mitigation of illness, ugliness and suffering are the goals, if this life is all we have, and if this planet is the only one that is habitable and accessible to us, Epicurean ideals can trump the Epicurean reluctance to engage in vexatious political action. Direct and useful scientific enquiry for the common good – even if no prizes are won, no particular fame or esteem is achieved – is another source of meaning in life. Even an indirect participation in science that involves taking an interest in the scientific researches of others and discussing them with our friends offers a form of connection to the physical world and a commitment to the welfare of the living things within it.

This attitude to science and philosophy is not necessarily the one that our governments have adopted. Vast sums are poured into the development of military technology, and to speeding up technological discoveries that will increase the domestic product, to increasing productivity, and to transforming natural resources into consumer goods and waste products. But development and growth are not aims of the Epicurean, and the study of science is not made desirable by the goal of enhancing the GDP and inventing better tools of warfare. A government that adopted as its immediate goal the reduction of human suffering rather than wealth production, backed by an appropriate and appealing philosophy, would 'choose and avoid' differently.

The Epicureans emphasized that inventions and innovations, both techno-logical and social, are our work, arising from our own minds. 'Human nature was taught and constrained to do many things of every kind merely by circumstances ...', Lucretius says, expressing deep ambivalence about these powers of ours and their application:

> Navigation, agriculture, city walls, laws, arms, roads, clothing, and all other practical inventions as well as everyone of life's rewards and refinements, poems, pictures, and polished statues of exquisite workmanship, all without exception were taught by experience and the inventiveness of the energetic mind, as humanity progressed step by step. People saw one thing after another become clear in their minds until each art reached the peak of perfection.
>
> (Lucretius *c.* 55 BCE: 176; bk V, ll. 1449–56)

Civilization, he points out, has given us perfections and comforts, but it has also produced mass, indiscriminate slaughter, the loss of life at sea, and epidemic diseases against which humans are defenceless, as well as the corruptions of greed and the taste for luxury. 'Gold and purple ... plague human lives with cares and weary them with war ... human beings never cease to labour vainly and fruitlessly, consuming their lives in groundless cares' (ibid.: 175; ll. 1422–31).

Feelings of meaninglessness and alienation are the side effects of the power over nature we have achieved since ancient times. Philosophy – and Epicureanism is especially well suited to this task – can remind us of our kinship with the rest of nature and the fragility of existence. It can insist on the difference between meaningful work and enslavement to an economic machine, and the difference between the cultivation of a truly pleasant life and the pursuit of unnecessary and ultimately unsatisfying goals and ambitions.

Notes

1 On Epicurean theology, see Farrington 1938.

2 Epicurus fourth–third century BCE: 31 (Vatican Sayings, no. 52).

3 On Spinoza's Epicureanism, see Lagrée 1994.

4 See Cicero's *On Ends* (Cicero 45 BCE: bks 1 and 2) for his most thorough challenge to Epicureanism.

5 'Plutarch presents two poles: the public glory of intellectual, political, and military achievement on one side; and the shady, woman-filled disrepute of the Garden on the other. Throughout the treatise, Plutarch associates the "rites" of Epicureanism ... with women, darkness, nighttime, and oblivion, and contrasts this characterization of the Garden with the noble, light filled, virtuous world of the men he views as the true philosophers and best generals and statesmen of Greece and Rome' (P. Gordon 2004: 228). On life in the Garden, see Frischer 1982.

6 For studies of particular Epicurean themes, see Warren 2009; and Clay 1983. There is a compact survey in Wilson 2015.

7 Or the maturation of eternally existing 'seeds' – the texts are not perfectly unambiguous.

8 See Wilson 2008: 85–111.

9 On the Stoic defence of suicide, see Griffin 1986.

10 The expensive and possibly fruitless search for extraterrestrial life (of which the Epicureans themselves were convinced) is hard to explain as other than a strange manifestation of the human desire for friendship.

10 Koheleth and the meaning of life

THADDEUS METZ

Introduction

Ecclesiastes stands out as the clearest instance of what one could call 'Biblical existentialism' (with Job being the next runner up). More than any other book of the Hebrew Bible, i.e. the Tanakh for Jews and the Old Testament for Christians, Ecclesiastes is naturally read as considering whether meaning can be found in an earthly life, and firmly concluding that it cannot.

Its opening chapter begins with, 'Utter futility – said Koheleth – Utter futility! All is futile!' (1.2), and the last of the quotations ascribed to Koheleth ends on the same note: 'Utter futility – said Koheleth – All is futile!' (12.8).[1] Although the words 'meaningless' or 'insignificant' are not used, talk of 'futility', or what is sometimes translated as 'vanity', connotes much the same concept. The key theme of the work is that human life on earth is pointless, akin to 'the pursuit of wind', another recurrent phrase in it.

Koheleth (or *Qoheleth*) is a Hebrew word for gatherer, often rendered as 'teacher' or 'preacher', while the title of the book ascribed to him, Ecclesiastes, is a Greek word for assemblymen or those who have gathered. There has been substantial debate about who Koheleth was, whether there was an additional author of Ecclesiastes beyond him, and when this book was written, with proposed dates ranging from the time of Solomon in the 900s BCE to that of Persian influence around 450–330 BCE to that of Greek influence *c.* 330–180 BCE.

Even supposing the latter time frame is accurate, Ecclesiastes remains one of the first written texts in the Western, monotheist tradition to address the theme of meaningfulness explicitly, and, above all, to posit its absence from our lives. It (along with Job) originated the tradition of nihilism or pessimism that in the modern era has been carried forward by Arthur Schopenhauer (1851b), Leo Tolstoy (1882) and Albert Camus (1942a). In fact, many, if not most, of these philosophers' arguments can be found in this text that predated them by at least 2,000 years.

This chapter critically discusses the most salient arguments pertaining to meaning to be found in Ecclesiastes, that is, the ones that take up the most space or are repeated in the text and those that have been particularly influential in the Western tradition of philosophy. These are considerations about: the mortality of humankind, the undeserved allocations of benefits and burdens we receive, and the inability to control our fate. Focusing on these respects in which there is, for Koheleth, 'no real value under the sun' (2.11) means that this chapter sets aside other claims about meaning to be encountered in Ecclesiastes. For example, it does not address Koheleth's claims that our lives are futile insofar as they are repetitive (1.4–1.9), forgotten by others (1.11, 9.5, 4.16) and exemplify what we today would call 'epistemic injustice' (9.14–9.16).

Fleeting, mortal lives

It is well known that it is difficult to find any reference to an immortal soul in the Hebrew Bible. A plain reading of it suggests that those who composed it believed that there is a God who transcends the earth and determines what happens on it, but not that any of us will reunite with God forever in a Heaven.

It is not merely that there is an apparent absence of reference to an immortal soul in the Hebrew Bible, but that there is, moreover, the presence of scepticism about it, particularly in Ecclesiastes. One major source of Koheleth's conclusion that life is futile is his belief that no one will survive the inevitable death of their body. Several of the relevant passages are poignant:

> I decided, as regards men, to dissociate them [from] the divine beings and to face the fact that they are beasts. For in respect of the fate of man and the fate of beast, they have one and the same fate: as the one dies so dies the other, and both have the same lifebreath; man has no superiority over beast, since both amount to nothing.
>
> (3.18–3.19)

> For the time of mischance comes to all. And a man cannot even know his time. As fishes are enmeshed in a fatal net, and as birds are trapped in a snare, so men are caught at the time of calamity, when it comes upon them without warning.
>
> (9.11–9.12)

> Even if a man lives many years, let him enjoy himself in all of them, remembering how many the days of darkness are going to be. The only future is nothingness!
>
> (11.7–11.8)

These and still other clear references to death (e.g. 3.20–3.21, 9.9–9.10, 12.6–12.7) indicate that their author is distraught at the prospect of a 'return to dust' (3.20) since it entails that all is futility.

This position has been extremely influential amongst Western philosophers of life's meaning, particularly since the medieval era. Those sympathetic to it have usually been led to hold some kind of supernaturalism, the view that a necessary condition for meaning in life is the existence of a spiritual realm, specifically one that includes an immortal soul (e.g. Tolstoy 1882; Morris 1992; Craig 1994). There is, however, divergence amongst supernaturalists between those who believe we have a soul, such that meaning is possible for us, and those who, like Koheleth, do not believe we have a soul, and so believe that meaning is impossible for us.

The usual way that philosophers these days criticize Koheleth's position is by suggesting that, even though all of us might well be mortal, some of our lives have more meaning in them than others. The lives of Albert Einstein or Nelson Mandela intuitively are more meaningful than, say, those that may have been spent 'cultivating one's prowess at long-distance spitting or collecting a big ball of string' (Wolf 2010: 104). Furthermore, there are those who not merely deny that immortality is necessary for a meaningful life, but also contend that immortality would be sufficient for a meaningless one. Perhaps an immortal life would unavoidably get boring (Williams 1973) or would have to repeat itself (Smuts 2011).

Undeserved goods and bads

A second, distinct rationale for the conclusion that all is futility, to be found in Ecclesiastes, appeals to the amount of injustice in our earthly lives. In particular, Koheleth often conceives of justice in terms of desert, with desert determined by our efforts, and he notes how often we do not get what we deserve for what we have done. He has in mind the claims that those who have chosen poorly receive benefits they do not deserve, and that those who have chosen well receive burdens they do not deserve.

One example involves the unfairly universal distribution of the burden of death. 'For the same fate is in store for all: for the righteous, and for the wicked; for the good and pure, and for the impure ... That is the sad thing about all that goes on under the sun: that the same fate is in store for all' (9.2–9.3; see also 2.14–2.16, 3.17).

However, there are myriad additional examples of undeserved conditions in the text. Those who are oppressed do not get comforted (4.1). One works hard to build up wealth, only to be dissatisfied upon obtaining it (4.8, 5.9), or to see it squandered (5.12–5.13), or to see someone else enjoy it and not oneself (6.2). A good or upright person suffers harm, while a wicked person flourishes (7.15, 8.14). A man 'who is pleasing to God' is not chosen by a woman, who instead selects a man who is displeasing to God (7.26). Scoundrels receive burial rites, whereas the righteous are forgotten and not honoured (8.10). In addition, Koheleth remarks,

I have observed under the sun that
The race is not won by the swift
Nor the battle by the valiant;
Nor is bread won by the wise,
Nor wealth by the intelligent,
Nor favor by the learned.

(9.11)

And it does not stop there. For just two more examples: 'He who digs a pit will fall into it; he who breaches a stone fence will be bitten by a snake' (10.8).

Life does seem to be in vain or absurd insofar as the upright, the courageous, the wise, the educated and the hard working do not flourish, whereas the wicked, the cowardly, the foolish, the ignorant and the lazy do flourish – and, still worse, insofar as the latter receive the goods that the former had laboured to produce (2.12, 2.18–2.21)! Contemporary philosophers of meaning also continue to find this rationale compelling. As with the previous rationale, many drawn to this one appeal to a supernaturalist conception of what could make life meaningful. Since justice is clearly not done in this, earthly world, in order for anyone's life to be meaningful, there must be another, spiritual world in which desert is meted out, presumably by God to souls that have outlived the death of our bodies (e.g. Camus 1942a; Davis 1987; Craig 1994; Quinn 2000).

Some critics of this reasoning contend that it is precisely the presence of injustice, at least in the form of undeserved harm, that offers our lives at least one major opportunity to obtain meaning. Returning to the example of Mandela, his life seems to have been meaningful because of the racial injustice he successfully helped to overcome. Peter Singer (1995) has argued that meaning in life comes particularly from acting from the moral point of view, and especially from doing what one can to reduce pain and dissatisfaction (one may add: of innocents); Singer's own life has arguably been meaningful by virtue of what he has done to prevent the infliction of unnecessary suffering on animals. From these perspectives, undeserved harm does not render everyone's life unavoidably futile, but rather can be what gives some lives a point.

Unpredictable predestination

By far the two most influential meaning-related views from Ecclesiastes are grounded on considerations of death and desert. However, there is a third recurrent theme from the text that is philosophically important and is still discussed, concerning the lack of control we have over our fate.

Koheleth routinely mentions two respects in which life is futile for us not being in charge of the course of our lives. For one, he contends that what befalls us is largely a function of God's will. 'Whatever happens, it was designated long ago and it was known that it would happen; as for man, he cannot contend with what is stronger than he' (6.10; see also 7.13–7.14).

For another, even though God knows what will happen to us, we do not. Sometimes Koheleth makes this point in the context of death, pointing out how ridiculous it is not to know that one is just about to die (8.7, 9.12). Other times, however, the point is broader, that we cannot predict much of our future and are in that respect not in control of our lives. 'Just as you do not know how the lifebreath passes into the limbs within the womb of the pregnant woman, so you cannot foresee the actions of God, who causes all things to happen' (11.5; see also 3.22, 6.12, 8.17, 10.14).

These days, philosophers would frame these points in more secular terms, namely those concerning a complex, deterministic universe. At the level beyond subatomic particles, it appears that all events, including the choices we make, are necessitated by prior events. In addition, the events that influence our choices and their outcomes are too many and too complicated for us to be able to predict much. So, even if there is no God who is in charge of our lives, it still appears that we are not in charge of them. And that arguably renders them meaningless.

Although this pessimistic rationale has not been as influential as the others discussed above, nevertheless it, or something like it, was behind some of Immanuel Kant's inclination to maintain that we must believe that we have a kind of freedom that is not subject to natural laws. Kant (1790) thinks of life's meaning in terms of our 'highest good', the final end that human beings ought to pursue. For him, that is the state of affairs in which happiness is proportionate to virtue, with virtue requiring the ability to act on laws that we give ourselves and that are not laid down for us by nature, God or anything else.

While Kant would have been 'incompatibilist' about meaning being possible in a determined universe, in the twenty-first century those who are more 'compatibilist' have emerged. As the debate about free will has lately shifted away from narrowly moral considerations of blame to a broader array of evaluative and normative issues, some have contended that a meaningful life is compatible with a determined universe (Pereboom 2002–3; Arpaly 2006; Pisciotta 2013). No doubt they would also argue that determinism further facilitates a reasonable degree of prediction about how our lives will unfold, at least much more than would exist if indeterminism were rampant.

Conclusion: how one is to live

In closing, note that Koheleth does not suggest that mortality, injustice and a lack of control over one's fate means that there is literally nothing of value in life. He repeatedly says that it is worthwhile for a person to seek out pleasure, and worthwhile only to do so. '[T]he only good a man can have under the sun is to eat and drink and enjoy himself' (8.15; see also 3.13, 3.22, 4.6, 5.17, 9.7–9.9, 11.9). What Koheleth is suggesting is that even if a life cannot have a point or be significant, it could be pleasant. Happiness is one thing, and meaningfulness is another. Even if he is incorrect that all is futility, he is right to draw a distinction between futility and misery (cf. Metz 2013: 59–74).

Note

1   All quotations are taken from Ecclesiastes, in *Tanakh: The Holy Scriptures* (Koheleth c. 450?–180 BCE/ 1985: 1441–56).

11 Epictetus and the meaning of life

A.A. LONG

Stoicism, the philosophy that Epictetus (*c.* 50–138 CE) professed and taught, did not investigate life's *meaning* as such, but Stoic philosophers offered a rich array of answers to the two main questions this modern expression is generally taken to raise: first, "Why is the world the way it is?" and second, "How can we live lives that are subjectively fulfilling and objectively worthwhile?" To the first question the Stoic response takes the world or "nature" to be an entirely physical structure, bodily through and through, providentially organized to provide the best possible life for rational beings; in this sense the world is defined as a universal city (*kosmopolis*) or the "habitation" of gods and humans. Answers to the second question elaborate on this cosmological thesis by positing that human beings are innately equipped (subject to appropriate education and training) to make the best of their lives in all contingencies they encounter, and by so doing contribute their own specific excellence as cosmic citizens to the world's rational organization.

These Stoic responses to the "meaning of life" question are distinctive because they combine theism with what has been called "objective naturalism" (Seachris 2013). The principal divinity that Stoicism invokes is not, as god is typically construed, a supernatural or spiritual entity, but the physical power, equivalent to nature (*physis*), that permeates and determines all particular bodies, and provides the world as a whole with its causality and coherence. What Stoics ideally seek to connect with in their quest for a fulfilling life is the rationality embodied both in their own minds and in the divinely determined processes of their natural environment. They seek, in the words of the great Stoic logician Chrysippus, to become self-aware "parts of the whole," to live "according to nature," and to deploy their "experience of natural events" in ways that are socially beneficent and personally gratifying (Diogenes Laertius third century CE: 7.87–88).

The Stoic term that corresponds most closely to "meaning" of life is *telos*, to be translated by purpose, end, or goal. Like other ancient philosophers, Stoics built their ethical theories around elucidation of life's *telos*; and like other philosophers again, they understood by that expression a human life's ultimate objective, in striving for which everything else is, or should be, subordinate and no more than instrumental. The name for this ancient philosophical project, taken generally, was happiness or flourishing (*eudaimonia*), and it included subjective and objective components. Pleasure, self-satisfaction, good feelings, sense of achievement, friendship and love, public recognition, service to family and community – all of these could figure in ancient philosophers' constituents of the *telos*, as they do in modern philosophers' accounts of a meaningful life. What ancient philosophers, however, emphasized above all else in their ethics was quality of mind and character, captured collectively in the notion of virtue (*arete*) and correctness of reason and understanding (*orthos logos*). In Stoicism this ingredient of the *telos*, and thereby of life's meaningfulness, was not only paramount but so decisive that nothing outside the self's direct capacity to control, not even pleasure or external success, was counted a necessary ingredient of the good life. The ideal Stoic was taken to be someone who, thanks entirely to the cultivation of reason, would live optimally in any situation, even when subject to unjust punishment like Socrates, or like the Cynic Diogenes with no creature comforts. In Epictetus especially, to whom I now come, this focus on the mind and on self-empowerment became the central feature of the Stoic philosophy he presented to his students.

***

Born a Phrygian slave and emancipated as a youth at Rome during or soon after the imperial rule of Nero (54–68 CE), Epictetus made his mark as the philosophical teacher of young men in the resplendent city of Nicopolis in North Western Greece. One of his students named Arrian, who later became a distinguished administrator and author, made a record of Epictetus's lectures, and it is these *Discourses*, together with the summary of them known as the *Handbook*, that constitute what we refer to as the works of Epictetus himself. The main subject of this material is not an outline of Stoic theory (which Epictetus will have expounded to his students in other classes) but advice on the application of the philosophy to oneself and one's daily life. Epictetus interrogates his students in dialogical ways that we may liken to modern therapy and psychoanalysis, getting them to imagine and confront difficult situations concerning personal and family relationships, their fears and ambitions and, especially, challenges to integrity that they are likely to experience. Epictetus does not speak, in so many words, of a *meaningful* life, but his recorded work provides an in-depth exposition of what such a life, according to Stoic values and Stoic world view, would involve.

Many of his characteristic thoughts and recommendations are encapsulated in the following text, which sums up the teaching of the *Handbook*:

> How long will you [a representative student or reader] delay thinking yourself worthy of the best, and making reason your decisive principle in everything? You have received the doctrines you ought to endorse, and you have endorsed

them. What sort of teacher, then, are you still waiting for, so you can transfer the correction of yourself to him? You are not a boy any more, but already a full-grown man. If you are negligent now and lazy and always procrastinating, and settling on the day after tomorrow and the next as when you will take yourself in hand, you will fail to see that you are making no progress but spending your entire life until you die as an ordinary person. Right now, then, think yourself worthy to live like a grown-up making progress; and take your view of the best to be the rule that you never transgress. And whatever you encounter that is painful or pleasant or popular or unpopular, keep in mind that *now* is the contest, and here right now are the Olympic games, and that postponement is no longer an option, and that your progress is saved or ruined by a single day and a single action. That is how Socrates perfected himself, by attending to nothing except reason in everything he encountered. You yourself too, even though you are not yet Socrates, ought to live as someone who wants to be a Socrates.

(Epictetus *c.* 108 CE: §51)[1]

Epictetus does not presume that lives come endowed from the cradle with merit or rights simply in virtue of being human. His outlook is teleological through and through, but the felicitous ends that are built into human nature are achievable only and solely by the effort and commitment that individual persons exhibit on their own behalf. As Epictetus explains here, instruction in Stoic philosophy and assiduous practice of its precepts are essential to the project of making something of oneself. The students he is addressing are on the threshold of careers in such professions as military and government service, law, and education. The aim of the Stoicism he expounds is not to equip them to distinguish themselves in any career specifically, but to turn them into, what he quaintly calls "professional" human beings, and so be ready for anything that comes their way (Epictetus *c.* 108 CE: 2.9.1–7) .

Reading this passage, then, as a recipe to confer meaning on one's life, we can extract the following notions as necessary conditions that it requires of persons – maturity, sense of urgency, commitment, progress, self-assessment and self- monitoring, achievement, objective excellence, and narrative coherence. I list these notions without any intention of prioritizing one over another. Some of them, for instance maturity, achievement, and objective value or excellence, are regularly included in contemporary accounts of life's meaning or conditions of meaningfulness (Wolf 2007). It is widely supposed that lives, to be meaningful, need aims and achievements beyond pleasure and basic welfare (Luper 2014), aims and achievements that transcend the particular desires of individuals, and that meet standards of value that are generally accepted to be worthwhile.

Epictetus, however, would be misrepresented if we took him to be adumbrating criteria of meaningfulness that apply across the board, so to speak. His focus on reason and "the rule of the best" presupposes the theistic and psychological doctrines that I outlined in the first paragraph of this essay. He spells out those doctrines in the following passage taken from a discourse entitled *On providence*.

> It is sufficient for non-rational animals to eat and drink and rest and procreate, and do everything that each kind of animal does. For us, on the other hand, to whom God has also given the power of attending to things, these animal activities are no longer sufficient, but unless we act appropriately and systematically and in agreement with our individual nature and constitution, we shall no longer attain our end ... God introduced the human being to be a student of himself and his works, and not merely a student but also an *interpreter* of these things. Therefore it is wrong or shameful (*aischron*) for a human being to begin *and* end where the non-rational animals do. He should rather begin where they do and end where nature has ended in our case. Nature ended at studying and attending to things and a way of life in harmony with nature.
>
> (Epictetus *c.* 108 CE: 1.6.14–22)

As we generally use the word "nature," we have in mind states of affairs that are normal or regular, if not invariant. Epictetus buys into that usage when he enumerates the activities of eating, resting, and so forth. Human beings in virtue of being animals behave accordingly or naturally, and cannot live otherwise. It is as natural for us to eat and sleep as it is for other animals. We cannot choose these aspects of our human identity. They are a given. By contrast, the nature that Epictetus posits as distinctively human and divinely mandated is normative, not a given. Nothing in your basic animal make-up compels you to value reason and understanding above eating and sleeping, and to become an interpreter of the world's significance and your place therein. What is at stake here, as Epictetus never tires of saying, is choice, volition, long-term purpose. We can opt out of our normative nature, and "end where the non-rational animals do" but, in that case, we also opt out of living a meaningful life.

Earlier in this discourse, Epictetus prepares for his treatment of normative human nature by commenting on the teleology exemplified in the relation between light, color, and vision, and in the efficacy of sexual attraction for procreation. Such natural signs of biological purposiveness give content to the interpretive role that Epictetus assigns to human beings as distinct from other animals. Plato and Aristotle had long ago traced the beginnings of philosophy to human interest in the investigation of nature. In Epictetus we come close to the idea of nature as a book, a semiotic system that is incumbent on us to study and respond to if we are to live up to our full human potential. On this construal, life does literally have a meaning, the meaning embodied in how we interpret the signs of natural or divine teleology.

We can flesh out this conception in its historical context by drawing a contrast with Epicureanism, which had been the principal rival philosophy from Stoicism's beginning, and is an unremitting target of Epictetus. The Epicurean universe is a purely mechanical structure of aimless atoms moving in infinite void. Taken universally the Epicurean world has no meaning because everything it contains, including gods and humans, exists as the outcome of matter in purposeless motion and not by design. Value is entirely a function of sensation and perception, with pleasure the foundation of good and pain of bad. Human life, according to Epicurus, has an objective *telos* in the sense that everyone naturally seeks pleasure and avoids pain. Philosophy serves this hedonistic goal by identifying tranquility as its optimal state of mind, by undermining beliefs that stand in its way such as the badness of death and the desirability of wealth and social status, and by cultivating prudence as the mindset appropriate to rationalizing one's desires so as to achieve a life that maximizes pleasure and minimizes pain. A quiet and simple life spent with friends and without political involvements is the Epicurean recommendation for fulfilling this goal. No further achievement is required to render life purposeful and fulfilling.

Epictetus challenges Epicurus by calling into question the consistency of his own life with a philosophy that situates all positive value in pleasurable sensation. "What is there in you that deliberates, that examines every detail, and that forms the judgment that the flesh itself is the leading constituent of our nature? Why do you light your lamp and toil for us and write so many books? Isn't it to prevent our ignorance of the truth?" (ibid.: 1.20.18–19). As the founder of a highly successful philosophical school, Epicurus lived a life that could be judged philanthropic in its primary motivation and replete with meaning in the sense of having social and historical significance. It was a life, moreover, according to Epictetus, that displayed Epicurus's virtual Stoicism in its cultivation of rationality as the supreme human faculty. What it chiefly lacked, on his view, was the theistic underpinning of reason's supreme value for Stoics – value grounded not in reason's prudential efficacy (though it had that, of course) but in being the faculty to connect the inner trajectory of life with external events (be they favorable or otherwise), and thus provide a sense of homeliness and affinity in the world.

I choose the words "homeliness" and "affinity" to draw attention to one of Stoicism's most innovative and powerful concepts, expressed in Greek by the term *oikeiosis*. Drawing metaphorically on the notions of home and kin and ownership, *oikeiosis* expresses the affinity and sense of belonging that living creatures feel naturally for themselves and their offspring. By extension, Stoics argued, with the development of reason human beings can and should (if they are to flourish) adapt themselves to feel at home in the world at large, making homeliness applicable to whatever circumstance they find themselves in. Underlying this project is the theism that I outlined at the beginning of this article. Holding that the world in its entirety is providentially governed and causally coherent, Stoics took it as axiomatic that one's particular spatio-temporal situation could not be otherwise than it is. What is up to us and entirely free from external determination is how we interpret and respond to our experience, moment by moment. Hence Epictetus tells his students to say "Bring on me now, O Zeus, whatever situation you will, for I have the means and the resources granted to me by yourself to bring honour to myself through whatever comes to pass" (ibid.: 1.6.37). Another leading Roman Stoic, Seneca, expresses the same thought in the following way:

> Let us keep our distance from fortune as much as we can. But the only way we can do that is through an understanding of ourselves and of nature. Let us know where we are headed and where we come from; what is good for us and what is bad; what to pursue and what to avoid; what reason is, which distinguishes objects of pursuit and avoidance, soothes the madness of our desires, and checks the savagery of our fears.
>
> (Seneca 62–65 CE: *Moral Letter* 82.6)

Epictetus, as we have seen, cajoles his students, urging them to think of themselves as Olympic athletes, readying for a contest, facing decisive challenges, teetering on the brink of absolute success or failure. His hyperbolical tone might seem to betoken an intensely elitist notion of a meaningful life, as if you have to compete and win in order for your life to be marked by any achievement worthy of note. This impression is not entirely wrong; for the Greek word *arete* that we often translate by "virtue" is better rendered by "excellence." In denoting the goal of life, as *arete* does in Stoicism, superlative achievement is in question: you cannot exhibit *arete*, and simply be ordinary, such as being unhappy when things do not work out as you would have liked, and exultant when you win the lottery. But the extraordinariness that *arete* signifies has nothing to do with success in the sense of accomplishment marked by external criteria, like completing a work of art, or finding a cure for cancer, or winning an election. The best way to express Epictetus's main point is to think of yourself, your character, and your emotional disposition as the objects of the challenge or competition. Prowess and progress, as he uses these words, apply to every situation, however humdrum, that calls for a deliberate response or social interaction. What is at issue may be simply one's reaction to an insult or a mundane disappointment, or it could be a situation calling for a decision that affects the lives of others. In all cases, the determining factor to count as a significant Stoic achievement is the appropriateness of the judgment, efforts, and emotional affect that persons display, especially in difficult circumstances. Another way to capture the relevance of this philosophy to notions of meaning is to say that the world, for a Stoic, makes sense to the extent that we take ourselves to be masters of our own fate.

Socrates' courage, resolution, and equanimity conferred a meaning on his life that needs no commentary to count as exemplary. Epictetus describes it in sporting images that any modern reader will find appealing and germane to this book's topic: Socrates, he says, played the ball well, with the ball he had to deploy being the hemlock poison he was required to drink and the cheerful demeanor he chose to exhibit to his grieving friends (Epictetus *c.* 108 CE: 2.5.18). Like his competitive language, it might seem as if exhibitionism is a necessary component of a meaningful life according to Epictetus since he repeatedly praises the way admirable persons show themselves, and treats displays of weakness or failure to live up to appropriate standards as shameful. But the relevant audience of the display is not a set of external observers but the literary self that he is representing to his students. Its purpose is to confront and ask them how they would judge their own behavior if they were observing it in others. In a particularly effective discourse, he envisions a father who is so distraught by his daughter's sickness that he cannot bear to stay at her bedside (ibid.: 1.11). Is he acting from love, the father is asked? Looking for sympathy, he retorts that he is acting "naturally." To which Epictetus responds that the father's abandonment of his child is completely contrary to the nature of love.

We are to understand that if the distraught father had supported the girl, this action would have been not only the ethically appropriate one but also an objectively significant response because it would have required him to overcome purely self-centered and gut reactions. Knowing at what emotional cost a person does the right thing may be sufficient to elevate actions from being merely ordinary into something we report with praise. Epictetus's subject matter focuses on mundane difficulties (for instance, illness, anxiety, anger, a lawsuit, disagreeable relatives) because these difficulties invite responses that fall within our control to handle thoughtfully rather than reactively and impulsively. Individual actions are hardly sufficient, taken by themselves, to provide a whole life with meaning, and we should not suppose that success at surmounting problems is a necessary criterion either. It looms so large in Epictetus because the essence of his Stoicism is autonomy, self-determination, and freedom from external constraint. One's actions, then, are meaningful in so far as they are what we deliberately and freely choose for ourselves. It is that intention that confers meaning on them.

Epictetus sets the bar for a meaningful life very high, but the height is relative to the personality and natural endowments of individuals. Only a few have the potential to become suitable subjects for public recognition and eulogistic biography. What he takes to be more generally available to people is the achievement of self-knowledge and excellent performance of social role, as father, brother, wife, soldier, magistrate, etc. As he puts it: "Only consider at what price you sell your own will and choice, if for nothing else, that you not sell it cheap. But what is great and exceptional perhaps belongs to others, to Socrates, and those who resemble him" (ibid.: 1.2.33).

***

How, then, in sum may we assess the interest of Epictetus for modern investigation of the meaning of life? For those who find meaning in their relationship to God, Epictetus will appeal through his conviction that the world's ultimate cause is a supreme being who wishes us well and who has delegated to our minds a portion of its own rationality. Since, however, his Stoic divinity is immanent and present within the processes of life itself, the main thrust of his philosophy is quite compatible with the notion that "there is sufficient meaning for human beings in the human world – the world of familiar, and even humdrum, doings and experiences" (Blackburn 2007: 190) Epictetus strongly endorses the need for an account of life's meaning to "distinguish between the animal self and the rational self" (Metz 2013: 88). He would be less sympathetic to notions that the meaning of life requires "some decision about what we want our life as a whole to accomplish" (Luper 2014: 200). This would probably strike him as grandiose and insufficiently attentive to the episodic nature of day-to-day existence. Epictetus lays great stress on achievement, but what he urges his students to achieve is not fulfillment of a specific life plan (which can easily lapse into megalomania or lack of balance) but the disposition to aspire to be at their best at all times. That aspiration is his principal contribution to the meaning of life.[2]

Notes

1   All translations of Epictetus in this essay are by the author. A complete modern translation of Epictetus is listed in the bibliography.
2   For further exploration of the themes of this essay see Long 2002 and Stephens 2007.

12 Sextus Empiricus and the meaning of life

SVAVAR HRAFN SVAVARSSON

Sextus Empiricus was a late second century Pyrrhonist, a radical sceptic, who claimed no knowledge. In fact, he claimed no beliefs. He would therefore not assert anything about the meaning of life, or whether there is one. Nevertheless he has a story to tell (or rather an experience to report) about himself and other sceptics that is offered – as was common in ancient times – in terms of their final end or goal.[1] These are people who seek tranquillity or, more accurately, the absence of anxiety (the literal meaning of the Greek word *ataraxia*). That is their goal. He does not say whether it is anything more than just their goal. It then turns out, according to Sextus, that they reach their goal. And insofar as they successfully rid themselves of anxiety, they do so precisely at the expense of belief. Sextus gives an account of the sceptical process that leads to this result. He explains the equal persuasiveness (or equipollence) of conflicting appearances and accounts, which forces sceptics to suspend belief. He describes the basis of the sceptics' actions, given that they have no beliefs. And he relates how it happens that sceptics become tranquil. Although his sceptical arguments have retained much of their force and interest through the ages, not least in the early modern period, his account of tranquillity, even if the very point of his Pyrrhonism, has not impressed (see Popkin 2003). On the contrary, it has been suggested, most famously by David Hume, that the very anxiety that the sceptics sought to avoid is a more likely result of their scepticism.[2] Not all of Sextus' accounts are crystal clear. In order to clarify how sceptics reach their goal and become tranquil, it is necessary to explain their suspension of belief and their living in the absence of beliefs.

But first, to understand the goal in question, their coveted tranquillity, we have to know what kind of anxiety the sceptics wanted to leave behind. They started out anxious because they found themselves faced with "the anomaly in things and puzzled as to which of them they should rather assent to" (*PH* 1.12). This initial intellectual kind of anxiety prompted their investigations into the nature of things, since they hoped to overcome it by arriving at the truth. Although this description may bring to mind accounts of wonder, if not epistemic discontent, as a spur to philosophy, Sextus makes no claim about the generality of this experience. He nevertheless implies that it is characteristic of intellectual talent (*PH* 1.12). Notwithstanding such talent, the sceptics proved unable to settle the various conflicting accounts of reality, having consistently found them *equally persuasive* (the precise meaning of which we shall leave aside for the present). Or perhaps more accurately, because of their talent they proved exceedingly adept at eliciting this balance of persuasiveness. In fact they offered methods of doing so, the so-called 'modes', the most famous of which are named after the little-known Aenesidemus and the completely obscure Agrippa.[3] At all events, they were compelled to withhold their assent to any claim about reality based on some account, given that they were invariably faced with a contrary claim based on a different account. In short, they were compelled to suspend belief. One would have thought that this impasse left them as troubled as before, as David Hume intimated, having failed to reach the truth through their investigations. But their experience was completely different. Having suspended belief, they found themselves rid of their intellectual anxiety. As Sextus explains: "when they suspended belief, tranquillity in matters of belief followed fortuitously" (*PH* 1.26). (The last word in this passage is likely to raise eyebrows. We shall return to it at the end.)

Now we can better understand the tranquillity in question. It rests on suspension of belief as a result of scrupulous investigations. Having realized this, the sceptics now say that their goal is this tranquillity in matters of belief and the concomitant "moderation of feeling (*metriopatheia*) in matters forced upon us" (*PH* 1.25). They therefore actively seek suspension of belief in all matters in order to attain this goal. If they failed to reach suspension of belief, this kind of tranquillity and moderation would elude them. But in order to suspend belief, they must investigate accounts for the various contrary appearances. And their investigations must be conducted in earnest, since it is of paramount importance that they are actually *compelled* to suspend belief, whatever they might wish to do. Their suspension must be genuine, not feigned, for feigned suspension implies that the opposed accounts are not really equally persuasive and fail to compel suspension of belief. Such a procedure would undermine their tranquillity. In what sense then do they investigate? The purpose of their investigations is to secure their tranquillity. They do not, as sceptics, investigate with the explicit aim of establishing the truth or falsity of some account, nor does Sextus claim that they do. Are they thereby disingenuous, subversively unphilosophical? That depends on whether they can fairly and rigorously investigate accounts – whether a Stoic account of virtue or an Epicurean account of pleasure, or a purported refutation of both – and simultaneously hope to find them equally persuasive. They could be charged with being biased from the outset, convinced that equal persuasiveness will ensue. And no doubt they will have become accustomed to that result. But we should still respect the restraints on their investigations, for even as they seek and hope for tranquillity, it will not come about unless they approach each account of reality, for and against the various appearances, with as much rigour and fairness as is needed to compel suspension of belief. At the same time, in order to reach their goal, they must become hypercritical and armed to the teeth with every kind of argument designed to upset any positive and negative account of reality, lest they forfeit their tranquillity. This is an unusual plan, significantly differentiating the sceptical disposition from that of other philosophers, whom the sceptics called 'dogmatists' on account of their entertaining of *beliefs* (in Greek, 'belief' can be expressed by *dogma*, although *doxa* is the usual word). The sceptics do not hope to find truth, but rather tranquillity in matters of belief.

Fundamental to the sceptic's hope is the experience that having beliefs entails being anxious. Of course much depends on what the sceptics mean by 'belief'. Sextus never mentions degrees of belief. Beliefs are of one kind and one either has them or not. And having one means that one accepts as true some claim concerning reality, about which there is or could be controversy. But a life without beliefs seems odd, even unrecognizable, as a human life. Our actions and the direction of our lives depend, at least to some extent, on our beliefs. Sextus is aware of the problem, and that it is a genuine problem. He explains what replaces beliefs in the lives of the sceptics. They live by their appearances, what appears to them to be the case, without any commitment to the truth or falsity of these appearances. Appearances are beliefs without commitment, or "without strong inclination or adherence," as Sextus says (*PH* 1.230). It is the commitment – in the sense of accepting that things really are (or are not) as they appear to one – that causes anxiety. Anything can appear to the sceptic to be the case. Furthermore, appearances can originate in the same way as beliefs. In order to explain these features of sceptical appearances, we must go through Sextus' account of the journey that leads to suspension of belief.

Sextus guides us through the paradigmatic Aenesideman modes that lead to suspension of belief. He starts by juxtaposing appearances of different observers and thinkers at different instances, suggesting that one can match any appearance with a contrary appearance. For example, it appears to some (most) that honey is sweet, but to others (the sick) that it is not, and it appears to some that there is a god, while to others it does not so appear. He then scrutinizes the accounts that are given of these appearances. In the light of these accounts, he can find no reason to accept one of the appearances as true, as revealing reality or the nature of things, rather than the other, implicitly ruling out the possibility that contrary appearances are both true. He does not give priority to what appears to be the case to the majority of people, to normal or healthy people, or to clever people. Given that he has no means of preferring one to the other, he suspends belief about which of them is true. Or, to be precise, he is forced to suspend belief, whether he wants to or not. Although a sceptic need not be party to the controversy, he may well be. In that case, he juxtaposes what appears to him to be the case and what appears to someone else to be the case, or to himself in different circumstances. It could, for instance, appear to him that there is a god, although in the end he will suspend belief about the existence of god. But yet it may still appear to him that there is a god, and it might later appear to him that there is no god. He still has his appearances, even though he suspends belief. These two attitudes go together.

Sextus uses the notion of persuasion to explain what happens. When confronted with contrary appearances, he tells us that the sceptic suspends belief because of equipollence. This equipollence is explained as equality with regard to being persuasive and unpersuasive. The sceptic is in stalemate because of the equal persuasiveness of different accounts for contrary appearances. This explanation could be interpreted to mean that he himself actually is just as persuaded by one account as the other, or perhaps that he is equally unimpressed by them. This would be a balance of persuasiveness, and the sceptic would suspend belief. But this interpretation can hardly be correct, for Sextus also allows, surprisingly enough, that the sceptic may actually be persuaded by one account rather than another, even though he still suspends belief. That persuasion is reflected in the fact that, despite suspending belief, the sceptic may retain what appears to him (he cannot but suffer appearances), or, sometimes, even change his mind and be persuaded of the contrary appearance. Sextus must have something else in mind. It is not that the sceptic himself necessarily is equally persuaded of contrary appearances, but that, having noted that different observers and thinkers (not excluding himself) are persuaded of contrary appearances and having investigated the accounts of them, the sceptic – because of his argumentative insights and skills – has no means to decide by which account he ought to be persuaded, even if it just so happens that he is persuaded by one of them. He asks himself: ought I to be persuaded by what in fact happens to persuade me rather than by what persuades others? That is the question that he cannot answer, in light of the opposed accounts, because of which he is compelled to suspend belief. For example, Sextus says that he can be persuaded that honey is sweet (*M* 8.53), presumably because he is not sick. He is evidently not at the same time equally persuaded that honey is not sweet. Again, Sextus advances against some theses the consideration that, given his experience, in the future equally persuasive counter-theses might be proposed. Obviously he is not actually persuaded by these future and as yet unformed counter-theses. It is because he cannot adjudicate between the different but equally authoritative accounts that he suspends belief. The equal force of the accounts for contrary appearances cancels the epistemic normativity of any one account, even if it leaves intact what the sceptic finds himself persuaded of at the moment, for whatever reason, good or bad.

Because he has no beliefs, the sceptic speaks and acts on the basis of what appears to him, or, as Sextus sometimes puts it, what happens to persuade him. What are these appearances that replace beliefs in the sceptic's life? Sextus emphasizes the passive nature of what appears to the sceptic, often characterizing it as an affection (*pathos*), saying that "it lies in feeling and unwilled affection" (*PH* 1.22). This feature also distinguishes appearance from belief, which involves the active contribution of assent or commitment to the appearance as true. Because of equipollence, the sceptic is not such an active contributor and does not give his assent. He does not willingly pass judgement on the truth of the appearance. In fact, suspension of belief itself is a clear example of such an affection, a passive reaction to equal persuasiveness. Nevertheless, one could say that the sceptic assents to his appearances in the sense that he acknowledges that he has specific appearances and not others. And he need not be unaware of the reasons for his appearances. He can explain why he has particular appearances and not others. He can explain why honey appears to him to be sweet, namely because he is not sick. He could point to some argument for a thesis of some kind as the source of his appearance, but note that it was "merely persuasive, and that for the moment it persuades them [the sceptics] and induces assent" (*M* 8.473). He attempts to clarify the persuasion (or appearance) in question by comparing it to a physical or emotional affection. There are many things that can persuade the sceptic, like other people, such as clever rhetoric, forceful arguments, cultural background, family and friends, his or her own interests. And we should note that Sextus never rejects reasoning as the source of the sceptic's appearances. As he says, "the sceptic is not barred, I think, from thought, if it both arises from arguments that passively strike him appearing evidently to him and does not at all imply the reality of the things thought" (*PH* 2.10).

Here, though, we encounter a problem in Sextus' account of the sceptic's life. For in an important chapter on the criterion of the sceptic's actions (*PH* 1.21–24) he seems to talk as if sceptics just imitate what they take to be ordinary life, unreflectively reacting to external stimuli on the basis of their observations. If that is what he has in mind, sceptics are not much more than shallow mimics, pretenders, minimally reflective, even if tranquil. They have in fact been portrayed as such, and not without justification (see Striker 2010).

Sextus emphasizes the passivity of the sceptic's appearances. As noted above, this passivity signals the absence of the active contribution of assent to the truth or falsity of the sceptic's appearances. But Sextus adds that the sceptic conducts his life by following what he calls observation (*tērēsis*) of life. This is a term of art borrowed from the Empiricist school of medicine, which was closely associated with Pyrrhonism, as Sextus' cognomen indicates: Empiricus. A statement of Galen's reveals the close connection between the sceptic's criterion and Empiricist medical practice: "The empiricist's attitude towards medical matters is like the sceptic's attitude towards the whole of life" (Galen *c.* 150–90 CE-a: 82).

According to this school, medicine is best practised on the basis of observation and experience. In his account, Sextus records an importation into Pyrrhonism of a distinction between the evident (as something immediately apprehensible) and the non-evident (as something only inferentially apprehensible), i.e. between observing the evident and inferring the non-evident. Observation latches on to the evident and dispenses with reflection on anything beyond the evident. Because of this distinction, the Pyrrhonist practical criterion can be taken to indicate a view according to which the sceptic acts only on the basis of what he passively observes without reflection. But the adoption of this medical distinction turns out to be misleading, since it is fundamentally different from a distinction the sceptics drew between the apparent and the real. (For clarity's sake I refer to the Pyrrhonist notion as 'apparent' and to the medical notion as 'evident', although in both cases, versions of the Greek *phainomenon* are being used.) In claiming that the sceptic utters and acts on the basis of what appears to him or her, Sextus is not implicitly contrasting what is immediately apprehensible with what is only inferentially apprehensible. He does not claim that the sceptic only acts on the immediately apprehensible, except arguably in his account of the observation of life, discussed below. The contrast that Sextus relies on is rather between how things appear – however the appearance is generated, immediately or inferentially – and how things really are. Even the evident, just as the non-evident, may not really be as it appears. For Sextus, what is non-evident is in each case just the object of investigation, for every such object may really be different from its appearance. Only in that sense does the sceptic suspend belief about the non-evident, since he makes no claims about how things really are. Sextus is actually aware of this confusion and later breaks rank with the Empiricists. He does so by criticizing them for harbouring dogmatic sentiments and then opens Pyrrhonism up to another medical school's rejection of the Empiricist distinction, namely that of the so-called Methodists. This confusion calls for a short explanation.

According to Sextus, observation of life is fourfold. First it is based on the human capabilities of perceiving and thinking. Although he is not emphasizing critical reflection as such a capability, he reminds his readers that the Pyrrhonist has typical human qualities, including the capacity to reflect. The second item on the list is necessitation of affections. Here Sextus only mentions as examples thirst leading to drinking and hunger to eating. The third item on Sextus' list refers to following laws and customs. It has usually been taken to imply that the sceptic passively acquiesces in the values that have been inculcated in him through the customs and laws of his culture (see Bett 2010). Sextus regards them as a collection of shared experiences that the Pyrrhonist has access to in his life, in the same manner as the Empiricist doctor has access not only to his own observations (*autopsia*) but those of others (*historia*), as a repository of observations and experience. Fourth on the list is the teaching of expertise. This claim is the typically Empiricist one that observation and experience are sufficient for imparting skills. Sextus later (*PH* 1.237–40) returns to this issue and criticizes the dogmatic tendencies of Empiricism, namely their claim that the non-evident is inapprehensible, while applauding the Methodist notion of the evident. He suggests that it is closer to the sceptical notion of the apparent, since it is wider and includes inferential reasoning. The sceptical criterion of action is then made to harmonize with the Methodist outlook through the second item on his list. The necessitation of affection accommodates not only what is evidently observed, but also what the Empiricists take to be objects of inferential reasoning.

But what does all of this have to do with tranquillity? That state is the result of suspension of belief. It does not depend on a particular way of life, so long as that life is lived without beliefs. Different sceptics can have different appearances and thus lead different kinds of life. But Sextus says about the sceptics that "when they suspended belief, tranquillity in matters of belief followed fortuitously" (*PH* 1.26). It is strange to suggest that the sceptics become tranquil *fortuitously*, i.e. by chance. In order to explain the sceptics' aiming at tranquillity in matters of belief, Sextus tells a story of the painter Apelles, who gave up trying to paint foam frothing from a horse's mouth and, by instead throwing the sponge at the painting, created a perfect picture of the sought-for foam (*PH* 1.28–29). We can safely assume that sponge-throwing is an unreliable method for creating images of difficult subjects. To add insult to injury, Sextus uses the following imagery: "But when they suspended belief, tranquillity followed as it were fortuitously, as a shadow follows a body" (*PH* 1.29). But it is not a coincidence that shadows follow bodies. The explanation, somewhat deflationary, is again to be found in the Empiricist school of medicine.

Tranquillity, on the Pyrrhonist account, is analogous to health on the Empiricist account, as Sextus intimates at the end of his *Outlines of Pyrrhonism*, when he compares the sceptic, "who wants to heal by argument the conceit and rashness of dogmatists" (*PH* 3.280), to a doctor fighting bodily afflictions. Pyrrhonism is therapeutic like medicine. The Empiricist explanation of the origins of treatments is, like that of the Pyrrhonists, given in terms of chance. Galen's account in *An Outline of Empiricism* is succinct.[4] He says:

> Those cases of knowledge are said to come about spontaneously which come about by chance or by nature; by chance, as when somebody who has a pain in the back of his head happens to fall, cuts the right vein on his forehead, loses blood, and gets better.
>
> (Galen *c*. 150–90 CE-a: 44–45)

This account is not intended to show that one should let oneself fall (or miraculously fall by chance) when one has a headache, in the hope of losing just enough blood, but that one has come to expect, from this experience, that a headache may be alleviated by bleeding. In the same way Sextus explains the advent of tranquillity as the chance result of suspending belief in the face of equipollence. The result has been noted, and if one wants to attain tranquillity, one needs to suspend belief, in the appropriately rigorous manner, not by deciding to suspend belief, but by being forced by equipollence to suspend belief. And that requires the talents of a sceptic.

Notes

1   The preserved works of Sextus are the *Outlines of Pyrrhonism* (= *PH*), in three books, and *Against the Dogmatists* (= *M*), in eleven books. The latter work comprises two separate groups of books, of which the last five deal with logic, physics, and ethics, while the first six address specific sciences. The first book of the *Outlines* is a general introduction to Sextus' Pyrrhonism. See Sextus Empiricus 150–200 CE.
2   See especially *A Treatise of Human Nature* (Hume 1739–40) I.iv.2.
3   Aenesidemus was a first century BCE philosopher who, having broken with the sceptical Academy of the day, revived the ideas of Pyrrho of Elis (365/60–275/70 BCE).
4   There is a longer explanation at the beginning of Galen's *On the Sects for Beginners*; see Galen c. 150–190 CE-b.

13 Avicenna and the meaning of life

NADER EL-BIZRI

Directives

This chapter addresses *the meaning of life* through a *neo-Avicennist* perspective that reflects on the entailments of meditations on *the question of being* by Avicenna (Ibn Sīnā, d. 1037 CE). To avoid anachronism, the purposes of this *exercise-in-thinking* are not exegetical per se, nor are they aimed at being part of Oriental Studies, or at solely abiding by the dominant conventions of historiography, philology, and codicology in the antiquarian documentation of the history of *Falsafa* (Arabic/Islamicate philosophy). My perspective is rather set in the context of theorizing about *the meaning of life* as a theme of inquiry in contemporary philosophy, and doing so in continuation of the pathway that I have taken elsewhere on the question of consciousness (El-Bizri 2016: 45). The aim herein is to recover the speech acts from the illocutionary propositions of Avicenna as a pre-modern thinker, to disclose their latent intentions, while eschewing prolepsis, parochialism, or anachronism.

The consideration of *the meaning of life* as a theme of inquiry within our neo-Avicennist thought-experiment takes into account that Avicenna did not reflect directly on this matter. This entails that any attempt to analyse Avicenna's philosophical oeuvres in that context has to be mediated via leitmotifs from his thought. Consequently, a conceptual re-appropriation and extension of Avicennian concepts within our neo-Avicennist perspective leads us to reconsider Avicenna's ontological reflections on *the question of being* as a basis for our philosophical consideration of *the meaning of life* (El-Bizri 2016: 45–53).

To begin our inquiry, we need to account for the fundamental elements in Avicenna's thinking about the question of being (*al-wujūd*) as this was primarily undertaken by him in terms of his meditations on the modalities of necessity (*al-wujūb*), contingency *qua* possibility (*al-imkān*), and impossibility (*al-imtināʿ*) within the framework of a pre-modern causal-naturalized ontology (Avicenna 1000–37a, 1000–37c, 1000–37d, 1000–37e, 1000–37f, 1000–37g; El-Bizri 2000, 2001, 2006, 2010, 2011, 2014). This will be followed by a consideration of Avicenna's thinking on the connection and distinction between mind and body, and the consequences this has on his contemplation of *the question of being*, which will in turn be brought to bear upon *the meaning of life*.

Modalities of being

The question of *the meaning of life* is closely related to the question of what it is 'to be' rather than 'not to be'.

Avicenna took the question of being to be the most fundamental in his philosophical thinking, as mediated via his logical and ontological consideration of the modalities of necessity (*al-wujūb*), contingency-possibility (*al-imkān*), and impossibility (*al-imtinā'*).

Avicenna argued that the impossible being (*mumtani' al-wujūd*) cannot exist, and that the affirmation of its existence entails a contradiction. The impossible is what necessarily does not exist. Two examples of impossible beings are a squared-circle and a unicorn. The former is logically impossible per se, while the latter is experientially impossible on the grounds of what is empirically known about animals. The squared-circle cannot be imagined, drawn, simulated, or modelled. It is a category mistake by definition. As for the unicorn, it can be imagined, drawn, simulated, and modelled. It could be approximated by fitting a white horse with a synthetic horn, or perhaps, one day, manufactured with bio-technologies. However, it suffices here, for the purposes of our exercise, to affirm that the impossible is what necessarily does not exist, logically or experientially, and that the affirmation of its existence entails a contradiction.

The contingent qua possible being (*mumkin al-wujūd*) is that whose existence or non-existence is neither impossible nor necessary. It is ontologically neutral in the sense that affirming or negating its existence does not entail a contradiction. There is therefore nothing inherent in the essence of the contingent *qua* possible that gives priority to its existence over its non-existence, or vice versa. It is essentially what exists or does not exist, not due-to-itself, but due-to-what-is-other-than-itself (*bi-ghayrih*). The contingent comes to be due-to-what-is-other-than-itself, its existence is distinct from its essence, hence, its being is derived from a source other than itself. It is also maintained in being or annihilated by something other than itself.

As for necessary being (*wājib al-wujūd*) it exists in such a way that it essentially cannot but exist, and the affirmation of its non-existence entails a contradiction, since it is impossible for it not to be. However, necessary being (*wājib al-wujūd*) can either be as such due-to-itself (*bi-dhātih*) or due-to-what-is-other-than-itself (*bi-ghayrih*).

The Necessary-Being-due-to-Itself (*wājib al-wujūd bi-dhātihi*) is beyond the Aristotelian categories. It is without definition or description, since its essence is none other than its existence. It is Pure Existence without determinateness (Avicenna 1000–37a: 262–63; 1000–37c: 65; 1000–37e: 36–39, 43–47, 350–55; 1000–37g: 255, 261–65, 272–75, 283–85). Consequently, and in order to avoid the use of the verbal 'to be' that entails an autotelic tautological self-pre-dication of *being*, all that can be uttered about *necessary-being-due-to-itself* is: '*hunālika*' – 'there is'. 'There is' *Being without a determinate being* (El-Bizri 2000, 2001, 2006, 2010, 2011, 2014). This discloses the transcendental char-acter of *the question of being*, since it is noetically thought by way of concepts without becoming transmuted into an immanent psychical entity that can be further fetishized. Necessary-Being-due-to-Itself is *one and only*, given that if there were two, then they are not each due-to-themselves per se, since differ-entia are posited as what distinguishes them from each other, and in being as such, they are co-dependent. Necessary-Being-due-to-Itself need not refer to anything other than Itself for it to be, and it is impossible for it not to be.

Thinking now about the necessary-being-due-to-something-other-than-itself (*wājib al-wujūd bi-ghayrih*), it is necessary condition insofar as it exists in actuality, that in being actual *in concreto*, its existence is affirmed rather than its negation. However, it necessarily exists in actuality not due-to-itself but due-to-something-other-than-itself (*bi-ghayrih*). Its existence is granted to it from what is other than itself; it hence exists owing to a causal source that is external to its essence. The necessary-being-due-to-something-other-than-itself is a contingent-being-in-itself that has been brought from a potentiality to an actuality by what is other than itself, whether as the causal source of its being, or as what sustains it in existence, or shields it from other causes that could annihilate it. Therefore, an ontological difference exists between *Being* qua *Necessary-Being-due-to-Itself* and a *being* qua *a-necessary-being-due-to-something-other-than-itself* (Avicenna 1000–37a: 262–63; 1000–37c: 65; 1000–37e: 36–39, 43–47, 350–55; 1000–37g: 255, 261–65, 272–75, 283–85; El-Bizri 2000, 2001, 2006, 2010, 2011, 2014).

Avicenna's analysis of the ontological modalities of being is entangled with his account of the connection and distinction between essence *qua* quiddity and existence *qua* being. This resonates with the Aristotelian '*tode ti*' (the 'thisness' of a present extant thing, its '*haecceitas*' or 'singularity in identity') and the hard to apprehend '*to ti ēn einai*' ('what it is for something to be the thing it is'). Such phrases, along with the Aristotelian categories, all refer back to '*ousia*' ('substance'; 'subject'; 'essence'), which is implied by the various meanings of being (Aristotle fourth century BCE: *Metaphysics* (Theta and Zeta)). This *ousiology* carries resonances too with the Kantian thesis in which *being* is not posited as a real predicate that can be added to the concept of a thing, but is logically the copula of a judgment (Kant 1787: A598/B626). Ultimately, Avicenna's Necessary-Being-due-to-Itself overcomes the Aris-totelian essentialist *ousia*-based substance metaphysics (El-Bizri 2000, 2001).

'Flying person'

The question of being is closely connected with Avicenna's 'flying person' thought-experiment (Avicenna 1000–37b: I.1, 15–16; El-Bizri 2016: 45–46), which begins with the hypothesis that I have been generated at a stroke as a fully grown adult, with sense-perceptions shrouded in such a way that nothing is perceived by me in a sensory manner. Hence, if in that hypothetical situation I do not perceive my own limbs or organs, or have any sensation of external bodies, not even the air buffeting me, then I can still affirm the existence of what, in an Avicennian parlance, would be my 'soul'. Thus self-consciousness is affirmed independently from bodily sensation or corporeality. The existence of my soul (self/ego) is distinct from my body and is disclosed via the unity of self-consciousness in the immediacy of introspective self-reflection (Avicenna 1000–37c: III.1, 2.319–24; El-Bizri 2016: 45). What here concerns us is not the question of consciousness, but the fact that the *field of being* is hypothetically detachable from any of our somatosensory systems (El-Bizri 2016: 46). The soul is seen by Avicenna as 'the first entelechy of a natural body with organs' (Avicenna 1000–37b: I.4, 40). The mutual exclusivity of the mental and the corporeal is existentially subsumed under the overarching genus of *generated beings*, and entails an antinomian ontological monism that is dialectically coupled with an ontic substance dualism (El-Bizri 2016: 46). The individuation of the soul is subject to physical laws in the life-world that governs embodied beings, but without consciousness being explained on the basis of physiology (ibid.: 47).

The soul is affected by the physical while being non-physical, and by having intentional directionality towards what is other than itself, in the noetic and behavioural senses, through lived situational experiences and the meanings they project in embodied life. These are the basis of individuating consciousness. The occurrence of thinking, and being self-conscious of it, as in the 'flying person' thought-experiment, is itself a tautological affirmation that 'there is [*being*]' rather than 'there is not'. The *flying person* is connected with otherness insofar as its being is granted to it from *what is other than itself* (ibid.: 51–52). If I am connected to others by empathy, analogy, expectations of reciprocity, symmetry, or, in ethical terms, by being ready to be responsive to their call, to their pain or joy, and with conscience, then this raises the question of how others may experience their life-world – they are possibly feeling in similar ways to me and to each other, showing intersubjective empathy, and exchanging meaning about situational lived experiences through language (ibid.: 52). In the thought-experiment, not only is a soul affirmed but also, insofar as the *flying person* in question is thinking, *there is* rather than *there is not* is affirmed. Meaning is not therein reducible to a Cartesian 'I think therefore I am' but more essentially that 'there is [*being*]' as given from otherness. This is not the situation of a windowless *monad*, but rather the individuated soul in embodied life, thrown into existence in *being-towards-what-grants-being* in the course of its inner-worldly being-towards-corporeal-death (Such a picture recalls Heidegger's existential analytic of *Dasein's being-towards-death* and Levinas' mysterious future as *Otherness* after death – and the hypostases of *what-gives-being* as: 'Es gibt … Sein' [Heidegger 1927: §2], and '*il y a*' [Levinas 1979: 25–26]).

Eschatology? Immortality?

The Avicennian rational soul that is distinct from the body, despite being individuated by it, is immortal and survives bodily death (Avicenna 1000–37b: V.4, 227, 231). The individuating ghost-embodiment is posited with fading levels of ontological reality, which nonetheless retains the form of the proprioception of the sensory-motor composition of the body in a residual bodily-self-image that accompanies the rational soul with its kinetics and mnemonics (El-Bizri 2016: 47–48). The soul is affected in its individuating embodied life by situational experiences, memories, and imaginings, which condition what is retained of its *phantom-bodily-self-image* after its bodily death, and will be recollected by that immortal individuated soul after the demise of its mortal body; as if glimpsing itself in an auto-scope disembodied perspective as an out-of-its-body experience (ibid.: 47–48). The body dies when the soul departs from it, freed for its other-worldly destiny and thus liberated from incarceration in the material realm of generation and corruption. The situation of the 'flying person' turns embodiment into a coffin; entrapping the self with no interactions outside its inner monologues, and held back from activating its arrested will, since its bodily limbs are immobile and atrophied. Corporeal being is not moved by itself, but via a substance other than itself, and this applies to the human body that is not movable by itself but only through its ensoulment, since the soul is the life-essence of the living being.

Grosso modo, the ontological question of being in Avicenna underpins metaphysical reflections on ontic situational lived experiences in the flesh in an inner-worldly embodied psychosomatic life, along with eschatological imaginings of the other-worldly afterlife of a soul (*al-nafs*) as individuated by inner-worldly-embodiment, albeit in separation from the physical body in corporeal death. If the ontic situational lived experiences in the flesh in an inner-worldly embodied psychosomatic life are marked by hardship and toil, or are unbearable to the point of wishing relief through bodily death, then the eschatological imagining of the other-worldly afterlife of the soul can occasion a promise of hope. The soul is readied in its embodied psychosomatic life for *being-towards-the-afterlife* in its *being-towards-what-grants-being*. This is meditated upon from the standpoint of also thinking of humans as *bodily-mortal-existents* who are thrown into existence in *being-towards-corporeal-death* (not simply a Heideggerian 'being-towards-death'). Embodied living is a borrowed existence granted by *what gives being* to an indebted *bodily-mortal* existent in the flesh. The human soul that survives bodily death is all along granted its being by what is other than itself. Such a soul is orientated towards its source in its self-realization, by way of actualizing its potentiality-to-be in embodied life and the thereafter (Gardet 1952: 37, 67). Such a soul's imagined immortality is marked by what happens in its individuating embodied life in terms of lived experiences that facilitate or hinder its orientation towards its source after bodily death. A soul comes into a body, and in the course of giving the soul its identity, the body facilitates or hinders that which allows the soul to be optimally in communion with the logos or intellect at work in the universe. This happens from the standpoint of preparing the return of the rational soul to its source, following its separation from the body in corporeal death.

A soul is moulded by an embodied life, and this character is retained in the destiny of an immortal disembodied soul (El-Bizri 2016: 48). A non-physical trace of the form of the past body is retained in the soul's self-consciousness. The rational soul that is individuated by way of its embodied life exists necessarily through what is other than itself, while being contingent-in-itself. *There is being rather than nothing* insofar as the thinking soul is self-conscious of its being. Moreover, there is temporal continuity in the non-reflectivity of self-awareness and its immediacy without an inherent objective content, either as consciousness of the body or as the faculties with a *mnemonic* sense of self-identity in the flow of consciousness after bodily death. The retention of the *what-has-been* of self-awareness with the *what-might-be* of protention, both let the past and future become co-entangled with presence (Avicenna 1000–37b: V.3, 38–54, 210–16, 234–35; El-Bizri 2016: 49–50).

Onto-theology and divinity?

Being is *what-is-given* to generated existents as temporal borrowed existence insofar as they are subject to corruption. Thinking can therefore be a mode of thanking *what-gives-being* not only in embodied life, but also in what might follow bodily death as the afterlife of an immortal individuated soul in its destined return to the source of the *being* of beings. The indeterminacy of *Necessary-Being-due-to-Itself* as the mystery of *what-gives-being*, is metamorphosed into a determinateness in being that is *sublated* into a determinate Existent. Being-itself (as indeterminacy in being) is being-for-self (as determinateness in being) that is also being-for-other; since determinateness in being-itself as being-for-self entails a dialectical differentiation from what is other than itself (El-Bizri 2006, 2010, 2011).

Given that every existent is a necessary-being-due-to-something-other-than-itself, and that such existents do not cause each other in a causal cycle where the cause is itself an effect, then the totality of existents constituting the entirety of the world and life is itself necessary-due-to-what-is-other-than-itself. This is the case in spite of Avicenna's thesis of *the co-eternity of the world with the source of its being* as founded on a neo-Platonist account of emanation (*al-ṣudūr; al-fayḍ*) in cosmological theosophy (El-Bizri 2016: 51). *The One* as the superabundant overflowing source of being emanates otherness from itself, whether deterministically or by willing it.

Emanating otherness from sameness, is followed by a return or ascent of the emanated back to the source. This takes the form of an analogical continuum in a grand hierarchical chain of being (*scala naturae*). If emanation is an expulsion, in a descent which posits an ontological difference between the emanated and its source, it is nevertheless the case that what is emanated is ever-connected to its source of being and is attracted to it by way of ascent through self-realization. The human being is placed in-between the worldly realm of the flesh and the transcendent domain of spirit, in being a rational soul individuated by its embodied life. The ascent of the soul towards the higher realms of the chain of being is only undertaken by its intellective faculties, and what is longed for in such attraction to the source is *goodness* per se; for the source is the affirmation of being and the negation of privative non-being.

Thrown into the existential possibilities of a temporal embodied life, the soul is only released into actualizing its return to its source after bodily death. This is the Avicennian account of the *mabda'* qua initiation, and the *ma'ād* qua return, as aetiological eschatology and salvific soteriology (Michot 1986: 30–43) in the self-sending and self-withdrawal of being; as an expulsion from the source in emanation and as an attraction back to it in the return. This picture has hermeneutical and exegetical resonances with the interpretation of religious scripture recited upon the bodily-perishing of a mortal human: '*We are God's and to Him we shall return*' ['*innā li-llāh^i wa innā ilayh^i rāji'ūn*'] (Qur'ān, 'The Heifer' ['*al-Baqara*'], verse 156 [2.156]).

Meaning/meaninglessness!

The meaning of embodied life can be onto-theologically grasped as *being-towards-what-grants-being* within inner-worldly being-towards-corporeal-death. Reflection upon bodily demise can become opened up to the mystery of other-worldliness as a future released into a mode of being that is detached from embodiment, and takes the form of *pure thought*. It is through thinking that *the question of being* is attended to within a mortal's lived experiences in the world while being-towards-corporeal-death. It is by way of this that *the meanings of life* can be disclosed as ponderings over *what-grants-being* via otherness. The meanings of living become un-concealed by way of thinking about *what-self-grants-being* in the movement of expulsion in *emanation*, and *what-self-withdraws-being* in the movement of attraction as *return*. The meaning of being calls for thinking about otherness as *what-gives-and-with-draws-being*.

What calls for thinking about this question of being is meaning-generating, even if the locus of such generation of meaning is itself lacking in meaning. Otherness remains at work within selfhood by generating meaning in being-with-others, even when seeking isolation and self-sufficiency; for to survive away from contemporary life is still to inherit ways of doing, thinking, acting, and making, that are not one's own but have rather been handed down. Hence privacy (even at the level of the 'flying person') is already indebted to otherness. Moreover, even if modern science discloses the structure of the material universe, and that it is not concerned with humanoid-meaning, the meaningfulness of scientific research as an activity of disclosing the principles of matter remains meaningful. My life-world in being-with-others provides pointers as to how I give meaning to my life, even via everyday busyness and engagement with others (falling in love, parenting, working with others, being subject to social norms and state laws, etc.). Even when not attending to the question of my own being, which itself is meaning-generating, I nonetheless give meaning to my living in the flesh in the here and now; or I find meaning in my past destining towards my presence; or I project its momentum as my future horizon of inner-worldly possibilities; or I give meaning via an onto-theological turn that pictures my being-towards-corporeal-death as an antici-pation of a posthumous afterlife, or, more agnostically, simply in wishing to leave a historical trace to posterity.

To state or believe that life is meaningless requires an argument, which is itself a mode of generating reasoned meanings through argumentation, even when assuming the voice of scepticism. Moreover, if the self-refuting nature of such belief is not proven disputation – if there is no argument – then the exis-tential experience of lived situations of angst, nausea, carelessness, hedonism (attitudes that may be associated with looking at life as meaningless) will still yield meaning, at least through actions and behaviours, or the lack thereof found in detachment and heedlessness. For meaninglessness becomes oddly meaningful in the sense that it affects mood, attitude, comportment, and choices. Moreover, if everydayness requires communicative relations of being-with-others, then these too carry meanings, otherwise none of the basic needs can be satisfied. Even in seeking self-sufficiency, or by begging, or depending on charity, some manifestations of communicative meaning are affirmed. Even seeking hedonistic lifestyles, and hence seeing only bodily pleasures as modes of affirming life in its biological reality, requires some toil and labour, or that we be of service to others, or appeal to them – and this reinserts the one who rejects meaning within the sphere of exchanging communicative meanings with others. The nihilist is forced to affirm meaning in action by way of being-with-others, even if this is undertaken in order to have the luxury of refuting meaning in argumentation (perhaps earning a living as a philosopher by doing this!), or by seeking a lifestyle of bodily pleasures.

An inquiry into the meaning of life in our age, independently of Avicenna's thought, must take into account the possibility that we are ordered about in response to modern technology (*das Wesen der modernen Technik*) as 'en-framing' *Ge-Stell* (Heidegger 1954: 13–44). If we are framed and posited as a 'standing reserve' of energies, as 'human resources', this is not entirely of our own doing, since technology shapes our modes of thinking, longing, saying, and doing. The mystery of the question of being calls for thinking about our own being-in-the-world (Heidegger 1927, 1954), or the meaning of our lived situational experience. Otherwise, we are turned into resources of energy that are driven by commodity-fetishisms in quotidian dealings that are ever-framed by technicity in shaping the expectations of ever-readied action in everydayness. Thinking about being opens up a liminal leeway within this network, by way of meditating on what it means *to be* in the facticity of living in the flesh and against the background of contemplating the mystery of what grants and withdraws being. Even if we do not feel confident about the meaning we project onto our life – for motivation, or for solace, or for being comforted by others in loss and bereavement, with regard to anguish about our own mortality, or in standing judged by a divinity in an onto-theological eschatology – nevertheless the mystery of the purpose of being is at times saturated with meaningfulness by what is thrust upon us from *otherness* in life.

Responsibilities are placed upon us in quotidian dealings. We assume them wilfully; or they surge from a call of conscience to sacrifice for the sake of others with whom we are bonded in love or friendship; or we are brought together in a commonwealth through a civic sense of duty, dignity, honour, or compassion; or we onto-theologically ponder over the mystery of being when we cannot define it. These are signifiers of the life and death instincts of felicity and ruin (Freud 1920), and of how we engage with the will of others as they impinge upon us, or in how we project our will on them. If the meaning of life becomes itself ontologically saturated with meditations on the phenomenon of being drawn to the source of our being, then living becomes itself a way of actualizing such a return with the least resistance and hardship. Even though Dante's *Divina Commedia* describes a different eschatology from that of Avicenna, both thinkers picture a neo-Platonist journey of *the return of the soul to its source of being*; accordingly, such epic attraction back to *what-grants-being* ought not to begin from what is allegorically described as being akin to an *inferno*. If the meaning of life is underpinned by the grand picture of an attraction of the soul back to its source, as ontologically marked by its intimate, inexplicable longings, then the pathways for such an ascent will be labyrinthine and tortuous. However, it remains the case that from an Avicennian perspective, such mystical love for the source is best granted its onto-theological meaning via the way in which the intellect (*al-'aql*) guides meditations in this ontic life to reveal how best to return to the One in the thereafter ...

14 Maimonides and the meaning of life

ALFRED L. IVRY

The man to whom this essay is dedicated would not have recognized his name as given above. He answered to the Arabic name of Abū 'Imran Mūsa ibn Maymūn ibn 'Abdallah al-Qurtubi al-Andalusī al-Isra'īlī (delineating his Cordovan, Andalusian and Israelite origins), and to the Hebrew name Moshe ben Maimon (from which the Greek "Maimonides" is derived). To his Jewish readers he was commonly known as "the *Rambam*," an acronym standing for "Rav (rabbi) Moshe ben Maimon," or simply as *Rav* or *Ram* (Rabbenu Moshe), *the* rabbi of the age. His age was mostly in the twelfth century (1138–1204), but as the *Rambam* he remains the pre-eminent rabbi of all times, at least from the Middle Ages to today, for all who value the Talmudic interpretation of biblical law on which rabbinic Judaism is based.

Maimonides is also widely regarded as the foremost and certainly the most famous of medieval Jewish philosophers, the author of *The Guide of the Perplexed*. In that work, Maimonides presents an image of God and His relation to the world that is diametrically opposed (mostly) to the image depicted in his rabbinic works. However different in genre, Maimonides' rabbinic and philosophic compositions both attest to his finding the meaning of life to consist in striving to understand God's nature and to live accordingly. As people differ in their understanding the nature of divinity, Maimonides offers diverse ways to live meaningfully, and does not demand one standard of meaning for all. To this day, scholars differ whether his rabbinic or philosophical work best expresses his personal choice for the meaning of life.

Maimonides' rabbinic stature is based primarily on two legal compendia he penned, the one a commentary on the *Mishnah*, the first stratum of the Talmud which contains the discussions and decisions of the rabbis in Palestine roughly from 100 BCE to 200 CE; and the other a compendium of Talmudic law, organized topically and decisively, shorn of the dialectical argumentation of its source. He called this book *Mishneh Torah*, which could be taken as the "Repetition of the Torah," or as the "Reiteration of the Law," and he claims that studying it and the Pentateuch only should suffice for most Jews, effectively rendering study of the Talmud itself unnecessary (cf. Kraemer 2008: 323; Davidson 2005: 197).

It is somewhat ironic that Maimonides achieved great renown among his co-religionists, for his codifying the laws of the Talmud and unilaterally prescribing correct procedures in all aspects of the law posed a great threat to the unique form of religiosity that rabbinical Judaism had cultivated for hundreds of years, namely, the study of the Talmud. Sanctioned as the Oral Law, regarded (by the Pharisees and their rabbinic descendants) as first given at Sinai together with the Written Law, the Talmud was treated as the ongoing pre-eminently Jewish connection to the Divine. Appreciating and mastering its arguments were thought to bring a person near to God's presence. This study of the Talmud was not, therefore, merely an intellectual or legalistic exercise, it was fundamentally a spiritual and religious act that could and should be pursued throughout one's life.

Maimonides' *Mishneh Torah* threatened to turn this open-ended and never-ending study of the law in all its possible theoretical entailments into a codified and dogmatically decisive body of law, to be consulted rather than studied; its brilliance as a code of law a questionable substitute for the spiritual rewards to be experienced in pondering a portion of the Talmud. And indeed, while Maimonides' rabbinic *opera* were greatly admired for their mastery of the Oral Law, they did not achieve the success he would have wanted, as study of the Talmud in its traditional form continued in his day and subsequently (until today, among orthodox Jews) to be the unique expression of Jewish religiosity.

For its part, the *Mishneh Torah*, as a code of Jewish law, was intended to facilitate correct observance of the law, even as it implicitly deprecated further intellectual preoccupation with that law. As a legist, Maimonides was strict in his demand that the law be followed, his fidelity to orthopraxis complementing his ostensibly orthodox beliefs. His negative attitude towards the traditional study of the Talmud may be explained in part by his desire to accommodate a new syllabus of learning within Jewish life, that of Western science in all its manifestations. He wanted to make room intellectually in Judaism for those subjects that had been deemed "foreign" and unwelcome since late classical times, when Greek culture had first clashed with nascent rabbinic Judaism. The Talmud was in part a wall erected to create a virtual reality within the historical "real" world of exile and frequent persecution in which Jews lived. That wall, or "ocean" of Talmud, as it was called, served to protect its followers, but also segregated them from the literary and scientific achievements of the Greco-Roman world. The hostility of that world, re-enforced by Christianity, had distanced Jews from involvement in it.

This negative attitude of Jews towards science began to change following the spread of Islam in the seventh century, and the subsequent translation of Greek texts in philosophy, medicine, astronomy and other sciences into Arabic, the lingua franca of most Jews at that time. Beginning in the ninth century, Muslim intellectuals, known as *falāsifa*, picked up the trails forged by the ancient Greeks, commented on their studies and added to them. Careful for the most part to distinguish their scientific and philosophic investigations from the tenets of Islamic theology, these philosophers and scientists presented an ostensibly neutral body of learning religiously, one which Jews could endorse. Still, before Maimonides' writings there were few Jews who dared to study and comment on the scientific world that was now available to them, who were prepared to widen their intellectual horizons.

In his Commentary on the Mishnah and in his *Mishneh Torah*, Maimonides already indicates, though relatively briefly, his familiarity with the major philosophical currents of the Western tradition, Aristotelian, Platonic and Neoplatonic. In an eight chapter introduction to the Mishnah *Avot* ("Fathers") in his commentary on that work, Maimonides adopts nearly all of Aristotle's teachings in his *Nichomachean Ethics,* following an adaptation given by the tenth century Muslim philosopher Alfarabi (cf. Maimonides 1168: 67). Similarly, in the first of the fourteen books that comprise the *Mishneh Torah*, Maimonides offers a brief précis of the metaphysical beliefs he feels all Jews must accept, notwithstanding their considerable Neoplatonic origins; and then follows that with a discourse on laws relating to moral dispositions and ethical conduct, largely drawn from Aristotle (Maimonides 1170–80: 43–64).

It is, though, in his *Guide of the Perplexed* that Maimonides fully indulges his admiration for the whole body of science that most of his peers still regarded as off-limits and threatening to Jewish survival. He writes in the foreword of the book that he wrote it to enlighten a student who had to leave him prematurely, before he had fully informed him of the issues and doctrines involved in the conflict between the Occasionalist beliefs posed by Muslim theology and the "scientific" tradition of philosophy headed by Aristotle and Plotinus that Maimonides favored. The student was unsure of the correct logical methodology to employ in this encounter, and Maimonides had to insist that religious beliefs should conform to the knowledge proven by empirical experience and logical reasoning to be demonstrably true or highly probable. A religious tenet, however sincerely asserted, could not exist in the realm of unbounded imaginative possibilities. God Himself, however unique His being, could not do or be that which logic showed was self-contradictory.

Maimonides used the science and cosmology of his day to argue for the existence and oneness of God, a unity of being so absolute as to sever His essence from all attributes and (direct) relationships to a world that He had ostensibly created. The image of an impersonal and unchanging, unaffected deity is familiar to us from Aristotle and Plotinus, and was adopted as well by some of Maimonides' Muslim predecessors, but is antithetical to the image of God presented in the Bible, the personal God of Judaism, Christianity and Islam. Maimonides' first task in the *Guide*, therefore, was to interpret the biblical depictions of God in non-literal, metaphorical terms; to allegorize God's encounters with man. The Bible was written in an exoteric, mythical style, Maimonides believes, to conform to the beliefs and customs of its time, many of its laws reflecting pagan practices deemed necessary in ancient times.

The prophetic encounters with God and angels are all, to Maimonides, human projections of what the prophets (correctly) conceived to be the will of God, universal truths conveyed in popular and particularistic fashion for the people addressed.

This allegorization of the biblical narrative and psychological interpretation of prophecy has the effect of shifting the meaning of the story from a particular time and place to a universal plane. While the history told and laws ordained are specific to the people of Israel, and meant to ensure their survival and well-being, the political and personal ideals espoused are relevant to all peoples and times. Maimonides thus sees the Bible as transcending its contingent historical origins, offering a meaningful life to all persons who seek it. Nevertheless, his immediate concern is to administer to the spiritual needs of his people, all his people. Thus, while the *Guide* is explicitly written for the select few who can appreciate the philosophical issues raised and who understand the scientific claims discussed, it also often depicts the allegedly affective behavior of a personal God, making assertions that seem to contradict or are contrary to Maimonides' more radical assertions. While this may well be a strategy to conceal his true beliefs, Maimonides is also in this manner giving the average person what he craves. For Maimonides believes it his responsibility to reach all his people with whatever amount of true teaching and guidance they can tolerate, even if that means transmitting matters in half measures and misrepresentations.

The meaning of life, then, for Maimonides, is not to be conceived only for himself and other philosophers. Lives vary, and there are all types within a community, each one searching in one way or another for meaning and happiness in life. The *Guide* to some degree, and the *Mishneh Torah* to a much greater degree, offers an implicit response to the quest for a meaningful life that can satisfy all members of the community. Ideally, though, as expressed in the *Guide*, the meaning of life is to be found in discovering the divine presence in all of nature, in the study that leads from the natural sciences to metaphysics to the One, culminating in an intellectual communion with and passionate love for that eternal being we call God (Maimonides *c.* 1190: 618–28). This enables the individual intellect to experience a taste of immortality, to the extent that it participates in universal truth. The rational faculty of the person arriving at this juncture will be filled with ecstatic joy and happiness, though the more individual faculties of the soul are not involved in it. The only psychic faculty that may endure is the acquired intellect, consisting of depersonalized universal principles of eternal and thus divine being.

Maimonides thus presents immortality, in the *Guide*, as an intellectual *cum* spiritual achievement available only for the select few, those who can appreciate the joy to be had in loving an unknowable God, with no personal reciprocity or individuated immortality of the soul. This belief accords with that of Maimonides' contemporary, Averroës, who in a number of treatises devoted to Aristotelian and post-Aristotelian views of the soul and intellect, propounded the view that became known as monopsychism; the belief that the only part of a person's soul that endures after death is that perfected intellect which becomes united with the immediate source of all forms on earth, the "Agent Intellect," there being no individual or personal survival of the soul.

Maimonides, while not analyzing the faculties of the soul in great detail, agrees implicitly with Averroës' monopsychist view, and like him presents it as the ultimate life experience for a select few (cf. Ivry 2008: 124). Like his Muslim counterpart too, Maimonides effectively ignores a more democratic entailment of the theory, namely that a person may attain immortal stature by acquiring knowledge, and thus conjoining, with but one eternally true principle of being; and for Maimonides, this knowledge need not depend on prior mastery of an entire science.

This may be inferred as well from Maimonides' teachings à *propos* of the Mishnah's opening statement in *Sanhedrin* 10 that "all Israel has a portion in the world to come," in which Maimonides presents a doxology of thirteen principles of the faith, belief in which allegedly ensures immortality. As Maimonides' prior remarks there had just shown, "the world to come" was an amorphous and controversial concept in Judaism, and the thirteen principles of belief that Maimonides enumerates require more explication than he provides to be fully understood by the typical reader of the Mishnah. Yet Maimonides holds out the promise of immortality, however understood, to those who have a partial and imperfect grasp of the truth.

It may be argued that this Mishnah commentary assertion of immortality, and the happiness it affords the believer, is more dogmatic than philosophical. Maimonides himself was suspected of not believing in (the traditional understanding of) resurrection and the messiah, though he included them as principles of the faith. Rhetorical and vague though it may be, however, Maimonides' holding out a promise of immortality to the uneducated mass of his people attests to his concern for more than just the elite; a lowering of the intellectual bar to meet the vast majority of his community, gain their trust and lead them to meaningful lives.

That concern for the welfare of the entire people is the thrust of Maimonides' moral as well as political teachings throughout both the Commentary on the Mishnah and the *Mishneh Torah*. Adopting essentially Aristotelian teachings in ethics and political philosophy, Maimonides views the Torah and rabbinic tradition as attempts to give meaning to life on both a personal and collective level. The law addresses the typical person, not the exception, and all must conform to its demands for the sake of social and political coherence. Observance of the law disciplines a person's behavior and leads to appreciation of the virtuous life as ordained by revelation. Moderation in all things is the standard, except for expressions of anger, which should be banished and only feigned (by a ruler) for strategic purposes. In a further deviation from Aristotelian teachings, Maimonides praises the humble and self-effacing man rather than Aristotle's proud and self-satisfied benefactor of society.

Maimonides' personal inclination towards ascetic practices is evidenced in his recognizing such behavior as that of a *Tzaddiq*, a "pious man," in contrast to the moderate but more indulgent lifestyle of one who is merely a "wise" person, a *Hacham*. The law is intended for the "wise" and the "pious," but the latter may go beyond the letter of the law to search its inner meaning.

Maimonides' recognition of the diversity of human experiences and the different degrees in which the meaning of life can be appreciated is apparent as well in his many medical writings. He arrived in Egypt already well read and tutored in medical treatises, taking the (translated) writings of Galen and Avicenna's *Canon of Medicine* as his main guidebooks. He served as physician to the vizier of Egypt and other notables in their palaces during the day, and returned home to hold a clinic for the community. Somehow he found the time as well as to write a number of medical textbooks, of both a general and specific kind. Throughout his medical works, as in his rabbinic and philosophical compositions, Maimonides insists upon the need to maintain a healthy lifestyle as a prerequisite for pursuing meaning in life. Indeed, the meaning of life requires a healthy body and soul, and he saw himself as guiding people to both perfections.

Maimonides' largest and most famous work is called *The Book of Medical Aphorisms* which encompassed all the fields of medicine then known. He divided the work into 25 treatises and 1,500 mostly Galenic "aphorisms," i.e. descriptions of diseases and prescriptions for their treatment. He devoted other treatises to specific medical issues, such as *On Asthma, On Hemorrhoids* and *On Coitus*. Maimonides announces, in the last named work (written for a Muslim notable), that he was instructed to write a guide that would aid the addressee "in the increase of sexual intercourse," and he does so (with some rather bizarre prescriptions), though pointing out to the intended individual that he is near emaciation in attempting to satisfy his large harem. Maimonides' own view on this issue is expressed in his treatise *On the Regulation of Health*, where he writes that "sexual intercourse harms most people ... Whoever wishes to remain healthy should shake the idea of sexual intercourse from his mind as much as he can."

Maimonides balances this negative attitude towards sexual activity, which clearly reflects his personal view, with a more positive stance elsewhere, attuned to the social norms and realities of his Muslim clientele as well as to the political/religious expectations of his Jewish co-religionists. He recommends the average person, be he Jew or Muslim, practice moderation in this area, not extremes of dissipation or denial of nature's urgings. He does not require that others find the meaning of life in denying the promptings of the flesh, as he does. For him, life has meaning to the degree that he exercises his intellect to reach, through scientific understanding of nature and the cosmos, an appreciation of the Divine providence that pervades the world. That appreciation is transformed into love of God and communion with the eternal principles of being, the ultimate meaning he finds in life.

15 Aquinas and the meaning of life

EDWARD FESER

Thomas Aquinas certainly has a thoroughly worked out view about the meaning of life. You might even say that it is the central theme of his work. This is so even though, as far as I know, he never actually addresses the question "What is the meaning of life?" Or to be more precise, he never addresses the question in exactly those terms. Indeed, the question, in its now familiar formulation, may be a distinctively modern one – asked only after it started to seem that life might *not* have any meaning, whereas for the medievals it was obvious that it does.

In what follows, I will begin by setting out the elements of Aquinas's thought that imply an answer to the question. As we will see, some of these elements derive from Aquinas's philosophical influences (and in particular from Aristotelianism and Neo-Platonism), and others derive from the Christian tradition. Next I will consider why Aquinas did not explicitly address the question in the terms now familiar, and why modern philosophers do. I will also discuss the way in which modern philosophers tend to think that any attempt to answer the question is bound to be problematic, and why Aquinas would not agree with them about this.

Many readers are bound to suspect that Aquinas's approach has something to do with God. It does, but not exclusively, and not in the way modern readers tend to suppose.

Natural ends

Nothing in Aquinas's philosophy can properly be understood apart from his commitment to Aristotelian essentialism and teleology.[1] Essentialism is the thesis that every natural object has, as a matter of objective fact (rather than as a matter of human convention, say), an essence or nature. That is to say, there is a fact of the matter about what it is and what its characteristic properties and activities are. Among the features that are grounded in a thing's essence or nature are teleological features. That is to say, just by virtue of having the essence it has or being the kind of thing it is, every natural object is directed toward the realization of certain distinctive ends or goals. For instance, an oak tree is naturally directed toward the realization of ends such as sinking roots into the ground, taking in water through them, producing acorns, carrying out photosynthesis, and so forth.

Natural objects are to be contrasted with artifacts such as watches, beds, and computers, and mere aggregates like a pile of stones that formed at random at the bottom of a hill. Nothing is *naturally* directed toward functioning as a watch, for example, because watches are human inventions. That certain bits of metal count as watch gears, a minute hand, etc., is relative to human interests, and that the whole collection has the end or goal of telling time is also relative to human interests. An artifact like a watch lacks the *intrinsic* or "built-in" teleology that an oak tree or other natural object has. And an aggregate like the random pile of stones doesn't have even the extrinsic or observer-relative teleology of a watch. Even a stone has a certain minimal teleology – it tends naturally toward ends like resisting pressure, falling toward the ground when dropped, etc. – but the pile *qua* pile has no natural tendencies over and above the sum of those of the individual stones that make it up.

For Aristotelians like Aquinas, the intrinsic teleology of a natural object entails an objective standard of *goodness* and *badness* for the object.[2] A thing is good to the extent that it realizes the ends toward which it is directed by virtue of its nature, and it is bad to the extent that it fails to realize these ends. For example, an oak that sinks deep and solid roots into the ground is to that extent a good oak, and an oak which due to disease or damage fails to do so is to that extent bad. The senses of "good" and "bad" operative here are essentially those we have in mind when we speak of a good or bad *specimen* of a kind of thing. The oak with weak or sickly roots is a bad specimen of an oak because it doesn't fulfill the ends toward which oaks are by nature directed as well as an oak with strong and deep roots does. Obviously it is not *moral* goodness and badness that are in question here, but for Aristotelians like Aquinas, moral goodness and badness are a special case of these more general kinds. They have to do with the goodness or badness of *rational* beings, who can *choose* whether or not to pursue those ends toward which their nature directs them.

The distinction between the intrinsic teleology of a natural object and the merely extrinsic or observer-relative teleology of artifacts entails that watches and other machines are not good models for natural objects. There is no *objective, mind-independent* fact of the matter about whether something is a good or bad watch, because there is no objective, mind-independent fact of the matter about whether something counts as a watch in the first place. By contrast, there *is* an objective fact of the matter about whether something is a good or bad specimen of an oak, because there is an objective, mind-independent fact of the matter about whether something *is* an oak, and about *what it is to be* an oak.

For this reason, for Aquinas, God is not related to the world as a craftsman is related to his artifacts, as in William Paley's design argument.[3] To be sure, oak trees and other natural objects are in Aquinas's view created by God, and indeed would not continue in existence and operation even for an instant unless God were sustaining them in being. Still, even if an oak could *per impossibile* exist apart from God, it would still have as its natural ends such goals as sinking roots into the ground, producing acorns, etc. It would have them because being directed toward such ends *simply follows from being an oak*, rather than being an observer-relative feature like the time-telling function of a watch.

There is, then, a *point* to being an oak, and a point to being a natural object of any other kind. That point is for a thing to realize the ends toward which it is directed by virtue of its nature. For example, the point of being an oak is to do oak-like things – to sink roots into the ground, carry out photosynthesis, produce acorns, and so on.

Now, a human being is a natural object. The essence or nature of a human being, for Aquinas as for Aristotle, is that of a *rational animal*. The ends toward which we are directed by nature thus include animal ends, such as acquiring food and shelter, and mating and producing offspring. But what is distinctive about us as rational animals is the possession of *intellect* and *will*, and thus our distinctive ends are those of the intellect and will – the true and the good, respectively. That is to say, our intellects are by nature directed toward the end of understanding things, and our wills toward the pursuit of what the intellect perceives to be good ("good" being understood in the teleological and essentialist terms outlined earlier).

So, the *point* of human life is to realize these ends. But for Aquinas, not all the ends toward which we are directed by nature are equally significant. They are hierarchically ordered, with the lower ends existing for the sake of the realization of the higher ones, which are what make us distinctively human. In particular, our animal ends exist for the sake of realizing the ends entailed by our rationality – again, the pursuit of the true and the good.

What, specifically, does this involve? Aquinas examines various possible candidate answers to the question of what can fulfill us as human beings, and argues that several popular answers are mistaken (cf. Aquinas 1265–74: I-II, 2). It cannot be wealth that fulfills us, he says, because wealth exists only for the sake of other things which we might acquire with it. It cannot be honor, because honor comes to us only as a result of our realizing some other good, so that it cannot itself be the ultimate good. For the same reason, it cannot be fame. Moreover, fame might come about as a result of something bad instead of something good. It cannot be power, because power too is only a means to an end, and can also be exercised for bad ends as well as good ones. It cannot be pleasure, because pleasure is a by-product of realizing some good, rather than constituting the good itself. It cannot be any mere bodily good, because these are subordinate to the goods of the soul – that is to say, the goods of the intellect and the will. But it cannot even be the soul itself, in Aquinas's view, for the soul is a created thing, and no created thing can bring us perfect fulfillment. Only God can do that.

Here it is crucial to understand how Aquinas conceives of God.[4] Aquinas's metaphysics is built on the foundation of Aristotle's theory of actuality and potentiality. For Aquinas, any contingent thing can exist at all, even for an instant, only insofar as its potential for existence is actualized at that instant. If what actualizes it is itself a further contingent thing which requires actualization, we will be led into a vicious regress unless we suppose that the series of actualizers terminates with a cause of existence that is *purely actual*, with no potentiality that needs to be or indeed could be actualized. It just is, always and already, pure actuality. In this way it can be an *uncaused* cause; for since it lacks potentiality, it lacks the metaphysical prerequisite of being caused or needing to be caused.

This is, for Aquinas, what God essentially is. Now, as the purely actual uncaused cause of things, God is also the ultimate explanation of the world. Knowing God is thus necessary for the intellect fully to achieve its natural end of understanding the world. God is also the most perfectly good thing. For the notion of goodness as the realization of an end is on further analysis to be cashed out, in Aquinas's view, in terms of the notion of actualization. For example, the oak tree with strong and deep roots is to that extent a good oak tree because it has actualized its inherent potential for growing roots in a way the sickly oak tree has not. If God is *pure* actuality, then, he must be perfectly good. Being with God is therefore also necessary for the human will fully to realize its natural end of pursuing the good.

God is thus for Aquinas both our *first cause* and our *last end*, that from which we came and that to which we are meant to return. This theme of coming from God and going back to him was present in the Neo-Platonic philosopher Plotinus, and Aquinas makes of it the overarching theme of his *Summa Theologiae*, interpreting it in light of an Aristotelian metaphysics. He also grafts onto it a distinctively Christian conception of human destiny.

Supernatural ends

Everything described so far is, in Aquinas's view, knowable in principle by purely philosophical arguments and attainable in theory by means of our natural powers. Nothing from scripture or special divine revelation more generally is strictly necessary. That is why pagan philosophers like Aristotle and Plotinus could know as much as they did about God and about the point of human existence. The issues treated so far are matters of natural theology and natural law, not Christianity per se.

There are, however, two serious limitations to our natural capacities in these areas. First, there is a very wide divergence between what is possible in principle and what is actually achieved in practice. Because we are rational *animals*, our intellects and wills (unlike those of angels, which are incorporeal) are tied to bodies. Our intellects thus require sensory input in order to attain knowledge, and our senses provide only very limited information about the world (which depends on time and place) and are also prone to malfunction. Hence, we are bound to fall into serious errors when reasoning about matters far removed from ordinary experience. Knowledge of God's existence and nature is, even under the best of circumstances, likely to be only partial and mixed with error. Furthermore, the bodily appetites we possess *qua* animals can easily distract us from pursuing the highest goods. Hence we are bound to fall into serious moral error and to develop habits of behavior that pull us away from God.

Second, even the most perfect knowledge of God, and communion with him, of which we are naturally capable, is radically incomplete. It is highly philosophical and abstract, and requires the intellect to move as far as possible away from material reality, which is the natural focus of its attention. It is easier for us to grasp what God is not than what he is, and we need to resort to analogical rather than univocal language to say whatever we can say about God that is of a positive nature. Our wills also have to strain to take us beyond the pursuit of our earthly ends and toward our other-worldly highest end.

What Christianity reveals is the possibility of a *super*natural knowledge of, and communion with, God. "Supernatural" in this context has nothing to do with magic, ghosts, goblins, or any of the other things popularly associated with the term.[5] A supernatural end is one that is *above and additional to* a thing's natural ends and capacities. Using our natural capacities, our knowledge of and yearning for God is, again, bound to be largely mixed with intellectual and moral error. Divine supernatural assistance could prevent us from falling into such error. Using our natural capacities, our knowledge of and communion with God would also be, even in the best case, highly limited. Divine supernatural assistance could afford us a far more intimate knowledge of and communion with God – the *beatific vision*, a *direct apprehension* of God's nature that bypasses the limitations of the body.

Now, according to Christian theology, the human race was at its creation offered precisely these supernatural gifts, but rejected them. What the penalty of original sin entails is the closing off of the path to attaining the *super*natural end of the beatific vision (which still left open the possibility of a merely *natural, philosophical* knowledge of God), and the loss of the *super*natural assistance which would have prevented dysfunction in the operation of our natural intellectual and moral powers (which still allowed us to use those powers in an imperfect way). What salvation amounts to is the recovery of these lost supernatural gifts.

Incorporating this understanding of Christian theology into his system of thought, Aquinas thus takes human existence to have a *twofold* point. Human beings have as their natural end the knowledge of God which pagan philosophers at least approximated. They have as their *super*natural end the beatific vision, which is not possible apart from the special divine assistance which in Christian theology is called grace.

World without ends

Early modern philosophy was defined by, perhaps more than anything else, its rejection of Aristotelian essentialism and teleology. Early modern thinkers like Descartes, Newton, and Paley erased the distinction between natural objects (in the Aristotelian sense of "natural") and artifacts, treating *all* things as artifacts – in the case of plants, animals, stones, water, and the like, as artifacts of *God*. Just as the parts of a watch have no *intrinsic* teleology but only the *extrinsic* teleology imposed on them by a watchmaker, so too do living things and inorganic phenomena lack, on this view, any intrinsic teleology. Any teleology they exhibit must come from *without, extrinsically*, from the intentions of a divine designer. When later modern philosophers also threw this divine designer out of their picture of reality, teleology of even an extrinsic kind went with him. The world inevitably came to seem entirely without point or purpose.

There were, of course, still the purposes individual human beings have. But these became problematic in two ways. First, in the absence of any *intrinsic* teleology, any teleology grounded in the *natures* of things, individual human purposes appear arbitrary and contingent. There can be no such thing as a point *to human existence as such*, a point that is there whether or not particular individuals realize it, and the realization of which is, as a matter of *objective* fact, good and fulfilling for them. There can be only the purposes this or that individual *happens* to have, and since these purposes do not reflect anything in the very essence or nature of human beings, the goodness of their realization has no *objective* status.

Second, the very *existence* even of contingent individual purposes is problematic given the metaphysical picture of the world taken for granted by most modern philosophers. Again, on this picture, there is no *intrinsic* teleology of the Aristotelian kind, and neither is there any *extrinsic* teleology of the Paleyan kind. Everything that exists comprises, at the end of the day, only purposeless particles in fields of force. The purpose or teleology that human thought and action seem to exhibit must therefore really be reducible to something else (patterns of efficient causality rather than final causality), or altogether eliminable. Just as Darwinian explanations claim to show that there is no genuinely irreducible teleology in living things but only the illusion of it, so too do materialist explanations claim to show that there is no irreducible teleology in human thought and action.

This seems to be the origin of what modern philosophers characterize as the problem of the meaning of life. Common sense attributes purposes to our actions and sees purposes in nature as well. But the metaphysical picture accepted by most modern intellectuals, and for which they think they find support in modern science (though whether it in fact follows from modern science is a matter of controversy),[6] implies that there is no purpose in nature at all, and indeed that even the purposes we think we find in our own thoughts and actions are illusory. Thus are we led to ask "What is the meaning of life?" and thus do modern philosophers tend to think that the unavoidable answer is that there isn't any.

Aquinas never frames the question in quite that way precisely because he does not think of the world in the radically non-teleological terms that modern philosophers take for granted. What he does ask is what our "last end" consists in, which presupposes that we *have* some last end or other. When modern people ask "What is the meaning of life?," it is not because they are convinced that life does have a meaning or point and are simply wondering what, specifically, that meaning is. Rather, it is because they *doubt* that it has any meaning or point at all. (Compare the way in which we ask, rhetorically, "What's the point?," precisely when we have judged of some action that it *has no* point.) In short, whereas modern philosophers are essentially asking *whether there is* any point to human existence and incline toward a negative answer, Aquinas has no doubt that the answer to that question is affirmative, and addresses instead the question of what, specifically, the point of human existence is.

The reason Aquinas does not doubt that the answer is affirmative, it is important to emphasize, is not because of his theism, but rather because of his essentialist and teleological metaphysics. Every natural object has a point in the sense of a natural end, so that there can be no question that human beings have such an end. That would remain true even if, *per impossibile*, there were no God. *What* the point is would be different in that case, but it doesn't follow that there *wouldn't be* a point.

For this reason, Aquinas would not be impressed by some of the misgivings that modern philosophers express about attempts to answer the question about the meaning of life. Alan Lacey expresses such misgivings when he asks:

> [W]e cannot expect meanings to be handed to us on a plate, and even if they were, what use would they be to us? God may have his purposes in creating me, but why should I adopt them?
>
> (Lacey 1995: 487–88)

The problem with such remarks is that they presuppose that the point of human existence would inevitably be something *contingent*. They presuppose, for example, that if God created us, then our purpose is like the time-telling purpose which a watchmaker assigns to certain bits of metal, where he could just as well have assigned some other purpose instead, or no purpose at all. But that is, in Aquinas's view, simply not how creation works. When God creates a natural object of type *X*, its end or purpose derives from *the fact that it has the essence or nature of an X*, not from some arbitrary stipulation on God's part. Again, even if an *X* could exist apart from God, it would still have the natural end or purpose characteristic of an *X*.

Nor can it make sense, on Aquinas's view, to suggest that it might be good for a natural object to realize some end other than the one entailed by its nature. For what is good or bad for a thing is *defined by* the ends inherent in its nature. It is *metaphysically impossible* for it to be good for a thing to act contrary to those ends. Suppose an oak tree were granted intelligence and we asked it: "What use to you are the ends of sinking roots into the ground, producing acorns, carrying out photosynthesis, etc.? Why adopt those ends as your own?" The oak tree might answer: "What are you talking about? I'm an *oak tree*. How could it possibly be good for me not to pursue those ends?" In the same way, for Aquinas, it makes no sense to suggest that it might be good for us to pursue something other than the ends toward which *our* nature directs us. Contra Lacey, there can be no question of whether we should "adopt" them or find them of "use," any more than there is any question about our "adopting" or finding of "use" the nature of being rational animals. These ends or purposes, like our nature, and indeed because of our nature, are simply given to us and could not be otherwise.

Or at least, that is the case *given* something like Aristotelian essentialism and teleology. With that metaphysical background in place, the question of the meaning of life barely even arises, but can readily be given an affirmative answer when it does arise. Without that metaphysical background, the question arises in an obvious and urgent way, but seems impossible to answer except negatively.

Notes

1 For detailed exposition and defense of Aristotelian essentialism and teleology, see Feser 2014b.
2 For exposition and defense of this theory of value, see Feser 2014a.
3 For a detailed account of the relationship between Aquinas's views and Paley's, see Feser 2013.
4 For exposition and defense of Aquinas's arguments concerning the existence and nature of God, see Feser 2009: ch. 3. Cf. also Feser 2017.
5 For a detailed treatment of Aquinas's understanding of the supernatural and the controversies over its proper interpretation, see Feingold 2010.
6 In Feser 2008, I argue that a non-teleological metaphysics can be *read out of* the results of modern science only if it is first *read into* those results. The results of modern science are of themselves neutral between an Aristotelian and non-Aristotelian reading, so that which reading to adopt is ultimately a philosophical rather than scientific question.

16 Montaigne and the meaning of life

STEPHEN LEACH

In a letter to *The Times* dated 10 February 1970, Valerie Eliot, wife of the late T.S. Eliot, told the following story.

> My husband, T.S. Eliot, loved to recount how late one evening he stopped a taxi. As he got in, the driver said: "You're T.S. Eliot." When asked how he knew, he replied: "Ah, I've got an eye for a celebrity. Only the other evening I picked up Bertrand Russell, and I said to him: 'Well, Lord Russell, what's it all about', and, do you know, he couldn't tell me."

I shall argue that in the same situation Montaigne would have given a very succinct answer to the driver's question – polite, but as concise and to the point as the question itself. Montaigne? "Of course Montaigne is not one of the Greats" (Friedrich 1991: 2): an amiable fellow, pleasant company, but perhaps not an obvious first choice for advice in the face of the very deepest philosophical quandary?

On the contrary, I shall argue that Montaigne's answer is not only concise and to the point, but is the best answer that can be given to the question 'what's it all about?', or, 'what is the meaning of life?' In fact, I shall argue it is the only answer that it makes sense for a philosopher to give.

In short, I believe Montaigne would have answered: 'Work it out for yourself.'

> Since philosophy has not been able to find a way to tranquillity that is suitable for all, let everyone seek it individually.
>
> ('Of Glory', 1578–80: 572)[1]

Of course if Montaigne had given that answer, his cabbie might then have told a very similar story to Russell's: "only the other evening I picked up Michel de Montaigne and I asked him 'what's it all about?' and do you know, he couldn't tell me." He might say that, but he would be wrong.

There is something profoundly unphilosophical in the cabbie's expectation of an immediate answer and in his disappointment at not receiving one. Montaigne's answer, by contrast, is an invitation to philosophize. For Montaigne does not imply that since philosophy does not provide an immediate assertoric answer we should abandon philosophy – he does not say that the meaning of life is whatever we take it to be: not at all – rather, he suggests that since philosophy does not provide an answer upon which we can all agree, we are forced to use our own resources, to look around ourselves and to think for ourselves – which, of course, is the starting point of philosophy, the love of wisdom. In this sense – teaching us to think for ourselves – "it is philosophy that teaches us to live" ('Of the Education of Children', 1579–80: 146).

At this point the objection may occur to some readers that Montaigne is here concerned with finding meaning *in* life (in answer to the question 'what should I do?'), and not with finding the meaning *of* life (in answer to the question 'what do I know?'), either that or he has conflated the two questions.[2] In reply, I would not deny that these are two distinct questions. However, the objection misses its target because Montaigne's answer answers both questions, without there being any implication that either question is more fundamental than the other. Yet, although the two questions are separate, there is a relationship between them in that we have, I believe, a tacit understanding that our answer to either question may affect our answer to the other.

Montaigne's *Complete Works*, which, including his letters and travel journals, runs to over 1,300 pages; and is a book which famously exhibits all the twists and turns and inconsistencies of the author's own thinking over the entire latter part of his lifetime. And from this work I have extracted but a five-word paraphrase! However, in this instance, on this particular question, Montaigne is remarkably consistent: in word and deed he took his own advice.

His essays, a blend of philosophy and autobiography, are prefaced with a note 'To the Reader' of extraordinary diffidence:

> This book was written in good faith, reader. It warns you from the outset that in it I have set no goal but a domestic and private one. I have had no thought of serving either you or my own glory. My powers are inadequate for such a purpose. I have dedicated it to the private convenience of my relatives and my friends, so that when they have lost me (as soon they must), they may recover here some features of my habits and temperament, and by this means keep the knowledge they have had of me more complete and alive.
>
> If I had written to seek the world's favour, I should have bedecked myself better, and should present myself in a studied posture. I want to be seen here in my simple, natural, ordinary fashion, without straining or artifice; for it is myself that I portray. My defects will here be read to the life, and also my natural form, as far as respect for the public has allowed. Had I been placed among those nations which are said to live still in the sweet freedom of nature's first laws, I assure you I should very gladly have portrayed myself here entire and wholly naked.

Thus, reader, I am myself the matter of my book; you would be unreasonable to spend your leisure on so frivolous and vain a subject.

So farewell. Montaigne, this first day of March, fifteen hundred and eighty.[3]

This may be disingenuous: Montaigne *did* enjoy the success of his essays, and he admits to possessing his fair share of vanity. But, nonetheless, when we turn to the essays themselves, we find that this note *is* consistent with the character of the work and with further explanations of his aims:

> Lately when I retired to my home, determined so far as possible to bother about nothing except spending the little life I have left in rest and seclusion, it seemed to me I could do my mind no greater favour than to let it entertain itself in full idleness and stay and settle in itself, which I hoped to do more easily now, having become weightier and riper with time. But I find ... that, on the contrary, like a runaway horse, it gives itself a hundred times more trouble than it took for others, and gives birth to so many chimeras and fantastic monsters, one after another, without order or purpose, that in order to contemplate their ineptitude and strangeness at my pleasure, I have begun to put them in writing, hoping in time to make my mind ashamed of itself.
>
> ('Of Idleness', 1572–74: 25)[4]

Montaigne was convinced that his essays were worth more to him, as an exercise and as a ladder, than they would be to his readers, as a finished work.

The essays seem to have begun as little more than a journal of quotations from classical authors – Plutarch, Seneca and Lucretius were among his favourites – with additional marginalia by Montaigne himself. But Montaigne came to realize that there was no end to the project and that an undertaking that had begun in idleness was actually greatly ambitious:

> It is only personal weakness that makes us content with what others or we ourselves have found out in this hunt for knowledge. An abler man would not rest content with it. There is always room for a successor, yes, and for ourselves, and a road in another direction. There is no end to our researches; our end is in the other world.
>
> ('Of Experience', 1587–88: 996)

Thus, not only was he continually writing on new subjects but he was continually making additions to his older essays, not in order to polish them but because he was aware that there was more to be said.

Yet for all his quotations he strove to attain wisdom and not simply learning. Against those who would rest content with learning he gave the following advice:

> We take the opinions and the knowledge of others into our keeping, and that is all. We must make them our own. We are just like a man, who, needing fire,

should go and fetch some at his neighbour's house, and, having found a fine big fire there, should stop there and warm himself, forgetting to carry any back home. What good does it do us to have our belly full of meat if it is not digested, if it is not transformed into us, if it does not make us bigger and stronger?

('Of Pedantry', 1572–78: 122)

Gaining confidence with age, and with the success of the first editions of his Essays, it is noticeable that in the later essays the frequency of the quotations begins to diminish.

Some of what Montaigne says about the composition of the *Essays* is, incidentally, of interest not only for what it reveals of Montaigne's habits as a writer and philosopher but also for their illumination of the origins of the essay as a genre – for the essay is Montaigne's invention. One might have surmised, from the work of present-day academics and journalists, that the essay was invented by a Renaissance Platonist whose intention was invariably to arrive back, older but wiser, at his original starting point. But this was not Montaigne's way. His aim was always to move on. If we learn from his example, then good – "What is useful to me may also by accident be useful to another" ('Of Practice', 1573–74: 331) – but his aim was not primarily to provide *us* with answers. "I have no authority to be believed, nor do I want it, feeling myself too ill-instructed to instruct others" ('Of the Education of Children', 1579–80: 132).

In the words of his secretary on his journey to Italy:

Monsieur de Montaigne strenuously avoided passing over the same road twice.

('Travel Journal', 1580: 1101)

The same can be said of his writing.

Admittedly, he keeps returning to the subject of himself, but that is because he is fascinated by his own changeability and inconsistencies. He is not morbidly introspective but he is aware that whatever the subject under discussion – 'Pedantry', 'Prayers', 'Idleness', 'Honorary Awards' – his writing is as much or more revelatory of himself than of the prima facie subject. "I study myself more than any other subject. That is my metaphysics, that is my physics" ('Of Experience', 1587–88: 1000).

Aside from himself, other recurrent themes include friendship, human frailty, the variety of custom, and death. Death was a major preoccupation. "I am by nature not melancholic, but dreamy. Since my earliest days, there is nothing with which I have occupied my mind more than with images of death" ('That to philosophise is to learn to die', 1572–74: 72). In this essay, Montaigne seeks consolation in the face of death not from Christianity but from "our mother Nature," to whom he gives the following speech:

> Imagine honestly how much less bearable and more painful to man would be an everlasting life than the life I have given him. If you did not have death, you would curse me incessantly for having deprived you of it. I have deliberately mixed with it a little bitterness to keep you, seeing the convenience of it, from embracing it too greedily and intemperately. To lodge you in that moderate state that I ask of you, of neither fleeing life nor fleeing back from death, I have tempered both of them between sweetness and bitterness.
>
> (Ibid.: 81)

Given Montaigne's preoccupation with death, and his view that "our end is in the other world" ('Of Experience', 1587–88: 996) it might be thought strange that the Essays say almost nothing about "the other world." In the words of his biographer, Philippe Desan: "Montaigne was not prepared to meddle in theology and was forced to approach religion as a custom. This expedient had at least the advantage of calming people's minds. He was born a Catholic and was determined to remain one, not by personal choice but by customary obligation and respect for traditions" (Desan 2017: 109).

In this area it is difficult to distinguish between those omissions that were politically expedient and those that are philosophically significant. However, in Montaigne's recollection of a riding accident in which he was knocked completely unconscious for over two hours the consolations of the Christian faith are again conspicuous by their absence. In the following passages he recounts the first moments of coming round:

> It seemed to me that my life was hanging only by the tip of my lips; I closed my eyes it seemed to me, to help push it out, and took pleasure in growing languid and letting myself go. It was an idea that was only floating on the surface of my soul, as delicate and feeble as all the rest, but in truth not only free from distress but mingled with that sweet feeling that people have who let themselves slide into sleep.
>
> ('Of Practice', 1573–74: 327)

> It would, in truth, have been a very happy death; for the weakness of my understanding kept me from having any judgment of it, and that of my body from having any feeling of it. I was letting myself slip away so gently, so gradually and easily, that I hardly ever did anything with less of a feeling of effort.
>
> (Ibid.: 330)

He tells us that recollection of this incident came to affect his philosophy in that it confirmed his previous suspicions:

> I believe that this is the same state in which people find themselves whom we see fainting with weakness in the agony of death; and I maintain that we pity

them without cause, supposing that they are agitated by grievous pains or have their soul oppressed by painful thought. This has always been my view ... I could not believe that with so great a paralysis of the limbs, and so great a failing of the senses, the soul could maintain any force within by which to be conscious of itself; and so I believed that they had no reflections to torment them, nothing able to make them judge and feel the misery of their condition, and that consequently they were not much to be pitied.

(Ibid.: 327–28)

It was almost as though Montaigne had now had a foretaste of a possible "other world," or of non-existence and the entry to it – and, behold, it was very good. "This recollection, which is strongly implanted on my soul, showing me the face and idea of death so true to nature, reconciles me to it somewhat" (ibid.: 327).

Within the body of the *Essays* it is generally agreed that a change of emphasis occurred in or about 1576, when Montaigne turned away from the stoicism that had characterized his early essays and instead turned towards scepticism, and that coinciding with this move his essays become lighter in tone. Admiration for scepticism is explicit in 'An Apology for Raymond Sebond' (1575–76, 1578–80) and it remains an influence thereafter. Without making drastic alterations to his earlier essays, he now abandoned the attempt to face death as a stoic:

If we have not known how to live, it is wrong to teach us how to die, and make the end inconsistent with the whole. If we have known how to live steadfastly and tranquilly, we shall know how to die in the same way .... it seems to me that death is indeed the end, but not therefore the goal of life; it is its finish, its extremity, but not therefore its object. Life should be an aim unto itself, a purpose unto itself ... Among the many other duties comprised in this general and principal chapter on knowing how to live is this article on knowing how to die; and it is one of the lightest, if our fear did not give it weight.

('Of Physiognomy', 1585–88: 980)

He came to realize that our ephemeral nature is a condition of our happiness. Security is boring, whereas: "Difficulty gives value to things ... To forbid us something is to make us want it" ('That our Desire is increased by Difficulty', 1575–76: 564–65) In other words, we want adventure – but not too much, or else, as is well known, 'it'll end in tears'.

So, without discovering any form of transcendence or reliable tranquillity, Montaigne, I believe, settled for some form of sceptical ambivalence. Despite his riding accident, he had to admit that he knew nothing, with any certainty, of "the other world." "As for me, I know neither what death is like nor what it is like in the other world. Perhaps death is something indifferent, perhaps desirable" ('Of Physiognomy', 1585–88: 981). Thus, unable to point to either the presence or the absence of life's larger context, he could not declare life to be meaningless. However, he could proclaim its absurdity. This he does resoundingly in his essay on vanity, which concludes with this pronouncement (made by a god at Delphi):

> There is not a single thing as empty and needy as you, who embrace the universe; you are the investigator without knowledge, the magistrate without jurisdiction, and all in all, the fool of the farce.
>
> ('Of Vanity', 1585–88: 932)

Life is absurd because, as was pointed out by Epicurus, and as was perhaps intimated to Montaigne by his riding accident, disappointment at nothingness is not a disappointment that we shall ever actually experience; and yet – since we are not wholly rational creatures – it is a disappointment that we still fear, now, in life.

As was noted by a later devotee of Montaigne, William Hazlitt, in comedy and tragedy, this absurdity, rooted in rationally unjustified optimism, permeates not only the philosopher's study but the entirety of our social lives.

> Man is the only animal that laughs and weeps; for he is the only animal that is struck with the difference between what things are, and what they ought to be. We weep at what thwarts or exceeds our desires in serious matters: we laugh at what only disappoints our expectations in trifles … To explain the nature of laughter and tears, is to account for the condition of human life; for it is in a manner compounded of these two!
>
> (Hazlitt 1819: 1)[5]

In both cases – comedy and tragedy – we are surprised by disappointment; and sometimes too we are surprised by joy. Rationally, we ought not to be, but we are – for, to reiterate, and as Montaigne knew full well, we are not wholly rational.

> If others examined themselves as attentively, as I do, they would find themselves, as I do, full of inanity and nonsense. Get rid of it I cannot without getting rid of myself. We are all steeped in it, one as much as another; but those who are aware of it are a little better off – though I don't know.
>
> ('Of Vanity', 1585–88: 931)

We can, like Montaigne, come to appreciate the absurdity of our existence, but in doing so – whether or not we are a little better off – we neither transcend nor reduce its absurdity. But, don't take my word for it …

Notes

1 All of the dates of composition in this essay have been taken from the table of contents of Montaigne's *Collected Works* edited by Donald Frame (Montaigne 1580–92). (While not providing an answer as succinct as Montaigne's, Russell may not have been quite as dumbfounded as the cabbie's story might lead us to imagine. In 1931 he received a letter from the philosopher Will Durant, a letter of a standard format, in which Durant asked many of the well-known public figures of the day "What is the meaning or worth of human life?" Russell replied "I am sorry to say that at the moment I am so busy as to be convinced that life has no meaning whatever, and that being so, I do not see how I can answer your questions intelligently./ I do not see that we can judge what would be the result of the discovery of truth, since none has hitherto been discovered" (Russell 1968: 205).)

2 See the introduction to Tartaglia's *Philosophy in a Meaningless Life* (Tartaglia 2016a).

3 The first edition of Montaigne's *Essays* was published in 1580. The first 'complete' edition was published posthumously in 1595.

4 Montaigne retired to his family estates in Bordeaux in 1571 at the age of 38. However, he later returned to public life, travelling to Italy in 1580 in search of a cure for his kidney stones – but also for political reasons; and becoming mayor of Bordeaux in 1581. Montaigne was a skilled negotiator, trusted by both Catholics and Protestants, in the wars of religion that ravaged France during his later life.

5 "Death mingles and fuses with our life throughout" ('Of Experience', 1587–88: 1031).

17 Descartes and the meaning of life

JOHN COTTINGHAM

A modern problem?

None of Descartes's writings contain a French or Latin phrase that could be rendered in English as 'the meaning of life', so it might at first seem that the topic of the meaning of life is simply absent from his philosophical thinking. One might go further and suggest that the very question of whether human life has a meaning is one that belongs to a much later phase of philosophical inquiry. Think, for example, of Martin Heidegger's description of human beings as 'thrown' into existence, or of Jean-Paul Sartre's 'nausea', his horror at realizing that we humans are simply here, facing the brute contingency or facticity of things.[1] This kind of disorientation, arising from a sense that human life has no ultimate meaning, may seem a particularly modern phenomenon, originating perhaps with the declaration of Nietzsche's madman in *Zarathustra*, that by killing God we have 'unchained the sun from its moorings' and lost any sense of purpose and direction in our lives (Nietzsche 1883–85: §125). Such existentialist anguish may seem worlds away from the 'age of reason' to which Descartes is often said to belong,[2] or from his project for establishing indubitable metaphysical foundations for his scientific system.

In philosophy, however, there is seldom anything new under the sun, and though the external circumstances of human life have changed beyond recognition since the seventeenth century, the fundamental problems of the human predicament are the same as they have always been. The very phrase 'there is nothing new under the sun' comes of course from the Bible, from the book of Ecclesiastes (1.9), dating from several centuries before Christ, and together with the famous phrase 'vanity of vanities, all is vanity' (1.2), it is a timeless expression of the anguish that can arise from the seeming pointlessness and absurdity of human life. The question of the ultimate significance, if any, of human existence, is as old as the human impulse to philosophize, and although it may not be explicitly addressed in Descartes's works, its implicit importance for his outlook is manifest at many points in the way his philosophical system is developed and structured.

Descartes was certainly no stranger to doubt and disorientation, growing up at a time when many of the old certainties were being eroded. Galileo's discovery of the phases of Venus and the moons of Jupiter in 1609, when Descartes was a schoolboy at the Jesuit College of La Flèche, constituted the first hard observational evidence undermining the foundations of the old earth-centred system which had held sway for so many centuries, and it must have made the young Descartes acutely aware of how even the most entrenched beliefs could turn out to be shaky. Many years later, in *Meditations on First Philosophy* (1641), he vividly describes the sensation of having 'fallen unexpectedly into a deep whirlpool' which so tumbles him around that he can 'neither stand on the bottom nor swim up to the top.'[3] It could be suggested that this is merely a rhetorical flourish, and that the meditator's quandary is in any case a purely theoretical one, regarding the epistemic status of previously accepted beliefs. But we should perhaps beware of retrojecting onto Descartes too much of the comfortable, detached stance of today's professional academic philosopher. It is of course true that the *Meditations* start with an epistemic problem, the search for 'stable foundations' in the sciences.[4] But in the course of the subsequent waves of systematic doubt that characterize that search, Descartes conjures up extreme and 'hyperbolical' scenarios of 'demons, dreamers and madmen',[5] questioning even his own ability to reason coherently from moment to moment, and ending the First Meditation with the nightmare scenario of being cut off from the light and having to struggle amid 'inextricable darkness'.[6] The way Descartes charts the route out of this darkness takes us to the heart of his theistic outlook, which has manifold implications for our status as human beings and the meaning of our existence.

From doubt to God

In a famous summary of his escape from universal doubt, Descartes says: 'Observing that this truth, "I am thinking, therefore I exist" was so firm and sure that the most extravagant suppositions of the sceptics were incapable of shaking it, I decided that I could accept it without scruple as the first principle of the philosophy I was seeking.'[7] Elsewhere, he describes 'I am, I exist' as the Archimedean point on which he will base his philosophy.[8] One view of Descartes's ambitions here sees him, in effect, as a precursor of modernity, the independent, autonomous inquirer who proposes to establish a comprehensive philosophical system entirely from his own resources. On this view, Descartes's approach contains the seeds of a modern secular perspective according to which humanity cannot rely on external or transcendent powers to help him in the quest for truth and meaning, but has to undertake the task essentially on his own, employing the tools of autonomous reason.

But a closer scrutiny of Descartes's more detailed arguments in the *Meditations* reveals that underpinning the meditator's seemingly solitary search for truth is an independent reality on which he is totally dependent. Even the certainty of his own existence is a flickering candle which could go out at any moment. 'I am, I exist, that is certain, but for how long? For as long as I am thinking. For it could be that were I totally to cease from thinking, I should totally cease to exist.'[9] Descartes goes on to use the fragility of his thinking as a decisive indicator of his complete dependence on a power greater than himself. Indeed, even the process of doubt could not get under way unless there were an objective structure of meaning that is not dependent on his own mind, but calls forth his spontaneous assent. The 'natural light' of reason that informs the Cartesian quest from first to last turns out to depend, like everything else, on an infinite and perfect creator, the source of all truth and goodness. In support of this Descartes deploys a number of complicated arguments for God's existence, but there is considerable force in the interpretation of Emmanuel Levinas (1982: 91ff.) according to which what is described in the Third Meditation is not so much an inference as an *encounter*, the encounter of the finite mind with the infinite – that which the mind recognizes by awareness of its own incompleteness and finitude, but which it is unable properly to grasp or encompass. As Hilary Putnam puts it:

> What Descartes is reporting is not a step in a deductive reasoning, but a profound religious experience, an experience which might be described as the experience of a *fissure*, of a confrontation with something that disrupted all his categories. On this reading, Descartes is not so much proving something as *acknowledging* something, acknowledging a Reality that he could not have constructed, a Reality which proves its own existence by the very fact that its presence in my mind turns out to be a phenomenological impossibility.
>
> (Putnam 1986: 42)

Once the finite human mind has discerned its dependence on this infinite creative power, it can only submit to it in wonder and adoration. 'Here let me pause a while', says the meditator at the end of the Third Meditation, and 'gaze with wonder and adoration on the beauty of this immense light, so far as the eye of my darkened intellect can bear it.'[10]

The theistic vision that is central to Descartes's metaphysics has important implications for the significance of human life. The initial impression from the passage just referred to from the close of the Third Meditation is that Descartes is content simply to affirm the traditional Catholic doctrine of the 'beatific vision' found for example in Thomas Aquinas (*c.* 1259–60: III, §1, ch. 37–48) – the idea of the contemplation of God in the next world as the ultimate goal and purpose of our existence. As Descartes puts it:

> Just as we believe through faith that the supreme happiness of the next life consists solely in the contemplation of the divine majesty, so experience tells us that this same contemplation, albeit much less perfect, enables us to know the greatest joy of which we are capable in this life.[11]

This seems to take Descartes in a very 'Platonic' direction as far as the meaning of life is concerned. He might appear to be agreeing with the Socratic dictum that all life is a preparation for dying,[12] and hence that our embodied nature, as creatures of flesh and blood, is pretty much irrelevant to the true meaning of our existence, which is to contemplate the divine in the next world (with imperfect anticipatory glimpses in this world). If this were the whole story, there would perhaps be considerable justice in Gilbert Ryle's famous denunciation of Descartes as promoting the myth of the 'ghost in the machine' – an incorporeal spirit lodged in a mechanical body (Ryle 1949: ch. 1). And one might conclude that the only human properties relevant to our existence having any meaning must be 'spiritual' properties – the properties of the immaterial soul that will live on after death. But although these Platonic elements in Descartes's thinking cannot be denied, they are very far from exhausting what Descartes has to say about the human condition and what gives meaning to our lives.

Human nature in Descartes

The first indication that the true meaning of our existence cannot depend wholly and entirely on the immaterial soul appears in the Sixth Meditation, where Descartes expends enormous effort in showing the value and importance of human sensory experience for human health and well-being. Descartes describes a system of mind–body correlations, where a given physiological state gives rise to a specific brain state which in turn is correlated with a specific sensation (e.g. of hunger, thirst, pleasure, pain). He continues:

> The best system that could be devised is that [a given brain state] should produce the one sensation which, of all possible sensations, is most especially and most frequently conducive to the preservation of the healthy man. And experience shows that the sensations which nature has given us are all of this kind; and so there is absolutely nothing to be found in them that does not bear witness to the power and goodness of God.[13]

Here Descartes is clearly speaking in a different register from that found in his official dualistic immaterialism. On the immaterialist picture, 'this I' (*ce moi*), the individual subject of consciousness, is identified with 'the soul, by which I am what I am'; and it is declared to be 'entirely independent of the body and capable of existing without it'.[14] In the Sixth Meditation, by contrast, Descartes's attention is directed not to the incorporeal ego, but to the real human being – what he elsewhere calls *le vrai homme*,[15] that is to say, a creature of flesh and blood, the subject of the whole spectrum of sensory and emotional experience that is the signature of our embodied existence. And the benevolence of God is displayed not merely in the good of contemplation held out as the ultimate destination for the soul, but in the psychophysical laws that govern our human nature and enable us to flourish.

So what, for Descartes, is the meaning and purpose of our embodied existence as human beings? To answer this question we need to move from Descartes's metaphysics and epistemology to his ethics, the branch of philosophy which he hoped would emerge as the crowning achievement of his system:

> By 'morals' I understand the highest and most perfect moral system, which presupposes a complete knowledge of the other sciences and is the ultimate level of wisdom. Now just as it is not the roots or the trunk of a tree from which one gathers the fruit, but only the ends of the branches, so the principal benefit of philosophy depends on those parts of it which can only be learned last of all.[16]

Nowadays we tend to think of a moral system as having to do with rules and principles of conduct, but Descartes, following the older Aristotelian model, thinks of it in terms of the development of virtues of character that will enable us to flourish and achieve happiness. His specific concern is with the emotions and passions, which he regarded as the key to human happiness, and which form the subject of his last published work, *The Passions of the Soul* (1649). And again, despite the immaterialist connotations which the word 'soul' in the title might have for the modern reader, the main focus is on our specifically *human* nature. For the human being, *le vrai homme*, is for Descartes a kind of 'compound' creature – what he elsewhere calls the 'substantial union'[17] of soul and body. And it is this union that is the key to our living richly rewarding lives:

> The soul can have pleasures of its own. But the pleasures *common to it and the body* depend entirely on the passions, so that those human beings whom the passions can move most to the highest degree are capable of tasting the greatest sweetness of this life.[18]

Many earlier systems of ethics, most notably ancient Stoicism, were very wary of the passions, as being potentially subversive of our peace and fulfilment. The guiding idea was that the life of rationality and virtue would be free of passion. But Descartes explicitly distances himself from this kind of stance. 'The philosophy I cultivate', he wrote to a correspondent, 'is not so grim or savage as to reject the employment of the passions; on the contrary, it is here that I believe all the sweetness and joy of this life is to be found'.[19] He nevertheless acknowledges that the passions do often lead us astray, by making some goods seem more significant and important than they really are, with the result that we end up feeling 'dissatisfaction, regret, and remorse'.[20] So for a human life to be a flourishing and worthwhile one, though it should not be passion-free, it nevertheless needs to find a way to bring the passions into line with our rational perception of the good.

Descartes's resulting theory of the good life, one in which the passions have a worthwhile place, draws partly on the old Aristotelian idea of training and habituation as the key to a virtuous existence, but this is now informed by a new and ambitious conception of what falls within the scope of such training. Descartes saw philosophy as a unified system, where ethics and science were integrated into a single organic system of knowledge, and he developed a striking vision of how the results of physiological science could be harnessed to the service of ethics. He wrote to a correspondent in 1646 that his results in physics had been 'a great help in establishing sure foundations in moral philosophy';[21] and when he published his treatise on the *Passions* in 1649 he explained that his goal was to give an account of the passions *en physicien* – from the point of view of a physical scientist.[22] Descartes envisaged a systematic programme for the re-training of our psychophysical responses. He laid great stress on how even animals that lack reason can have their responses modified by training – so that for example a gun dog, naturally disposed to bolt at the sound of gunfire, can be trained to freeze.[23] If we can re-program the working of the passions in animals, how much more should we be able to do it in our own human case?

Descartes's ambitions here connect with the general aspiration he expressed in the *Discourse on the Method*, namely that the new mathematical and mechanical science he hoped to found would enable human beings to become 'masters and possessors of nature'.[24] But 'nature' here would not just be the physical environment we inhabit, but our own human nature as well. Scientific mastery would extend to manipulation and control not only of the world around us, but also to the mechanisms of our own bodies, whose material structure and laws of operation are for Descartes in principle no different from the mechanisms and structures found anywhere else in the universe. Science, for Descartes, thus opens the door to a practical recipe for virtue, since it is now in our power to re-program ourselves, armed with scientific knowledge of how our psychophysical responses operate. 'Even those whose souls are most feeble' observes Descartes in the *Passions*, 'would be able to gain an absolute mastery over all the passions, if enough effort were devoted to training and guiding them.'[25] The 'training' proposed is aimed at nothing less than adjusting the pattern of brain movements (*les mouvements du cerveau*) and their associated feelings – a systematic reprogramming of our inherited and acquired psycho-cerebral responses.

The route to meaning: control or submission?

From this necessarily very brief sketch of Descartes's scientific goals and their application to psychophysiology and ethics, some fascinating questions arise about his underlying picture of the meaning of human existence. One may wonder in particular about how his scientific ambitions relate to the theistic vision that (as we saw earlier) informs the metaphysical journey described in the *Meditations*. Answering these interpretative questions is not easy, partly because Descartes is such a liminal figure, standing at the threshold of the modern age, yet also with much of his thought rooted in the worldview of his medieval and classical predecessors. Thinking of Descartes as the herald of modernity, one of the chief inaugurators of mechanistic explanations in science and of the modern quantitative approach to physics, invites us to see him as an essentially independent thinker, keen to break free from the authority of past tradition. On this interpretation, which seems to be supported by some of the ways in which Descartes talks about his grand scientific ambitions, Descartes in a certain way anticipates the modern idea that, armed with tools of science, we can take charge of our own destiny. In terms of how we should live, this approach points forward to the thinking of Friedrich Nietzsche and those who followed him, according to which humans beings, or at least those who are strong enough, need to reach forward in a courageous act of will and generate meaning and value in their lives from their own resources (Nietzsche 1882: §335).

Such ideas are, however, ultimately alien to Descartes's way of thinking. The notion of 'self-creation', or the idea that our own free and autonomous choices could in themselves make our lives meaningful, is radically at odds with Descartes's conception of human freedom. The clearest description of this conception is to be found in the Fourth Meditation:

> In order to be free, there is no need for me to be capable of going in each of two directions; on the contrary, the more I incline in one direction – either because I clearly understand that reasons of truth and goodness point that way, or because of a divinely produced disposition of my inmost thought – the freer is my choice.[26]

The summit of human freedom, for Descartes, is not some detached power of 'plumping' for one course of action rather than another, but rather the spontaneous assent to what is revealed by 'reasons of truth and goodness' – what Descartes elsewhere calls the 'natural light', implanted in each mind by God. As Descartes frequently says in other places, when I clearly and distinctly perceive some simple proposition, such as 'two plus three equals five', so long as I attend to it, I cannot but spontaneously assent to its truth.[27] And the same goes for my perceptions of goodness – once I clearly and distinctly perceive some object as good, I cannot but judge it to be worthy to be pursued or chosen. Always presupposed, for Descartes, is an objective framework of truth, meaning and value which is ultimately laid down by God.

The upshot of all this is that the role of the will, for Descartes, is not to *decide*, as it were, what is good, or to be pursued, but rather to freely assent to the deliverances of the natural light. Having arbitrarily to turn in one direction or another when the truth is not clear is, says Descartes, the 'lowest grade of freedom'; the more desirable state for a human being is to be so enlightened by reasons of truth or goodness that only one course of action is possible.[28] This in turn takes us back to the theistic vision of the Third Meditation, where the meditator gazes in wonder and contemplates the 'beauty of this immense light.' To the Cartesian way of thinking, meaning and value flow from a source other than oneself, a source that floods the mind with such clarity that joyful and spontaneous acquiescence is the only possible option.[29] One might call this a 'submissive' conception of human freedom, but it is not 'submission' in the sense of being reluctantly coerced or constrained; rather, it is a spontaneous outflowing of the will in assenting towards what my (innately bestowed) reason perceives as good or true. But it can nonetheless be thought of as 'submissive' in the sense that what is assented to is something *independent of myself*, something whose truth or value commands my assent 'whether I like it or not' – as Descartes says of the properties of a triangle, which I must acknowledge willy-nilly, once I perceive them clearly.[30]

So how does this conception of 'freedom of enlightenment' (of human freedom as spontaneous assent to what is rationally perceived as true or good independently of me) connect up with Descartes's scientific and technological ambition that humans should become 'masters and possessors of nature', able to control the environment and even our own bodily patterns of response? The answer, it seems to me, is that Descartes's blueprint for controlling and managing the passions would be rudderless, it would have nothing to guide or direct it, unless it was informed by a vision in which human life has a meaningful place in the scheme of things ordained by a benevolent creator. The resources of science can be used to help humans in the pursuit of the good and the meaningful, only because there is, in the first place, objective goodness and meaningfulness that is independently worthy of pursuit. So Descartes would never have subscribed to the modern idea that what makes for a meaningful life is 'up for grabs', as it were; he would never have been tempted by contemporary 'expressivist' or purely instrumentalist conceptions of ethics, that cut ethics free from any substantive vision of the good, and simply aim to maximize the 'preferences' of individual agents or groups of agents.[31]

Descartes, in describing the blueprint for his new mathematical science, once observed that the search for final causes (or purposes) is 'utterly useless in physics'.[32] Certainly he saw scientific explanation as working through quantitative laws (such as the laws of motion), and warned against invoking the supposed purposes of the creator, which were 'hidden in the inscrutable abyss of his wisdom'.[33] But this does not entail that Descartes construed the cosmos as a meaningless concatenation of blind particle interactions. Physics may have no room for teleology, according to Descartes, but the cosmos is still a divine creation, whose laws of operation, he insists, bear the stamp of the divine intelligence that laid them down.[34] And in any case, while he thought that teleology is best left out of physics, there is ample evidence from the texts we have been looking at that Descartes regarded it as fully operative in the realm of human life. For though our bodies, like everything else in the quantitative universe, operate in accordance with the laws of corpuscular interaction, Descartes believes that human beings, through the gift of reason, can still orient their lives towards an objective source of meaning and value, and thus achieve fulfilling and meaningful lives. Whether, and if so how, the human longing for meaning can be fully satisfied in today's very un-Cartesian worldview, where God is typically taken out of the equation, is a question that contemporary philosophy has still not finally settled.

Notes

1 For 'thrownness' (*Geworfenheit*), see Heidegger 1927: §135; for 'nausea', see Sartre 1938.
2 For the use of this term to characterize the era of the seventeenth-century 'rationalists', see (Hampshire 1956).
3 AT VII 24, CSM II 16. In this chapter, 'AT' refers to the standard Franco-Latin edition of Descartes; 'CSM' refers to the English translation, and 'CSMK' to the English translation of the correspondence.
4 See the opening paragraph of the First Meditation.
5 The phrase is from Frankfurt 1970. For 'hyperbolical' doubt, see Descartes, Sixth Meditation, AT VII 89, CSM II 61.
6 AT VII 23, CSM II 15.
7 Descartes, *Discourse on the Method* [*Discours de la method*], 1637, Part Four, AT VI 32, CSM I 127.
8 See opening paragraph of the Second Meditation.
9 Second Meditation, AT VII 27, CSM II 18.
10 AT VII 52, CSM II 36.
11 AT VII 52, CSM II 36.
12 Plato, *Phaedo* (*c.* 380 BCE), 64a3–4.
13 AT VII 87, CSM II 60.
14 *Discourse on the Method*, Part Four, AT VI 33, CSM I 127.
15 *Discourse on the Method*, Part Five, AT VI 59, CSM I 141. See further Cottingham 2006: ch. 1, §3(d).
16 Preface to the 1647 French translation of the *Principles of Philosophy*, AT IX 14–15, CSM I 186.
17 See Descartes's letter to Elizabeth of 28 June 1643, AT III 691–92: CSMK 227, and letter to Mesland of 9 February 1645, AT IV 166: CSMK 243.
18 Descartes, *Passions of the Soul* [*Les passions de l'âme*], art. 212, AT XI 488, CSM I 404. emphasis supplied.
19 Letter to Silhon of March or April 1648, AT V 135, CSMK 330.
20 Letter to Princess Elizabeth of Bohemia of 1 September 1645, AT IV 284–85, CSMK 264.
21 Letter to Chanut of 15 June 1646, AT IV 441, CSMK 289.
22 AT XI 326, CSM I 327.
23 *Passions of the Soul*, art. 50, AT XI 369–70, CSM I 348.
24 *Discourse*, Part Six, AT VI 62, CSM I 142.
25 *Passions of the Soul*, art. 50, AT XI 370, CSM I 348.
26 Fourth Meditation, AT VII 57–58, CSM II 40.
27 Compare Third Meditation, AT VII 36, CSM II 25.
28 Fourth Meditation, AT VII 58, CSM II 40.
29 See Cottingham 2010.
30 Compare Fifth Meditation, AT VII 64, CSM II 45.
31 For 'expressivism', see MacIntyre 2016.
32 Fourth Meditation, AT VII 55, CSM II 39.
33 Fifth Replies, AT VII 375, CSM II 258.
34 *Principles of Philosophy* [*Principia philosophiae*] 1644, Part Two, art. 36, AT VIII 61–62, CSM 240.

18 Spinoza and the meaning of life

GENEVIEVE LLOYD

Bringing past philosophers into debates on contemporary issues has to be an exercise of imagination, though one informed by historically based textual analysis. It involves reflecting on what may be problematic in the kinds of questions we now ask, as well as trying to return in imagination to the past. The question of the meaning of life is, in its own right, perplexing – even before we enter into the complexities of bringing the past to bear on the present. In relation to our individual lives, we seem more able to make sense of lack or loss of meaning – as in debilitating states of grief or depression – than of its presence.

Concern with *the* meaning of life-in-general is commonly talked of in ironic tones. It is often treated as epitomizing silliness in philosophical enquiry – or even the silliness of philosophical enquiry itself. Yet it does seem of late to be attracting the serious interest of philosophers. There were already large and reputable volumes on the issue, before we representatives of the Great Philosophers entered the debate. It may nonetheless seem particularly strange to expect an answer derived from Spinoza. He does not explicitly discuss the question; and much of what he does say can seem to be at odds with even posing it. Yet he also offers some insights which seem to take him into that territory. At the very least, we can draw from Spinoza insights that may help illuminate what is at stake in the question.

Notoriously, Spinoza's world is a world without purpose – whether beyond or within it. He does not regard our lives – either individually or collectively – as sustained by any beneficent divine concern for the future of humanity. Yet his vision is not bleak. Spinozist lives are not inherently forlorn or lonely struggles. In his philosophy, there is nothing transcending the natural world that might provide life with an external meaning. Yet that lack seems in no way to detract from his articulation of ideals of the good human life. He repudiates free will, with its connotations of purpose. Yet he offers in compensation an enriched concept of desire as shaping human lives; and joy is integral to his central concept of *conatus* – the striving to persist in being.

On behalf of Spinoza, then, the first question I wish to pose is: what is required for something to count as an answer to our contemporary question of the meaning of life? On the face of it, an answer must offer something over and above an account of what it is to live well. Philosophers can offer advice about how best to live without invoking *meaning*. Moreover, it seems possible to reject the whole idea of the meaning *of* life, while offering prescriptions of how to live *meaningfully*. Think, for example, of a broadly existentialist approach – summed up in the dictum that the only meaning of life is what we ourselves provide through our autonomous projects and exploits. We see here some of the fault lines along which current discussion of the meaning of life divides: we can try to find meaning *in* our lives, without being committed to the claim that life itself *has* meaning at all.

What does Spinoza have to offer here? His philosophy does seem to provide answers to old philosophical questions about the nature of the good human life. It can also readily be construed as offering instructive examples of meaningful living – though of a kind very different from those that centre on the proper use of a supposed faculty of free will. Yet it is not clear that any of that really amounts to an answer to our question.

Speaking now in the role of adjudicator of the imagined debate, I wish to offer my own understanding of the prerequisites for something to count here as a genuine answer. It must, I suggest, offer some general truth about human existence, the acceptance of which can be taken as motivating – or at any rate *shaping* – the way we live, and as providing some basis of hope for the future. At their clearest, such answers point us towards a supernatural framing of human life; but there are also answers which do not postulate anything supernatural.

Answers which are framed by belief in the supernatural clearly point to something beyond human life that can coherently – even if unjustifiably – be regarded as providing it with meaning. It might be a set of divine commands, with the promise of reward or punishment in an afterlife. The answer might come instead through a narrative of progress towards a collective earthly goal. Ideas of the perfectibility of the human species, as well as talk of immortality, can subsume present realities into an idealized future. However, appeal to what is itself finite and limited is more likely to elicit scepticism about the power to bestow meaning.

The core of the challenge here has been articulated by Robert Nozick, at the conclusion of chapter VI of his book *Philosophical Explanations:* it arises from the sense of encountering limits. In seeking the meaning of life, we look for something wider, which supposedly gives meaning to what we started from. Yet whatever we then reach also has its own limits. So the original 'problem' surfaces again. Nozick observes that this suggests that the problem can be avoided or transcended only by something we cannot be outside, even in imagination – that the questioning is stopped only where there is nowhere else to stand (Nozick 1981b).

Nozick's comments help explain why it is that the most clear-cut versions of supposed answers to the question of the meaning of life are those which take a leap into a transcendent realm – to an afterlife of divine judgement, or at any rate to a postulated divine understanding of a purpose or rationale not grasped by human thought. Here, in what is traditionally construed as 'unlimited' being, the search for meaning stops; and where the search stops it becomes possible to talk of *finding* the meaning of life – as indeed theists often do.

Does Spinoza offer anything that might fit that general pattern – an external truth about human lives, capable of shaping the perception of their present reality and providing hope for the future? And, if he does offer such a truth, is it one which avoids the challenge raised by Nozick?

Stepping back into the role of Spinoza's spokesperson, let me now briefly reprise some relevant features of his version of the good human life. It does seem to be grounded in what he presents as metaphysical truths about the nature of human existence. For Spinoza, the good life centres on under-standing ourselves as integral parts of the totality of being. As bodies, we are dynamically embedded in the interconnected whole which is the material world. As minds, we are *ideas* of those bodies – finite modes within the corre-sponding totality of thought. Mind and matter in this system are the same reality, though 'expressed' under different 'attributes' of a perfect – though not transcendent – being, which he identifies as 'God-or-Substance'.

The *Ethics* (Spinoza 1677) offers descriptions of expansive lives of joy and hope, along with alternative descriptions of shrunken lives of despondency, bitterness or despair. Those descriptions reflect Spinoza's understanding of the nature of human existence. For him, ideally, an individual mind comes to apprehend itself – with ever increasing adequacy – as part of an interconnected totality, on which its existence depends. The clarity – and the affective intensity – of that understanding will wax and wane throughout our lives. As finite modes within a totality, we are vulnerable to antagonistic forces; but we are also capable of drawing strength from congenial ones. Ultimately we will cease to exist; yet during life we can come to an understanding of the inter-connections on which our being depends. The effort to attain and sustain that understanding is for Spinoza the key to the good life.

In the concluding sections of the *Ethics*, Spinoza claims that such a life, in its highest form, involves a mind coming to understand itself as an eternal idea in 'the mind of God'. The consensus of commentary on those luminous but elusive passages is that such lofty heights do not amount to individual immortality. Spinoza's 'eternity of the mind' is not located in a paradisal hereafter, to be attained through virtuous living. This raises for us the inter-esting possibility that Spinoza's version of the mind's 'eternity' might offer a secular analogue of belief in an afterlife. Might it then offer a truth about human existence, the understanding of which might provide meaning and sustain hope? And does it do so in a way that avoids Nozick's formulation of what is problematic about the whole idea of finding such meaning?

Formally, it seems promising to cast Spinoza as having an answer to our question. In grasping itself as a finite mode within the totality of thought, a mind does not locate the source of its meaning in another finite thing, concerning which the same search for meaning might arise. It is in understanding its inclusion in the whole of Nature – rather than in shifting its attention to a transcendent realm – that a Spinozist mind is supposed to find the meaning of its existence. But what exactly is the content of this self-understanding?

Many frustrated commentators – perhaps most vehemently, Jonathan Bennett – have dismissed those concluding sections of the *Ethics* as impenetrable (Bennett 1984: 357–72). As an attempt to give content to the meaning of life, Spinoza's doctrine of the mind's eternity may well seem to have the distinct disadvantage of being comprehensible – if at all – only to the most dedicated of Spinoza scholars. A 'meaning' that can neither be understood while we live nor projected into a hereafter, in which all might become clear, may seem unlikely to prove of much use as a source of general hope for the future.

Spinoza's account of the eternity of the mind is meant to be the upshot of the complex argumentative structure of the *Ethics* in its entirety – the ultimate consequence of his treatment of minds as finite modes of *Substance-expressed-as-Thought.* Stripped of its intricate underlying metaphysics, his injunction – that we should think of ourselves as parts of a whole – may seem an empty response to the challenge of articulating the meaning of life. There is nonetheless a crucial insight here, which bears directly on understanding our contemporary concern with the question.

Spinoza himself saw the truth that we are parts of a totality as more than a commonplace – even apart from its ultimate realization in the eternity of the mind. For him apprehension of that truth grounded an attitude towards human life which is capable of bringing some measure of acquiescence or tranquillity in troubled times. This insight into the human condition echoed some aspects of ancient Stoicism, but without the bleak sense of emotional disengagement that has become a common understanding of the Stoic legacy.

Outside his philosophical works, Spinoza expressed the point more informally, in a letter of 1665 to his friend Henry Oldenberg. Writing from England, Oldenberg had lamented the brutality of the current war between Dutch and English forces – a war he described as almost banishing all civilized behaviour from the world. In reply, Spinoza commented (referring perhaps to Democritus) that if some famous ancient scoffer could see their present condition, he would surely die of laughter. He insists, however, that the current turmoils move him neither to laughter nor to tears, but rather to philosophizing and to better observation of human nature, which should be neither mocked nor lamented. For human beings, he says, are only a part of nature, and he does not know either how each part agrees with the whole or how it coheres with other parts.

Part of the point of Spinoza's talk here of an acquiescence deeper than tears or laughter is something that can now sound familiar to the point of triteness: faced with troubles, we must learn to take a broader perspective, rather than being obsessed with our own little part of the world. However, there is also something more profound and unfamiliar in Spinoza's insights, throughout the *Ethics,* into the ways in which a thinking mind is itself immersed in the totality of being. For him a mind depends for its very existence on thus being a part of the whole. When we think, we do so *as* parts of a whole. That means in turn that a mind's well-being – its joy in persisting in being – resides in its persistent effort to understand its interconnections with other things. For Spinoza the good life resides in the mind's ongoing apprehension of those conditions of human life – the interconnections and interactions which make possible its own continued existence.

It is difficult for contemporary readers of Spinoza to engage with this talk of minds as themselves parts of a wider whole. We think more readily of our minds as located somehow outside totalities – as having an external perspective from which we can consider the rest of the world. However, in trying to imagine ourselves into Spinoza's view of minds-in-the-world, we can get some insight into what sense it might make to talk of the *meaning* of life.

In his treatment of the thinking mind as itself part of a whole, Spinoza offers a form of self-transcendence – of a kind that cannot itself be transcended – while yet staying firmly within the natural world. His version of God-as-Substance is the totality of being, of which we experience ourselves as part. We are not 'ideas' in Spinoza's 'mind of God' as pawns in another being's game – however beneficent that game might be. As minds, our very existence resides in inadequate understanding of the totality in which we are immersed.

Within that Spinozist frame, we can talk of finding the meaning of life by reaching beyond ourselves. However, the only form this can take is through better understanding ourselves as interdependent parts of a whole. We will not find the meaning of life in something else just as finite as us. But nor will we find it by reaching to something supposedly beyond Nature; or by treating Nature itself as some kind of separate higher being – a surrogate for a transcendent God. We will find it – or at any rate stop looking for it – only by reaching a fuller understanding of ourselves as interconnected living things, sustained by complex environmental conditions, reaching out to the whole of Nature.

Does this amount to an insight into the *meaning* of our lives? Yes, if that means an understanding of what it is to be alive – as an individual thinking human being. Grasping Spinoza's insight here depends on taking seriously his emphasis on the fact that a human mind exists *only* as part of an interconnected totality. The consequences of that view are often underestimated in interpretations of Spinoza's 'rationalism'. At one level, his philosophy does indeed insist on a complete correspondence between two rationally ordered structures: 'the order of thought' and 'the order of things'. Yet he insists also that an individual mind is itself a confused confluence of imagination and emotion, struggling for what clarity it can attain through the exercise of reason within the totality of things.

For all his apparent confidence in the power and adequacy of reason – which makes him rightly regarded as a 'rationalist' – there is a darker side to Spinoza's treatment of minds as part of the whole of Nature, which can have strong resonances in our own times. In chapter 16 of the *Theological-Political-Treatise* (Spinoza 1670), he observes that human reason is itself only a small part in the whole of Nature. The whole, he insists, is not constrained by the laws of that tiny part within it. Our minds may be sustained by the thought of ourselves as parts of a whole; but the other side of that thought is an intimation of our own cosmic insignificance.

Where has our consideration of Spinoza brought us? Has he offered an answer to the question of the meaning of life? Or should his contribution be seen rather as an exposure of what is problematic in the question itself, which might persuade us to stop asking it? It has elements of both approaches. For a Spinozist way of undercutting the question does not amount to a denial of the desire for meaning which prompts its being asked in the first place. To cease to seek is not necessarily to have found. Yet nor is it necessarily to be disappointed at having searched in vain.

Spinoza's talk of necessarily interconnected totalities – with its connotations of monist metaphysics and rationalist epistemology – is alien to much of contemporary philosophical thinking. Yet his emphasis on the interconnection of things resonates more broadly in contemporary preoccupations with the challenges of climate change. 'The meaning of life' takes on new dimensions when we confront the possibility that the earth might cease to sustain the fragile conditions under which life itself is possible. Perhaps it is here that Spinoza's glimpse of the convergence of the human and the cosmic might have most to offer.

Reading Spinoza now can strike off resonances, which he could not himself have envisaged, with contemporary appreciation of the ways in which human life is integrated into complex, fragile ecosystems. Much of that thinking is at odds with older ideas of humanity as the paramount species – as life's highest achievement, the apex of the natural order which shapes 'its' world from a position of supremacy within it. We now read Spinoza post Darwin; and in the light of more recent developments in evolutionary biology. We read him also with an increased understanding of just how 'deep' time is.

Spinoza contemplated a universe without purpose, whether benign or malevolent. However, he could not have envisaged that life itself would ultimately disappear. He could not have known that inevitable changes, long in the future, would ultimately make life on earth's surfaces, or in its oceans, impossible; or that those life-sustaining oceans themselves would eventually disappear. He did not know that life had emerged in a deep past in which chance and catastrophe mingled with unimaginably slow adaptation. Nor did he understand the extinction of species, which made possible the gradual emergence of thinking beings, capable of comprehending themselves as part of a world.

Some of the current resurgence of philosophical interest in issues of the meaning of life reflects concern with the significance – the upshot – of there being life at all. Thus construed, the question of life's 'meaning' may have no real answer. Yet the felt need to raise it can express a new realization of the fragility and vulnerability of the conditions of life. We are able now to comprehend that the conditions under which life can flourish will come to an end under the force of planetary change. We are also able to grasp the hitherto unthinkable possibility that, in a frighteningly more imminent future, those fragile conditions are under threat from the advance of human capabilities themselves.

Perhaps the need now to ask again old questions about its *meaning* can be a way of expressing a salutary apprehension of the fragility of life – and of humanity's ultimate insignificance within the universe, or perhaps even within a multiplicity of universes. Spinoza's tantalizing themes of interconnection might lead us to deeper reflection on the ways in which human thought itself is just a speck within an immense totality. Such reflection in turn might help us to shake the grip of more triumphalist ways of thinking of human reason, which are complicit in life itself coming under threat – before its time.

19 Kant and the meaning of life

TERRY F. GODLOVE

The question of the meaningfulness of human life does not, so far as I know, arise explicitly for Kant. At the same time, much of his thinking about knowledge, ethics, and religion is relevant to it. The question, then, is how best to approach the issue from a Kantian point of view. Is it a legitimate question and, if it is, how to answer? One approach – I do not say it is the only one – is to begin with a more tractable question, namely, with Kant's account of human action. The thought is that, when we understand what gives particular actions their distinctive character and depth – their "meaning" – we can then take up the larger question of the meaning of human life.

What sets human action apart is its distinctive motivational structure. We are, according to Kant, the sorts of creatures who can be pushed and pulled by empirical circumstances but who can also begin a series of events from within ourselves. Thus, to take a well-known example from the *Groundwork of the Metaphysics of Morals*, the shopkeeper who resists the temptation to overcharge an unsuspecting customer may do so from fear of being exposed – or from the thought that it would be wrong to treat the customer simply as a means of enrichment (Kant 1785b: 52; 4: 397).[1] In the first instance, even though, as we say, the fear is "mine," still, I am being moved by it; it is, as it were, an alien force. By contrast, in the second instance, I am acting on the thought – a thought I give myself – of what is right. As Kant puts it, "only a rational being has the capacity to act in accordance with the representation of laws, that is, in accordance with principles" (ibid.: 66; 4: 412).

Put another way, we can be motivated by a principle's object or its form. Perhaps the shopkeeper has in view some empirical characteristic of his customer – her race, say, or her standing in the community. On the other hand, the thought that persons must not be treated simply as things (i.e. simply as means to ends) makes no reference to any subjective ground of determination. Rather, it appeals only to the pure idea of duty, which Kant famously calls the categorical imperative. We act from duty when we treat others with respect;[2] that is, as capable – as we know we are – of acting freely.

Let us say that acting freely or from duty gives "meaning" to a certain class of human actions: ones with moral standing. Of course acting from duty does not exhaust the meaning of all human action; so much is implied in our foregoing discussion. Kant is as aware as anyone that the point of many actions will be exhausted by considerations of happiness or unhappiness and that persons vary as to where they find satisfaction. He makes this point forcefully in *The Metaphysics of Morals*:

> Only experience can teach us what brings us joy. Only the natural drives for food, sex, rest and movement, and (as our natural predispositions develop) for honor, for enlarging our knowledge and so forth, can tell each of us, and each only in his particular way, in what he will find those joys; and, in the same way, only experience can teach him the means by which to seek them ... [E]veryone must be allowed countless exceptions in order to adapt his choice of a way of life to his particular inclinations and susceptibility to satisfaction.
>
> (Kant 1797: 371; 6: 215–16)

The main point here seems to be to contrast the uniformity of duty with the variability of joy. It is never permissible to treat someone with disrespect, but whether I take satisfaction from his style of dress or from her cuisine – over such matters uniformity is neither natural nor desirable. Kant seems to be imagining diverse "ways of life" oriented within a univocal moral standard.

Elsewhere in the same work, Kant gives a second reason why there must be more to human action than virtue:

> But that the human being can be fantastically virtuous who allows nothing to be morally indifferent and strews all his steps with duties ... ; it is not indifferent to him whether I eat meat or fish, drink beer or wine, supposing that both agree with me. Fantastic virtue is a concern with petty details [*Mikrology*] which ... would turn the government of virtue into tyranny.
>
> (Ibid.: 536–37; 6: 409)

In other words, too much virtue can be crippling. If I find moral gravity in even the "petty details" of life ("beer or wine?"), not only will I likely miss out on joy, but I risk being unable to clear my mind to reflect when I am confronted with questions of real moral import. No doubt whether to drink beer or wine can be morally weighty; arguably, moral considerations can be attached to any prospective action. The point is that I cannot take each successive circumstance as an occasion for moral reflection – if only because the activity of reflection requires that I maintain a continuous train of thought. (For example: I am tired of life ... May I end it? ... But that would be to treat myself as an object ... But then it is impermissible.) I cannot, then, begin a new train of moral reflection at every moment.

Let us review. We are pursuing a Kantian answer to what is apparently a large, unwieldy question, "What is the meaning of life?" Our strategy has been to approach it by way of a smaller, more manageable one: What gives meaning to human action? To this question we now seem to have arrived at serviceable answer, namely, a balance of duty and joy – where there is no more one "right" balance than there is one right way of life. Many questions of clarification arise at this point, but we must put them to one side. Given this picture of human action, what about the meaning of life?

At this point we face some perplexity, for it may appear that our reflections thus far, rather than advancing our inquiry, have made it difficult or perhaps impossible to raise the general question of the meaningfulness of human life. After all, if I know what makes each of my actions meaningful as it arises, then what room is left for the general question? We might put the problem thus: at any given moment, I am confronted by circumstances which call for action of some sort. Some of these circumstances will be keyed to satisfaction or perhaps even joy of some sort (Time to walk the dog? Beer or wine?), and some will be morally weighty (how both to keep a promise and not betray an innocent). But, either way, I seem to have all the resources I need. If questions of duty do not arise, I will act on the basis of considerations of happiness. If the moment is morally freighted I may need to reflect as to what duty requires. Not that I will always recognize what my duty is; no doubt there will be hard cases, considerations of time pressure, fatigue, etc. The point is that I know that what gives the action in question its moment, its depth (in the *Groundwork*, Kant says its "sublimity"; Kant 1785b: 88; 4: 439) – in our terms, its meaning – is the fact that it draws duty (and so freedom) into play. Since, in this sense, I know what makes any given course of action meaningful then the general question as to the meaningfulness of human life may seem to find no purchase.

Kant's reply to this challenge, repeated throughout his mature authorship, turns on his insistence that we cannot view each episode of moral striving in isolation, but rather that we must view them as a whole, as a unity (e.g. Kant 1793: 177; 6: 154). Now, taken by itself, the act of taking a plurality as a unity is unexceptionable. In fact, it is pervasive in ordinary experience. Thus, when we cognize a straight line, we are taking a plurality of points as a unity (Kant 1787: A162–63/B203); again, when we cognize a house we are taking in the door and windows and roof as one thing (B162ff.). We may agree that the activity of taking a plurality as a unity is unavoidable in the context of mathematical judgment and of empirical perception. After all, we want to cognize *lines* and not just points, *houses* and not just doors, windows, and roofs. What about the context that interests us, the moral context? Why can we not rest content with cognizing particular actions as such?

Much is at issue for Kant in this question. At the heart of his philosophy is a story about what separates legitimate from bogus questions. In the *Critique of Pure Reason*, Kant argues that we can cognize objects only as they are given to our senses. Questions about how objects may be apart from how they affect us – how they may be when considered "in themselves" – are illegitimate. In a rare burst of high spirits, Kant writes

For if [a] question is absurd in itself and demands unnecessary answers, then, besides the embarrassment of the one who proposes it, it also has the disadvantage of misleading the incautious listener into absurd answers, and presenting the ridiculous sight (as the ancients said) of one person milking a billy-goat while the other holds a sieve underneath.

(Kant 1787: A58/B82)

In the more usual, austere language of the *Critique*, we fall into a "transcendental illusion" when we form for ourselves the idea of an unconditioned totality (A310/B367). Kant devotes much attention to documenting and then criticizing several such illusions, including those having to do with *soul* and *world*. No doubt I cognize the dog I walk and the tune I hum – but nowhere in experience do I encounter a substantial soul. Similarly, we experience objects large and small – but we cannot take in the world considered as an absolute totality. In each of these cases the problem lies in taking a plurality as a unity. That is, we unify this pain, that perception, this memory and that emotion into a bogus object: a soul (B422). Again, we unify this planet, that waterfall, this galaxy and that book into an illegitimate object: the world (A522/B550).

In asking after the meaning of life we represent ourselves as able to advance from the meaning of this or that particular action to the meaning of our actions as a whole. Is this advance like unifying points into a line, or doors and windows into a house – or is it like trying to milk a billy-goat?

Kant is aware that much is at stake. It partly motivates the second half of the *Critique of Practical Reason*. What is wanted is an argument showing the legitimacy of asking about the meaning of my actions taken together. In this work, the emphasis falls on explicating the notion of a "finite rational being." Were we purely rational beings our "highest good" would be exhausted by the notion of acting from duty, that is, by the notion of virtue. But, as we have seen, part of what it means to be both rational and finite is to pursue happiness as well as virtue. The highest good then, in the sense of the *complete* good for such creatures as ourselves, would be a world in which happiness is apportioned according to virtue (Kant 1788: 5: 110). Such a world would present a stark contrast to the world we live in, where, as we know, the rain falls equally on the just and the unjust. Thus, when we take all of our individual actions together (as a unity), Kant says we must aim at our "final purpose," that is, the creation of the highest good. At this point our central question recurs: Why must we take all of our actions as a unity? Why not rest content with the meaningfulness of each individual action as it comes? Here, in the *Critique of Practical Reason*, Kant answers by appealing directly to the categorical imperative: "the moral law commands me to make the highest possible good in a world the final object of all my conduct" (ibid.: 108; 5: 129). In one clear sense of the phrase, Kant is saying that promoting a world in which virtue is rewarded with happiness is itself "the meaning of life."

Now one reaction we might have to this account would be to say that Kant has hit on a concept of undeniable interest, that of the highest good. And we might want to concede that, as a concept, part of its interest lies in the natural way it fits with creatures who feel the pull of both duty and of happiness. And yet we might at the same time doubt that Kant has shown it to be of any *more* interest than this. That is, we might doubt whether he has shown that I am required to find a purpose or goal for "all my conduct," or, in our terms, that I am required to find the meaning of life. Note that this doubt might well come from deep behind Kantian lines, namely, from the thought that it is at least odd to have the categorical imperative commanding happiness in *any* form – even as a component of the highest good. In fact, that Kant's highest good should appear to us as objectively necessary on the grounds that it is required by the categorical imperative might itself smack of transcendental illusion.

Whether or not for this reason, five years later, in *Religion within the Boundaries of Mere Reason* (1793), Kant sets our pursuit of the highest good on a rather different footing. Here is the central passage:

> Morality really has no need of an end for right conduct; on the contrary, the law that contains the formal condition of the use of freedom in general suffices to it. Yet an end proceeds from morality just the same; for it cannot possibly be a matter of indifference to reason how to answer the question, *What is then the result of this right conduct of ours?* Nor to what we are to direct our doings and nondoings, even granted this is not fully within our control, at least as something with which they are to harmonize. And this is indeed only the idea of an object that unites within itself the formal condition of all such ends as we ought to have (duty) with everything which is conditional upon ends we have and which conforms to duty (happiness proportioned to its observance), that is, the idea of a highest good in the world ... This idea is not (practically considered) an empty one; for it meets our natural need, which would otherwise be a hindrance to moral resolve, to think for all our doings and nondoings taken as a whole some sort of ultimate end which reason can justify. What is most important here, however, is that this idea arises out of morality and is not its foundation ...
>
> (Kant 1793: 58; 6: 5, original italics)

Let us begin with the italicized sentence. We are imagining someone who tries to treat persons with respect and never merely as means to an end. The central thought in this passage is that, to such a person, morality must present itself in general, as well as in particular, terms. That is, this person tries to do, and is aware that she is trying to do, the right thing as circumstances arise. These particular actions must resemble one another, and must be appreciated as resembling one another, as species of a higher genera – after all, each is intended to be an instance of "right conduct." Thus, she cannot avoid the thought that she is attempting a certain *kind* of action. But just as particular actions require some intended result, so, too, does the general kind. I intend a particular act of promise-keeping to result in, say, the repayment of a debt. To be sure, what motivates my promise-keeping is not the repayment per se, but rather the realization that failure to repay would require using the lender simply as a means to an end. The crucial question is not, "At what does the policy of promise-keeping aim?" Promise-keeping is itself a part of the larger sphere of morality ("all our doings and nondoings taken as a whole"). The question is, "At what does the larger project of morality aim?" Kant answers, here as before: a world in which happiness is apportioned according to virtue.

What has happened to the meaning of life between 1788 and 1793? In one sense, nothing. In both the *Critique of Practical Reason* and *Religion within the Boundaries of Mere Reason*, the meaning of life is the pursuit of the highest good. The difference is that, in the later work, the impetus to pursue the highest good no longer comes directly from the categorical imperative, but rather from the following train of thought:

1   All actions must have some goal or end.
2   So, right conduct, as a kind of action, must have some goal or end.
3   The goal or end that best fits creatures who answer both to duty and to happiness is a world in which virtue is rewarded with happiness.
4   In other words, the goal of right conduct is the highest good.

Here the meaning of life, in the sense of the pursuit of the highest or complete good, emerges from a generic feature of human action (premise 1), from the unavoidability of taking our moral actions as a unity (premise 2), and from the most general contours of moral anthropology (premise 3).

At this point, for the second time in the course of our reflections, it might seem that we have reached a natural end point in thinking about the meaning of life. We know the meaning of individual actions (duty and happiness) and, conceding that one is required, we have a goal for them when taken together (the highest good). But, at least in the works we have been considering, Kant does not take our work as finished.

In the *Critique of Practical Reason* and again in *Religion within the Boundaries of Mere Reason,* Kant argues that intending to achieve the highest good requires me to believe that such a world is possible – otherwise, believing that is not possible, I would cease to pursue it. But to think that the highest good is possible requires believing that nature will one day reward virtue with proportional happiness. And that does not seem plausible; I have no reason to think the rain will, of itself, one day start to fall only on the unjust.

> Therefore the highest good in the world is possible only insofar as a supreme cause of nature having a causality in keeping with the moral disposition is assumed. Now, a being capable of actions in accordance with the representation of laws is *an*

intelligence (a rational being), and the causality of such a being in accordance with the representation of laws is his *will*. Therefore the supreme cause of nature, insofar as it must be presupposed for the highest good, is a being that is the cause of nature by *understanding* and *will* (hence its author), that is, **God**.

(Kant 1788: 101; 5: 125)

In other words, in committing myself to achieving the highest good in the world, I thereby commit myself to its possibility.[3] But the being capable of making rain respect virtue is God. So, *"it is morally necessary to assume the existence of God"* (Kant 1788: 105; 5: 125, emphasis in the original).

As Kant puts it in *Religion within the Boundaries of Mere Reason*,

Morality thus inevitably leads to religion, and through religion it extends itself to the idea of a mighty moral lawgiver outside the human being, in whose will the ultimate end (of the creation of the world) is what can and at the same ought to be the ultimate human end.

(Kant 1793: 35–36; 6: 6)

Talk of the "ultimate human end" certainly seems to bear on our question. Shall we extend the meaning of life from pursuit of the highest good in the world, to the moral "postulate" of the existence of God?

Not an easy question, and one about which Kant himself apparently had second thoughts. In the *Critique of Practical Reason*, Kant emphasizes that belief in God is "subjectively" and not "objectively" necessary: "Moreover, it is not to be understood by this that it is necessary to assume the existence of God *as a ground of all obligation in general* (for this rests, as has been sufficiently shown, on the autonomy of reason itself)" (Kant 1788:105; 5: 125–26). But then we seem to be thrown back on our initial puzzlement: if I know the "ground of all obligation," what further question can I have about the meaning of life? Kant himself seems to say as much in a much-discussed remark, written shortly before his death.[4]

In seeking a Kantian answer to the question of the meaning of life, we have transcribed an arc from individual human actions, to all our actions taken together, to belief in God; and we have seen that our motivating question can be raised and answered at any stop along the way. To take Kant seriously, at any such point, requires that we endorse the categorical imperative – the requirement that persons must be treated with respect. The question is whether this endorsement carries us all the way to belief in God, or merely to a commitment to the highest, most complete good in the world.

Notes

1   Reference to Kant's works will have the English translation followed by the "Akademie" edition volume and page: *Kant's Gesammelte Schriften* (Kant 1747–1802).

2 Kant gives several versions or "formulae" of the "principle of morality" and claims that they come to the same thing (Kant 1785b: 85; 4: 436). I do not have space to discuss these issues.

3 To its real possibility, not merely to its logical possibility. See Ferreira (2013).

4 "Religion is conscientiousness (*mihi hoc religioni*). The holiness of the acceptance [*Zusage*] and the truthfulness of what man must confess to himself. Confess to yourself. To have religion, the concept of God is not required (still less the postulate: 'There is a God')" (Kant 1795–1804: 248; 21: 81).

20 Schopenhauer and the meaning of life

ROBERT WICKS

When considering the question of life's meaning, there are some initial points to clarify. First, by referring to "the" meaning of life, a single, ultimate meaning is usually in mind. Second, although people ask about the meaning of *life*, the concern is often with the meaning of all *existence*, sentient and non-sentient, or alternatively phrased, the meaning of all *being*. Third, the query could be about the meaning of life, existence, or being in an objective, mind-independent sense, or alternatively, about the meaning of life, existence, or being "to me" or "to some person or people." Life, existence, or being may have no objective meaning, but it may have a conditional meaning to one or more people, even though that meaning will dissolve when they die.

Arthur Schopenhauer approaches the question of life's meaning by asking whether life is worth living in view of the objective worth of reality itself. According to him, ultimate reality or, following Immanuel Kant's terminology, the "thing-in-itself," is nothing more than an aimless, meaningless impulse, and by implication, so is life. Schopenhauer uses the word "will" (hereafter capitalized for clarity) to refer to ultimate reality, which he characterizes in the following excerpts:

> *Thing-in-itself* expresses that which exists independently of perception through any of our senses, and so that which really and truly is. For Democritus this was formed matter; at bottom, it was still the same for Locke; for Kant it was an *x*; for me it is *will*.
>
> (Schopenhauer 1851b: §61, 90)

> In fact, absence of all aim, of all limits, belongs to the essential nature of the will in itself, which is an endless striving .... Every individual act has a purpose or end; willing as a whole has no end in view.
>
> (Schopenhauer 1818: §29, 164)

> The will, considered purely in itself, is devoid of knowledge, and is only a blind, irresistible urge ...
>
> (Ibid.: §54, 275)

The will in itself is absolutely free and entirely self-determining, and for it there is no law.

(Ibid.: §54, 285)

Schopenhauer adds that Will as thing-in-itself is "one" beyond the distinction between one and many, that it is beyond the subject–object distinction, and that it is beyond space and time (ibid.: §23, 113; §25, 128). Insofar as Will constitutes the spatio-temporal world, it is also a morally objectionable being insofar as it manifests itself as an uncountable number of individuals dispersed throughout space and time that are in perpetual conflict with one another. The realm of living things embodies this conflict most intensely:

This world is the battle-ground of tormented and agonized beings who continue to exist only by each devouring the other. Therefore, every beast of prey in it is the living grave of thousands of others, and its self-maintenance is a chain of torturing deaths.

(Schopenhauer 1844: XLVI, 581)

... this strife itself is only the revelation of that variance with itself that is essential to the will. This universal conflict is to be seen most clearly in the animal kingdom. Animals have the vegetable kingdom for their nourishment, and within the animal kingdom again every animal is the prey and food of some other ... [The] most glaring example of this kind is afforded by the bulldog-ant of Australia, for when it is cut in two, a battle begins between the head and the tail. The head attacks the tail with its teeth, and the tail defends itself bravely by stinging the head. The contest usually lasts for half an hour, until they die or are dragged away by other ants. This takes place every time.

(Schopenhauer 1818: §27, 147)

In a straightforward sense, then, Schopenhauer understands the world to be essentially meaningless, fundamentally vicious, and morally objectionable, for reality is "Will" – a senseless impulse that manifests itself as a world that, in its sentient aspect, is filled with self-centered individuals that sustain themselves by devouring each other. Insofar as Will is a cannibalistic and morally repugnant entity, Schopenhauer concludes that it would have been better had this world and ourselves not existed:

In fact, nothing else can be stated as the aim of our existence except the knowledge that it would be better for us not to exist.

(Schopenhauer 1844: XLVIII, 605)

Schopenhauer is often met with disapproval for maintaining that people tend to be selfish and animalistic, that the world is worthless, and that it would be better if we, as well as all sentient, suffering beings, did not exist. His message resists easy assimilation and it underlies the common impression of his philosophy as having a distinctively pessimistic and misanthropic tone. The following is exemplary:

> If we want to know what human beings, morally considered, are worth as a whole and in general, let us consider their fate as a whole and in general. This fate is want, wretchedness, misery, lamentation, and death. Eternal justice prevails; if they were not as a whole contemptible, their fate as a whole would not be so melancholy.
>
> (Schopenhauer 1818: §63, 352)

There is some truth in the pessimistic assessment of Schopenhauer's vision of things, but it does not appreciate his understanding of a certain profound meaning that life can have. To see this, we can reflect upon the concluding statement of the first volume of *The World as Will and Representation*, which seems merely to reinforce his account of the spatio-temporal world as meaningless, but which contains an additional consideration that yields a tremendously meaningful and rebellious way to comprehend our earthly situation. He writes:

> … we freely acknowledge that what remains after the complete abolition of the will is, for all who are still full of the will, assuredly nothing. But also conversely, to those in whom the will has turned and denied itself, this very real world of ours with all its suns and galaxies, is – nothing.
>
> (Ibid.: §71, 411–12)

As noted, Schopenhauer maintains that each individual, sentient and non-sentient, is a manifestation of Will, and that when these manifestations assume the form of animals and human beings, desire dominates their lives. Our ordinary perspective of the world is consequently that of a being that is "still full of the will."

Contrasting with this condition, Schopenhauer identifies an exceptional, enlightened state of consciousness that stems from the extreme minimization of desire – a condition that is predominantly will-less, peaceful, and clear-minded. This is the ascetic's awareness, whose outlook Schopenhauer implicitly refers to above as that of someone "in whom the will has turned and denied itself." For Schopenhauer, anyone with an ascetic awareness will enjoy a state of transcendence and supreme satisfaction – that is, a profound meaning – that renders the ordinary world unimportant in contrast. He maintains that the spatio-temporal world is morally worthless as a manifestation of self-devouring Will, but upon adding that it appears to be "nothing" from the ascetic's perspective, he associates transcendence with a meaningful experience:

> If, however, it should be absolutely insisted on that somehow a positive knowledge is to be acquired of what philosophy can express only negatively

as denial of the will [i.e. asceticism], nothing would be left but to refer to that state which is experienced by all who have attained to complete denial of the will [i.e. ascetics], and which is denoted by the names ecstasy, rapture, illumination, union with God, and so on. But such a state cannot be called knowledge, since it no longer has the form of subject and object; moreover, it is accessible only to one's own experience that cannot be further communicated.

(Ibid.: §71, 410)

Schopenhauer is known for having despised Hegel and Hegelianism, but it is surprising how Schopenhauer's philosophy parallels Hegel's in the importance it gives to self-consciousness. Specifically, Hegel maintains that the world is the product of a growth process through which reality slowly becomes aware of itself, attaining self-awareness in the form of thoroughly rational and reflective human beings. Hegel's ultimate reality is not irrational Will, as we find in Schopenhauer's philosophy; it is a fundamentally rational being that through continual and accumulative patterns of opposition and reconciliation, grows logically from the single, timeless, abstract concept of pure and empty being into an organized, spatio-temporal world populated with self-conscious individuals. Despite how at the basis of Schopenhauer's philosophy, Will as a single, timeless, and aimless being is neither rational, conceptual, logical, nor implicitly moral in nature, Schopenhauer maintains similarly that Will becomes aware of itself in its manifestation as a world that contains self-conscious human beings.

Will may be aimless and meaningless, but with the emergence of human beings Schopenhauer discerns an answer to what our purpose is, by appreciating how he himself is a manifestation of Will that is coming to know itself through philosophical reflection in the form of human beings. Just as Hegel maintains that reality, understood to be a rational being, develops an awareness of itself through the course of human history and eventually attains philosophical clarity through him and other like-minded beings, Schopenhauer maintains that Will, understood to be a non-rational being, develops an awareness of itself through the course of human history and eventually attains philosophical clarity through him and other like-minded human beings. The two views run in parallel, although they differ on the nature of ultimate reality.

In Schopenhauer's case, what reality, or Will, comes to know about itself is not that it is developing into a perfectly rational, moral, systematically integrated being. It realizes instead that it is a horrible, morally repugnant being. Just as when a person looks into a mirror and is shocked to behold a monster, Will comes to realize that it is irrational, meaningless, suffering-producing, and cannibalistic. Schopenhauer concludes that the purpose of life is self-knowledge, namely, to understand that Will itself – the substance of reality – is a worthless, morally objectionable being. Only Will in the form of human beings can realize this, and this realization motivates a turn away from Will towards asceticism:

He knows the whole, comprehends its inner nature, and finds it involved in a constant passing away, a vain striving, an inward conflict, and a continual suffering. Wherever he looks, he sees suffering humanity and the suffering animal world, and a world that passes away. Now all this lies just as near to him as only his own person lies to the egoist. Now how could he, with such knowledge of the world, affirm this very life through constant acts of will, and precisely in this way bind himself more and more firmly to it, press himself to it more and more closely? Thus, whoever is still involved in the *principium individuationis*, in egoism, knows only particular things and their relation to his own person, and these then become ever renewed *motives* of his willing. On the other hand, that knowledge of the whole, of the inner nature of the thing-in-itself, which has been described, becomes the *quieter* of all and every willing. The will now turns away from life; it shudders at the pleasures in which it recognizes the affirmation of life. Man attains to the state of voluntary renunciation, resignation, true composure, and complete willlessness.

(Ibid.: §68, 379)

This reversal in perspective amounts to a struggle of Will with itself, where reflection appears in the human being, moral awareness dawns, and where the enlightened individual realizes that as it minimizes its desires, it minimizes the cannibalism in which Will is engaged in its various manifestations. Since such an enlightened person is constituted by Will, Schopenhauer regards the person's minimization of its desire as none other than an act of freedom and self-suppression on the part of Will itself to diminish its own power by increasing its metaphysical self-recognition. Schopenhauer consequently locates asceticism and its associated denial-of-the-will at the highest level of awareness, for the ascetic realizes that the spatio-temporal world is inherently devoid of moral value and that Will's inherent viciousness in manifesting itself as such, ought to be neutralized.

A question to ask at this point is why it does not make sense for individuals to commit suicide, if our deepest substance is a morally objectionable being and if it is consequently "better for us not to exist." The reason is that Schopenhauer's statement that it is better for us not to exist is saying that it would have been better had *Will* never been. Within the context of the broadest question of why there is something rather than nothing, Schopenhauer prefers nothing. But Will is, and an individual's suicide cannot affect this.

Schopenhauer also regards the typical motivations for suicide as implicit affirmations of Will, rather than suppressions or denials of it, having in mind cases where people feel hopeless, or where suffering is so severe that death is the only reasonable alternative. If hope were to arise unexpectedly or if suffering were to diminish in such situations, Schopenhauer maintains that the person's interest in remaining alive would immediately surge, indicating that despite a person's disposition to commit suicide under adverse circumstances, the person's will to live subconsciously persists.

A disposition towards suicide nonetheless underlies Schopenhauer's philosophy, but it has a different motivation and is located at a more fundamental metaphysical level than that of desire-filled individuals. Schopenhauer's most pressing moral interest is in relieving suffering, and to achieve this he realizes that the force that produces suffering, namely, Will itself, must be opposed. The denial-of-the-will – the stifling of Will as it manifests itself in the individual person – is thus seen as the ultimate pathway to peace. Rather than commit suicide as an individual, which would merely dissolve a person's consciousness and blend the person's body back into the field of the Will's cannibalistic self-devouring, the optimal moral path is to *live as long as possible* as an ascetic to minimize desire and reduce the energy of Will. The moral purpose of the ascetic's existence is to participate in tranquilizing Will at the metaphysical level.

With respect to the meaning of life, it is common for many people to find meaning in a great task to which they devote themselves wholeheartedly. Political leaders, for instance, often motivate their societies by defining a vital mission such as making their country great once more, as was expressed to the German population after World War I, or conducting war against a demonic enemy, as was put forth in those countries who fought against Germany in World War II. Further examples are working towards achieving a free and just world society, or working towards liberating one's country from corruption and oppression. By defining their lives in reference to such grand projects, people establish a single and solid meaning for themselves. Single-minded tasks on a smaller scale also provide satisfying life-meanings for people, such as working hard to sustain a family, community, or local institution.

Schopenhauer adheres to this same pattern and presents a meaning for life in reference to perhaps the greatest task of all, which is to wage a moral battle against reality itself, an absolute and unbeatable enemy. Given the magnitude of its being, this enemy generates the greatest sense of meaning in those who battle defiantly against it – a battle that is essentially against oneself.

This is a peculiar battle as Schopenhauer conceives of it, for it takes the form of a guerrilla war against one's inner being as Will – a being that manifests itself predominantly as a set of selfish, competitive, mutually devouring, morally insensitive individuals. To appreciate this war against one's inner being, let us consider Schopenhauer's argument that ultimate reality is Will with particular attention to the metaphors he uses to describe his quest for metaphysical knowledge. These illuminate how asceticism constitutes a subversive moral campaign against reality itself.

To a significant extent, although not entirely, Schopenhauer accepts Kant's view that our daily experience does not present to us how ultimate reality truly is. Schopenhauer describes our ordinary experience as a world of "objects" situated in space and time that are causally related to each other.

As he interprets and simplifies Kant's view, he holds that space, time, and causality are the basic forms of our minds though which we construct an appearance of ultimate reality. The problem of apprehending ultimate reality as it is in itself is thus the problem of apprehending it independently of the forms of space, time, and causality.

Since Schopenhauer finds it impossible to obtain metaphysical knowledge through scientific methods that analyze objects situated in space, he turns inward in his effort to apprehend ultimate reality:

> ... it is absolutely impossible to arrive at a comprehension of the *inner nature* of things on the path of mere *knowledge* and *representation*, since this knowledge always comes to things *from without*, and must therefore remain eternally *outside* them. This purpose could be attained only by our finding *ourselves* in the inside of things, so that this inside would be known to us directly.
>
> (Schopenhauer 1844: I, 12)

Schopenhauer achieves knowledge of the "inside" of things by realizing that he, like everyone else, knows his own body from the inside – a body that, as a physical object *per se*, he recognizes as being on a metaphysical par with every other physical object. He consequently introspects, sets aside thereby the forms of space and causality to leave only the form of time as a "thin veil" over his ultimate inner being, and attempts to apprehend an aspect of himself that is metaphysically elementary. He aims directly to apprehend an elementary aspect of himself that in addition to constituting his own inner being, could also constitute the inner being of any physical object. This he discovers in what he calls "will," a blind, aimless impulse that underlies his awareness and bodily action. Subsequently generalizing and describing all of reality as Will, he soon finds himself repulsed by the morally objectionable nature of this being, as discussed above.

With respect to the metaphors he uses, when Schopenhauer is considering whether scientific styles of inquiry can provide metaphysical knowledge, he concludes that the effort is futile, finding himself in a position similar to that of someone who is trying to enter a castle, but who can find no entrance:

> Here we already see that we can never get at the inner nature of things *from without*. However much we may investigate, we obtain nothing but images and names. We are like a man who goes round a castle, looking in vain for an entrance, and sometimes sketching the facades. Yet this is the path that all philosophers before me have followed.
>
> (Schopenhauer 1818: §17, 99)

So far I agree with Kant. But now, as the counterpoise to this truth, I have stressed that other truth that we are not merely the *knowing subject*, but that *we ourselves* are also among those realities or entities we require to know, that *we ourselves are the thing-in-itself.* Consequently, a way *from within* stands open to us to that real inner nature of things to which we cannot penetrate *from without.* It is, so to speak, a subterranean passage, a secret alliance, which, as if by treachery, places us all at once in the fortress that could not be taken by attack from without. Precisely as such, the *thing-in-itself* can come into consciousness only quite directly, namely by *it itself being conscious of itself;* to try to know it objectively is to desire something contradictory. (Schopenhauer 1844: XVIII, 195)

After Schopenhauer introspectively achieves a measure of metaphysical self-knowledge as Will, he articulates his philosophy thereafter. What goes unnoticed in his arguments are the subversive connotations of the leading metaphors for his quest for metaphysical knowledge, which present us with the image of penetrating a castle's or fortress's defenses by stealth. The connotations are subversive because they apply not only to his initial quest for self-knowledge, but to his subsequent project of negating what he discovers. The path through which Schopenhauer initially enters the castle, so to speak, to obtain knowledge of ultimate reality, is the same path through which he later enters to destroy the castle in his advocacy of asceticism, or denial-of-the-will, after having had the terrible surprise that the reality within – the philosophical treasure he sought in his quest to solve the riddle of the world – is morally repugnant.

When Schopenhauer refers to the path towards metaphysical knowledge as "a subterranean passage, a secret alliance, which, as if by treachery, places us all at once in the fortress that could not be taken by attack from without," a suggestion of guerrilla warfare comes forth, doubly applicable, for he is interested not only in penetrating the castle walls to know the castle from within, but also in destroying the castle in the form of an ascetic after realizing the horrors it contains.

In effect, then, the ascetic is a guerrilla fighter, or ninja, or secret agent of the highest metaphysical order, who wages a morally motivated war upon reality itself, conceived as blind Will. Not only, then, is there a directly experienced meaning in the condition of being will-less, insofar as Schopenhauer associates the ascetic's experience with the ecstasy of seeing God, there is also an absolute meaning in the ascetic's experience of participating in a metaphysical battle against an unbeatable, morally repugnant opponent through the denial-of-the-will.

Contrary to expectations, then, Schopenhauer's position that ultimate reality as Will is essentially meaningless does not lead to a hopeless pessimism. In the form of the ascetic, at least, and in anyone whose life-project engages in fostering the ascetic denial-of-the-will, either directly or indirectly, Schopenhauer's account of Will opens the door to an absolutely meaningful life as an advocate of peace and moral crusader at the highest level of existence. It involves a life so meaningful as to diminish in contrast, the significance of the infinity of space and time, and of all the sentient beings it contains. This is the sense in which we can understand the final sentence of the first volume of *The World as Will and Representation*, namely, that "to those in whom the will has turned and denied itself, this very real world of ours with all its suns and galaxies, is – nothing."

In reference to the meaning of our lives today, Schopenhauer would recognize all lifestyles that either directly involve the experience of the denial-of-the-will, or that foster or sustain that experience, as having an absolute and positive metaphysical meaning. In contrast, he would regard lifestyles dominated by wilfulness, selfishness, aggression, individuality, competition, exploitation, and viciousness, as essentially meaningless in the large scheme of things. The implications are thought-provoking, for they render people whose vocations involve, for instance, the humble task of delivering milk and food to a monastery of ascetics, as having metaphysically meaningful and respectable lives, and those who sustain institutions that wage war, construct armies, set populations against one another, and exploit other sentient beings, as having lives that are metaphysically meaningless.

21 Kierkegaard and the meaning of life

MARK BERNIER

Søren Kierkegaard (1813–1855) lived in golden age Denmark, at the eventide of the early modern period. He was born and raised (and died) in Copenhagen, the cultural center of Denmark; and as the son of a wealthy hosier, he was exposed to the significant cultural and intellectual happenings of the day. It was at this time, early in the nineteenth century, that the question of the meaning of life began to emerge in the form familiar to us now, as a topic in its own right, with an urgency reflecting a fundamental importance to the connection between "life" and "meaning." Kierkegaard is in the vanguard of this dramatic shift in thought, and his authorship can be read as a sustained meditation on the problem of meaning, developed from within the Christian perspective. His account is thus historically relevant, in that he is one of the first modern thinkers to take the problem of meaning as a fundamental crisis (or more accurately: *the* fundamental crisis). In what follows I will highlight some of the primary aspects of his position, how he understands the problem, and what he sees as the solution. The development of his thought follows a trajectory of the Christian concepts of despair and faith, which he treats existentially. He sees life as a fundamental task, one which has been rejected (despair) – the problem is that the self is *itself* the task, and to reject one's task is to reject oneself. This is the root of the existential crisis of meaning. According to Kierkegaard, meaning in life resides in accepting oneself as the task; but one can only secure meaning through a proper relation to God (faith).

This theme is touched upon throughout his work, but often indirectly. The broad range of his writings includes sermons, scriptural commentaries, reviews, essays, books, and thousands of pages of journal reflections.[1] But to highlight how he sees the importance of meaning, and the nature of the problem, I will focus on a well-known text from his journals; the Gilleleje entry from 1 August 1835. His analysis, we should note, is thoroughly Christian. Kierkegaard's father exerted great influence over the development of his son's attitudes and beliefs, and from him he received his father's melancholy disposition and stern Christian outlook – specifically, Danish Lutheran pietism, which emphasizes inherited sin, guilt and the need for individual piety. This Christian framework influenced Kierkegaard's understanding of the self and meaning, and set the stage for his rebellion against "Christendom" – the

Danish Lutheran Church was the official church of Denmark, and it was no more difficult to become a Christian than to have the good sense to be born in Denmark. Kierkegaard rightly noted that this reduction destroys the need for personal, individual faith, and cheapens the struggle he saw as implicit to being a Christian (themes he takes up against the Hegelian interpretation of Christianity influencing theological discourse in Copenhagen). The problem of meaning should be understood against this backdrop, motivated by his view of what it is to be a Christian individual and authentic self (these are identical for Kierkegaard), in a time and place in history when everyone in Christendom was already considered a Christian.

Understanding the problem

Kierkegaard's interest in the problem of meaning is clearly captured in a powerful, raw reflection dated 1 August 1835, written when he was 22 years old, several years before his authorship begins with *Either–Or* (1843).[2] The journal entry is noteworthy in that it is considered one of the earliest expressions of existential thought, and is widely cited as showcasing Kierkegaard's idea of subjective truth. But it just as plainly shows that Kierkegaard sees meaning as the central existential crisis; and it is to this crisis that the passage so powerfully speaks. While the whole entry is of considerable interest, we will focus on a few pivotal elements of his reflection.

> What I really need is to be clear about *what I am to do*, not what I must know, except in the way knowledge must precede all action. It is a question of understanding my destiny, of seeing what the Deity really wants *me* to do; the thing is to find a truth that is truth *for me*, to find *the idea for which I am willing to live and die*. And what use would it be if I were to discover a so-called objective truth, or if I worked my way through the philosophers' systems ... What use would it be to be able to propound the meaning of Christianity, to explain many separate facts, if it had no deeper meaning for myself and for *my life*? ... But to find that idea, or more properly to find myself, it is no use my plunging still further into the world .... One must first learn to know oneself before knowing anything else (*gnothi seauton*). Only when the person has inwardly understood *himself*, and then sees the course forward from the path he is to take, does his life acquire repose and meaning ... [emphasis original].
>
> (Kierkegaard 1835: I A 75, §5100)

What he describes in this passage is a profound existential crisis, where the problem of meaning is formulated as a personal question about whom he is meant to be. He does not turn outward, toward his circumstances, or engage in critical analysis to determine which religion or philosophical system is most likely true – as he says, "it is no use my plunging still further into the world." He turns inward: the absence of meaning is linked to a lack of self-knowledge. By grounding his approach in a crisis of self-knowledge, he makes the question of meaning one that must be answered by each individual (there is no universal answer). Meaning is the central problem to solve.

This is not, and can never be, an abstract puzzle, but is irreducibly personal. To treat the problem of meaning as a philosophical fact-hunting safari is to make a category mistake. He does not seek life's general meaning – which would have no meaning to him – but meaning for *his own life*. Note the important distinction he draws between two different imperatives: what he must know, and what he must do. He does not deny that one must seek knowledge about the world (objective philosophical truths have their place, as does knowledge of Christian truth); but meaning is not the conclusion of an argument. Obviously it is far more important for him to become clear about *what he must do*. Without this grounding in the textures of his own life, objective knowledge is unimportant. His concern, therefore, is not with general truths, but with how to live. But here, too, we must draw a distinction: his interest is not in categorical imperatives or moral laws, and he does not seek to maximize pleasure, or the means by which he can achieve a happy life. Rather, as he says, he seeks to understand his destiny, what God wants him to do with his life – "to find a truth that is truth *for me*, to find *the idea for which I am willing to live and die*." Such stark phrasing moves away (for example) from the theme of happiness, which has been a main area of philosophical inquiry since at least Plato. Kierkegaard's quest to determine *what he must do* does not refer to the good life; he does not ask "what kind of person should I be?" but "what should I live for?" – he seeks a fundamental answer to the question of the meaning and purpose of his life.

Let us linger with his dramatic phrasing for a moment. He describes the object of his inquiry thus: as an idea for which he is willing to live and die. What he seeks, then, is an "idea," but by qualifying it as one "for which he is willing to live and die," he suggests that it is meant to find concrete expression in his life. It is not simply descriptive, but involves a broad normativity about the purpose of his life as a whole (it must be normative, since he seeks to be clear about what he *must do*). The problem he faces takes into account his life as a whole. Note that death does not simply play a limiting function, indicating the end of life's duration – death imposes a test for what might count as an adequate response to the problem: the only answer that can satisfy is the one for which he is willing to live *and* die.

Still, we should ask, why does he need to find a truth for which he is willing to live and die? What motivates him? We will return to this issue in a moment, when we examine his concept of despair. But at this point, we can note that in the above passage he says his answer will provide "repose and meaning." This indicates that something is *missing*, and in its place there is a pervasive disquiet about his life. The missing element is the "idea" linked with "what he must do," where the answer is to be found in self-knowledge. As we have seen, the answer is not that he needs to develop his ethical compass; he is not having a moral crisis and neither does he seek mere descriptive knowledge of himself. What he has in mind is a theme he develops later: that the self has a task. Thus, what he seeks is to get clear on his *task in life* – this, I suggest, is the idea. An "idea" of a task that applies to one's life combines the elements of self-knowledge and normativity as the conduit for meaning. One's meaning in life is embodied in the task one must do; and taking up one's task is to secure meaning (we will return to this).

Note that the objective truth of Christianity (which he accepts) does not produce meaning, and may in fact pose a problem. The problem has already been mentioned above: that one can "be Christian" simply in virtue of being born in Denmark. In such a case, the Christian framework has no meaning for one's life – it is merely descriptive and not normative (in the sense in question), and does not present one with a task for which to live. As we have seen, Kierkegaard says that even if he were to fully understand Christianity, it would be empty "if it had no deeper meaning" for his life. This suggests that Christianity is at least potentially able to ground meaning for one's life – but one must appropriate it as an element of the task one has in life. Christianity must cease being only general and objective (systematic), and instead become individual and personal, as the primary factor that generates the problem of meaning: what is it that "the Deity really wants *me* to do"? Thus, for Kierkegaard, Christianity frames the question, but doesn't supply an answer; one must find the answer by turning inward.

The pervasiveness of the problem: despair

Kierkegaardian despair is a rejection of the task of becoming oneself, a failure to become what one wants to be, and an unwillingness to hope in God as the source of meaning for one's life. The only way to overcome despair – thereby securing meaning in one's life – is through faith in God. While we have seen that Kierkegaard personally experienced a crisis of meaning, he also views all of humanity as being in crisis (one that mostly goes unnoticed). This is the human condition of despair, which is at the foundation of his philosophical anthropology of the self. It is a systemic, pervasive condition, and it explains why we are in a crisis of meaning: we have *willingly* relinquished the divine ground of our existence, and are unwilling to hope in God.

According to Kierkegaard, despair is characterized equally by two attitudes that stand in conflict, a willingness and an unwillingness: we are unwilling to be what we are, and instead favor what we would prefer to be (Kierkegaard 1849: 14). The problem, however, is that we cannot rid ourselves of what we are, and we can never truly become what we want to be. This produces an underlying feeling of dissatisfaction with one's life, and with oneself, which for most of us remains largely undetected – yet we all suffer from the irreconcilable rift between what we are and what we want to be. And since we cannot bridge these two impulses of the self, we remain in despair.

Kierkegaard's sense of despair is first and foremost of a sickness of the self; there is something wrong at the foundation of human existence. Typically, however, when we think of despair, we think of the experience of a loss that triggers an affective collapse – we *fall into* despair, for example, when we hear that our beloved will not survive. Yet this runs contrary to the Kierkegaardian view, in that we are not passive victims, as we might be when we succumb to a physical malady. Despair is not a misfortune, or the result of an event, but an active mode, something we do to ourselves. In *The Sickness unto Death*, the pseudonymous Anti-Climacus writes: "every moment he is in despair he is bringing it upon himself. It is always the present tense" (ibid.: 17). Despair is thus not the result of an event from our past, but is a continually self-inflicted condition. If one is "in despair" one is in the active process of causing it.

It may be strange to think of despair as a condition we ourselves cause. But in its broad strokes, Kierkegaard's account follows the Christian view of sin, as a way of being, or standing, with respect to oneself and God. Despair can be viewed as an existential expression of this way of standing, realized in two forms – there is a willingness in despair, a primal choosing, which comes from our desire to be the self we want to be; this impulse is matched by an unwillingness to be what we are (in relation to the eternal God). The core which drives despair (sin) is the desire for self-fashioning. Yet when we take up the task of self-fashioning in this way, on our own terms, we experience a crisis of meaning, since we lose the ground of our being, and we are unable to become what we desire.

While not everyone will accept Kierkegaard's Christian account of this, the experience he tracks of existential despair obviously will be familiar to many of us. There is a feeling, which occasionally enters our consciousness, that we lack a purpose in our life (a "destiny," as he writes in his journal), and that we are in danger of somehow "failing" to be what we were meant to be. It is a feeling unlike almost all other feelings: not a moral failure (which is typically accompanied with expressions of guilt or regret), but a feeling that emerges in a combination of anxiety and underlying hopelessness. There may be a sadness in us about our lives (what medieval Christians explained with the concept of *acedia*), a sense we are too *weak* to take up the task of living; or we may move in *defiance* against this feeling, to push to become something we choose to be, to fashion our own path.[3] Kierkegaard suggests that weakness and defiance are the two primary forms of despair (discussed at length in *The Sickness unto Death*), manifesting as evidence of our sickness and inability to find sure footing. He uses the Christian frame to explain this instability and hopelessness as a loss of the eternal, a break from God as the ground of our existence.

One way to approach this issue is to ask whether the suffering of despair is meaningful or not. Suffering *can* be meaningful – why not the suffering of despair? However, consider the following. It is one thing to suffer in life, and not to have an answer for it, when suffering is the result of external conditions beyond one's control; we may question God's will, or the blind luck of the universe, perhaps resigning ourselves to the way the world is. One can perhaps find, or assign, meaning to one's suffering in such cases. But it is an entirely different sort of crisis when you yourself are the cause of your suffering – not through some distant past event you brought about in a moment of weakness or ignorance, but as an ongoing condition. How can we say that this is meaningful suffering? This is the strange and difficult terrain into which Kierkegaard delves. The concept of despair at work here is not of a condition resulting from the loss of a good which is necessary for happiness, but instead is a pervasive existential nihilism – a despair over oneself.

Kierkegaard's position, however, is not simply that the self has a task, but that the self *is* the task. According to the pseudonymous Anti-Climacus, the self "is indeed itself, but it has the task of becoming itself" (ibid.: 35). There is an incompleteness in our existence, a fracturing between what we are and what we want to be, which provides a groundwork for the task: to secure a meaningful life through a unified identity. Kierkegaard's point is that when you are the task, willing to do or not do the task is identical with whether or not you will to exist – it reduces to Hamlet's question, to be or not to be (Bernier 2015: 33). Despair is thus the active turning away from oneself, one's existence, not as a result of external circumstances, but as a condition constituted by an unwillingness to be what one is, coupled with a drive to establish one's own self. This is the dialectic of despair, and what causes the existential crisis of meaning.

Faith: a solution to the problem

The loss of meaning characteristic of existential despair is overcome through a supernatural reconciliation with the divine. This is the great achievement of faith, which is a wholehearted commitment to trust God with the good in one's life. The act of despair involves a break from the eternal – and the eternal is necessary for meaning in life. Faith heals this sickness of despair through a reconciliation with the eternal ground of one's existence.

The structure of Kierkegaardian faith is important to understanding how it overcomes despair. In *Fear and Trembling*, faith is described in terms of a "double movement" (Kierkegaard 1843: 29). The first movement, which is called *infinite resignation*, is a movement to absorb all the sadness one has in the world, all the pain of despair, and to face it without collapse – he compares this to an old legend, of a shirt one sews with tears that protect better than armor (ibid.: 38). At the outset, you must have the courage to commit to this world with all your heart, in such a way that the meaning in your life is constituted through this commitment. But the world can offer no lasting foundation for meaning; you must reconcile yourself to this loss, and as much as possible come to terms with it. Infinite resignation is the acceptance of, and reconciliation with, this loss – by making your sorrow part of your identity. The ones who make this movement perfectly are like dancers who leap beautifully into the air, but land with hesitation because "they are really strangers in the world" (ibid.: 34). The price of reconciliation is closure to being at home in the world.

In the second movement of faith one makes the dancer's leap, accepting that the world can no longer be one's home, but then does something impossible after the closure of resignation: the dancer lands gracefully, transforming "the leap into a gait" as though perfectly at home in the world again (ibid.: 34). One returns to the world, not in the closure of resignation, but to a life with meaning. Faith is constituted by the double movements of the dance, always leaving the world only to reclaim it with meaning. What makes this return possible is a shift: to *trust* God completely for the meaning in one's life. The dancer who thus returns has already absorbed all the sorrow of despair and the closure of resignation, but the possibility of meaning has been restored through the eternal – "by virtue of the fact that for God everything is possible" (ibid.: 39).

If faith were only for a future life, it would not be faith – it must be for *this life* (ibid.: 17). It is because faith is for this life that meaning can be restored – otherwise one has only *resigned* – since meaning is constituted in temporality, according to each individual's life, through our worldly commitments, our history, our relations. This is not an act of self-mastery (which led to despair), since trust in God requires that one relinquishes the project of one's own self-fashioning. Faith is to accept what we are, and to rest "transparently in God" (Kierkegaard 1849: 82). This is the fulfillment of the task of the self, the condition in which despair has been "completely rooted out" (ibid.: 14), which allows for the individual constitution of meaning in each person's life, as the task of the self is embraced.

Notes

1 Kierkegaard's authorship poses a challenge of interpretation, since he wrote several of his most important books under pseudonyms. The use of pseudonyms was common enough in Denmark at the time, though Kierkegaard uses the device not simply to write under another name, but to write from a different perspective. He denies, however, that these pseudonymous perspectives represent his own point of view – these are not his works, and he insists that they be counted as separate from what he wrote in his own name. He writes: "So in the pseudonymous works there is not a single word that is mine, I have no opinion about these works except as a third person, no knowledge of their meaning except as a reader" (Kierkegaard 1844: 551). For our purposes, if we gently bracket this larger interpretive issue, it will not distort our understanding of his account of the problem of meaning.

2 The journal entry is written a year and a day after his mother's death (31 July 1834), in the same year he came to believe that he and his six siblings would all die before the age of 34. He discovered that when his father was a child, as a desperately poor and lonely shepherd in Jutland, he was so miserable he stood alone on the heath and cursed God. His father went on to become extremely rich, with a family of seven children. Yet because of what he had done, he was certain his riches were an ironic punishment from God, and that he would live long enough to watch all his

children die before they reached the age of 34. Kierkegaard was convinced his father was right; in fact, his mother and five of his siblings died prematurely. This realization shook him to the core, and likely explains the urgency galvanizing him in the years approaching his 34th birthday; but it also is instructive for understanding why the question of meaning personally came to grip him.

3 There is a remarkable similarity between St Thomas' treatment of the vicious extremes of hope, and Kierkegaard's account of despair. St Thomas places hope as the mean between *desperatio* (the abandonment of hope) and *praesumptio* (the arrogance of one who relies on God's mercy without the effort of trying to become worthy). In Kierkegaard's account, these two extremes roughly become weakness and defiance (respectively), and collectively constitute the existential condition of despair – remarkably, there is no evidence that Kierkegaard was familiar with St Thomas' view; see Bernier 2015: 62–64.

22 Marx and the meaning of life

AMY E. WENDLING

Introduction

Marx's work has important implications for understanding human suffering and so for the meaning of human life. Capitalism promises to end suffering through a rising standard of living for some. But it does so at a cost, by actively causing suffering for others. Capitalism thus requires some to be comfortable while others are miserable. Those who accept this feel that individual economic gain is a suitable trade off for actively causing human suffering.

Some do, in fact, accept this. But many do not. Capitalism relies on both groups: on the predators and on the compliant. To accomplish this it circulates a good many false beliefs. For Marx, relying on false belief is itself an important form of human suffering: this form of suffering often goes on without explicit awareness on the part of the sufferer.

The removal of false belief, in itself, does not distinguish Marx from other philosophers. Plato and Kant, Hegel and Descartes: all wish to escape the images on the cave's walls. What distinguishes Marx is the connection between the project of living without false belief and the question of human suffering. Once defined properly, human suffering, quite simply, must be alleviated in any and all possible forms. Marx's philosophy seeks to clear the obstacles to this alleviation. A large part of his task will be to reformulate the ideas of the possible and impossible, since the limits of these will have been determined by false belief.

Judeo-Christian peoples merge their narrative of suffering with a narrative of redemption: too frequently, too swiftly, and without proper differentiation among types of suffering. As we shall see, even Marx struggles with the narrative of suffering and redemption. However, Marx's most important questions surface only when we separate the narrative of suffering from that of redemption. What forms of suffering, both bodily and spiritual, do not redeem? What if some forms of suffering not only do not redeem, but hobble and curtail the sufferer's possibilities? What if suffering is not simply senseless, but pernicious and damaging? And, finally, what if the most acute sufferings are tied directly to the bourgeoisie's rising standard of living, and so to the very domination it exercises? That is, what if all of the most acute human sufferings are linked?

Ruling idea one: undifferentiated suffering

The science of undoing false social belief has its own terminology. Marx speaks of ideology; following him, Gramsci speaks of hegemony. No term, however, captures the idea Marx seeks to explicate here as perfectly as that of a "ruling idea." The term is his own from *The German Ideology*, and so that is the term that I shall favor here.

For Marx, the question of false belief is connected to the question of material suffering because human ideas are dependent, more or less directly, on the systems of material production that found any given society. A society that operates with a structure of domination will produce a series of beliefs that mirror this structure.

These beliefs are what Marx calls the ruling ideas. He writes:

> [T]he ideas of the ruling class are in every epoch the ruling ideas: i.e. the class which is the ruling *material* force of society, is at the same time its ruling *intellectual* force. The class which has the means of material production at its disposal, has control at the same time over the means of mental production, so that thereby, generally speaking, the ideas of those who lack the means of mental production are subject to it. The ruling ideas are nothing more than the ideal expression of the dominant material relationships, the dominant material relationships grasped as ideas; hence of the relationships which make the one class the ruling one; therefore, the ideas of its dominance.
>
> (Marx and Engels 1846: 172–73)

Once ruling ideas become socially dominant, not only the working classes but also the bourgeoisie are in their grip. Even something manifestly untrue can function as a ruling idea, particularly once it is linked to other, complementary ruling ideas in a network of false belief. Furthermore, ruling ideas may contradict one another so long as each still serves to shore up the nexus of domination.

The bourgeoisie produces many ruling ideas about human suffering. This essay explores five of them. The first of these is the idea of undifferentiated suffering.

Two conditions make it possible to regard individual economic gain as a suitable trade off for actively causing human suffering. First, the failure to make individual economic gains has to be seen as a kind of suffering. Second, before alleviating suffering can be traded for worsening suffering, all suffering has to be of the same kind.

The first condition gets its power from a society in which the poor are actively penalized, and in which they have few social networks on which to rely: the kind of society portrayed in Engels's (1845) text *The Condition of the Working Class in England*. In this society, the failure to make individual economic gains, such as a minimum wage, can really be the difference between life and death.

But the concept of "individual economic gain" can also be used to describe the difference between earning $105,000 and $75,000 a year, a raise that behavioral economists have identified as a kind of "happiness threshold" (Kahneman and Deaton 2010). The failure to get a minimum wage and the failure to get this $30,000 raise are clearly not the same kind of suffering. They can appear to be such only because both are classified under the leveling ideas of "economic gain" or a "rising standard of living."

This sets the stage for the second condition, which actively falsifies the nature of suffering, treating it as if it were all of the same kind: as if even small gains in comfort could compensate for great offenses to human bodies and consciousness. Discerning differences between types of suffering, and ranking them with respect to one another, will be required in order to unwind the ruling idea of undifferentiated suffering. We will also need to distinguish between suffering, which has an existential dimension, and "mere" pain or discomfort.

Elementary analysis will show that even very excellent human comforts cannot excuse things like slavery and death. They may not even be able to excuse things like long work hours. If more of us are to reject the trade-off between individual economic gain and actively causing human suffering, we will need to be able to see this.

Ruling idea two: bodily suffering

Many of the stock marketing images used to deploy suffering are distinctly bodily images. In the United States, advertising on television and social media offers spectacles of injured and hungry animals, or spectacles of hungry people, especially children, usually in other countries even though the children in our own also suffer from food insecurity. In response, we are asked to write a check that sends monetary aid. Such aid is inevitably quantified as a small amount, comparatively, in the context of the check writer's resources.

These commercials are run alongside ads for snacks masquerading as health foods, faster Internet providers, and credit score services: as a thing to buy among others. This confirms the first ruling idea of undifferentiated suffering. All the discomforts are positioned as if they were relatively equal in weight, both to each other and to the suffering children and animals. Actually, the costs of the other advertised commodities could be traded many times over for the pittance asked to help suffering children or animals. The ads make this explicit: the viewer can help "for the price of a cup of coffee a day."

Clearly, the sufferings of hunger and injury are painful. They have, in addition, an existential dimension that is not to be minimized. However, the spectacle of hungry or injured children or animals functions in an insidious way, abetting the spectator's ability to look away from the very economic structures that produce hunger and injury.

Firstly, the viewer is asked to take responsibility for the hunger and injury only by producing a small amount of money, not by changing his standard of living, lifestyle, or beliefs, or by recognizing that the economic systems that enabled his wealth may make much money blood money. The very smallness of the amount illustrates how little such people and animals' health and welfare is worth. This reassures the spectator of his great comparative economic wealth, both making him feel better about himself and threatening him with what might happen should he lose this wealth. He is allowed to indulge his shopping instinct to boot.

Secondly, such images encourage the spectator to focus on bodily suffering rather than on moral, spiritual, intellectual, and imaginative suffering. Discomforts that capitalism easily alleviates for the wealthy, bodily discomforts in particular, become the exclusive focus of his attention.

Higher-order suffering can even result directly from comfort-seeking behaviors. I replace the air-conditioning unit at my house from one that cools the house to 78 degrees Fahrenheit to one that cools it to precisely 72 degrees, but for two years afterward, I struggle with anxiety about paying off the debt I have thereby incurred. I have traded comfort for anxiety. The air conditioner is felt to be a need, while the anxiety remains invisible as a cost. A form of suffering that is both existential and bodily, anxiety expresses itself in ways that, while seldom well hidden from the sufferer, are notoriously disconnected from their true causes.

The basic structure is addiction, a contemporary form of the suffering Marx called alienation. Indeed, addictions to shopping and sufferings from debt are among what psychoanalyst Thomas Svolos calls "the new symptoms" (Svolos 2017: 113–25).

While Marx never forgot the bodily pain of the proletariat, he was also concerned with its higher-order sufferings. The proletariat worked only to live, and to live just in the limited sense of continuing its biological facticity, a situation Marx also called alienation. But alienation was not simply limited to inadequate food and a short life span. Alienation encompassed wounds inflicted on the proletarian intelligence, imagination, and spirit.

For these reasons, Marx's famous 1844 account of alienation is also a comprehensive theory of human suffering (Marx 1844: 71–77). Marx charts four moments: the proletarian is alienated from the object she creates, from the activity she performs, from participating in creating the notion of human nature, and from other human beings.

The proletarian is alienated from the object she creates. Others use it and not her. Material deprivation is, of course, a kind of physical pain and suffering. But it is also a higher-order suffering. The pleasure that I get from consuming or using an object that I have created is different and higher in quality than the pleasure I get from consuming or using an object that someone else has created. Pleasure is not simply consumption, but the back and forth between subject and object, between imagination and the material world, that occurs in using something designed by oneself. The pain, then, of being separated from objects that one has created is not simply the loss of the object, but the loss of one's intentionality in the creation. The shopper repetitively consumes prefabricated commodities whose precise pleasures are designed for him both in form and substance: all to no avail, since the very thing he seeks cannot be found in such an object.

This is closely related to the second moment of alienation, in which the proletarian is alienated from the activity of creation itself. Instead of amplifying her capacities for innovation and imagination, her labor becomes boring and monotonous. Since longer hours are spent at this boring and monotonous activity than at any other kind, she learns to hate and disavow her own activity. She no longer enjoys her labor experience, not simply because it is dangerous or hard, but because it does not actualize her abilities to enjoy it while she is doing it. Against such a backdrop, all labor is a kind of suffering: a ruling idea that exploits its association with pre-modern narratives that link labor and suffering. Once this idea rules, I feel free only in not-labor. I seek an activity that is aggressively coded as non-labor. To be is to shop.

While the first two forms of alienation thus have clear comfort dimensions, they also have higher-order dimensions. The third and fourth forms of alienation are both exclusively higher-order forms of suffering. They are also, respectively, the subjects of the next two sections.

Ruling idea three: ontological suffering

As Simon Skempton observes, the third moment of Marx's account of alienation, the idea of species being, is not well understood (Skempton 2010: 101). In English, the word "species" invokes the discourse of biology, and is loaded up with the idea of a fixed and determined human essence. But Marx actually has the opposite of this in mind. He believes that the human essence is malleable, and takes this malleability explicitly as its own object in a creative act of redefining the human genus. Marx's idea thereby widens the scope of the Aristotelian idea of a second nature.

In the third form of alienation, proletarian and bourgeois alike accept ontologies of the human being amenable to capitalism. One ontology of the human that capitalism tends to highlight and prefer is suffering itself. To be human is to suffer.

Marx's thought worries about the identification of humanity with suffering because doing so forms an excuse for capital's exploitation of the working classes, and even an excuse for capitalist alienation. As a concept, defining humans as beings who suffer relies on the idea of undifferentiated suffering. What distinguishes one form of suffering from another becomes less important if suffering is what unifies human experience. In practice, identifying human beings with suffering risks enabling the worst forms of suffering, since the worse the suffering, the more authentic the human experience.

And so, apart from the minor bodily discomforts that must be eradicated at all costs, capitalism likes for us to think that all really terrible suffering is necessary. When we regard suffering as a part of what it means to be human, this plays right into capitalism's hands. So long as suffering defines the human condition, capitalism need not acknowledge that many very terrible forms of suffering are historical artifacts that it creates and exacerbates. We are also unlikely either to discern which sufferings are most grievously unjust or, should we discern them, to agitate for their removal, since such suffering has become pivotal to our definition of what the human is.

Once humans are identified with suffering, it paves the way for definitions of nature and human nature that extend the capitalist project. Nature is miserly and only has a limited number of resources; so say Malthus, Smith, and Burke. Material wealth for a few can only be bought at the cost of suffering for the many. In light of this, human nature is individualistic and competitive.

Similarly, some can live without illusion – that is, with philosophy – but, as Plato affirms, this requires leisure. Leisure is only possible for a few who are relieved from their work duties by the entitlements of slavery or wage slavery: it will hardly be possible for all humans. To those humans for whom it is not possible, Stoicism says: suffering is an inherent part of the human condition, unavoidable, and to be integrated rather than alleviated. Suffering redeems, adds Christianity. To be human is to labor, says Locke. Yuck, says Nietzsche; but then his project risks reinvigorating the preceding Greco-Roman value system.

Reconfigured into the forms most amenable to capitalist exploitation, these forms of thought are entrenched. That they contradict one another makes the attempt to unwind them harder still, as one can trade Plato for Locke, or vice versa, without abandoning the nexus. And Marx's demand is nothing less than that we should abandon them all.

Suffering human nature, the natural world it responds to, and the possibilities for human society that it enables or refuses: all are illusory forms of thought that falsely define the limits of the possible and the impossible. For Marx, the meaning of human life, then, is to remake human nature and, with it, the limits of the possible and the impossible. Like many philosophies, his is a project of freedom.

Ruling idea four: predatory suffering

The fourth ruling idea reactivates a classical idea, born of slavery, that domination conditions leisure, and that leisure makes truth and freedom possible for some. In response, Marx does not simply argue that this is not moral, though that is certainly true. He argues that it is not possible.

Freedom for some not only should not be bought at the expense of freedom for others: it cannot be bought at this expense. Domination itself produces illusory thinking, and for everyone. As domination escalates, so does illusion. Unwinding illusory thinking will also require unwinding domination: the great *modus tollens* of Marxist theory.

Marx thought that alienation cut human beings off from one another, making us see one another as hostile competitors in a world of scarcity, allowing for little solidarity. This loss reduces the possibilities for friendship, love, and other forms of social feeling. It separates us from others and burdens us with a constant and escalating mistrust. It makes empathy impossible. At best, relationship is a détente. When the *zoon politikon* becomes the *homo economicus*, she finds herself totally alone.

Such failures of relationship are among the higher-order sufferings. The relationships of the dominator survive no better than those of the dominated: in fact, they may be worse. New empirical work on the loss of empathy in powerful persons corroborates Marx's insight here (Useem 2017). A team of neuroscientists tested the motor resonance or "mirroring" response, thought to be active in empathy, of a group of high-power participants (Hogeveen et al. 2014). The motor resonance of the high-power group decreased relative to other groups. Dacher Keltner's work documents what may be an allied phenomenon, studying how power, once acquired, leads to "empathy defects," "diminished moral sentiments," "self-serving impulsivity," "incivility," "disrespect," and "narratives of exceptionalism" (Keltner 2016: 101).

Understanding all sufferings to be the sufferings of physical comfort allows the dominator to escape the truth that he also suffers at the hands of the capitalist system of production. His higher-order sufferings become invisible or unimportant to the concept of suffering: and, with this, also invisible to him. In fact, he suffers from domination itself. The acute sufferings of the dominated and the most poignant sufferings of the dominator, different though they may be, are linked.

Conclusion: teleological suffering

If capitalist thought forms still allowed us to experience empathy, it would be easy enough to get caught up in the examples from Engels's *History of the Working Class in England*. Typhus. Rickets. Barely enough cubic feet of air, in workplaces and at home, to breathe, and then polluted by coal in the cities. Breasts dripping with milk at a factory job, with an infant – no doubt hungry, and often drugged to abate the effects of this – left at home in the care of a five-year-old child. Punishments of the workhouse that include getting locked in a closet for days, sexual abuse, and limited food of poor quality.

We could update the list for our own working poor: inadequate toilet breaks while at work (Linder 1998); malnutrition, including both hunger and obesity (Albritton 2009); disproportionate incarceration, including at immigrant detention centers; and, continued difficulties around parental leave and quality childcare, especially for those working wage-labor jobs.

These sufferings experienced by the working classes were and are something more than mere pain. As Engels put it, "insecurity is even more demoralizing then poverty" (Engels 1845: 131). And so the suffering is not only pain in the breasts but anguish and frustration at the inability to feed one's infant while also working to support oneself; or a fuller than usual table, but the anxiety of not knowing when the present cycle of work opportunity will end; or steady work, but accompanied by the fear of never knowing when immigration officials will appear to put you in a detention center.

At the same time as the sufferings of the proletarian class worsened, enormous wealth was created. Scientific manipulations of nature became the norm. Legal codes became a significant way of negotiating power for the propertied classes. Unlike those who simply celebrated these achievements of the bourgeois social class, Marx noted that they were grounded in the sufferings of the proletariat. Marx's main criticism of this structure is its injustice: it produces great wealth, leisure, and beauty for some at the expense of hobbling, stunting, and torturing many others. For this reason, individual economic gain is an insufficient excuse for continuing the sufferings of the proletariat. And so Marx seeks for a different kind of explanation. Political revolution redeems the suffering proletariat. We might call such an explanation for suffering teleological.

The problem with teleological suffering is that it functions as an excuse for absolutely anything. It can even function perversely: as cause for worsening human suffering in order to hasten a revolutionary outcome. And though Marx utterly rejects the palliatives of Christianity, in which earthly sufferings are redeemed in heaven, this rejection does not extend so far as the teleological structure itself. The issue worsens when many political revolutions arrive, though they were neither where nor as Marx envisioned. In light of this, the revolution that would justify suffering functions only as a deferred or postponed promise: little better, in the end, than heaven.

The explanation of teleological suffering, be it Christian or be it Marxist, is very valuable to the bourgeois world, so long as it takes the form of a deferred promise. It explains suffering, but it doesn't require us to do anything about it: or, at the very least, what is to be done is unclear. In this way, teleological suffering itself functions as a ruling idea.

23 Mill and the meaning of life

FRANS SVENSSON

I

In the beginning of his essay *Utility of Religion*, John Stuart Mill maintains that

> [i]f religion, or any particular form of it, is true, its usefulness follows without other proof. If to know authentically in what order of things, under what government of the universe it is our destiny to live, were not useful, it is difficult to imagine what could be considered so.
>
> (Mill 1874: 403)

But the evidence against the truth of religion is steadily increasing, according to Mill. It has therefore become time for us to ask: what good is "the belief in religion, considered as a mere persuasion, apart from the question of its truth" (ibid.: 405)? Given the utilitarian framework within which Mill is working, there is but one thing that is desirable as an end in itself, namely happiness, or, what for Mill comes down to the same thing, welfare. The question he proposes that we should ask thus concerns in what respects, if any, religion, when "considered as a mere persuasion, apart from the question of its truth," is "indispensable for the ... welfare of mankind" (ibid.)? There are two parts to this question, according to Mill. On the one hand, we can ask what the *social* benefits of (belief in) religion may be. And on the other hand, we can ask what religion does for the *individual* – "what influence [it has] in improving and ennobling individual human nature," and thus in promoting the individual's happiness or well-being (ibid.: 406).

After having rejected several possible suggestions for ways in which religion may be indispensable from a social perspective, Mill goes on to suggest that there is one important respect in which its usefulness to the individual cannot plausibly be denied. Because of the many flaws or shortcomings of our earthly lives – e.g. their brevity, their cosmic insignificance, the disappointments and suffering that they involve – there is, he says, "a craving for higher things" (ibid.: 419). In order to find meaning or purpose, or to maintain a serious interest, in our lives, we need conceptions of something greater, more perfect, and longer lasting than ourselves, with which we can connect in our thoughts and feelings. And religion, in its many different manifestations, indeed supplies such conceptions, according to Mill. He writes thus:

> Belief in a God or Gods, and in a life after death, becomes the canvas on which every mind, according to its capacity, covers with such ideal pictures as it can either invent or copy. In that other life each hopes to find the good which he has failed to find on earth, or the better which is suggested to him by the good which on earth he has partially seen and known.
>
> (Ibid.)

Mill clearly thinks that the satisfaction of our "craving for higher things" is crucial to individual happiness. For one thing, it will protect us against suffering from experiences of existential despair or emptiness. For another, the cultivation of thoughts and feelings directed towards things "grander and more beautiful than we see realized in the prose of human life" is itself, in Mill's view, an essential element in a flourishing or fully happy life for us as humans (ibid.).[1] But even if our craving, as Mill puts it, "finds its most obvious satisfaction in religion," it does not follow that religion, even in this respect, is indispensable for human happiness or welfare (ibid.). There still remains the possibility that there might be some other alternative, one without any supernatural elements, which, if cultivated to the same degree that religion often is or at least traditionally has been, would satisfy our "craving for higher things" equally well as, and in some respects perhaps even better than, religion. And Mill proposes that there indeed exists an alternative that is, upon reflection, not only equal but superior to religion with respect to satisfying the relevant craving. This alternative is humanism, or as he (a bit curiously) often refers to it, the Religion of Humanity.[2]

In Section III below, I will sketch the main features of Mill's humanistic alternative, and also present the two reasons that he offers for thinking that humanism is indeed superior to religion. Then, in Section IV, I will consider three different questions that might be raised in relation to Mill's humanism. I will end, in Section V, with a few concluding remarks. First of all, however, in Section II, it may be worthwhile to say a few more things about why it matters for Mill whether there is some alternative to religion that could satisfy our "craving for higher things." Something should also be said about one thing Mill is *not* directly concerned with in his discussion of how our craving can best be met or satisfied, namely an objective meaning of life.

II

There are at least two reasons why the question of whether there is an alternative to religion that can satisfy our "craving for higher things" is important to Mill. One of them we have encountered already, namely to establish whether religion is or is not indispensable for human happiness. The second and, I take it, more important reason, however, is that it matters normatively, in Mill's view, whether there is such an alternative. According to Mill's utilitarian ethic, happiness is the only thing that is desirable for its own sake. And because of this, happiness is also, according to Mill, the source of all practical or normative reasons. If there is an alternative that can satisfy our "craving for higher things" even better, or to an even higher degree, than religion (in any of its forms), then that alternative is also more conducive to individual happiness or welfare. We would thus have stronger reason to cultivate that alternative in our lives than to cultivate belief in religion.

We should notice that Mill is not concerned, at least not directly, with the question of what, if anything, may constitute the *objective* meaning, point or purpose of life. If there were anything such as an objective meaning of life, then it would presumably be useful for us to know about it in order to be able to make as fully informed judgments as possible about how we ought to live our lives. But whether that objective meaning could be turned into a conception, the cultivation of which would be capable of effectively satisfying our "craving for higher things," would have to be investigated separately. Suppose, for example, that "we learned that we were being raised to provide food for other creatures fond of human flesh, who planned to turn us into cutlets before we got too stringy" (Nagel 1971: 721). This would, it seems, be an important piece of information to take into account when we deliberate about what we can do to promote the welfare of our own species. It might, for instance, suggest that we need to find some way of protecting ourselves against the human-eaters if or when they come for us. But it would not constitute very promising material for developing a "high conception" that could help us maintain a serious interest in our lives.

III

In Mill's view, we need not "travel beyond the boundaries of the world which we inhabit" to find "a large enough object to satisfy any reasonable demand for grandeur of aspiration" (Mill 1874: 420). We might turn instead to humanity, or to "the idealization of our earthly life, the cultivation of a high conception of what *it* may be made" (ibid., emphasis in the original). It seems plausible that some amount of idealization is indeed needed here in order for Mill's proposal to get off the ground. The history of mankind does, after all, include many examples of lives that are quite far from constituting models of inspiration and awe. In *Auguste Comte and Positivism*, Mill therefore suggests that we should conceive of "Humanity, or Mankind, as composed, in the past, solely of those who, in every age and variety of position, have played their part worthily in life. It is only as thus restricted that the aggregate of our species becomes an object deserving our veneration" (Mill 1865: 334). Once we have a suitably idealized conception of humanity clearly before our minds, however, the idea of playing a part in humanity's progression – of, as it were, continuing the work of the great benefactors of mankind in the past (Mill mentions Socrates and Christ, among others) – is one that could acquire great power over our thought and feelings, according to Mill. It could make us "see in the earthly destiny of mankind the playing out of a great drama, or the action of a prolonged epic," as "all the generations of mankind become indissolubly united into a single image" (ibid.). Mill even suggests that humanity needs us (which an altogether perfect Being presumably does not!). In the "great drama" of humanity, each of us has a role to carve out and play as well as we can.

But even if our "craving for higher things," as per Mill's proposal, can indeed find its satisfaction not only in religion but also in humanism, it may still be asked if there is any reason to think that humanism can satisfy our craving more effectively, or to a higher degree, than religion. Mill thinks that there is. First of all, he argues, humanism

> is disinterested. It carries the thoughts and feelings out of self, and fixes them on an unselfish object, loved and pursued as an end for its own sake. The religions which deal in promises and threats regarding a future life, do exactly the opposite: they fasten down the thoughts to the person's own posthumous interests; they tempt him to regard the performance of his duties to others mainly as a means to his own personal salvation.
>
> (Mill 1874: 422)

One advantage of humanism, in Mill's view, is thus that, in contrast to religion, it is free from any temptation to identify with its object out of concern primarily for oneself and one's own good. The cultivation of a high conception of humanity and its potential, instead involves the nurturing of thoughts and feelings directed at something "grander and more beautiful" than ourselves solely for *its* own sake. And such elevated or noble thoughts and feelings are themselves important elements of human happiness.

Furthermore, humanism does not require anything such as "torpidity," or a "positive twist in the intellectual faculties," on the part of its followers, whereas religion, according to Mill, does (ibid.: 423). In particular, Mill suggests that no intellectually alert and honest person "should be able without misgiving to go on ascribing absolute perfection to the author and ruler of so clumsily made and capriciously governed a creation as this planet and the life of its inhabitants" (ibid.).[3] Since humanism does not contain any supernatural elements, and in particular no assumptions about an altogether perfect creator and ruler of this world, it avoids this problem entirely.

IV

Several questions can of course be raised regarding Mill's humanism. Here I will briefly consider three such questions. The first two concern potential drawbacks or disadvantages of humanism in comparison to religion, whereas the third instead concerns motivation.

1

One question that someone could ask is whether humanism, in contrast to religion, might not leave our "craving for higher things" at least partly unsatisfied due to its inability to make sense of our lives in relation to the universe as a whole. As for instance Thomas Nagel points out (without any particular reference to Mill): "Since the universe cannot be identified with the human world, [humanism and its relatives] do not really give us a way of incorporating a conception of the universe as a whole into our lives and how we think of them" (Nagel 2010: 11–12). Many forms of religion, on the other hand, do offer conceptions of "some kind of all-encompassing mind or spiritual principle ... [which] is the foundation of the existence of the universe, of the natural order, of value, and of our existence, nature, and purpose" (ibid.: 5). Insofar as being able to conceive or think of ourselves as existing in harmony with the universe as a whole is part of what our "craving for higher things" involves, the relevant forms of religion would seem to have a clear and important advantage over humanism.

But thinking of ourselves as existing in harmony with the universe as a whole is *not* an essential part of our "craving for higher things," according to Mill.[4] History, he argues, teaches us that people have indeed been able to develop and derive meaning or purpose in their lives from e.g. a high conception of their *country*. And if people have been able to do that, then why would they not be able to do the same with respect to the, in comparison with their country, larger object of humanity or mankind? Humanism does certainly take us outside of ourselves as individuals. Furthermore, even "if individual life is short," as Mill puts it, "the life of the species is not short; its indefinite duration is practically equivalent to endlessness," and it is, in addition, "combined with indefinite capability of improvement" (Mill 1874: 420). So why should it not be possible to develop this into something that, if properly cultivated, would be capable of satisfying our "craving for higher things"?

2

Humanism, as we have seen, is meant to constitute a way of meeting or satisfying our "craving for higher things," without having to "travel beyond the boundaries of the world which we inhabit." Humanism does not contain or hold out any prospect to the individual of a life after this one, but instead maintains that a high conception of humanity's potential "offers ... a large enough object to satisfy any reasonable demand for grandeur of aspiration" (ibid.: 420). But, someone could ask, does not the absence of any prospect of an afterlife constitute a respect in which humanism is really at a disadvantage when compared to those forms of religion that do hold out such a prospect?

Is not the prospect of a life after death quite important in order for people to maintain a serious interest in their lives?

In response to this question, Mill suggests that a further lesson from history is "that mankind can perfectly well do without the belief in a heaven" (ibid.: 427). As evidence for this, Mill on the one hand refers to the ancient Greeks, who, he writes, "neither enjoyed life less, nor feared death more, than other people," even though they "had anything but a tempting idea of a future state" (ibid.). On the other hand, he refers to Buddhists, whose "creed recognizes many modes of punishment in ... future ... lives, by the transmigration of the soul into new bodies of men or animals," while "the blessing for Heaven which it proposes as a reward ... is annihilation [or] the cessation, at least, of all conscious or separate existence" (ibid.). Neither of these examples is perhaps entirely uncontroversial. But let us simply assume here that Mill is right. It could still be asked whether *humanism* can allow us to get on "perfectly well ... without the belief in a heaven." Mill thinks it clearly can. By cultivating humanism, he argues, we will come to identify with the feelings, thoughts, and deeds of other people to such an extent that any concern that we might have had before about whether we will ourselves move on to another life after this one, will become insignificant to us. Rather, we will "up to the hour of death live ideally in the life of those who are to follow" us (ibid. 426).

3

The third and final question that I shall raise here is this: Is the cultivation of humanism, in Mill's view, meant to bring with it an exclusive concern in each person for the good of mankind? Is the good of mankind meant to become our sole motive, end or objective in everything that we do? Mill's answer to this question is clearly no. Humanism is rather supposed to be compatible with – or, perhaps better, to encourage – what Mill calls *individuality*.[5] As he famously argues in chapter 3 of *On Liberty*, it is indeed a necessary constituent of a humanly happy life that one makes one's own choices, using one's "faculties of perception, judgment, discriminative feeling, mental activity, and even moral preference," instead of just imitating what other people do (Mill 1859: 262). Thus, if humanism were *in*compatible with individuality, then it seems that would, in Mill's view, constitute a decisive objection to it. Instead we may perhaps think of humanism, as Mill conceives of it, as involving the adoption of a kind of general narrative framework for one's life. Within this framework, the exercise of individuality in the shaping of one's life will acquire meaning or purpose in virtue of its being part of the "great drama" of humanity.

V

It is time to sum up. While for many of us earthly life is certainly not only a vale of tears, it is, Mill suggests, still flawed in important respects. As a result of this, there is in us "a craving for higher things," which "finds its most obvious satisfaction in religion." But there is also a non-religious (or non-supernatural) alternative, according to Mill, which, if cultivated to the same degree that belief in religion has often been, can satisfy our craving just as well as, and in at least two respects even better than, religion. The alternative that Mill has in mind is humanism, or as we saw him put it, "the idealization of our earthly life, the cultivation of a high conception of what *it* may be made." There are at least two reasons why humanism is superior to religion, in Mill's view. First of all, in contrast to religion, humanism does not provide any temptation to identify with its object mainly as a way of securing personal benefits in a life after this one. And secondly, humanism (again in contrast to religion) does not commit us to any intellectually unsettling belief in an altogether perfect Being who is supposed to be the author and ruler of such an imperfect creation as the world that we presently inhabit. Since Mill believes that happiness (or welfare) constitutes the source of all normative reasons, and the satisfaction of the "craving for higher things" is crucial for a happy life, it follows that there is stronger reason for us to cultivate humanism than religion.[6]

Notes

1 In Mill's own account, it was one of the "marked effects" that his thinking underwent as a result of the depression that he suffered in 1826, that he "for the first time, gave its proper place, among the prime necessities of human well-being, to the internal culture of the individual [...] I had now learnt by experience," he continues, "that the passive susceptibilities needed to be cultivated as well as the active capacities, and required to be nourished and enriched, as well as guided" (Mill 1873: 145ff.) And in the light of this, Mill suggests that his reading of, in particular, Wordsworth's poetry came to have an important impact on him. "Wordsworth's poems," he writes, "expressed, not mere outward beauty, but states of feeling, and of thought coloured by feeling, under the excitement of beauty. They seemed to express the very culture of the feelings, which I was in quest of" (ibid.: 151).

2 Mill maintains that even though humanism does not contain any supernatural elements, it still meets the essential conditions for constituting a religion (Mill 1874: 422; 1865: 332f.). I will not pause here to consider the reasons that he offers for this. Furthermore from now I shall set aside the label Religion of Humanity and instead stick simply to humanism.

3 For a classic statement of this kind of criticism of religion, see Hume 1779: parts X and XI.

4 Nor, I should say, does Nagel think that it is. (Nagel does not seem to think that there is anything such as a general craving for higher things at all. Rather, he suggests that some people have such a craving, while others do not.)

5 See, in particular, Mill 1859: ch. 3; but also Mill 1865: 335–39.

6 I am grateful to Paul Carron, Daan Evers, and Lisa Hecht for providing comments on an earlier draft of this chapter.

24 Nietzsche and the meaning of life

RAYMOND ANGELO BELLIOTTI

Although acknowledging that no guarantees are manifest, Nietzsche stakes his faith in the union of robust will to power and a maximally affirmative attitude toward life ("amor fati"). After advancing and defending interpretations of robust, moderate, and attenuated wills to power, and connecting these versions to prospects for constructing meaning in human life, both the insights and shortcomings of Nietzsche's account blossom. Nietzsche's celebration of grand aristocrats striving for lofty, personal ideals coalesces uneasily with the attainment of a salutary sense of community required for broader, human development.

In his most famous parable, Nietzsche announces the death of God (Nietzsche 1882: §125). The allegory transmits several messages. The forum is the market place – the center of commerce, the focus of modern life, and the symbol of dominant culture. The bearer of the news is a madman: to deny God's efficacy in a Europe dominated by Christian religion would strike the masses as deranged. Moreover, the madman, already stigmatized as an aberration within society, with his lantern is the bearer of special insight; the distinction between madman and genius may be thinner than commonly supposed. The news itself is not a banal assertion of atheism but rather an observation of historical trajectory: the notion of God either is or will soon be unworthy of belief even if the masses are currently unaware that cultural conditions no longer support fervent religious belief and practice. The development of science and technology spawns explanations that were previously supplied only by robust belief in God, his powers, and his Grand Design. Faith in God in earlier decades had energized everyday life, but that conviction is weakening and is rapidly transforming into merely a series of institutional religious routines and rituals animated more by habit than by fervent passion.

The dramatic, poetic conclusion that we have wiped "away the entire horizon" underscores Nietzsche's contention that without zealous religious belief and practice, our standards of truth, foundations of meaning, and understanding of transcendent redemption evaporate: without God the world of Being collapses, and only the world of Becoming, which precludes inherent meaning, remains. We have all "murdered" God in the sense that we constitute a culture in which integrity, intellectual cleanliness, and pursuit of truth undermine continued, passionate religious belief. The "scientific conscience," which in its quest for objectivity, absolute truth, and universal application is a sublimated form of the "Christian conscience," fuels the death of God. Thus, with typical irony, Nietzsche claims that God was "murdered" by the very Christian morality that was originally needed to invoke Him (ibid.: §357).

Glad tidings?

As recognition of "the death of God" gains currency, Nietzsche anticipates that human beings will acknowledge that the cosmos is inherently meaningless. Accordingly, no *meaning of life* awaits our discovery: human existence as such lacks meaning. Moreover, whether human beings can construct fragile *meaning in their lives* becomes problematic: individual human beings lack guarantees that they can accrue meaning within social life.

The death of God extinguishes the source of foundational meaning and engenders the specter of nihilism. "Nihilism" is the condition of the spirit which occurs after we recognize that our highest values have devalued themselves. With the further recognition that there are no foundations for inherent meaning, values seem arbitrary, goals lack purpose, and horizons of understanding wither away. How shall we reconstruct ourselves without God? What new myths will be necessary? Must we not become our own gods?

Nietzsche is concerned with the links between culture and a tragic view of life. The specter of nihilism suggests that the most critical human values and meanings are up for grabs, and Nietzsche cannot guarantee that human beings will respond energetically to the possibilities opened within the nihilistic moment. For him, the loss of a secure foundation for our dearest substantive beliefs suggests that we must ultimately choose under conditions of radical uncertainty. Human reason cannot redeem our predicament. Some of us will shrink back in horror. We will resign ourselves to bitterness and self-pity, and conclude that all is lost ("pathetic nihilism"). Some of us will refuse to relinquish the fantasy of a transcendent world and blissful afterlife ("passive nihilism") (Nietzsche 1883–85: pt II, "The Soothsayer"). Others will accept cosmic meaninglessness and use it as a point of departure for grand creativity ("active nihilism"). Having "killed" God by developing science and technology, and by creating the social conditions that provide compelling explanations for natural phenomena that in previous ages were explainable only by reference to God, we must now come to grips with the aftershock of our cultural accomplishment (see e.g. Nietzsche 1882: §§108, 283, 343, 382).

Nietzsche is an unapologetic active nihilist. Embracing cosmic meaninglessness as the springboard to creative possibilities; reveling in radical contingency; relishing the human condition fully while recognizing its tragic dimensions; re-creating the self; and rejoicing in liberation from imposed values and meanings are at the heart of active nihilism. Active nihilism places paramount value on this life and this world, since there are no others

The criterion of power grounds Nietzsche's version of active nihilism: exertion, struggle, and suffering are at the core of overcoming obstacles, and it is only through overcoming obstacles that human beings experience – truly feel – their power. For those courageous enough to cheerfully reject their conviction in the divine, the death of God promises creative opportunities. An active nihilism can rejuvenate will to power, not by returning to a historically obsolete pre-Christian, Homeric (master) morality, but through celebration of contingency and the creation of new values. The best of us must become our own gods.

Will to power

The precise definition of "will to power" is a matter of ongoing scholarly dispute (see e.g. Kaufmann 1974; Clark 1990; Reginster 2006; Soll 2012; Belliotti 2017). My view is that generic will to power, or will to power as such, can be described only vaguely: it is a second-order desire to have, pursue, and fulfill first-order desires; it bears a relationship to confronting and overcoming resistances and obstacles; and is related to the pursuit of excellence and personal transformation, as well as to experiences of feeling power (Belliotti 2017: 163–66). Typically, when interpreters and Nietzscheans invoke "will to power," however, they are speaking not of the indefinite generic version I have adumbrated, but of *robust* will to power. Accordingly, I will begin by describing that version.

First, Nietzsche insists that robust will to power requires ever-increasing challenges and confrontation with greater resistance in order to grow. Robust will to power cannot be satisfied by recurrently confronting and overcoming the *same* level of resistance or reiterations of power that renege on relentless self-overcoming, the pursuit of excellence, and insatiable growth. Second, the quest for Nietzschean self-perfection is crucial, as an ideal that cannot be attained but can be approximated through our indefatigable strivings. Third, robust will to power implies the struggle for pre-eminence, which invokes aspiring for distinction and establishing domination of a sort. Fourth, Nietzsche celebrates how the activity of robust will to power results in an increase in *power itself*, understood as an increase in the capability of an agent to affect outcomes – power increases only when ever-increasing challenges (or at least different ones) and confrontations with greater resistances take place. Fifth, Nietzsche's grandest aspiration is the marriage of robust will to power to his highest value, a maximally affirmative attitude toward life ("amor fati"). Robust will to power increases the possibility of that union by invoking the dimensions of self-overcoming, pursuit of excellence, the struggle for pre-eminence, establishing the foundations for distinction and domination, increasing power, and persistent growth. The activity of robust will to power so conceived will almost certainly reflect and sustain a maximally affirmative attitude toward life.

Accordingly, *robust will to power* is

1   a *strong* second-order desire to have and pursue first-order desires; and
2   a *strong* second-order desire to confront and overcome significant resistance and obstacles, and thereby feel power while satisfying those first-order desires;
3   in service of recurrent self-overcoming and the pursuit of excellence.

Satisfying will to power is thoroughly paradoxical. For it is only a transitory moment of deserved fulfillment, immediately followed by dissatisfaction, that spawns ongoing activity. Satisfaction of robust will to power is not even a relatively stable or lingering state of affairs; instead it amounts to a temporary moment or experience that must be immediately followed by additional striving. Although effete forms of will to power may well aspire to lingering contentment or more enduring (and pleasurable) satisfaction, robust will to power – the genuine article for Nietzsche – harbors no such illusions. Value, as always, glistens most strikingly in the process, and recurrent activity, of robust will to power.

On this rendering, how might robust will to power not attain (transitory) satisfaction? The possibilities are numerous. Lacking or being unable to pursue first-order desires would stymie the activity of robust will to power and thereby deny satisfaction. The failure to confront or to overcome resistance while pursuing first-order desires would also chill satisfaction. Thus, if one agent established a monopoly of domination in his or her domain of activity, that agent would not have suitable "enemies" to overcome. The agent's monopoly would be self-defeating to the aspirations of robust will to power. This is why pre-eminence, distinction, and domination should not imply the elimination of worthy competition. Likewise, if the competition is too daunting the agent will be unlikely to overcome it and robust will to power will be frustrated. Another source of frustration arises from overcoming only moderate resistance that does not produce the feelings of power or promote the increase of power. Any of these ways of frustrating robust will to power is also likely to thwart self-overcoming, the pursuit of excellence, and growth.

I propose describing various levels of will to power in terms of the intensity of their desire to overcome serious resistance that directly affects the possibilities for self-overcoming, the pursuit of excellence, and experiencing feelings of power. Nietzsche insists that all human beings embody will to power to some extent. As the fundamental instinct of life, will to power cannot be forfeited or waived by living beings. *Robust* will to power, among other things, *seeks explicitly* to confront and overcome *serious* resistance.

Following this train of thought, *moderate will to power* is:

1   a *measured* second-order desire to have, pursue, and satisfy first-order desires; and

2   a *measured* second-order desire *to be prepared* to overcome (but not seek out) serious resistance and obstacles, and thereby feel some power in satisfying those first-order desires;

3   in service of steady self-overcoming and the pursuit of improvement.

That is, those embodying moderate will to power will accept and strive to overcome serious resistance if it presents itself but will prefer to attain their goals without that challenge. As such, those embodying moderate will to power will experience the feelings of power less frequently and less intensely than those exercising robust will to power, and will self-overcome and approximate excellence less often and more tepidly.

Finally, we must account for the type of will to power embodied by Nietzsche's most "contemptible" and "despicable" human being: the last man (Nietzsche 1883–85: 5). Last men exert themselves minimally and avoid suffering religiously. They are shallow, narrow egalitarians, who pursue a superficial "happiness" that extinguishes their possibilities for intense love, creation, longing, striving, and excellence. The highest ambitions of last men are comfort and security. They are the extreme case of the herd mentality: habit, custom, indolence, egalitarianism, self-preservation, and muted will to power prevail. Last men embody none of the inner tensions and conflicts that spur trans-formative action: they take no risks, lack convictions, avoid experimentation, and seek only bland survival.

Last men fail to take responsibility for the persons they are becoming; offer facile excuses for their shortcomings; seek only the blandest hedonistic com-forts; and conform abjectly to dominant social ideas in order to highlight their non-threatening nature and to satisfy their compulsion for external validation. As such, the last man represents the path of least resistance: easy accommodations and effete aspirations replace the arduous task of self-realization. Notice that the last man is not an agent of evil. The short-coming that in Nietzsche's eyes makes the last man the most despicable, the most contemptible, and the most injurious person, is his severely attenuated will to power.

Accordingly, *attenuated will to power* (a variant embodied by last men) is:

1   an *enfeebled* second-order desire to have, pursue, and satisfy first-order desires; and

2   a *considerable* second-order desire to avoid confronting serious resistance and obstacles in satisfying those first-order desires;

3   in service of establishing, maintaining, or increasing tepid pleasure, com-fort, and communal peace.

Those harboring attenuated will to power will often abandon the pursuit of their first-order desires if the process of satisfying them is too arduous. Instead, they will conjure up and pursue new first-order desires that appear more easily fulfilled. Attenuated will to power still implies the ongoing second-order desire to have, pursue, and fulfill first-order desires, but aspires to avoid facing serious resistance and does not explicitly seek recurrent self-overcoming and excellence. Accordingly, those embodying attenuated will to power experience the feelings of power rarely and fortuitously (Belliotti 2013: 126–36; 2017: 163–66).[1]

Constructing meaning in a human life

Although Nietzsche often excoriates romanticism as an intellectual movement, his own work exudes much of the same impulses. The Romantics valued integrity, sincerity, and readiness to sacrifice one's life for a cherished ideal (see e.g. Berlin 1966a). They replaced the ancient Greek desire for internal peace, harmony, and tranquility, with insatiable yearnings to approach infinity, to create and stamp a legacy upon nature, and to struggle and soar. Romantics were convinced that the excitement and possibilities of the world could not be fully exhausted and that no final, fixed answers to specific questions of how to live were accessible. They perceived themselves as people of continuous action, generating and creating, constantly transforming themselves afresh, as they propelled forward as a microcosm of a vast cosmic design, renewing themselves recurrently. By allowing their seemingly infinite natures to rise to greater and greater heights, they transcended toward divinity. Mirroring the flow and endless self-creativity of the cosmos, the Romantics' indomitable wills, their ceaseless process of deconstruction, re-imagination, and re-creation, animated their passions and constituted the meaning of their lives. For the Romantics, reality is not a stable state of affairs, but a dynamic process of change, and human beings emerge wholly within that process, of which they are partially constitutive. Human beings are seen as being at one with nature, sharing with it the spirituality of their innermost beings. Creative artists are celebrated as heroic, and art is rendered the object of religious attitudes.

Nietzsche, too, understands life as a bold narrative, a relentless project of self-creation, aesthetic creativity, or grand striving underwritten by robust will to power. Such a portrayal likens life to literature and art. But do we then live to curry a favorable audience? Do we exert our energy and enthusiasm into the world in order to win fans, admirers, and critics appreciative of our performances or artistic creations? Not necessarily. While a life well-lived merits applause from the public, this recognition is not the core of crafting a meaningful human life.

Nietzsche intimates that we construct and experience the meaning in life through our emotions and passions. Moreover, through our reason we connect our lives to wider values that produce meaning. Creativity is not merely producing something somewhat original. Creativity is a self-examination and self-exploration that affects the creator. Creative activity spawns self-transformation.

Accordingly, vigorously meaningful lives conjure the metaphor of pogo sticks (Belliotti 2001: 78–84). We bound from goal to goal and from desire to desire, as each (temporary) satisfaction impels us to new imaginings and pursuits. Although we take time to savor our accomplishments, we are excited by the process and continue the quest. The best among us will represent the full process of Nietzschean becoming – recurrent deconstruction, re-imagination, and re-creation – the virtues of the active nihilist. To prepare to even approximate a higher human type, we must pass through "three metamorphoses" of discipline, defiance, and creation (Nietzsche 1883–85: pt I, "On the Three Metamorphoses"). The spirit, like a camel, flees into the desert to bear enormous burdens (the process of social construction); the spirit, like a lion, must transform itself into a master, a conqueror who releases its own freedom by destroying traditional prohibitions (the process of deconstruction of, and liberation from, the past); but the lion cannot create new values, so the spirit must transform itself into a child, whose playful innocence, ability to forget, and capability for creative games signals the spirit's willing of its own will (the processes of re-imagination and re-creation). This cycle continues until we die or lose the human capabilities required to participate. At all stages, learning informs the process. New understandings and findings propel us forward.

Although it may be criticized for not including sufficient respite and time to savor, Nietzsche's process nevertheless highlights the deficiencies of viewing life as a simple journey to a particular, fixed, final goal. At its best, the metaphor of the pogo stick underscores our need for faith, understood as conviction, choice, and action in the face of radical uncertainty. As Nietzsche reminds us, our project of self-creation is our greatest aesthetic mission in life. The metaphor of the pogo stick celebrates how spurred engagement underwrites meaning and value in our lives, and confirms Nietzsche's view of process values.

Following Nietzsche, our growth and suffering are often connected. The Italian proverb, which generously predates Nietzsche, testifies *Ciò che non mi distrugge mi rende più forte* ("What does not destroy me will make me stronger"). Although not a literal truth, its trajectory bears currency. The loss of adolescent innocence as we gain worldly experience, of the sense of infinite possibilities as we make choices that narrow our imaginings, of boundless hope as we bury loved ones, of transcendent power as we suffer debilitating disease, of inflated self-esteem as love turns sour, all this can trigger growth and meaning … or self-destruction. We must integrate the tragic, painful aspects of human experience into our reality. Evil, suffering, death, and the loss of what is closest to us are also part of life. Adversity need never merely be adversity unless we permit it to be. Adversity can be refashioned into practical advantage where the will to do so is resolute. But life offers no guarantees.

Getting what we want too easily, without struggle, induces boredom more predictably than simply accomplishing a goal. The classic, sometimes irritating, adage merits attention: "Only things that take great effort to acquire are worth having; nothing worthwhile comes easily." Perhaps even Nietzsche's annoying warrior rhetoric exudes a kernel of truth: wars, as horrible as they are, provide stunning opportunities for meaning. Apathy and indifference, total immersion in the mundane, are unavailable. Collective narcolepsy and prostrate, complacent faithlessness evaporate. We understand viscerally and not merely rationally, the radical indeterminacy of life: the dread of cosmic exile and the longing for infinite redemption.

What does the pogo stick suggest if not Nietzsche's psychological doctrine of will to power as I have interpreted it? The second-order desire to have and pursue first-order desires promotes the ongoing engagement required for meaningful lives; the desire to confront and overcome resistance in attaining the goals of first-order desires supports creative use of suffering in service to self-overcoming and the pursuit of excellence that spurs ever-increasing engagement; the yearning to feel power as one's capabilities and dispositions to affect outcomes increasingly fuels the bearer's zest for and faith in life; the lack of a fixed, final goal reminds the bearer that ongoing activity is the trajectory of life; and the insatiable nature of will to power underscores the proposition that the elusiveness of final fulfillment is good news.

For Nietzsche, meaning is not purely an objective matter. We are never in a neutral position to evaluate our perceptions and beliefs against the world as such. Our interpretations are within the realm of our experiences of the world and we cannot ascend to a point outside our world. We cannot appeal to an entirely atheoretical perception of pure, uninterpreted states of affairs. The realm of truth is within the realms of experience, reason, and passion. Human beings cannot access truth or knowledge outside these realms. Although no single, privileged position that could freeze truth claims and sanctify interpretations once and for all is accessible to us, that need not imply that all interpretations are equally sound (Belliotti 2017: 198–205).

Concerns

Nietzsche's perfectionism is individualistic and aristocratic. As such, he does not intend his normative message to be embraced by everyone. In fact, he speaks only to the few who have the potential to understand fully the tragic nature of life and yet still affirm life in all its dimensions. The crucial ingredients that define higher human beings, for Nietzsche, are the capability to endure great suffering and turn it to practical advantage; the impulse to exert high energy and enthusiasm in projects requiring uncommon creativity; and full participation in the ongoing process of personal deconstruction–re-imagination–re-creation. For the greatest among us, our paramount artistic project is crafting a grand self.

Numerous of Nietzsche's specific pronouncements are troubling and unpersuasive. To mention a few: championing an unrepentant elitism; deflating the social dimension of human productivity; unsqueamishly extolling an aristo-cratic class that would "use the great mass of people as their tools" (Nietzsche 1886: §257); insisting that only a few among us can attain robustly meaningful lives; obscuring the suffering of numerous human beings by glorifying the cultural artifacts generated by a few; and amplifying the virtues of interior life. In sum, Nietzsche's perfectionism instructs the vast majority of us to devote ourselves only to nurturing the excellences of the greatest exemplars in our society and it empowers the greatest exemplars to embrace our sacrifices and use our services with a good conscience. Contra Nietzsche, excellences, personal achievements, intelligence, and creative powers can all be exemplified by common people. We are not all either herd animals or cultural geniuses. Nietzsche identifies, as do many philosophers, excellence too closely with intellectual activity. Apart from his romantic worship of military battle, he sees genius only in art, music, philosophy, and science. While we should not easily disparage the life of the interior, it is woefully insufficient for engaging the world. Private fulfillment is less purposeful than public involvement that requires passionate identification with particular communities. Such activity – horror of horrors – means mingling with the herd. Human beings have a need for belonging; and much fear, insecurity, selfishness, and anxiety arise from the frustration of that need. This need does not flow from a herd instinct, at least not in a pejorative sense, but is a prerequisite for a highly textured and robustly meaningful life. The lack of an acute sense of belonging undermines the development of the self. By stressing the virtues of grand strivers and by connecting them only tenuously to those not of the same rank, Nietzsche undermines a healthy sense of community to the detriment of broader, salutary human development.

Note

1   Of course, the three versions of will to power I describe need not be taken as an exhaustive catalogue. Those so inclined may sketch intermediary versions that bridge the gaps between strong, moderate, and attenuated will to power.

25 Ortega and the meaning of life

PEDRO BLAS GONZÁLEZ

A clear and succinct account of the Spanish philosopher José Ortega y Gasset's philosophy of the meaning of human existence is that man must learn to live within himself; to *ensimismarse* (Ortega 1939: 180).[1] *Ensimismamiento* means self-reflection, the opposite of *alteración*, which equates to living without respect for our circumstances. For Ortega, the reflective life makes a distinction between human existence and human life. The former is an existential category, while the latter denotes biology. Yet in Ortega's thought, contemplation is not merely detachment from the world. In profoundly ironic fashion, Ortega suggests, self-reflection enables man to take a respite from the world by calling attention to the existential plight of subjectivity in the objective world. Reflection allows man to locate himself in his surroundings, which make up part of an individual's circumstance. Thus, as an existential being, man is capable of projecting himself out of the background of nature – like a sculpture in high relief.

The world, which comprises but a portion of man's circumstance, is made coherent through the hierarchy of values from which man must choose. Man, on the other hand, through existential inquietude, must turn his glance inward toward himself in order to interpret human experience. Ortega's ideas on the meaning of life are rooted in the interplay of *ensimismamiento* and *alteración*. These two Spanish words are the anchor of authenticity and inauthenticity, even though these words do not convey the same meaning found in the thought of other existentialists. Ortega's work is wrought through with these two concepts, which serve as the glue that unifies his metaphysics, which in turn, is imbued with philosophical anthropology.

Ortega's 1939 essay "The Self and the Other" is a fine exposition of what the Spanish thinker views as the tension between man's inner life and the demands made by the world he inhabits (ibid.: 178). When man lives life outside himself, that is, by ignoring his existential inner constitution, this forces man to "act mechanically in a frenetic somnambulism" (ibid.). The importance of *ensimismamiento* is that it enables man to recognize that human life is ruled by insecurity. The reflective glance that *ensimismamiento* demands gives meaning to life by transforming it from human life, which is merely a biological category, to existence, which denotes existential self-reflection. *Ensimismamiento* affords man the possibility of self-rule, unlike animals, which live in perpetual *alteración*.

Because it is not possible for man to turn his back on the world on a permanent basis, Ortega argues, man must take a stand within himself. Even though this form of inward reflection cannot be sustained indefinitely, it helps man understand the role that his life and circumstances play in the greater scheme of human reality. Hence, before man can reflect on the nature of the self, he must first find himself immersed, as it were, in physical reality. After many trials and tribulations, disappointments and disenchantment with the structure of human reality, man comes to understand that human life is essentially a shipwrecked existence. Ortega says that man is shipwrecked in several places throughout his complete works, which consist of twelve volumes in Spanish. However, the existential condition of being shipwrecked does not entail that human existence is devoid of meaning and purpose, or that man is alienated from the world, as is often asserted in the work of other existentialists. For Ortega, to be shipwrecked means that life must be made coherent by every individual. Man is a differentiated being who must come to terms with this existential reality. Human life is encountered by people as a singular reality. Man is responsible for making sense of his own existence.

Man discovers that the human condition is imbued with difficulty and limitation. Ortega argues that difficulty and limitation teach man that human life is insecure. He explains: "Life is our reaction to the basic insecurity which constitutes its substance. Hence, it is an extremely serious matter for a man to find himself too much surrounded by apparent securities. A consciousness of security kills life" (Ortega 1932: 161). Ortega argues that the discovery of human reality and the human person comes about as a three-step process of discovery.

The first stage of man's discovery of human reality is the realization that reality cannot be deformed in order to suit everyone's desires. That would deface and trivialize human reality. According to Ortega, individual perspective cannot override the structure of objective reality. Two basic components of objective reality are life as resistance and the insecurity (and limitations) of the self. By addressing the contingencies of objective reality and life itself, man eventually discovers a way to save his circumstances.

The initial stage of man's confrontation with human reality, as Ortega explains it, is to find oneself among a dizzying array of objects and other people, which serve to eventually help man discover his inner constitution. But first, man must come to the realization that life is ruled by insecurity. During the initial stage of the discovery of interiority, man turns away from the world by turning inward. In this stage, man realizes that he is not just one more object that helps constitute the world. This stage of self-reflection, which Ortega refers to as the turn inward, takes tremendous individual effort. This is what Ortega refers to as a temporary freeing from the slavery of the world: "This inwardly directed attention, this stand within the self, is the most anti-natural and ultra-biological of phenomena" (Ortega 1939: 186).

While the initial stage of discovery is that man finds himself shipwrecked in the world, the second stage begins when man turns inward. This is what Ortega refers to as "saving our circumstances." The second stage of discovery is a crucial component of *ensimismamiento*; for even to live as a recluse on a mountain top, away from other people, necessitates that man exist within himself first. The turn inward is a necessary step in man's understanding of the objective world and human reality. The apparent distance created between man as a being in a circumstance (the world), and man the inward, time-oriented being who is aware of life as a circumstance itself, comes about through reflection on the nature of man as a differentiated being.

Turning himself into the object of self-reflection, man calls attention to the question of meaning in human life. What man discovers in the second stage of auto-gnosis is that human existence is the root reality – the radical reality – from which all other reality can be made coherent. This does not imply that man is alone ontologically, only that the world exists for a self that finds itself situated in it. This realization enables man to encounter meaning in his daily dealings with the world.

Hence, the fundamental importance that Ortega places on the second stage of self-reflection – the turn inward – is that man is subsequently able to cultivate ideas about the world and human reality. In other words, man's pre-reflective existence in the world is never encountered authentically, Ortega argues, until man is provoked into self-reflection. As a physical being, existing animal-like in the physical world, man lives in *alteración*. This is why the cultivation of ideas serves as a guide for man to live in the world. The latter fosters in man a form of freedom that animals are not privy to. Thus, ideas enable man to maneuver through human existence with the modicum of understanding that man, as a differentiated being in a world of inanimate objects, can attain. This activity is not undertaken as a luxury, but rather as a necessity for survival. Ortega stresses that the second stage of self-discovery takes great initiative on man's part. As a consequence, Ortega asserts that there is nothing natural in man seeking to make himself knowledgeable about the world, and ultimately, of his own existence. The latter is an act of will that originates in *amour propre*. Unlike Aristotle, Ortega does not believe that man has a predisposition for knowledge, especially self-knowledge.

The second stage of the turn inward, which Ortega regards as man's embrace of *ensimismamiento*, is a necessary step in not allowing human life to become dehumanized – what he refers to in *The Revolt of the Masses* as demoralization. The form of objectification that Ortega is concerned with is akin to the "Not-me" aspect of objective reality that Fichte points out. The question for Ortega is not whether the world can be comprehended objectively in the absence of man, or whether man can be himself without the world-as-circumstance, but rather that "I am I and my circumstances"

(Ortega 1914: 45). Ortega seeks to find a common ground between idealism and realism.

This is important for several reasons. As a young man, Ortega went to Germany to study in what he referred to as the "citadel of Neo-Kantianism." He was interested in introducing German philosophy to the Spanish people. While studying in Marburg with Paul Natorp and Herman Cohen, from 1905 to 1908, Ortega became steeped in Neo-Kantianism. Subsequently, he came to reject the sterility of this form of thought, which he believed had little to contribute to the philosophy of life. The other main reason for Ortega's discontent with Neo-Kantianism had to do with Spanish culture, and more specifically, his belief that Neo-Kantianism was incompatible with the temperament of the Spanish people. The question of the meaning of life in Ortega's work is rooted in his idea of vital reason.

While writing for newspapers as a young man, Ortega's work stylistically came to embody respect for clarity, which he viewed as the ultimate respect that a thinker can have for readers. This is one reason why Ortega came to eschew neologisms, and the sterility he encountered in many philosophy journals. In terms of philosophical thought, Ortega can be considered a Germanophile. He wanted to blend German philosophy, its stout dialectic, with the often mercurial Spanish temperament. This task focused Ortega's philosophical prowess through the recognition that practical reason – for him, the vital reason – ought to work in the service of life. This is another way in which Ortega's thought manifests an existential dimension.

Thus, equipped with a newly found understanding of his role in human reality, man, in the third and final stage of self-discovery, encounters the world in a new light. No longer shipwrecked as an entity among inanimate objects and other people, man appropriates himself as a being that can come to guide his own existence; to a greater degree than when he viewed himself as shipwrecked. The significance of the third stage is the realization that man is a being that humanizes the universe. What Ortega means is that man brings values to the world. In other words, man's greatest contribution to the physical universe is to supply it with meaning. No doubt the universe, its laws and processes, fulfill a purpose. Yet purpose and meaning are not the same thing, as far as meaning in human existence is concerned.

One essential trait of meaning in Ortega's work is that it is not to be sought out consciously. Part of the significance of Ortega's three stages of discovery, which amount to man seeking security in ideas, is that by doing so he becomes better equipped to confront objective reality. Ideas ennoble man. *Ensimismamiento* fosters a level of engagement with being that enables man to live "within himself" and thus avoid becoming objectified. Yet by turning inward, Ortega does not suggest that man can remain in a meditative state. Instead, *ensimismamiento* proactively confronts the demands and exigencies of physical reality. This is one way in which it can be said that "I am I and my circumstances."

However, it would be a *malentendu* to suggest that Ortega's ideas on the nature of man's circumstance merely mean that man always finds himself in a situation. This is only true at a superficial level of engagement with the world. The broader understanding of circumstance, which serves as the source of meaning in life in Ortega's thought, has to do with man's ability to cultivate a vocation. For thought, according to Ortega, is not an existentially vital characteristic of man; it becomes static and worn thin by clichéd usage.[2] This is not so much a critique of thinking as a clarification of what it means for man to have an inner life that directs its attention and creativity to the external world. Thus, ideas allow man to be more than an animal, for animals are characterized by *alteración*. This implies that animal life may display purpose, but not meaning. This is part of what vital reason signifies in Ortega's thought.

Ortega explains this as such: "Observe that this marvellous faculty which man possesses of temporarily freeing himself from his slavery to things implies two very different powers; one, his ability to ignore the world for a greater or lesser time without fatal risk; the other, his having somewhere to take his stand, to be, when he has virtually left the world" (Ortega 1939: 181). The question of meaning in human life, within Ortega's thought, is grounded in his understanding of man's inner life, or what he believes *ensimismamiento* conveys about human existence. The basic reality that man discovers in the world is his own existence as a problem for contemplation. This is what Ortega means by radical reality. Radical means root. Yet, as we have already seen, this is not easily discovered by man. In other words, to find himself man must first discover himself shipwrecked in the world. This not only creates a sense of disorientation, but also the need to understand his surroundings. This, in turn, necessitates self-understanding. As a consequence, man can achieve a modicum of self-autonomy over his handling of and interpretation of reality, even though not necessarily reality proper. Ortega's metaphysics pays homage to man; the being for whom metaphysics is necessary. This means that Ortega's philosophy of life is a philosophical anthropology.

In attempting to answer the question "what is man?" Ortega branches out into other metaphysical categories. However, the latter cannot take place in the absence of man as an existential being, who must labor diligently in order to achieve even a minimum level of auto-gnosis. This is why the meaning of life in Ortega's work cannot be divorced from the notion of having-to-do (*quehacer*). *Quehacer* can be conceived as having to address mundane problems of day-to-day life. Yet we must also keep in mind that Ortega's pragmatic Spanish temperament viewed mundane tasks as being precisely the kind of activities that make life meaningful.

In an essay published in 1910, entitled *Adán en el Paraíso* (Adam in paradise), Ortega first presents the idea that human existence is the ultimate reality from which subsequent aspects of reality can be made coherent. This is what Ortega means when he argues that radical reality is to be understood as the fundamental reality. Ortega argues that human existence encounters itself in the world in the life of differentiated persons. In other words, the fabric of self-awareness makes it possible for man to know the world. What enables man to know the world is precisely what allows for a meaningful life: ideas that help man manage life. By cultivating ideas man finds that he can forge an existential path for himself in the physical universe. This not only entails the exercise of free will but also a measure of existential security. For man in pre-history, seeking food, water and shelter had profound implications as they were life-saving. This is the ultimate form of having-to-do (*quehacer*), which is a theme throughout his complete works, especially in *Meditations on Hunting* and *Meditations on Quixote* (1914), where he first writes of life as vital reason. In *Meditations on Hunting*, Ortega addresses the question of man and his circumstances as such: "Life is the dynamic interchange between the individual and his surroundings, and his surroundings include his own emotional and intellectual responses to life's problems" (Ortega 1943: 8).

Every person must come to terms with his existential constitution, which presents human existence as a problem for reflection. Man's essence, Ortega is wont to say, is essentially always a becoming. Man is a work in progress, as it were. This is why life, experienced from the inside out, is a drama and narrative. Man becomes the novelist of himself, Ortega suggests, because he is a character in his own drama. This does not mean that man's life is insubstantial. On the contrary, man's entire life ought to be devoted to the cultivation of the self. Not to do so is to lose oneself in the vast array of inanimate objects of the world, and thus to live in *alteración*. Inauthenticity is not so much a condition of maladjustment to the world, but the result of man's inability to cultivate the self. Ortega writes: "The fate of culture, the destiny of man, depends upon our maintaining that dramatic consciousness ever alive in our inmost being, and upon our feeling, like a murmuring counterpoint in our entrails, that we are only sure of insecurity" (Ortega 1939: 191).

The existential component of Ortega's thought conveys a sense of self that man can only gain through a turn inward; toward interiority. Interiority forms an essential level of being that man must not only discover but continually cultivate throughout life. This is why man, who finds himself shipwrecked in the world, and saves his circumstance by reflecting on it, can easily recoil back into animal existence. Because the world offers man opportunities to lose himself in the vast array that makes up the physical world, man is in constant danger of never getting hold of himself, existentially speaking.

A meaningful life regards itself as distinct in kind from nature. Yet, as we have already seen, this does not signal a radical break with the world. Instead, by realizing that circumstances vary for different people, the reflective person must settle on the realization that some perspectives are inappropriate for cultivating an authentic account of human existence. Man's quest for meaning cannot be satisfied through a self-conscious effort. That would make meaning and happiness a continually shifting target. Instead, the road to meaning is paved with reflection on how best to appropriate our personal circumstances. This can be an overwhelming quest, though, for it confronts man with the realization that life is dangerous. This is why Ortega dismisses Nietzsche's contention that man should live dangerously ... for life is already dangerous enough.

One of the implications of the turn inward toward interiority is that this task cannot be shared or substituted with the life of another person. We must learn to live with our own non-interchangeable circumstances. At the root of man's turn inward we realize that we need a plan of attack. This is the role that ideas play in human existence. But ideas are not ready-made. This is why ideas in Ortega's work must serve life: vital existence. As such, ideas in the form of vital reason serve an existential end. He writes that, "thought is not a gift to man but a laborious, precarious and volatile acquisition" (ibid.: 193). The kind of thought that Ortega espouses is not pure reason but vital reason. Thinking is a task that man undergoes for sheer survival. Ultimately, thinking must be a function of vital existence. The fruits of thought allow man to encounter life in a proactive manner. Action is not determined by doing constant blind battle with reality, the world and other people. Instead, action underscores man's ability to have a plan to live in the world.

According to Ortega, action must not be associated with mere activity. Action for its own sake is what Ortega refers to as voluntarism. In its crudest form voluntarism leads to stupefaction, which in his estimation, is the vilest form of *alteración*. *Alteración* promotes a corrosive lack of meaning in human life. Instead, action must be guided by a form of self-reflection that guides human behavior. The form of reflection that enables man to lead a meaningful existence is self-reflection that comes about through man's reflective turn inward (*ensimismarse*). *Ensimismamiento*, an act of authenticity for Ortega, works in the service of life. This leads to what Socrates considered the good life. Reflection, Ortega argues, is forced upon man in order to comprehend the contingencies of the physical world. While reflection is a necessity and not a luxury, its antithesis is intellectualism. Ortega explains: "The heaviest of these chains is 'intellectualism'; and now, when it is imperative that we change our course and take a new road – in short, get on the right track – it is of the greatest importance that we resolutely rid ourselves of this archaic attitude, which has been carried to its extreme during these last two centuries" (ibid.: 197).

Ortega's critique of intellectualism views it as responsible for eroding the conditions that make the prospect of a meaningful life difficult to attain in modernity. Intellectualism is the result of *alteración*. Thinking for thinking's sake, Ortega suggests, is an aberration. Hence, we realize that Ortega's idea of a meaningful life is grounded in man having to take a stand within himself in order to face the order of human reality. A life lived by grasping at intellectual values – often desperately – is an artificial life. A life held captive by action that springs from *alteración*, and which can only be satiated by taking recourse in further action, is a life dominated by *alteración*. As far as meaning in human life is concerned, a life of action leaves very little time and creative imagination for knowing how best to act – how to live without succumbing to objectification. This is what Ortega means when he says in *The Revolt of the Masses,* "And such is the simple truth. The whole world – nations and individuals – is demoralised. For a time this demoralisation rather amuses people, and even causes a vague illusion" (Ortega 1930: 135).

Notes

1 And equally, of course, that woman must learn to live within herself. Such qualifications apply to the shorthand 'man' throughout this chapter.
2 "In words which, merely from having been worn down, like old coins, are no longer able to convey their meaning to us with any force, we are accustomed to calling this process: thinking, meditation" (Ortega 1939: 181).

26 Wittgenstein and the meaning of life

REZA HOSSEINI

The current literature on the meaning of life among analytic philosophers is founded upon a couple of delicate distinctions with far-reaching implications. Firstly, a great deal of effort and care has gone into establishing "meaningfulness" as a normative category distinct from "morality" and/or "happiness." The idea is that although traditionally philosophers would appeal to morality or happiness to give an account of what makes a good life or good action, there are other things that we usually take into consideration when we contemplate ways of justifying a course of action; things that are neither shaped by our need for happiness nor guided by moral considerations, and which we do because they have a capacity to make our lives more meaningful. And it seems that most of us don't think that any random thing could have that capacity. We wouldn't think, for example, that the sum total of all the times we had ice cream, overslept, brushed our teeth, took selfies and filtered them, or stayed home to play computer games, are serious candidates for what would make our lives meaningful. We might prefer to think of things like gardening, friendships, our jobs, mastering an art or a craft, travelling to faraway continents, raising children, meeting someone by accident and meeting them again (for the heart is pounding). There seems to be something in common in the second list which is not there in the first list. Eating ice cream is good but not in the same sense that travelling is. One wouldn't be proud of eating ice cream in the same way that one would be proud of travelling and learning about other cultures. Meaning, as a normative category, could be of help in explaining the differences, even if only partly.

The second distinction in the literature is between the cosmic and the individual conceptions of life's meaning, which is translated into a distinction between "the meaning of life" and "meaning in life." The assumption is that an answer to the question of life's meaning in its individual sense is not contingent upon arriving at or having an answer to the question of life's meaning in its cosmic sense. One could have a meaningful life, so the argument goes, even if one fails to provide an answer to the questions about the purpose of life on earth. The impatient cry of "What is the point of it all?" wouldn't undermine a philosopher's search for what, if anything, could confer meaning on one's life in its individual sense.

Keeping these distinctions in mind, we can now turn to Ludwig Wittgenstein and his way of looking at the question of life's meaning. Wittgenstein never wrote in a systematic fashion about "meaning" as a normative category, but his reflections offer important insights about the very phenomenon of inquiring into life's meaning, and the variety of ways it manifests itself. For all we know he was not interested in engaging in first-order philosophical inquiry into the meaning of life. His writings on value, broadly construed, are predominantly driven by second-order questions. In other words, on the whole his contribution to the question of life's meaningfulness is a grammatical contribution. The kinds of questions he asks and the observations he shares are more often than not "grammatical remarks." His questions are not aimed at finding the "essence" of life's meaning; rather, he asks many questions about the grammar of life's meaning. There are ways in which Wittgenstein's body of texts could offer insights about the nature of inquiring into life's meaning, but to appreciate them we would need to leave aside or to bracket the search for the essence of life's meaning, and embrace second-order inquiries, that is, inquiries about the varieties of inquiring into the meaning of life. He would ask questions such as: Is it possible to communicate successfully the "sense" of a theory of life's meaning? Why do we commit certain acts and find meaning in them (waking up before dawn to bow down in prayer, burning an effigy, kissing the photo of a dead man while remembering his ashes scattered to the wind, etc.)? Would my life become meaningless if I failed to find justificatory reasons for my actions? Why is it that some "very intelligent and well-educated people" come to believe in things that others consider to be obviously false? (Wittgenstein 1933–35: §336)

Questions such as these, and Wittgenstein's attempts to make sense of them, are scattered throughout his writings, from his diaries (two edited collections of which can be found in *Culture and Value*, and *Public and Private Occasions*, for example) to his public lectures and notes (*Notebooks 1914–1916*, "A Lecture on Ethics," *Lectures on Psychology, Aesthetics and Religious Beliefs*, "Remarks on Frazer's Golden Bough," and *On Certainty*). In addition, many commentators appeal to biographical anecdotes in discussing their take on Wittgenstein's philosophy of life. It is normal to see that, for example, a sentence by Wittgenstein in a letter or a simple remark in passing to a friend has become decisively important in a certain commentators' reading. Indeed, many of his personal remarks about value have an aphoristic quality, offering often important insights into the nature of our search for meaning. As a result, if someone is interested to know what Wittgenstein would think of life's meaning, they are bound to hear many dramatic stories of what Wittgenstein said, did, or what not. Although attention to his extraordinary biography could be helpful in understanding his philosophy of life, in what follows I will focus on what I think is his key contribution to the current issues and questions in the rapidly growing literature on life's meaning.

I

In an edited collection such as this book, which sets out to highlight the great philosophers' thoughts on life's meaning, commentators from different backgrounds share their thoughts on their favourite philosopher's account of life's meaning. Now if we were to examine these views in search of at least one fundamental element common to all, there might seem to be a splendid chance of arriving at a principle or theory of life's meaning. And even if we failed to arrive at a theory that could survive all objections, we might have the feeling that somewhere in this book there must be something that has the capacity to make us change our whole "way of seeing." We might feel like Ben Horne in David Lynch's *Twin Peaks*, in the scene where he is holding in his hands "the Koran, the Bhagavad-Gita, the Talmud, the Bible, New and Old Testaments, the Tao-Te-Ching," and telling Audrey that "somewhere in here are the answers I seek." We might say: somewhere in this book there is the answer to the question of what would make a life meaningful.

But the philosophers we are writing about might themselves have had the same urge or "tendency to look for something in common to all the entities which we commonly subsume under a general term" (Wittgenstein 1933–5: 17). It makes sense to assume that their goal, too, was to find that common element shared by all the conceptions of life's meaning. But if that is the case, why is it that theories of life's meaning haven't reached a final conclusion on that awesome thing which could confer meaning on all lives? Wittgenstein thinks that such vast discrepancies between various strands of theories of life's meaning are bound to occur.

In his early works, Wittgenstein tried to draw the boundaries, or limits, between what could be said meaningfully and "what lies on the other side of the limit," and he argued that all the problems of philosophy are a result of misunderstanding or trespassing over this boundary. In this line of argument, utterances of value cannot be expressed in meaningful propositions. The inexpressibility of value has to do with the "structure" of the world. In "A Lecture on Ethics," he goes on to claim that writing about value or the meaning of life would entail a total re-evaluation of the structure of our language and what it is capable of communicating. For a person to offer a theory of life's meaning which was indeed a *true* theory of life's meaning would be most extraordinary; it would be so extraordinary that, metaphorically speaking, "this book would, with an explosion, destroy all the other books in the world" (Wittgenstein 1929: 46). What Wittgenstein seems to be saying is that if we were to write the true book on the meaning of life we would need to dismantle the whole boundary between what could and could not be said meaningfully. He recognizes our wish to say something about the ultimate value of life but at the same time he was concerned that in attempting to do so, one could be exposed to all sorts of extravagances of the mind. He didn't offer a theory of life's meaning; he didn't have one and he was not interested in acquiring one because he believed that a theoretical way of looking at the question of life's meaning was not the right way. It wouldn't do justice to the varieties of ways we experience the question of life's meaningfulness or its answers.

If that is the case, then, what is the so-called "right way" of looking at the question of life's meaning according to Wittgenstein? I think he would have it that the knowledge of the meaningfulness of one's life is more like a knowledge of how to draw connections between various aspects of one's life, a know-how capacity to integrate different parts into a unified whole. It is a knowledge that is not reducible to a straightforward theory. There is something about life, the varieties of life experience, that makes it evade all theories. There is, in Martha Nussbaum's words, a "complexity, a many-sidedness, a temporally evolving plurality" about life, which is often missing in the "explicit theories" of life's meaning (Nussbaum 1990: 283). We would need an approach that accommodates the complexities which made us begin our inquiry in the first place.

But what kind of knowledge is this and can we acquire it? Yes, but not by taking a course on the meaning of life. The key to someone's understanding of life is to pay attention to what Iris Murdoch calls their "total vision of life":

> When we apprehend and assess other people we do not consider only their solutions to specifiable practical problems, we consider something more elusive which may be called their total vision of life, as shown in their mode of speech or silence, their choice of words, their assessments of others, their conception of their own lives, what they think attractive or praiseworthy, what they think funny: in short the configurations of their thought which show continually in their reactions and conversation. These things ... one may call the texture of man's being or the nature of his personal vision.
>
> (Murdoch 1956: 80–81)

In other words, Wittgenstein would say there is a "texture" for one's conception of life's meaning which makes it almost tangible; there is so much in the eyes, he would say. Attention to these "fine shades of behaviour" of the kind Murdoch alludes to would help us arrive at a holistic picture of an understanding of life. We might call it a "confessional" approach toward the question of life's meaning, as opposed to a "theoretical" approach. The aim of a confessional approach is to acquire an understanding of human life that is embodied in (some)one's "total vision of life." Taking one's life to be meaningful or meaningless, in this view, has less to do with securing a theory of life's meaning and more with one's total vision of life. For one might come to accept the claim that fulfilling God's purpose is the ultimate meaning of life and yet fail to see God's will in what one experiences in life. Or, one might conclude that orientating one's life toward projects of objective value could make one's life meaningful and yet fail to do so. The problem with the half-hearted believer and the naturalist might be that the one is increasingly feeling that things do not add up, and the other one doesn't see it in his heart to act upon his passion for an objectively valuable project – covering the expenses of a mortgaged life in the suburbs is his lifelong project. Or, they might be struck by something that threatens all theories of life's meaning, a feeling that Leo Tolstoy aptly described as "the arrest of life" (Tolstoy 1882: 7).

Wittgenstein has written about the variety of ways this experience manifests itself; for example a passage in the "Koder Diaries" reads:

> A human being lives his ordinary life with the illumination of a light of which he is not aware until it is extinguished. Once it is extinguished, life is suddenly deprived of all value, meaning, or whatever one wants to say. One suddenly becomes aware that mere existence – as one would like to say – is in itself still completely empty, bleak. It is as if the sheen was wiped away from all things.
> (Wittgenstein 1930–37: 207)

What is it that has ceased to illuminate that life? Wittgenstein's notions of "aspect-seeing" and "aspect-blindness" could help us here. In aspect-seeing one comes to see an aspect in the object of one's visual experience. "I contemplate a face, and then suddenly notice its likeness to another. I see that it has not changed, and I see it differently" (Wittgenstein 1953: 193). The change, in other words, is not out there, it is in the eye. And the "expression of a change of aspect is the expression of a *new* perception and at the same time of the perception's being unchanged" (ibid.: 196).

Likewise, if seeing an aspect is a capacity within us that we cultivate, it would make sense to talk of not having the capacity to see an aspect. Wittgenstein calls it "aspect-blindness" (ibid.: 213). And, as I have argued elsewhere, for Wittgenstein aspect-blindness is not limited to pictures: "One can be aspect-blind to various experiences in *life*" (Hosseini 2015: 50). That is, the way we experience life's meaningfulness is similar to the way we see an aspect. About the person to whom the light of life seems to be extinguished, Wittgenstein might say here "what is incomprehensible is that *nothing*, and yet *everything*, has changed" (Wittgenstein 1946–49: 474). With a change of aspect, a life has changed. Now the awakenings, the daily small talks, what Goethe calls "the demands of the day," all seem to stand in need of justification. We were able to live our "ordinary life" quite successfully before the light was extinguished. Wittgenstein always showed an involved interest in the way we acquire or lose a "picture" or a way of looking at the world. A person, for example, would say "God's eye sees everything" and Wittgenstein responds:

> I want to say of this that it uses a picture. I don't want to belittle the person who says it ... We associate a particular use with a picture ... What conclusions are you going to draw? ... Are eyebrows going to be talked of, in

connection with the Eye of God? ... If I say he used a picture, I don't want to say anything he himself wouldn't say. I want to say he draws these conclusions.

(Wittgenstein 1938: 71–72).

How does such a person arrive at a picture of the world in which the eye of God is of importance but not His eyebrows? Why would we contemplate His words and never think about His accent? What are the implications of seeing the hands of God in one's life? On many occasions Wittgenstein refers to the ways, "Life can educate one to a belief in God" (Wittgenstein 1914–51: 86) or, how a certain "upbringing" is required to arrive at a religious way of looking at the world. For example, one might grow up in an environment where the sunrise means something special and one might keep seeing it as something special. However, one could get used to the specialness of the sun and in due time start to doubt whether it is indeed that special. The sun might then begin to look indifferent. Wittgenstein seems to think that often a change in one's picture of life happens like this. Things "break, slide about, cause every imaginable mischief" and one begins to see things differently (ibid.: 71). The darkest hours of one's life could pass right in front of a rising sun. Consider, for example, this passage in Wittgenstein's diaries:

After a very difficult day for me I kneeled during dinner today and prayed and suddenly said kneeling and looking up above: "There is no one here." That made me feel at ease as if I had been enlightened in an important matter. But what it really means I do not know yet. I feel relieved. But that does not mean, for example: I had previously been in error.

(Wittgenstein 1930–37: 193).

The gestalt shift from the belief that "God's eye sees everything" to the realization that "There is no one here," is not just a shift from one opinion to another. We might not be able to say in any unambiguous terms what caused this major shift but, Wittgenstein might suggest, that could sum up someone's life. He wants to know what it takes to let go of a picture of the world and embrace another. The varieties of human response to the phenomena of life interest him; the "strangeness" of human life and the "ceremonial" nature of many activities in our lives interest him. In short, he takes an involved interest in the things that happen in "the abyss in the human heart" (ibid.: 183).

But why is it that he refrains from a first-order engagement with the question of life's meaning? That is, why is it that he doesn't advance a principle or a theory of what could confer meaning on our lives? It seems that Wittgenstein is of the conviction that bringing forth a theory of life's meaning somehow entails the assumption that life could be familiarized; that it could be put within the framework of a system of understanding of the world, say – a scientific or a religious worldview. Theories of life's meaning, whether they are naturalist, supernaturalist or pessimist, take it for granted that, ultimately, things can be explained, and Wittgenstein finds that difficult to accept. He writes at the end of the *Tractatus*, "the whole modern conception of the world" is based on the "illusion" that "the so-called laws of nature" could explain everything. Thus,

> people today stop at the laws of nature, treating them as something inviolable, just as God and Fate were treated in past ages. And in fact both are right and both wrong: though the view of the ancients is clearer in so far as they have a clear and acknowledged terminus, while the modern system tries to make it look as if everything were explained.
>
> (Wittgenstein 1922: §6.372)

In contrast, a person who is not convinced that things could be explained away would be receptive to the quintessential way of philosophical life, that is, to the life of wonder: Not because "the world is a fine place and worth the fighting for," but because it exists (Hemingway 1940: 488). For this person: "It is not *how* things are in the world that is mystical, but *that* it exists" (Wittgenstein 1922: §6.44). That things are here and that things that are here tend to burn out or to fade away; that people from the dawn of time find themselves in the world: if we think about it freshly and innocently, we would be able to see that the ways we make sense of the world could be as awe-inspiring as all the things that made us think in the first place. On many occasions Wittgenstein points at this mode of seeing life and always tries to understand the varieties of human response to the world of the wind and the rain, to enduring memories, to the things we do and see in ourselves and in the lives of others, and the fact that, "My life consists in my being content to accept many things" (Wittgenstein 1933–35: §344). As a passage in "Remarks on Frazer's Golden Bough" illustrates:

> That a man's shadow, which looks like a man, or that his mirror image, or that rain, thunderstorms, the phases of the moon, the change of the seasons, the likeness and differences of animals to one another and to human beings, the phenomena of death, of birth and of sexual life, in short everything a man perceives year in, year out around him, connected together in any variety of ways – that all this should play a part in his thinking (his philosophy) and his practices, is obvious, or in other words, this is what we really know and find interesting.
>
> (Wittgenstein 1931: 6)

This way of approaching the phenomena of life is on the whole at odds with the approach of many philosophers to whom life is there to be explained away. The theorist of life's meaning might say life is just there and it wouldn't be constructive to dwell upon rudderless questions about the strangeness of human life. One is to get used to the strangeness and set forth a theory to show us what makes our life meaningful. Put differently, theorists of life's meaning would give us a theory but it would be in exchange for the initial astonishment we have "when the world hits us" (Clack 2002: 27). Wittgenstein is skeptical of such a transaction. He thinks no theory could do justice to the endless varieties of human responses to the phenomena of life, or to what Emerson once called "the language of these wandering eye-beams" (Emerson 1848: 341). From this vantage point one could get a sense of the kinds of questions Wittgenstein asks and the kinds of solutions he finds "interesting."

27 Heidegger and the meaning of life

WENDELL O'BRIEN

After he got over being a baby, Heidegger's whole life was a path of thinking, or a following of a path, and sometimes the forging of a new one. His path was one of twists and turns – apparently a U-turn in one place. What this means here is: We should expect Heidegger's thinking about the meaning of life to take different directions at different times.

Heidegger's works before and after *Being and Time*

Martin Heidegger gave lectures at the University of Freiburg (now published in English translation) several years before the 1927 appearance of his magnum opus *Being and Time*. The theme of these early lectures is "factical" human life, which comes already packed full of meaning. Life is self-sufficient. It requires nothing outside itself in order to be fully meaningful. The thing to do is to develop a full appreciation of the depth, immediacy, and intensity of life. It is in these that the meaningfulness of life lies.[1]

Many years later, Heidegger gave us more writings relevant to the meaning of life. These pieces are diffuse and often poetic, and it is difficult to say exactly what Heidegger's view of meaning in them is. One Heidegger scholar has argued that, in "[l]ater Heidegger," the meaning of life is to be *a guardian of the earth* (Young 2014: 232; see also Young 2002). Others have suggested all kinds of things: thinking; waiting for the return of the gods; letting things be; living poetically; listening to language speak; overcoming metaphysics and the "enframing" (*Gestell*) of the technological worldview and learning to dwell with things under the sky, on the earth, with mortals and gods; and on and on.[2]

It is no wonder there are so many widely divergent interpretations of the later works. One finds in them sentences that verge on unintelligibility to English and American readers, sentences such as: "What in the thing is thingly?" "The thing things." "Thinging, things are things." "If we let the thing be present in its thinging from out of the worlding world, then … we are the be-thinged … ones." "The gift of the outpouring [from the jug] stays the onefold of the fourfold of the four." And "Preserving farness, nearing preserves nearing in nearing that farness."[3] But much of Heidegger's later material is quite interesting when it is readable.

Here, however, I will focus on *Being and Time,* Heidegger's best known and most influential work.[4]

What *Being and Time*'s primary questions are and how they sound

In *Being and Time* Heidegger's theme (verbally) is not "life" but "Being" and "Human Being." There are two primary questions in *Being and Time*: "What is Being?" and "What is the *meaning* of Being?"

These are weird questions. We want to ask what the dickens Heidegger has in mind. But if we want to read Heidegger with charity, rather than dismiss his project as senseless and turn away to a better book by someone else (maybe Bertrand Russell), we will read his book and try to make sense of his questions and project. I believe we can, to some degree at least.

The question of Being

As human beings, we already have a dim, vague, implicit, and preconceptual understanding of Being, one that tends to be right but also contains errors. If we did not have this initial understanding, we could not use hammers, relate to other people, or deal with the entities around us. We could not even ask the question of Being and seek to answer it. It is our nature to want something better and clearer than the dim understanding we already have. A *philosopher*, especially, wants more. If she is anything like Heidegger, she wants a *fundamental ontology.* She seeks an understanding of Being that is conceptual, explicit, determinate, bright, and as correct as can be. But it is not easy to seek or find such an understanding. It is hard because, as Michael Inwood puts it, "the being of beings is not as localized, as conspicuous, or as independent of ourselves as are the mating habits of giraffes" (Inwood 1997: 21).

With that, I think, we see some sense in the question of being. More sense to the question comes – and a step toward answering it is taken – with the realization that Being is different from beings. I am a being, and so is my dog, apparently. But Being is not a being; it is not an entity of *any* sort. It is not even the *totality* of beings and entities; nor is it God, if He exists.

The question of the *meaning* of Being

The question of the *meaning* of Being is what we are most concerned with here. What precisely *is* it to ask this question? I could give no better answer than the one given by Charles Guignon:

> [T]o ask about the *meaning* of Being is to ask about how things come to show up as *counting* or *mattering* in specific ways in relation to our lives (where the

word "meaning" is used in the sense in which we say "This book meant a lot to me" or "That affair didn't mean a thing").

(Guignon, in Guignon and Pereboom 2001: 185)

Many philosophers, including "Analytic" philosophers like Thomas Nagel, take the question of the meaning of *life* to be the question of whether anything *matters*, and, if so, *how* it does (Nagel 1987: 95–107).[5] I will then take Heidegger's question about *the meaning of Being* to be equivalent to the question of *the meaning of life*, the theme of this whole volume. It seems to me that Heidegger's use of "Being" in preference to "life" is explained more by verbal than by substantive matters. By 1926 or 1927 he has come to think that the concept(s) of "life" is both too narrow and too broad. And the word itself is hopelessly ambiguous. Moreover, Heidegger wants to avoid words, such as "life," that might identify him with certain movements he wants to be no part of.

Why ask this question of the meaning of life (of Being)? Heidegger scholar W. Julian Korab-Karpowicz writes: "The question of the meaning of being is the deepest problem of life for every human being" (Korab-Karpowicz 2017: 109). I believe Heidegger would agree with this statement and would assent to the suggestion that the statement captures a conviction of his that partly motivates *Being and Time*. But Heidegger also thinks it is *important* to ask this question, especially *now* in 1927. (That's the rest of the motivation.) The question of the meaning of Being (life) is both *deep* and *important now to ask*.

Why is it so important to ask the question now? A short answer is that the worldview of modern science, which has trickled down to nearly everyone in the West, has left us with a problem about how anything can have meaning or value. We ourselves are supposed to inject value into an in-itself valueless and meaningless world. But we seem to have no basis for doing that. The result is we are unable to regard one way of life as "better" or "higher" than another, and there is a widespread sense of loss of meaning. That is bad and dangerous. "The concern with confronting this wide-spread loss of meaning in modern life is one of the central aims of *Being and Time*" (Guignon 2001: 187).

What Heidegger planned and what he actually did

In writing *Being and Time*, Heidegger's original plan was to approach the question of the meaning of Being in general by way of an examination of the meaning of one particular (kind of) being, namely, *Dasein*. But Heidegger completed only one-third of *Being and Time*, and he never did get around to addressing the question of the meaning of Being as such. He did, however, say plenty about the meaning of Dasein and its mode of Being.

Dasein

"Dasein" literally means "being there," or "being here" – which of these is the better literal translation is unclear, but that's neither here nor there – and in ordinary German usage it means "life" or "existence." Heidegger gives his own technical definition of it: *Dasein is the being for whom its Being is an issue.* Dasein is, in effect, the human being, or human life, since, as far as we know, it is only for human beings that Being is an issue. I am a Dasein and you the reader are another Dasein, but my dog is not a Dasein, and neither is yours, if you have one. Dogs don't think about stuff like Being and the meaning of life. In what follows, then, I will sometimes use, in addition to "Dasein," alternative English expressions like "human being," "person," "existence," and "life" instead of "Dasein." I will not use "dog."

Dasein, the human being, has no essence. What it *is* depends on its choices and *actions*. We are primarily *agents* (not detached observers or knowing subjects). What we *are* is determined by what we *do*.

Different people make different choices and do different things. So the Being of one person is (to some degree) different from the Being of another. And the meaning of one person's life may be quite different from the meaning of another's. "Everyone answers [the question of the meaning of being] alone; and therefore, our answer is not always valid for others" (Korab-Karpowicz 2017: 109).

There is no such thing as interior Dasein. We are not minds trapped inside our own heads, trying to get out, wondering whether there really is an "external" world, and if there is, how to get to it. There is no "problem of our knowledge of the external world." The very internal–external distinction is dubious in this context. The Being of Dasein as such is essentially *Being-in-the-world.*

The meaning of life

When he writes *Being and Time* Heidegger does not think that there is any universal meaning of life to be discovered, the sort of meaning a firm believer in God might look for or claim to have found. Heidegger writes, "'Behind' the phenomena of phenomenology there is essentially nothing else," and "The 'nothing' with which anxiety brings us face to face, unveils the nullity by which Dasein, in its very basis, is defined" (Heidegger 1927: §7, §62).

Nonetheless, it still makes sense to ask about meaningfulness and the meaning of life, for life *is* (or can be) meaningful and have meaning in it.

What is the meaning of life (human existence) in *Being and Time*? And what makes life meaningful? There are several possible answers. I will discuss three of them. I will not argue strenuously that any one of them is the correct one – correct in expressing Heidegger's standpoint (on his path). The answers may be consistent with each other; or they may be inconsistent. The reader who wants a single answer must read *Being and Time* carefully – and then reread it several times *more* carefully, consulting the best commentaries along the way – and make his or her own decision about the matter. I will, though, mention some potential problems many readers might see in Heidegger's stances, and some objections.

Care as the meaning of life

Heidegger says the meaning of the Being of Dasein as such is *care* (*Sorge*). He writes: "Dasein's Being reveals itself as *care*"; "Being-in-the-world is essentially care"; "[Dasein is] an entity whose Being must be defined as 'care'"; and, speaking of the Being of Dasein, "Its existential meaning is *care*" (ibid.: §8, §39, §41).

Care is a primordial structural totality, a unity that can neither be "torn asunder" nor traced back to special acts or drives like willing or wishing. Nonetheless, it does have a structure, a threefold one. The three items in the structure are: (1) Being-*already*-in-world; (2) Being-*ahead-of-itself*; and (3) Being-*alongside* or Being-*with*-(other people, beings, and entities in the world). Heidegger puts it like this: "[T]he Being of Dasein means ahead-of-itself-Being-already-in-(the-world) as Being-alongside (entities encountered within-the-world) .... This Being fills in the signification of the term '*care*'" (ibid.: §41).

Being-(already)-in-the world signifies a person's *past*, her "thrownness" and its implications. We don't originally decide to exist; we don't create ourselves and choose the kind of world we want to live in. We just find ourselves in a world with obligations, tasks, tendencies, and so forth that derive from the past – our history, and the history of our community. What I am now, what I must do now, may depend, for example, on a choice I made years ago, or it may depend on history of the community I find myself thrown into.

Being-ahead-of-itself has to do with the *future*. This aspect of our Being Heidegger calls "projection." Dasein projects itself (or its Being) toward any of a range of future possibilities. Dasein, then, has (or *is*) potentiality for various modes of Being. Being-alongside or Being-with has to do with the *present*. Heidegger calls it "fallenness." Dasein is not solitary. Dasein essentially and primordially lives in the world, encountering entities and beings, some of which are other Daseins (human beings) and some of which are not. A human being could not exist at all if there were not a world to be in, a world in which there are other beings and entities to encounter and relate to. So the Being of Dasein, human Being, is through and through *temporal*. It comes from the past, abides (with others) in the present, and faces the future.

Heidegger's "care" is not some particular emotion like worry. It is general primordial *concern* and *solicitude*. A human being essentially concerns himself or herself with what is at hand, and he or she takes care of (is solicitous about) others. People and things necessarily *matter* to us. If they didn't, life would be *meaningless*, perhaps even *impossible*. Maybe, then, one could indeed justifiably attribute to Heidegger – whether or not he would like it – the view that care is the meaning of life, or at least what makes life meaningful.

All this may be difficult for the non-German reader to make sense of. But one thing clear is that Heidegger's thinking in *Being and Time* is plainly at odds with thought that places the meaning, sense, or secret of life (or Being) in anything like indifference, disengagement, detachment, or non-attachment – thought found in, for example, *The Bhagavad Gita* and certain veins of Daoism, Buddhism, and Stoicism. Richard Polt writes: "Although Heidegger does not directly say so, his language of 'care' is an implicit criticism of all philosophies of detachment. Human beings can never become … radically indifferent" (Polt 1999: 79).

Sometimes we *feel* indifferent, detached, disengaged, at peace, calm, unconcerned. Heidegger does not deny this. But he holds that even these are modes of care or concern – *deficient* modes. But, if he were to allow the possibility at all, what would Heidegger say of someone who truly achieved a state of complete non-attachment or realized nirvana in this very life? He would probably say something like what Polt says here:

> Someone who has truly reached absolute indifference is not Dasein anymore, but has entered another state of Being, either nirvana or vegetation, that is unintelligible to those of us who still dwell in the world.
>
> (Ibid.: 47)

Although care seems to me to be a reasonable candidate for the meaning of life, I might vote against it, if I had to vote at all. Certainly, those who think that there is something to the philosophy of detachment – a philosophy embraced by many great thinkers of our heritage, both Western and Asian – would vote "No" or (more likely) abstain.

Time as the meaning of life

Because Heidegger regards life as thoroughly temporal, and because he goes on to say that the meaning of care itself is time, one might reasonably hold that, for Heidegger, the meaning of human existence is *time*. After all, the very title of his book is *Being and Time*, and Heidegger says, "Our provisional aim is the Interpretation of *time* as the possible horizon [context or frame of reference] for any understanding whatever of Being" (Heidegger 1927: 19). He also says temporality is the "meaning" of Dasein's Being (ibid: §5). Moreover, without time to exist in, Dasein could not exist at all: time is the ground of the very possibility of Dasein.

In Heidegger's usage, the word "time" does not mean ordinary clock-and-calendar time. Time of the latter sort is associated with a theoretical conception according to which time is an endless, one-directional succession of instants. This less important sort of time has become the standard and ordinary sense of time. But it is not fundamental. It is *derivative* from the kind of time that is of the greatest importance.

The most important and fundamental sense of time is *primordial* time. I cannot find anything like a *definition* of this "primordial time" in *Being and Time*. But Heidegger does provide characterizations of it that give some indication of what it is supposed to be. Here, in brief, are two of them. (1) Primordial time is *Dasein's temporality*. Dasein has a present, a past, and a future. These three are "ecstases." Temporality lies in these ecstases. *"Temporality is the primordial 'outside-of-itself' in and for itself"* (ibid.: §65). The *essence* of temporality is "a process of temporalizing in the unity of the ecstases" (ibid.: §65). Clarifying "temporalizing," Heidegger writes: "The future is *not later* than having been, and having been is *not earlier* than the Present" and "Temporalizing temporalizes itself as a future which makes present in the process of having been" (ibid.: §68). Make of this what you can. (2) Time is a matter of *significance*. In time things are *important* to Dasein. "Our future and our past ... are meaningful to us in everyday life because they are relevant to our current practical concerns" (Polt 1999: 107).

I suspect that time will not strike many readers as a good candidate for the-meaning-of-life position. There are several reasons this is the case. (1) True, without time to live in, we couldn't exist at all. But that can be said of many things: space, air, water, food, shelter, tobacco, and so on. The adoption of time as the winning candidate seems arbitrary. (2) "The meaning of life is time" may very well just *sound* wrong to your ear. If Nietzsche can trust his nose, why can't you trust your ear? (3) Heidegger's reasoning here appears empty and circular: the meaning of Dasein is time; time is a matter of significance; so the significance of Dasein is significance, the meaning of meaning is meaning.

Authenticity as what makes one's life meaningful

There is a plausible alternative to the results of the reasoning above. It is that, for Heidegger, the meaningfulness of life lies in *authenticity* (*Eigentlichkeit*). Young writes: "Authenticity is Heidegger's account of what it is to live a meaningful life" (Young 2014: 146). Heidegger's treatment of authenticity and the web of issues surrounding it is among the most important, influential, and interesting things in *Being and Time*.

"Proximally and for the most part" we live in the realm of "average-everydayness," in which we just follow the crowd. We take on social roles. We give in to peer pressure, or just conform mindlessly. We follow social conventions, doing what "one" does and refraining from what "one" does *not* do. Suppose my baldness bothers me. How should I respond to this fact? "Wearing a wig is an acceptable response, whereas attempting to shave the heads of everyone else so that I am no longer exceptional is not" (Inwood 1997: 26). In this I follow the dictates of "The Man" or the "They." It is "They," not I, who determine what and who I am, the choices I make, the actions I take. "They" run my life, I don't.

This kind of existence is *inauthentic*. One has a dim sense that there is something wrong with it. At some level of my being I feel that I myself should determine who I am, what choices I make, and the shape my life should take. I have a sense of self-betrayal. So there is something bad about the average-everyday-inauthentic mode of existence. But there is an upside to it as well. It brings with it a feeling of security. It brings comfort, and it tends to produce tranquility. All that *sounds* good.

What we are really doing in the inauthentic life, however, is fleeing from ourselves and trying to evade *death*. Like everyone who pays taxes, I know I'm going to die. But "They" never die. By identifying myself with "Them," I gain (an illusory) sense of immortality. And then I can forget about my death and let it remain something I just don't think about.

Heidegger believes that simply won't do. I must, in order to be an *authentic* person, face up to death. I must pound it into my head that my death is indeed mine, real and utter annihilation, unavoidable, and *could happen at any moment*. An authentic person anticipates death. Her mode of Being is "Being-toward-death" or "running-forward-into-death" – not literally, as in running forward toward the top of the cliff, but rather running forward toward her death in *thought*. Heidegger nowhere recommends suicide.

In this vivid awareness of her death, a person realizes the *finitude* of her existence and of the possibilities open to her. She realizes the preciousness of her life, and gets a sense of the waste in squandering it in the life of the "They." In brief, authenticity is a matter of making one's *own* choices, determining *oneself* the kind of person one is going to be and (as long as it lasts) the way one's life is going to go. Then one resolutely lives in accordance with those decisions and choices. This gives *shape* and unity to one's life, creates *focus*, gives one a sense of purpose, importance, and urgency, and therefore makes one's life genuinely *meaningful*.

The spur to the movement toward authenticity is provided by the experience of profound *anxiety*, a rare mood or "attunement" in which one encounters the meaninglessness of everything and is thrown back on confronting the question of one's own Being. Because I, Wendell, am feeling anxious and realize I could die at any minute, I cannot further discuss this anxiety and how it works.

None of this means Heidegger's thinking here is radically individualistic. A person draws his or her choices from the well of tradition, from the heritage of his or her community.

I believe that most of my readers will consider authenticity the best of the three possible answers Heidegger gives to the question of the meaning of life in *Being and Time*. However, some (mistakenly, perhaps) find the idea that a person should have his or her death constantly (or often) in mind rather *morbid*. And it is not something every great thinker would accept. Spinoza, for instance, writes: "A free man thinks of death least of all things, and his wisdom is a meditation of life, not of death" (Spinoza 1677: IV, §67). Is Spinoza right?

What about the man who chooses to lead an immoral life? After all, there are about as many villains as heroes in our heritage. And what about the man who authentically chooses and resolutely follows the inauthentic, but comfortable and tranquil, life dictated by "The Man"? Questions remain.[6]

Notes

1 Those interested in Heidegger's early Freiburg thought should begin with (Campbell 2012), and then follow Campbell's lead to other sources.
2 The essays, lectures, and addresses in which Heidegger's later thinking is communicated may be found in several ready-to-hand collections, among them: Heidegger 1971b, 1938–55 , 1927–64.
3 All these examples are taken from Heidegger 1971b.
4 My treatment of *Being and Time* makes liberal use of the interpretations of Charles Guignon in the introduction to Heidegger in Guignon and Pereboom 2001 and Young 2014. I have also found the writings of Richard Polt and Michael Inwood extremely helpful.
5 The chapter on "The Meaning of Life" is all about whether and how anything matters,
6 In writing this piece I have benefited from pointers and suggestions from Scott Campbell, Daniel Dahlstrom, Charles Guignon, Michael Inwood, Ted Kisiel, Julian Korab-Karpowicz, Richard Polt, Robert Scharff, Thomas Sheehan, Mark Wrathall, and Julian Young. They will likely be dismayed by the result, if they read it at all, but I am grateful to them nonetheless.

28 Sartre and the meaning of life

JOSEPH S. CATALANO

The task before me is to write an account of Sartre's view of the meaning of life so that it "will not be a work of historical reconstruction but rather a means to put the history of philosophy into direct action." Having spent the good part of the last thirty years reading and writing about Sartre, I am pleased to offer my answer. I will proceed in four stages that loosely reflect the development of Sartre's own thought, while I will nevertheless permit myself to look forward and backward at each stage.

These stages are, first, the formation of our own personal "project," that is, the way our daily actions fit within our general view of the meaning of life. As very young children, our thoughts and actions go this way and that. But gradually, by five or at least ten years of age, in interacting with others, we form for ourselves a general pattern for how we shall pursue the task of giving meaning to our lives, even if this be that we think life meaningless. Later conversions will always be possible, although the longer we stay in a project, the more difficult change becomes. The second stage is that our early interactions with others help us to form our general pursuit to give meaning to our own lives. We may call this stage the adult–child relation. Third, we work out our personal and daily pursuit to give meaning to our own lives amidst the forces of history that surround us on every side. Finally, each life reflects its own project and that of all humans.

As the above stages indicate, there is development in Sartre's thought. Nevertheless, there is a general theme that runs throughout all his reflections on our pursuit to give meaning to our lives. *All of the philosophy of Jean-Paul Sartre has this moral imperative: one must align oneself with the more disadvantaged members of one's society, attempting to see the world from their perspective and then help to bring them up to your more advantaged position.* This collective responsibility falls upon all of "us," – the well-fed, relatively safe and fortunate of the world, even if we think we deserve our position in society. This moral imperative is nicely summed up in one of Sartre's earliest essays, *Existentialism Is a Humanism*. I still like this early work on humanism, and particularly the ending:

> Tomorrow, after my death, some men may decide to establish Fascism, and
> the others may be so cowardly or slack as to let them do it. If so, Fascism will

then be the truth of man, and so much the worse for us ... Does that mean that I should abandon myself to quietism? No ... if I ask myself "Will the social ideal as such ever become a reality?" I cannot tell, I only know that whatever may be in my power to make it so, I shall do.

(Sartre 1946: 358)

"Whatever may be in my power to make it so, I shall do." A colleague of mine, who does not particularly like Sartre, nevertheless gives credit to his practical conviction: that he taught a generation of scholars that they must go out into the streets and get involved. Sartre gave out pamphlets and associated himself – *his body* – with numerous causes of injustice that he saw in Paris. In this, he scandalized many of his contemporaries who did not think it professional of him. For Sartre, one's philosophical thoughts must overflow into action as much as this is possible.

I have referred to Sartre's early attitude toward humanism, but it is important to add that later in his writings, Sartre distinguished between a bourgeois humanism and an existential humanism. In its final form, this bourgeois humanism implied a world without God or free humans, in which there are no meaningful answers to seek concerning the significance of human existence, since all the answers are already part of the furniture of the world and merely have to be uncovered by science. Bourgeois humanism served the rich and powerful, since adhering to the doctrine of survival of the fittest, it stressed the needs of a rising French middle class over the destitution of the poor. An existential humanism that looks at the world from the perspective of the most disadvantaged, however, seeking their immediate help, was always possible ... but never put into practice. It must be noted that these are the thoughts of an atheist. For Sartre, there is no God, but there is freedom and responsibility. With this in mind, we can now begin our reflection on the four stages listed above.

First stage: the project

Being and Nothingness is a complex and dense work, and yet Sartre invites us, the readers, to work out the adventure of his book along with him. He informs us that he is writing this book about how we are each related to all reality, and says he recognizes that you, the reader, no doubt wish to know his general perspective on his task. He invites you to follow him:

Now this very inquiry furnishes us with the desired conduct; this man that *I am* – if I apprehend him such as he is at this moment in the world, I establish that he stands before being in an attitude of interrogation.

(Sartre 1943: 4)

Every human life is filled with meaning because it is the birth of the question of the meaning of existence. The existence of even one person fractures reality, creating order and hierarchy – what we call our "world." True, without human existence, dinosaurs, for example, would have existed, but so would gusts of winds and the countless movement of particles and snowflakes, which we are told are each different from one another. Why should a snow flake, unique and irreplaceable, be less important than a dinosaur? The only answer is that we see a closer connection to our own life between the existences of those large beings who roamed the Earth than we do to fading snowflakes. Sartre terms the infinite complexity of things without order, "being-in-itself," or simply the "in-itself." A human existence is termed a "for-itself" because, as we question reality, we relate all things to ourselves. Nevertheless, we could not exist without the in-itself, for we arise from the in-itself; although for Sartre there is no reason why this should be so.

Every human being is born to be a philosopher – recall the countless "why"s of every child – but only a few, such as represented in this volume, embrace the task as a way of life. But, each life pursues the answer to the question of the meaning of existence in its daily pursuits, in what Sartre terms its "project." Consider a teenager who does not have a clear notion of what they wish to do with their life and goes to school to help him or her decide. Still, that itself is a major decision, a project. If our young person were to awake each morning and question whether it is best to be going to school, or rather to drop out and start working, then a nervous collapse would be the answer. The possibility of dropping out always exists, but is kept in the background until such time as one is ready to consider it a viable option. Otherwise, one retains one's project, or more specifically, one's fundamental project.

In Part Four of *Being and Nothingness*, Sartre writes, "My ultimate and initial project – for these are but one – is, we will see, always the outline of a solution of the problem of being," and he adds, "But this solution is not first conceived and then realized; we are this solution" (ibid.: 463). Our solution to the problem of being is the concrete ways we live our lives. The two most general ways are to accept this responsibility in good faith or attempt to flee from it in bad faith. *Being and Nothingness*, which proceeds from the abstract to the concrete, does indeed describe in more detail our many ways of attempting to avoid our responsibility for being an individual and to thereby avoid a personal solution to the problem of being. This would be difficult to understand unless one realized that Sartre had already reflected on World War I and was seeing the beginnings of World War II, as well as experiencing the pervasiveness of such bad-faith phenomena as anti-Semitism in his own French society.

Indeed, as he was writing *Being and Nothingness*, Sartre seemed to realize that he needed to explain his moral position in more detail and thus he promised an ethics that would appear soon. It never appeared, but we now know that it was written, and it has been published posthumously as *Notebooks for an Ethics*. The work is interesting for it is a detailed examination of the various ways in which those in power subordinate others for their own benefit: this inner restructuring of a budding freedom is not innocent: "One does not make use of the oppressed as a machine, contrary to what is often said, but as a limited freedom" (Sartre 1983: 328).

But let us return to *Being and Nothingness*. In Part Three, section three, "Concrete Relations with Others," Sartre attempts to give a general description of our basic attitudes that we have toward each other. I have always thought it the weakest part of his work, the one place where he attempts to do to too much too quickly. Still, in retrospect, rereading these words in light of his later works, the basic theme becomes clearer. He divides his discussion into three parts. The first concerns love, language, and masochism; the second, indifference, desire, hate, and sadism. And then a last section about the "we." The first two sections all have their clue in the reflection on love. The basic notion is simple. There is love that is a gamble, respecting the freedom of both the lover and beloved, and love that seeks security by attempting to keep freedom only for oneself. (This all comes out beautifully in Sartre's study of Flaubert, where the father wanted his son to be a doctor like himself, or at least a lawyer, and not waste his time writing stupid novels.) Sartre writes:

> This unrealizable ideal which haunts my projects in the presence of the Other is not to be identified with love in so far as love is an enterprise; i.e., an organic ensemble of projects toward my own possibilities. But it is the ideal of love, its motivation and its end, its unique value.
>
> (Sartre 1943: 366)

The distinction here and elsewhere in this section is between an act and an ideal; but this can be confusing since every act includes an ideal. The ideals that Sartre has in mind are bad-faith ideals: those that do not involve belief in change, those that want the other, the beloved, to offer a mirror to oneself, so that we can see our own progress while the beloved remains constant. It is not ownership that is desired in the ideal of love; rather, something deeper, namely, a freedom fixed forever on one's own freedom and on one's body in all its details: "How good am I to have eyes, hair, eyebrows and to lavish them away tirelessly in an overflow of generosity – This is the basis for the joy of love when there is joy: we feel that our existence is justified" (ibid.: 371).

All these attitudes can be in good faith if one respects the freedom of others. Only masochism is always in bad faith, and what Sartre writes is interesting: "Masochism therefore is on principle a failure. This should not surprise us if we realize that masochism is a 'vice' and that vice is, on principle, the love of failure" (ibid.: 379). Thus the moral challenge: Try! If you fail, well you fail; but it cannot have been failure you sought, for then you would never have truly tried.

I mentioned a third division in this section; it is the "Mitsein," Heidegger's notion of our "being with another." For Sartre, our being with others is only something we achieve by our efforts; it is not something we are born with.

Second stage: the adult–child relation

All philosophical works are written by adults who tend to forget what it was like when they were children. It is natural, and Sartre is no exception, at least in his early philosophical works. It was only when he decided to write about Genet and then later to reflect in detail on the life of Gustave Flaubert that Sartre began to examine the vulnerability of every child, at least until five or six, and frequently later. The relation should be one of love as an "enterprise," that is, allowing the child to grow and discover its own adventure in life. Sartre was aware that the children of slaves, the oppressed, the very poor, are frequently deprived of that opportunity through no fault of their own – or that of their parents. But in his study of Genet and Flaubert, Sartre comes upon middle-class oppression. The massive study of Flaubert, *The Family Idiot*, is the most comprehensive study, but the shorter study of Genet – still about 600 pages – has its own distinctive features, especially as it clearly expresses how Sartre the atheist can distinguish between true good and real evil:

> For the specialist, magistrates, criminologists, sociologists, there are not *evil* acts: there are only punishable acts. For the man in the street, there are evil acts, but it is always the Others who commit them. Genet wants to reveal to the former that Evil exists and to the latter that its roots are to be found in themselves.
>
> (Sartre 1952: 490)

At the heart of Sartre's sympathetic study of Genet is our misguided pursuit to find the meaning of life in the ownership of things. Strangely, Genet wants to be a property owner and become a member of acceptable society. But he is too quickly judged as a thief, and thus whatever he owns is considered to be stolen, whether this is true or not. Genet is judged by the "good" people of the world, and this judgment reaches deep within the youth: "The child Genet is the inhuman product of which man is the sole problem. How to be accepted by men?" (ibid.: 46). Remarkably, Genet accepts his role: yes, he will be an outcast, but a pure outcast, the "saint" of the rejected.

Third stage: the forces of history

The two volumes of Sartre's *Critique of Dialectical Reason* are devoted to showing how our individual lives work out their meanings in the complex material world in which we live. Let us begin with a great note of optimism. We live in a unique period in which for the first time we have at hand the means of guiding our future historical development. This was not always true. Sartre uses the example of Chinese peasants who, in order to make their land arable, deforested it and were thereby themselves the cause of floods. Floods, of course, are also caused by nature; but the point here is that the very intention to plant crops hid the counter-finality of a land barren of trees. While it was impossible for the Chinese peasants to foresee the result of deforesting their land, the message of the *Critique* is that we are now capable of such foresight and consequent control of our actions. The dialectic is thus a specific type of intellectual effort. It is a rethinking, born of Hegel, Kierkegaard, and Marx, as well as of the countless efforts to form unions and organize against those who would use humans as tools for their own profit. The world should be a better place than it is, but, with all our failures, the good acts of countless humans have had their effects. Sartre writes:

> Thus when we claim *anyone* can carry out the critical investigation, this does not mean it could happen at any period. It means anyone *today*. What then does "anyone" mean? We use this term to indicate that, if the historical totalization is to be able to exist, then any human life is the direct and indirect expression of (the totalizing movement) and of all lives precisely to the extent that it is opposed to everything and to everyone.
>
> (Sartre 1960: 50)

Another way of putting this general claim is that there is a meaning and a truth to history, to the extent that we can each understand our inclusion within a web of ever-widening, open-ended totalizations that ultimately give us "One World," even as we are thereby distinguished as *this unique person.*

Nevertheless, this great optimistic note must be balanced by the unfortunate ways in which we have let the rich and powerful peoples of the world keep the collective historical benefits to themselves, using and directing human efforts to make humans always suspicious of their fellow humans. Their success is so widespread that they have forged our institutions to reflect "scarcity" as the meaning of our history: there will never be enough for all and so each person had better take care of themselves. Sartre writes:

> Nothing – not even wild beasts or microbes – could be more terrifying for man than a species which is intelligent, carnivorous and cruel, and which can understand and outwit human intelligence, and whose aim is precisely the destruction of man. This, however, is obviously our own species as perceived in others by each of its members in the context of scarcity ... The first movement of ethics, in this case, is the constitution of radical evil and of Manichaeism.
>
> (Ibid.: 132)

Scarcity – there will never be enough for all; second, a Manichaeism that proclaims that good is the destruction of evil rather than an attempt to do good itself; and finally, the placement of radical evil in the dangerous poor and disadvantaged who appear capable of threatening our possessions – these are the three main moral facets of our instituted forces of history that keep us distracted from doing real good. We keep this hell alive through the constant rebirth of enemies. Sometimes these dangerous others are "over there," but no, they are under our feet; or banging the doors of our safe homes. Now, perhaps, we are safe from them; that is, I am safe from you and you are safe from me – but who knows what will happen?

Indeed, relevant to our contemporary American political position under Donald Trump, Sartre notes that the French colonization of Algeria was only partly initiated for capitalistic gains; more important than cheap labor, was the need to forge the Muslims into the subhuman, dangerous *other* that needed to be tamed and governed, for their own good, and for the good of the established order.

Individually, it is impossible for any one person to change history, but we can and do form what Sartre terms "groups-in-fusion," which is to say that at certain times when the conditions are right, our individual acts can unite freely with others to overcome oppression. I do what I can *here*, knowing that, if you could, you would be *here* with me to help; and reciprocally, you know the same of me. Still, for Sartre, this "we" is something constituted from our individual actions. "The only practical dialectical reality, the motive force of everything, is individual action" (ibid.: 322).

Final: how each life reflects history

Regardless of how the forces of history work upon us, there are still personal and family dramas. Indeed, the longest and most exhaustive study by Sartre is about a middle-class French family, the Flauberts.

Achille-Cléophas and Caroline Flaubert had plans for their children, and, as Sartre observes, when parents have plans then their children have destinies. Achille, the first born son, fulfilled his destiny by becoming a doctor like his eminent father, and Caroline, the only daughter, made a good match in marriage, just like her mother, after whom she was named. Only Gustave, the second son, did not seem able or willing to conform to the family plan. He paid a price for his resistance. Sartre does not mince words: "Gustave's relationship with his mother deprived him of affirmative power, tainted his relationship to the word and to truth, destined him for sexual perversion; his relationship with his father made him lose his sense of reality" (Sartre 1971–72: II, 69).

Do parents have this much influence over a child? Usually parental presence is tempered by the influence of relatives and friends; but when the family structure is tight, as it was with the Flaubert family, the infant can enter the real world only through the family. But, if through lack of love this door to the real world is closed, only one other path beckons the infant: that of the imaginary. (Later, the child or adolescent may choose death.) Thus, the infant Gustave Flaubert chooses the imaginary. Too young to put a bundle of cloths over his shoulder and leave the home in which he felt unwanted, he found a way – as do many others – of keeping his fragile body at home while living elsewhere. In this way, from his earliest years until he was about seven, Gustave Flaubert gave himself over to his daydreams and seemed always to be in a stupor. He was incapable of the quick learning which already characterized his older brother and would later characterize his younger sister too. In comparison, Gustave seemed to be a dunce. Nevertheless, by ten or eleven years of age, he who could not read was already writing with exceptional competence. "Indeed, let us not forget," Sartre writes, "that from his thirteenth year the cards were on the table, Gustave wrote books and letters, he had permanent witnesses. It is impossible to take liberties with facts so well known" (ibid.: I, 46).

Through three large volumes in French and five in English by the excellent and dedicated work of Carol Cosman, Sartre traces the relentless way the Flaubert family never accepted their son. Even when he had attained fame, they regarded him as the "family idiot," one who could never cut it as a doctor or even a lawyer. What makes the elaboration of this drama so telling and relevant to our present day is the way Gustave Flaubert's life and writings, especially *Madame Bovary*, reflect the almost hopeless historical situation of France, simmering under the defeat of Napoleon and looking for its own way out of resentment – much as we in America are looking for a way out of our own failure to sustain a middle class. We, in America, with the help of the other prosperous nations, can feed the world and give to all a decent life – the industrial revolution accomplished that – but the rich and powerful are afraid to live in a world in which the average person has the same freedom and opportunity to live the adventure of giving meaning to all existence which they themselves possess ... and squander. Sartre writes, "Our species has set out upon the road of no return toward self-domestication" (ibid.: I, 98).

Still, the constant message by Sartre is that change, both individual and social, is always possible. All of Sartre's philosophy details how the meaning of each life reveals the meaning of existence for all humanity. We can accept this burden or attempt to flee from it in bad faith. No other philosopher except Marx has written with such dedication on this one theme. Sartre summarizes his relation to Marx in this way: "It must be clearly understood that the rediscovery of scarcity in this investigation makes absolutely no claim to oppose Marxist theory or to complete it. It is of a different order" (Sartre 1960: 152, n. 35). This "order" is freedom, which is one with the efficacy and value of individual efforts. That is a very big difference.[1]

Note

1 This chapter builds upon Catalano 2010.

29 Beauvoir and the meaning of life

JONATHAN WEBBER

Simone de Beauvoir's first published philosophical treatise was her short book on absurdity and morality, *Pyrrhus and Cineas* (Beauvoir 1944). It is rather unfortunate that this book was not available in English until sixty years later. Her work in moral and political philosophy in the 1940s rests crucially on this book's central argument, so the reception of that thought in the anglophone world has been stymied by a lack of attention to that argument. And this book contains her only sustained consideration of absurdity and the human condition, so the reception of her existential philosophy has been distorted.

Beauvoir does not make herself easy to understand in this book. Her attention meanders, in the classical French essay style developed by Michel de Montaigne, through various responses to the problem of absurdity in the history of thought, illustrated along the way by examples from Christian theology, medieval European politics, the history of art, and the development of the sciences. All this erudition somewhat obscures the book's argument, which is, as we will see, well worth articulating in splendid isolation. For it connects the problem of absurdity with the question of the grounding of morality to form a single innovative contribution to both existential and moral philosophy.

Absurdity and existentialism

The book opens with a dialogue between Pyrrhus, King of Epirus in the third century BCE, and his adviser Cineas about a plan for world domination. Pyrrhus declares that he will first conquer Greece and Cineas asks what he will do after that. Pyrrhus responds that he will then conquer Africa, to which Cineas replies with the same question. This continues until Pyrrhus has run out of lands to conquer, at which point, he says, he will rest. But then, asks Cineas, why not just rest straight away? His implication is that this life of rest would be no less meaningful than the world domination that Pyrrhus has planned.

Beauvoir argues that Cineas does have a point. Each project we pursue has a goal that we value while we pursue it, but once we have completed the project we move on to a new goal, a new value, and the old one no longer seems so important. We can even take up this perspective before the project is completed, reflecting on our goal and asking why we value that rather than something else. Should we accept the implication of this reflective stance, that values are only temporary illusions generated by our projects? Should we accept this nihilist conclusion that Cineas is hinting at?

Beauvoir's view is that we simply cannot accept this. Pursuing projects with values at their core is not an optional feature of human life like keeping pets or reading newspapers. We cannot just give it up. Beauvoir holds to the existentialist view that the pursuit of projects is the very structure of our being. On this view, the structure of our being commits us to taking our values seriously, even though on reflection those values can seem entirely arbitrary. But this ability to step back and question our own values is equally fundamental to our existence, she argues, so we cannot just ignore that either.

We seem to be left not with nihilism, but with absurdity. We seem condemned to taking seriously some set of values while being aware that we have no justification for them. This is the problem Beauvoir sets out to address. In its existential aspect, it poses the question of whether our lives and the activities that comprise them can have any real meaning or value. In its moral aspect, it poses the question of whether there are any objective values that constrain the range of projects that it is acceptable for us to pursue. Beauvoir's strategy is to solve the existential aspect of the problem through its moral aspect.

Pyrrhus is not Sisyphus

Albert Camus famously crystallizes the problem of absurdity, as he sees that problem, into the image of Sisyphus being condemned to continuously roll a rock to the top of a hill only to see it roll back down again. Although his short treatise on absurdity, published two years before Beauvoir's, provides plenty of other examples, his use of this image as the book's title and its concluding chapter makes it definitive. Beauvoir's choice of Pyrrhus as her defining example of the pursuit of projects stands in sharp contrast to *The Myth of Sisyphus* (Camus 1942a), even though she does not directly mention that book anywhere in her analysis of absurdity.

For Pyrrhus and Sisyphus differ in three important ways. Pyrrhus is planning a sequence of conquests of different lands, each land presenting different challenges, but Sisyphus merely repeats a single project. Pyrrhus knows full well that one fine day he will run out lands to conquer, but Sisyphus is condemned to roll his rock for all eternity. And, perhaps most importantly, Pyrrhus is engaged in a world filled with other people pursuing their own projects, whereas Sisyphus is embarked on an inherently solipsistic enterprise.

In all three ways, Pyrrhus resembles the human condition where Sisyphus does not. The structure of human existence does not condemn us to repeating a single project over and over again. It is true that for most people a large part of life is absorbed in the repetitive cycle of maintaining the conditions required for staying alive and healthy. But it is not inherent in the human condition that life must be entirely devoted to its own maintenance. Rather, to an extent that depends on the individual's economic circumstances, staying alive provides the necessary grounds for the pursuit of other projects.

The end of staying alive, so long as it is achieved, is therefore an example of what Beauvoir calls a 'point of departure' (*point de départ*). When an end is achieved, she points out, it does not simply disappear from the world as a new project is undertaken. Rather, it remains available to serve as the required basis for a new project. Not only does Pyrrhus differ from Sisyphus in being engaged in a sequence of different projects, but each project in that sequence provides part of the ground required for the next one. Previous success in rolling the rock up the hill makes no difference to Sisyphus as he embarks on the project again. Pyrrhus, by contrast, could not hope to conquer Africa without first building a larger army by conquering Greece.

Points of departure

Beauvoir's point is not merely that an achieved end can serve as a means to further ends. It is rather that it thereby remains valuable. But this value does not require it to feature as a means in my own further projects. For that would require that its value as a means derives from the value of the ends pursued in those further projects. Those ends in turn would seem not to be genuinely valuable unless their value would persist once they had been achieved, which would require them to be deployed as means in yet further projects, and so on. For the value of my achieved end to rest on my using it as a means requires that we are each like Sisyphus in having an infinite chain of projects ahead of us, when in fact like Pyrrhus our ambitions must be finite.

It is thus important that we do not live solipsistic lives like Sisyphus, according to Beauvoir, but are instead like Pyrrhus in pursuing our projects in a world of people who pursue their own projects. The value of our achieved ends is not that they can function as means to our own further projects, but that they can function as means to projects generally, whether these are our own projects or the projects of other people.

But this value still cannot depend on the achieved end being deployed as a means. There are two reasons for this. One is essentially the same as the reason why this value cannot be conferred by the end being a means to my own projects: it would require an infinite chain of projects, the end of each being deployed as a means in the next. Even if human history is infinite, it would be vanishingly unlikely that any specific end of mine, once it is achieved, forms part of such an infinite chain. It would thus be overwhelmingly likely that all of my ends are in fact devoid of any real value.

Equally importantly, we have not yet seen any reason why the means deployed in someone else's project should thereby be valuable for me. It would be valuable for that person, because they value their end and the means is required for achieving that end. But this does not make the end objectively valuable. Neither does it make the means valuable for me, even though it only exists as a means for someone else because it was once an end that I valued achieving. The device that I have invented, for example, might be valuable to you if it helps you succeed in your project, but that does not make it valuable for me, especially as your project might be opposed to mine.

The value of a potential means

Beauvoir argues that the continuing value of an end that has been achieved must therefore lie in its status as a *potential* means, rather than in its *actual* use as a means. If the value of my achieved end rests on its mere possibility of being used as a means, then this does not require that any further actual project is valuable, so does not require that my end forms part of an infinite chain of projects. And for the same reason, it does not require that anyone else's projects are valuable to me, so does not require that my values coincide with anyone else's.

Why should we conclude from this that an achieved end has value as a potential means, rather than that it has no value? Beauvoir argues that we cannot accept the idea that an achieved end has no value. It is the structure of human existence, on her view, that we pursue projects, which requires that we value achieving the ends of those projects. We are existentially committed to valuing our ends, which entails that we are committed to valuing their achievement, and so to holding that they will be valuable once they have been achieved. Our only option, therefore, is to accept that our achieved ends are valuable because they are potential means to other projects, whether those projects are our own or other people's.

The next step in Beauvoir's argument is her claim that this value of a potential means entails the value of the capacity to use it as a means. For the possibility of something being used as a means depends on there being the capacity to use it as a means. If that possibility is itself valuable, then so must be the capacity on which it depends. Since we have to accept that our achieved ends are valuable as potential means, therefore, we also have to accept that the capacity to set ends and deploy means in pursuit of them is itself valuable.

This capacity is, of course, nothing other than human agency as existentialism conceives of it. Beauvoir's argument has therefore led from the value of one's own ends to the value of human agency in general. If the argument is valid, then since you do accept the value of your own ends, you must accept the value of their achievement, so you must accept their value as potential means, so you must accept the value of human agency as the capacity to deploy your achieved ends as means.

This argument does not rely on human agency itself being a means or an end in anyone's project. The value of human agency that it establishes, therefore, cannot be a subjective value dependent on having some specific project.

Rather, what the argument concludes is that you must accept the value of human agency regardless of which projects you in fact pursue. That is, you must accept that human agency is objectively valuable. This is the basic moral conclusion that Beauvoir draws from her consideration of absurdity.

Authenticity as moral law

Immanuel Kant argued that morality consists in a single categorical imperative, to which we are subject precisely because we are rational agents who set our own subjective ends. He argues in his *Groundwork for the Metaphysics of Morals* (1785) that this imperative can be formulated in various ways, including what has become known as the formula of humanity, which declares that we must treat human agency as objectively valuable in itself. Beauvoir's conclusion in *Pyrrhus and Cineas* is a categorical imperative that closely resembles Kant's formula of humanity. Her argument for it resembles Kant's in broad outline, since both derive their categorical imperative from the structure of human agency itself.

This broad strategy avoids the need to postulate any source of moral command external to our own agency. If successful, it explains why we are subject to morality when other creatures are not. Perhaps most importantly, this strategy promises to show that obedience to the demands of morality is no threat to our own freedom. It is because the categorical imperative is entailed by the structure of our own agency, argues Kant, that we are not autonomous unless we obey it. Beauvoir's view is that authenticity, the recognition and expression of our true structure as human existents, requires that we respect the categorical imperative. For that structure of our existence entails that we are subject to that imperative.

This is not to say that Beauvoir has simply restated Kant's argument in different language. Beauvoir attempts to derive her categorical imperative directly from the structure of human agency as the pursuit of ends, whereas Kant's argument rests on a more general metaphysical theory of the realm of rational understanding and the world of sensory experience. Beauvoir's form of the argument thus does not require Kant's strict distinction between the rational and the sensory or his broader metaphysical theory. Neither does her argument entail the rejection of those aspects of Kant's philosophy. It would seem to be a strength of her argument that it does not entail any commitment on those controversial matters.

It is a little odd, however, that *Pyrrhus and Cineas* contains only a few brief and scattered comments on Kant and that these do not seem to acknowledge the parallels between her metaethical thought here and his. These sparse comments focus not on Kant's basic moral philosophy itself, but rather on his application of it, especially his assumption that it is always possible to obey the categorical imperative. Beauvoir's view is more pessimistic: given the conflicts between people around us, she thinks, we are inevitably condemned to sometimes breaking the moral law. We cannot always avoid acting immorally, she argues, which she equates with acting violently.

Morality and the meaning of life

Beauvoir's argument does conclude, however, that we must treat human agency as objectively valuable. This is not undermined by the fact that it will sometimes generate genuine dilemmas. Her argument also implies the further claim that we must consider this structure of human agency to be the foundation of all other values. Those other values can be divided into two kinds.

One kind are the objects, designs, ideas, theories, stories, and other items in the world that have been created by human agency, along with the items that make up the natural world. These are all potential means to our ends. Since there is no clear factual limit to the range of ends that people might formulate and pursue, there is no reason to limit this status to any specific set of items. We might agree that a potential means would not be valuable if the only ends it could be used to pursue were themselves ruled immoral by the categorical imperative. But given that the range of possible human ends vastly outstrips anyone's capacity to imagine it, perhaps we should not be confident that any item fits this description. If this is right, then we should consider all potential means to be valuable, with their value deriving from the value of the human capacity to deploy them as means.

The other kind of value is had by the ends that we pursue. Our ends are genuinely valuable, if Beauvoir's argument is right, precisely because they are expressions of human agency. This value is therefore derived from the value of human agency. This is how Beauvoir grounds her response to the existential aspect of the problem of absurdity in her response to its moral aspect. We are not, after all, condemned to value ends that are not really valuable. Our ends derive genuine value from being our ends. But this does not mean that any end we choose to pursue would be equally valuable, because the value of our ends is moderated by the moral law; ends pursued at the expense of other people's agency are not valuable. Their value as expressions of human agency is cancelled by their disvalue as suppressions of human agency.

Living a meaningful life in pursuit of genuinely valuable ends therefore requires obeying the categorical imperative to respect human agency. Projects that violate that imperative are absurd. Their ends are not valuable. But this is not the reason why one must respect human agency. For the conclusion of Beauvoir's moral argument in this short book is not the hypothetical imperative that if you want to avoid existential absurdity, then you must respect human agency. Neither is it the hypothetical imperative that if you value your ends, then you must respect human agency. It is the categorical imperative that you must respect human agency. Once this moral conclusion has been established, it can ground the existential point that projects are absurd if and only if they contravene that imperative.

The demands of authenticity

What does obedience to this categorical imperative amount to? Beauvoir does not provide a detailed answer to this question in _Pyrrhus and Cineas_, but addresses it in subsequent moral and political writings of the 1940s. She limits herself in this book to arguing that this imperative demands more than that our projects do not destroy or damage other people's agency. Rather, she argues, it requires us to secure for all people the conditions required to exercise their agency effectively. Poverty can absorb this capacity to formulate and pursue projects into the basic project of staying alive. Illness can sap the energy required to pursue projects. Lack of education can limit one's ability to imagine and develop new projects. We are therefore obliged, she argues, to promote wealth, health, and education for all people.

Beauvoir does not make her argument for this obligation clear. Why should our respect for the objective value of human agency require us to promote human agency, rather than simply avoid suppressing it? It might be thought that the answer to this lies in human agency being the foundation of all other values. The more people can exercise their agency, the more valuable ends and potential means there will be, so the more value there will be in the world.

Beauvoir's argument, however, could not support this consequentialist reasoning. For this reasoning could support an obligation to promote human agency only if we are subject to an imperative to maximize value. Beauvoir's argument does not entail such an imperative. And even if there were an imperative to maximize value, our efforts to liberate human agency from poverty, illness, and lack of education might not have the intended effect. For we could not control or predict whether the people we liberate would obey the moral law, so we would not know whether their liberation will have positive or negative consequences overall.

Perhaps her thought is rather that a project violates the moral law if any of the myriad means that it rests on have been produced in ways that suppress or destroy human agency. It is not obvious that avoiding this kind of indirect violation of the moral law would entail an obligation to promote better lives for everyone, rather than only for those involved in the production of the means that one deploys. But perhaps such a generalizing move could be supplied by considering the complex holism of the global economy, reasons to keep one's range of potential projects as open as possible, or both. Perhaps such considerations could also help to explain how one should decide in a situation where all the available options violate the categorical imperative.

However these questions are to be resolved, it seems clear that Beauvoir's argument in _Pyrrhus and Cineas_ is an innovative response to the existential problem of absurdity and a novel argument for the grounding of moral obligation. Her argument merits serious attention in both existential philosophy and moral philosophy. I have provided some more detailed analysis of it in my book _Rethinking Existentialism_ (Webber 2018), but there is much more work to be done to draw out the full philosophical significance of Beauvoir's unfortunately neglected argument.

To conclude this introductory analysis, we should return to the book's title characters. Which of them is right? The answer given by Beauvoir's overall argument is: neither. Cineas is wrong to imply that all projects are absurd, though he does succeed in bringing an important existential problem to light. Pyrrhus is wrong to value the project of conquering other lands, since the violence of this project violates the moral law needlessly. His project is absurd, but not for the reason Cineas implies. Rather, it is absurd because it is immoral.

30 Weil and the meaning of life

LISSA MCCULLOUGH

In the final years of her short life, Simone Weil's philosophical perspective was profoundly transformed by the unexpected religious turn that occurred in her late twenties.[1] The later Weil, now transmuted into a religious thinker, believed that the transcendent meaning of life is narrated in the story of Job, which she judged to be an utterly pure account of spiritual purification, the perfect exemplification of a human soul under trial. In the course of his endless afflictions, Job discovers a divine grace beyond every possible mundane consolation (Job 19.25–27; Weil 1970: 139).[2] Weil attests: "Supernatural compassion is a bitterness without consolation, but one that envelops the void into which grace descends. Let it be an *irreducible* bitterness, like the irreducible bitterness of the suffering one undergoes in the flesh …. [In Job,] the contemplation of human misery violently pulls us toward God" (Weil 1956: 281). Life's ultimate meaning, for Weil, is a transcendent contact with a reality that is most real to the one who suffers catastrophic loss of meaning, rather than to the one who is confident of life's meaning. Readers in search of "existential meaning" are likely to balk at the extremity of Weil's spiritual asceticism; she is profoundly skeptical with regard to not only commonplace social sentiments and naive optimisms but also to the most austere consolations resorted to by God-obsessed mystics and saints. In her view, even if they succeed in being self-lacerating ascetics and self-denying minimalists, in finding any consolation whatsoever they have their reward. This is because, for her as a Christian, crucifixion is the central mystery that grounds pure faith and renders joy transcendent. Transcendent joy is not merely a product of happy circumstances, destined to be demolished by a change in conditions, but is a redemptive joy that abides in the midst of abject affliction (*malheur*) and most extreme forms of suffering.

William James helpfully distinguished between the healthy-minded once-born soul and the sick soul (James 1902: lectures 4–7), but to contend with Simone Weil's notion of spiritual purity we must interrogate this distinction between sickness and wellness, recognizing it to be a social construct that is itself highly relative to truth conditions, to the exigencies of reality within which life is lived. Attitudes that appear healthy and adaptive in the context of undisturbed civil society suddenly become maladaptive under the conditions of a concentration camp. Souls that embrace their illusions greedily, without a second thought, appear quite hale from the point of view of privileged social life while being utterly deluded or nescient concerning the actual conditions of their existence.

The only meaning worth finding in life, ultimately, is spiritual salvation – identical to sanctification. The *true* meaning of life transcends life; all other meanings are conditional and ephemeral. Life as such persists as a supremely complex set of conditions, therefore life can have no meaning that is not essentially conditional, vulnerable to destruction or dissolution, except for one unconditional possibility that is a surd, an impossibility – that is, to be spiritually detached from all expectation of meaning, from the very notion of life's having a meaning. To live thus is to *transcend* in an authentically spiritual sense, in total detachment from illusion and consolation; it is to *live beyond life* in pure faith, embodying a supernatural compassion suspended in the void.

For Weil, truth trumps life. Life is a lie; only death is true.[3] The authentic saint is marked by a radical humility, a spiritual poverty, an uncompromising passion for truth that is extraordinarily rare precisely because *greed for life* is the fundamental corruption that motivates the living. Human beings are prone to cling to illusion precisely because we prefer falsehood to crucifying truth. As Matthew 16.25 avers, the truth will make you free, but it will do so by taking your life.

The natural joy experienced in life is beautiful, a grace to be loved and relished with religious awe, as God the creator is the giver of every such natural joy. But natural joy is grounded in a set of conditions that will pass. When the time comes that the conditional joy passes, we must choose the truth of reality (crucifixion) over illusions that console, conceal, and deny this bereft condition. This brings us to a core structural tenet of Weil's religious thought, which employs and enlarges Plato's distinction between necessity and the good (see *Republic* 6.493c; *Timaeus* 47e–48a). "One should ever be conscious of the impossibility of good, that is to say, of how much the essence of the necessary differs from that of the good" (Weil 1956: 410). Weil maintains that the world is necessity, not purpose (Weil 1968: 196). "The sensible universe has no other reality than that of necessity, as every phenomenon is a modification of the distribution of energy, hence is determined by the laws of energy" (Weil 1949: 293).

In consequence, when we reach the end of our natural energy, our will is rendered impotent and cast into the void. Our response to the shock of impotence is to wail, to rail, to lash out with *ressentiment*. There is a wrenching of every natural expectation in us; "meaning" fails, perhaps never to return. Weil employs the analogy of a cow reaching the end of her tether – suddenly brought to her knees: "End of using my energy" (Weil 1956: 179). On these grounds Weil rejected Henri Bergson's notion of *élan vital*, the energy of organic life, as a philosophical or spiritual basis on which to rely for meaning (Weil 1956: 167–68; 1949: 249). *Élan vital* offers nothing to the sufferer of extreme *malheur* whose afflictions extinguish all natural joy and natural energy, suddenly bereft of every foothold for worldly meaning by an infinite suffering without meaning. Only faith in the thought of God's voluntary self-emptying and crucifixion can offer a grace that reaches the soul in such a bottomless hell.

To know what is impossible for us by nature is the first opening to super-natural possibility, hence Weil considered it an urgent and essential task to formulate a logic of the absurd (Weil 1970: 182). Our life is nothing but impossibility, absurdity: with all our being we desire a good that does not exist – the existence of which is impossible – and on the other hand we suffer an ironclad necessity that exists but is not good. Really to experience this impossibility through suffering is to undergo a death more encompassing than a merely personal or bodily death. "Impossibility – that is, radical impossibility clearly perceived, absurdity – is the gate leading to the supernatural. All we can do is to knock on it. It is another who opens" (Weil 1956: 411–13). An attachment that contains an impossibility is a *metaxu* (ibid.: 222).[4]

Given that our life is an impossible attachment, nothing less than a wrenching absolute detachment – acceptance of the void – makes possible the initial birth of the spiritual capacity to be nourished by the light of a trans-cendent truth. It is our contradictory attachment to life – which we actively prefer to seeing and assenting to the truth of reality – that results in our incapacity to feed on light rather than on natural energy. "There is only one fault: incapacity to feed upon light; for in the absence of this capacity, all faults are possible and none is avoidable" (ibid.: 223). Ours is not to judge, since all human faults are worth the same. To be just, to be pure in spirit, it is necessary to be naked and dead (Weil 1989–2006: III, 96, my translation).

Light is the transcendent food that feeds the soul with beauty rather than worldly energy, if only we can detach from life and accept that death is the truth; that is, if we do not grasp at life, if we let it be conditional and beyond the reach of our will, we can simply *witness* reality without insisting on *having* it. Weil refers to this light as a supernatural beauty that is "imperceptible": meaning that the soul is no longer *feeding on* anything but is rather *fed by* a light in the void, a gratuitous grace that is perceptible only to a spiritually transformed capacity to see.

> Beauty is always a miracle. But the miracle is raised to the second degree when the soul receives an impression of beauty which, while it is beyond all sense perception is no abstraction, but real and direct as the impression caused by a song at the moment it reaches our ears .... Everything happens as though, by a miraculous favor, our very senses themselves had been made aware that silence is not the absence of sounds, but something infinitely more real than sounds, and the center of a harmony more perfect than anything which a combination of sounds can produce.
>
> (Weil 1951: 213)

This beauty is the face of the eternal "yes" (Weil 1970: 194); the beauty of God's creation is an absolute YES, a "yes" that is inaudibly audible in the effect of every heartrending song, captivating landscape, glorious saintly act, and the dark emptiness of the void.

Our experiences of beauty and suffering alike are manifestations of our desire. In beauty there is something irreducible, exactly as there is in physical suffering. Indeed, enjoyment of beauty is a "suffering" of the necessity embedded in reality, unaccompanied by pain; it is the appearance of necessity when it manifests itself as desirable. Whereas beauty gives joy through a sense of perfect finality, suffering imposes a sense of perfect emptiness of finality: absence of significance, futility, meaninglessness, void. Both beauty and suffering reflect the same irreducibility of reality *qua* real, an irreducibility that is impenetrable for the intelligence (Weil 1956: 308). The essence of reality lies in beauty, or "transcendent appropriateness" (ibid.: 515), for beauty is the manifest appearance of reality (Weil 1970: 341); and joy, Weil proposes, is the fullness of the sentiment of the real (Weil 1956: 222, cf. 360). The beauty of the world is the order of the world that is loved (Weil 1951: 170). Our joy in reality is ultimately a joy in God, the source of all reality, and this means that on the plane of events, "the notion of conformity to the will of God is identical with the notion of reality" (Weil 1949: 270). Because of its absolute sacrality, there is nothing beyond Beauty, Weil observes; or rather, "Good alone is more than beauty; but it does not lie beyond, it is at the end of Beauty in the same way as the point that terminates a segment of a straight line" (Weil 1956: 605).

Weil believed that a sense of beauty, however mutilated and distorted by the alienations and predations of modern life, remains rooted in the human heart as the most powerful incentive toward justice, faith, hope, and love. Just as the later Dostoevsky prophesied that "beauty will save the world," (Dostoevsky 1869: 356) so similarly Weil imagined that the power of beauty might some-how call forth a new impulse to purity in the decadent wartime civilization she observed destroying itself around her. She lamented that the modern world has "forgotten" this to its own catastrophic detriment, commenting that we "must have piled up a mass of crimes that have made us accursed for us so to have lost all the poetry inherent in the universe" (Weil 1956: 540). Beauty is the only value that is universally recognized, in Weil's view (Weil 1957: 103); it was the universality and inalienability of this value that permitted Weil to hope for an authentically *catholic* incarnation of Christianity right in the midst of a decaying former Christendom, displacing the ruins of compromised hieratical church traditions with the universal body of the secular world.

In her last notebooks, Weil pondered the existential paradox that is human life with a purity of insight into its absurdity that can only be compared with the genius of Kafka. "The hunger of the soul is hard to bear," she wrote, "but there is no other remedy for our disease" (Weil 1970: 286). Hunger as remedy? This is because the impossibility of satiating desire is the ultimate truth about it; the hope of satiating it is falsehood (Weil 1956: 60). The eternal part of the soul feeds on hunger. When the human vessel is shattered by necessity in the form of deprivation, suffering, degradation, wrenching demoralization and disillusion, the core absurdity of life comes to be nakedly exposed. There is only one option that remains available in the void: it is to begin *ex nihilo*, having nothing, being nothing. To begin this way, with an absolute beginning "outside" the terms and conditions of life, is the miracle of a faith beyond faith. Nothing is more fragile and fleeting than that upon which the afflicted soul relies for salvation. Salvation arrives as an impossible, paradoxical manifestation of supernatural good: a weightless, bodiless, unconditional joy infused with a light beyond visible light, a beauty beyond physical beauty, a truth beyond meaning, a life beyond death. The only pure and infallible good is supernatural good, Weil insists. These spiritual truths are ancient, but Simone Weil brought them forward into early twentieth-century Europe and made them palpable for the modern mind in the wake of the death of God.[5]

Notes

1 Simone Weil recounts this utterly unexpected spiritual transformation in her own letter, entitled "Spiritual Autobiography" in English translations, which appears in Weil 1951: 61–83.
2 Since most of Weil's work was only published after her death in 1943, and was compiled from notebooks produced over many years, references are made only to the original date of publication (whether in English or French).
3 Weil's notion that "life is a lie, only death is true" is treated in McCullough 2014: 22–24, 67–69.
4 This term, deriving from Plato's *Symposium*, means "middle-ground" or "in-between," and is traditionally used to indicate the manner in which oral traditions can be perceived by different people in different ways. Weil uses *metaxu* to mean "bridges between the world of the good and the world of the necessary" (Miles 1986: 30).
5 For my take on the cultural-historical contextual background from which Weil's religious thinking emerged, see McCullough 2017.

31 Ayer and the meaning of life

JAMES TARTAGLIA

A.J. Ayer sat in with the Vienna Circle, and enthusiastically embraced the logical positivism he thereby discovered. The result was *Language, Truth and Logic*, published when he was twenty-five. As becomes clear from the first paragraph, the project that most enthused him was that of discrediting large swathes of the history of philosophy. He wanted to terminate traditional, historically embedded discourses which he thought would otherwise run on interminably, and thus to his mind, fruitlessly, by establishing 'beyond question what should be the purpose and method of a philosophical inquiry'. This was feasible, he thought, because, 'if there are any questions which science leaves it to philosophy to answer, a straightforward process of elimination must lead to their discovery' (Ayer 1936: 45). Science might *not* leave anything for philosophy, then; it might have all the answers, or at least the resources to provide them – some contemporary physicalists still think it does (Rosenberg 2011). But Ayer left open the possibility of preserving something of the philosophical tradition, and the strand he liked best was the empiricist tradition stemming from Locke, the original 'under-labourer' for science. If science did leave questions for philosophy, however, they would have to be answerable in a science-like manner: decisively and through the application of technical apparatus – logic would be philosophy's substitute for experimental equipment. So legitimate lines of philosophical inquiry were to be closed down with the right answers, and the rest discredited as nonsense. Progress was in the air, and if philosophy was to help science achieve it, its most urgent task was to purge itself.

Ayer's main tool for this project was his principle of verification, according to which if a proposition is neither a tautology, nor an empirical hypothesis for which there is some possible sensory experience which would be relevant to determining whether it is true, then it is a metaphysical proposition; and all such propositions are literally senseless. Applying this principle allows him to take a uniquely hard line on religion in the sixth chapter, 'Critique of Ethics and Theology', which was primarily responsible for the book's early notoriety. Thus the assertion that God exists is nonsensical because no experience could help determine its truth. But equally, the atheist's denial of God is nonsensical, as is the agnostic's refusal to take a positive stance, which presupposes that the question is legitimate (Ayer 1936: 153). Believers, atheists and agnostics are all just talking nonsense.

With this kind of mind-set, it seems obvious what Ayer would have said about the meaning of life; but it is not explicitly addressed. Since the heyday of logical positivism, this thoroughly unscientific and thoroughly natural philosophical issue has been stigmatized as the ultimate embarrassment in the minds of many analytic philosophers. The stigma survived the decline of logical positivism – 'nearly all of it was false', Ayer later said[1] – and although the situation has now changed, it is still an issue which puts the wind up the more ardent physicalists and naturalists of today.

But Ayer did tackle the question at two significant junctures of his life.[2] The first was in 'The Claims of Philosophy', written around the same time as the introduction to the second edition of *Language, Truth and Logic*, in which Ayer described his classic as, 'in every sense a young man's book' (Ayer 1946: 7) – he was still only thirty-five. He had just successfully made it through World War II – a war he was honest enough to admit that he enjoyed (Ayer 1988a: 194).[3] And it was at this time that he turned to the meaning of life. Although he concludes that the question is nonsensical, he does not simply dismiss it with the principle of verification. Rather, he provides the most concrete argument for stigmatizing the question which I know of.

Ayer returned to the question in the year before he died, and given the connection he now made between this topic and the possibility of an afterlife, it was thereafter to preoccupy him right until the end, through reflections on the near-death experience which he famously underwent in the interim. By this time, Ayer's stance on religion had softened, to the extent that he was now happy to call himself an atheist. And his stance on the question of the meaning of life had softened too, for in his final broadcast interview, he said: 'I hold that life has no meaning independent of the meaning one is able to give it, but it doesn't follow from this that it's either nice or nasty'. I agree (Tartaglia 2016a); I would want to qualify talk of 'the meaning one is able to give it', but then so would Ayer. Ayer had enjoyed a long and successful life in philosophy, during which he had seen that the definitive answers he wanted in his youth had not been forthcoming; and he must surely have also seen that the answers he had endeavoured to provide were simply his own, contentious contributions to an ongoing historical conversation – an interminable one, I hope. As the anti-philosophy of positivism lost its grip over him, he became more willing to take a stance on two traditional philosophical issues that clearly mattered to him: he was an atheist and a nihilist.

'The Claims of Philosophy' is not primarily an essay about the meaning of life, but rather the nature of philosophy; it is interesting to see how he makes the connection.[4] He begins by distinguishing the 'pontiffs' and 'journeymen' of philosophy, which is a recasting of the distinction in *Language, Truth and Logic* between metaphysicians, and the legitimate philosophy of logical positivism and British empiricism. It is characteristic of the pontiffs to 'think it within the province of philosophy to compete with natural science', whereas the journeymen realize that 'the ideal of a metaphysical system that is anything other than a scientific encyclopaedia is devoid of any basis in reason' (Ayer 1947: 1–2). The new terminology is revealing: 'pontiffs' shows the connection in Ayer's mind between metaphysics and religion, and the fact that he is prepared to describe even philosophers of the status of Wittgenstein as 'journeymen', shows the depth of his commitment to the differential status of philosophers and scientists.[5]

Ayer says that 'The history of philosophy, as it is taught in the textbooks, is largely a parade of pontiffs', but that the journeymen have now taken over in England and America (ibid.: 3). What worries him, however, is that they suffer from 'a certain thinness of material'; the new philosophers were finding 'an unfortunate disparity between the richness of their technique and the increasing poverty of the material on which they are able to exercise it' (ibid.: 6). He thinks their salvation might be 'the reunion of philosophy with science'.

Why he thinks this is unclear to me. Journeymen clear away the linguistic confusions thrown up by the 'parade of pontiffs', as well as similar confusions arising from everyday talk, for which Ayer's examples are the problems of perception and other minds, and determining the significance of moral judgements (ibid.: 3). However, these are traditional problems of philosophy that pontiffs also address, except without the journeyman's presupposition that they must embody linguistic confusions. This presupposition is made because to acknowledge that the problems might be real, would be to entertain the possibility of a distinctively philosophical way of understanding the world addressed to answering such questions, which Ayer thinks would amount to challenging science. But the traditional problems are not thin unless you suppose they must be merely semantic. If you do, then it is not clear how merging philosophy with science is going to help; even if something distinctively philosophical survived, it is going to be thin if it is not actually science. Ayer mentions 'formal logic', 'the analysis of scientific method, 'the evaluation of scientific theories' and 'clarification of scientific terms' (ibid.: 3). But even if these tasks could not be performed by mathematicians and scientists, for some reason, they are the very tasks which generate Ayer's worries about thinness.

With hindsight, there is no detectable problem of thinness within Ayer's opus; which reflects well on him, but not his pontiff / journeyman distinction. Nevertheless he was worried at the time, having said at the end of *Language, Truth and Logic* that 'philosophy is virtually empty without science' (Ayer 1936: 201). There is little science to be found in Ayer, and although he could still cling to 'logical puzzles which the journeyman, who is relatively ignorant of science, may reasonably be called upon to solve' (Ayer 1947: 6), the situation, by his own positivist lights, was not sustainable.

So the future Sir Alfred Ayer, highly engaged public intellectual, looks to 'what the public expects of its philosophers'; and what they expect, he thinks, is to be told the meaning of life – whether by a journeyman or pontiff is inconsequential to them. Ayer's response is that they are asking the impossible, and that when this is seen, 'the problem is solved, so far as reasoning can solve it' (ibid.: 7). To begin to show this, he asks how it is possible for human existence to have a purpose.[6] For an individual, it is to intend to bring about a desired outcome; when thus engaged with our projects, the things we do have meaning for us. Since most of our lives are spent like this, it is only natural that we should wonder what the meaning of the whole thing is. And as Ayer says, a simple answer would be that 'all events are tending towards a certain specifiable end' (ibid.: 7). He has two responses. The first is that 'there is no good reason whatever for supposing this assumption to be true' (ibid.: 7). I would stop there and conclude that nihilism is the answer to the question of the meaning of life; and from his final broadcast, quoted above, it seems Ayer ultimately came to that conclusion too. But he goes on with a second response, and it is this line of reasoning which has remained influential (e.g. Nozick 1981a: 585ff.; Metz 2013: ch. 6; Trisel 2017).

He says that even if reality has been arranged to inevitably lead to a certain end, this would not tell us the meaning of life. Why not? Because, 'the end in question will not be the one that [we ourselves] have chosen' (Ayer 1947: 7). As such, from our own perspectives, the end will be 'entirely arbitrary' and so we will have not been provided with a justification for our existence, only an explanation of the facts of it. It can only be a brute fact that events tend towards this end, since 'what is called an explanation is nothing other than a more general description' (ibid.: 8). So since people curious about the meaning of life are asking *why* human beings exist and do the things they do, and want an answer that tells them something other than *how* they exist, the question cannot legitimately be answered.

Ayer now considers the possibility that reality was designed by a god, and that our purpose is to realize this god's purposes. Reiterating his previous two lines of response, he says, firstly, that there is no good reason to believe this, and secondly, that even though our lives would now fulfil a purpose, it would not be *our* purpose. It would just be a brute fact that the god chose this purpose, so again we would not have a justification, only a description. He then argues that the purpose could be of no practical significance to us. It would either be built into reality, such that we would be working towards it whatever we did; or, if we have a choice, we would have no reason to try to conform 'unless we independently judge it to be good' (ibid.: 9). Thus Ayer comes down decisively on Plato's Euthyphro dilemma: what the gods think on moral matters is totally irrelevant. Religion is generally irrelevant to the meaning of life, in fact, for if a religious hypothesis were true, it would simply mean that different brute facts hold from those the sciences tell us about. We would get a different story about *what we are*, but would learn nothing about *why we are*. So the question of the meaning of life is unanswerable. We should not regret that there is no meaning of life, because 'it is not sensible to cry for what is logically impossible' (ibid.: 9). We should not say there is or is not such a meaning, since these are not factually significant statements.

The whole argument turns on the assumption that we would have to choose the meaning of life; were it not our choice, it would be arbitrary and could not justify our existence. But if it has to be something we choose – if this requirement is supposed to be one which people who ask the question would recognize and accept – then the reason for asking, as regards the practical component of the question, must have been that people did not know what to choose. But then, given that the question also has a theoretical component about why we and the rest of reality exist, how could a choice that we make possibly provide the answer? Obviously it could not, so Ayer has prepared his 'unanswerable' conclusion from the outset.

However, the argument fails simply in virtue of the practical component, because if the choices we make may or may not be in accordance with the meaning of life, as our wanting to know the answer in order to choose how to live presupposes, then it is not a requirement on the meaning of life that we choose it; for if we might be getting it wrong, this must be in virtue of a meaning of life we are not choosing. It is simply a vacuous requirement on our living in conformity to the meaning of life, if we have a choice in the matter, that in order to do so, we must choose to live in conformity to it. If the meaning of life is X, and X requires me to live life Y, then I may have a choice over Y but not X; it is not a requirement on X that I choose it, but if I do want to conform to it, and I have a choice, then I had better choose Y.

The overall flaw to the argument might be summarized by saying that it would not make enough initial sense, prior to Ayer's diagnosis of senselessness, for somebody to ask the question of the meaning of life, if in doing so they were presupposing, as the diagnosis demands, that any suitable answer must be one which they themselves choose. I cannot sensibly ask where the cat is, while presupposing that any answer, such as 'on the mat', must be an answer chosen by me, rather than determined by the whereabouts of the cat.

But leaving that aside; suppose it became clear that the gods of Olympus have been ruling over us throughout history. They toy with our lives, and if they do not like what they see, they ensure we come to a sticky end. This would not tell us why there is a reality; but scientific cosmology cannot either, and if the gods seemed to understand, told us this knowledge was forbidden to mortals, and assured us that our lives are being directed in accordance with the meaning of life, then I see little ground for rational scepticism about their testimony. What reason would we have to do what they demanded? To keep them onside if we wanted to achieve our own, independently conceived goals, since things would not go well for us otherwise; and the same reason for making their goals for us our own. Those goals might jar with our moral reflections, but we would then have good reason to suppose our reflections were faulty; we might stick to our convictions, but a refusal to obey might preserve our consciences only at the cost of more suffering. We trust human experts when we do not personally understand, and we think we should; I imagine we would trust the gods. Only a fool would wantonly sin with the epistemic light shining on such a radical scenario.

As it is, we have no good reason to suppose that our lives are governed by a meaning of life, and we may resent those who think they are, on the basis of scant evidence, when this is used as a platform to undercut moral reflections. Ayer certainly did, and I think a general antipathy to the authoritarianism of religious belief explains the enduring popularity of his hard-line 'God would be irrelevant anyway' stance. Religion can easily offend contemporary individualism, as well as democratic pride in our ability to find the best available answers, which, given our actual situation, we must take individual and collective responsibility for. But such sentiments can skew philosophical reasoning and suspend common sense. At the end of his career, Ayer said he did 'not know whether it has been more of an advantage or a handicap to me as a philosopher that I am entirely devoid of any religious feeling'; that he would even raise this question shows how far he had moved (Ayer 1989: 345). I doubt it was a handicap, but I think his anti-religious feeling was.

Ayer says that the truth of a religious hypothesis could only tell us more about what reality amounts to, and hence could not provide the justification we seek. His reasoning follows Hume's principle that we cannot derive an 'ought' from an 'is'. But as Searle has argued, within a social setting this is not so obvious: presuppose the institution of promising, and it is quite easy – she uttered certain words, so she ought to pay the money (Searle 1964). Now you might reason that such institutions are merely social constructions within an ultimately meaningless, physical reality, to which the notion of 'ought' is alien. But the whole point of the meaning of life idea is that we do not occupy that kind of reality. If there were a meaning of life, this institution would be built into the fabric of reality. It would be a fact that our lives have meaning, within a reality whose nature explained its own existence. Reflecting on the Euthyphro dilemma, Wittgenstein said that the view that things are good because God wills them is 'deeper' than the alternative that God wills them because they are good, since the former, 'blocks off the road to any kind of explanation, "why" it is good; while the second interpretation is the shallow, rationalistic one, in that it behaves "as though" that which is good could be given yet some further foundation' (Wittgenstein 1930: 115). That seems right. If the meaning of reality is something I could know about, perhaps by emerging at death into a new understanding which encapsulates my present one, then now is not the time to be second-guessing God's will.

Where is the positive appeal to the idea that we must choose the meaning of life? Well, the idea of slaving away towards a goal that does not readily engage you is not appealing. We do this for money, which lessens the feeling of arbitrariness, but we do not much like the interim; we thank God it is Friday. We like to be easily engaged by our tasks these days, and technology provides more and more easy engagement; so some philosophers try to conceive certain, 'better' kinds of engagement as the meaning of life (Dreyfus and Kelly 2011), within a wider culture where the 'mindfulness' phenomenon has arisen from the concern that technology has made our engagements too fleeting. In this setting, the notion of a meaning of life, which alone makes sense of the question we inherited, starts to look rather dated. We recoil from a meaning which might keep us away from the activities that really engage us; especially if we cannot take the payday of paradise seriously. However what is not dated about the idea is that it requires us to think beyond even our most distant projects to ask what we are here for. Successfully dispel this kind of natural philosophical curiosity, and the terminus for the journeyman will be sooner than he thinks.

Ayer returned to the topic at age seventy-seven with 'The Meaning of Life', in which his heightened sense of mortality is never far from the surface. He says he has 'chosen to call' the meaning of life the possibility of an afterlife (Ayer 1988a: 180); but he soon comes around to the traditional question. The connection is made through a discussion of how belief in the rewards or punishments of an afterlife can affect how believers live; not altogether rationally, he thinks. Nevertheless, he grants that an afterlife is possible, if the requirements of a Lockean account of personal identity are met, while still thinking that death leads to non-existence. After rehearsing some reasons for thinking that death is nothing to fear, and that it is generally overdramatized, he admits he would like an extended life; but only because he belongs to a privileged minority ('the vast majority of the human race ... [lack] a tolerable standard of living for it to be rational for them to wish their miseries prolonged'); and only if he could return to the prime of his life, since in getting older 'one tends to live with less intensity' (ibid.: 187–88).

In going on to discuss what would nowadays be called meaning *in* life – glossed as 'the satisfaction that people receive for the character and conduct of their personal lives' (ibid.: 190) – intensity of engagement with our projects is at the forefront of his mind. He points out that there is no intrinsic connection between living a socially meaningful life and living one that is morally worthy – bad people have lived intense and significant lives – and he concludes that, 'there is no general answer to the question what constitutes a meaningful life', both because it will depend on the culture you live in, and because subjective criteria concerning engagement need not coincide with objective criteria (ibid.: 196). I think he was right, but much of the recent literature on this topic has been premised on the possibility of a general account. It has presupposed that a socially meaningful life must be positive, morally or otherwise; it has ignored cultural differences; and it has appealed to both subjective and objective criteria – in one prominent case, by trying to combine them (Wolf 1997b). However 'for the most part', Ayer says (Ayer 1988a: 190), the question has been directed to the meaning *of* life. On this, he says that even if there is one, those with faith in it cannot have known; so why does it matter to people? Because 'most people are excited by the feeling that they are involved in a larger enterprise' (ibid.: 193). Thus he comes back to intensity, and it is in this context that he mentions having enjoyed World War II.[7]

Not long afterwards, Ayer had his near-death experience. When he regained consciousness, he spoke of trying to cross 'the river' – the Styx on the way to Hades, he later presumed. He was unable to recall the crossing episode, but the part of the experience he did recall, about a light which was 'responsible for the government of the universe', was clearly a powerful hallucination, the verisimilitude of which shook him (Ayer 1988b: 200). In his subsequent reflections, he can be found lingering over the fact that C.D. Broad believed there was a good chance of an afterlife: Broad was an atheist, he did not want an afterlife, and he was a great philosopher – some would say better than Wittgenstein (ibid.: 203). Ayer concluded that, 'My recent experiences have slightly weakened my conviction that my genuine death, which is due fairly soon, will be the end of me, though I continue to hope that it will be'; there was no prospect of technology bringing him back to the prime of life now, so he wanted an end to it (ibid.: 204). Ayer subsequently tried to backtrack on that sentence with evident embarrassment (Ayer 1988c), but there was no need. Die with a coin for the ferryman, so long as you do not publicize the fact as a lesson.

Notes

1 He said this in a broadcast interview. My references to Ayer's broadcasts are taken from A.C. Grayling's programme for BBC Radio 4, 'The Meaning of Life according to A.J. Ayer'. It is available online at: www.bbc.co.uk/programmes/b05pw9tw.

2 It also came up briefly in the interim (Ayer 1973: 233–35), but I will focus on the two main statements.

3 He says most English people who did not experience great loss did, but the implication seems clear enough, and is amply borne out by his personal war story; see Rogers 1999.

4 For my view on the connection, see Tartaglia 2016b.

5 Wittgenstein was offended by the discussion of his work in this essay, and broke off all relations with Ayer; see Honderich 1990: xii. What did the damage, apparently, was Ayer saying of Wittgenstein that 'the effect of his teaching upon his more articulate disciples has been that they tend to treat philosophy as a department of psychoanalysis' (Ayer 1947: 5) – it is noteworthy that this particular 'journeyman' is said to have had 'disciples'.

6 Ayer hones straight in on the question, but some philosophers now take it to be thoroughly obscure (e.g. Mawson 2016). I do not think the meaning of life would have to ascribe a purpose to human existence, as Ayer would later agree (Ayer 1988a: 191), or indeed any purposes at all. But the possibility that it does is nevertheless a large part of what interests us; see Tartaglia 2016a: introd..

7 In the terminology of this paragraph, his 1947 argument conflates the meaning *of* life with meaning *in* life, and presupposes a general account of the latter in terms of subjective engagement.

32 Camus and the meaning of life

WILLIAM MCBRIDE

The year 2013 marked the centenary of Albert Camus' birth, and there is little doubt that it occurred in the midst of a Camus revival. I recall, for instance, walking through the lovely streets of Aix-en-Provence one day that summer, with enormous pictures of him hanging overhead. Philosopher, successful novelist and Nobel Prize winner, "rock star" *avant la lettre* – Camus, it would seem, had had it all; if only he had lived to his one hundredth year to continue reveling in his celebrity!

But there is another side to Camus' life that also touched me personally, on a gloomy Friday afternoon in Lille in January 1960. It was the first day back in class at the university, after the Christmas holidays, for Professor Jean Grenier. I was a student there that year. Grenier was a study in sadness: his former student become lifelong friend and correspondent, Albert Camus, had been killed in an automobile accident a few days earlier. The unspeakable absurdity of this totally unforeseen tragedy could not help but weigh heavily on all of us, Grenier by far the most of all.

One of Camus' very last publications, as it turned out, was a preface that he wrote to a new edition of Grenier's collection of essays, *Les Iles*, which Camus tells us he had first read at the age of twenty. This preface is a superb tribute to the book that, more than any other, Camus claims changed his life. Here is just one brief excerpt:

> For a young man brought up outside traditional religions, this prudent, allusive approach was perhaps the only way to direct him toward a deeper meditation on life. Personally, I had no lack of gods: the sun, the night, the sea ... But these are gods of enjoyment; they fill one, then they leave one empty. With them alone for company I should have forgotten the gods in favor of enjoyment itself. I had to be reminded of mystery and holy things, of the finite nature of man, of a love that is impossible in order to return to my natural gods one day, less arrogantly. So I do not owe to Grenier certainties he neither could nor wished to give me. But I owe him, instead, a doubt which will never end ...
>
> (Camus 1932–60: 262–63)

From the letters between Camus and his former teacher, those that have survived and have been published (to which the English translation of this Preface to *Les Iles* has been appended), there emerges a rather different image of Camus from what I take to be the stereotype of him: the handsome, dashing Resistance fighter and icon of the post-war existentialist wave that engulfed France and eventually much of the West. On the one hand, in these letters he at one point rejects the widely held view that, because he had lived in poverty as a child and through his student years, his early years had been unhappy. But, on the other hand, much of his later life was anxiety filled, not just because of the recurrence of tubercular symptoms that had first manifested themselves late in his high-school days and had caused him to spend an inactive year as an invalid, but also, later on, because of his wife's suicide crisis and ongoing psychological distress, and also, especially but not only in his early years as a budding author, because of self-doubts about his writing ability. Throughout Camus' career, Jean Grenier, a Catholic, a gentle, unconventional man with a strong affinity for Taoism, served as his confidant and supporter. Camus' short thesis in partial fulfillment of the requirements for his *diplôme d'études supérieures*, on Christian metaphysics and neo-Platonism, was written under the co-direction of Grenier, who had been promoted to a university-level position by the time of Camus' brief involvement in higher education. The "mystic" side of Camus' thought, of which some commentators have taken note, has its roots in these early interactions and studies.

Camus was a mystic, yes, but "un mystico senza Dio," as Aniello Montano has called him. As Montano reports at the opening of his essay by that title (Montano 1994: 285), Camus asserted, in an article published in *Le Monde*, that he did not believe in God, but that at the same time he was not an atheist. Montano rightly stresses the very strong weight that Camus always placed on human suffering in sustaining his disbelief: As the old, familiar question goes, how could a God, if real and omnipotent, allow so much suffering in this world? This question comes to the fore especially in Camus' great novel, *The Plague*, in which the Algerian city of Oran is besieged by the plague and cut off from the rest of the world while many of its citizens, including many innocent children, die helplessly. Father Paneloux, one of the central characters in the novel, gives a sermon in which he lays out the traditional Christian case that this calamity is at once an expression of God's wrath, to be sure, but also an invitation to the citizenry to become reconciled with God and hence an instrument for ultimately achieving a higher good. Doctor Rieux, who at the end is revealed to be the narrator of the novel, cannot accept the priest's story. The whole situation is absurd, but the two of them work together to try to mitigate the suffering.

The word "absurd" is the key to comprehending Camus' view of the meaning of life. It is the opening and central theme of his most influential philosophical work, *The Myth of Sisyphus*, written at roughly the same time, and published in the same year, 1942, as his equally influential novel, *The*

Stranger. The essay, while it ranges over other topics such as the relationship between philosophy and fiction, is initially presented as a study of the connection between the absurd and suicide: the question of whether the latter can be seen as a solution to the absurd. The absurd, Camus gives us to understand, is neither a human characteristic nor a quality of the world, but is rather the ineluctable disparity between the two, humans and world. The widespread resort to "rationality," to reasoning, in the attempt to bridge this gap is doomed to failure. So, too, are the various would-be solutions, often by means of religious faith, proposed by those whom Camus calls the existentialist philosophers, most notably Kierkegaard – solutions that Camus dubs "philosophical suicide."

Several background details are worth noting here. First, the idea of absurdity has strong roots in early Christianity, with which, as I have already noted, Camus had acquired considerable familiarity. Perhaps most famous is the statement of the early church father, Tertullian, *"Credo quia absurdum"* – I believe inasmuch as it is absurd – referring to the fundamental Christian doctrine of a God become man and dying for men's sins. This same notion plays a large role in Kierkegaard's thinking. When Camus was a student, a book was published, written in French by an exiled Russian philosopher, Lev (or Leo) Chestov, entitled in translation *Kierkegaard and the Existential Philosophy* (Chestov 1934). Camus devotes several pages of *The Myth of Sisyphus* to Chestov, who was if anything more extreme than Kierkegaard in insisting on the need to take a leap of faith in the face of absurdity. Meanwhile, one of the most highly respected French academic philosophers, Jean Wahl, published his *Etudes Kierkegaardiennes* in 1938. Wahl regarded Jules Lequier – a man of the mid-nineteenth century who committed suicide by swimming out into the Atlantic Ocean and not turning back, in an apparent attempt to prove the reality of human freedom against all the philosophies and cultural trends that he saw as denying it – as "the French Kierkegaard." Camus mentions Lequier very briefly near the opening of *The Myth of Sisyphus* as being one among very few of the "thinkers who refused a meaning to life" to have actually carried out that refusal in practice (Camus 1942a: 6). It may come as no surprise to learn that Jean Grenier's doctoral dissertation focused on Lequier, whose fairly extensive writings, previously unpublished except for one essay (one which, as it happens, played an important role in the life of William James), Grenier edited.

By contrast with those whom he has designated as the existentialist philosophers, Camus advocates what amounts to an heroic stance in the face of the absurd: to rely on ourselves alone as creators of value, as creators of the only reality that there is once the illusion of another world has been abandoned. There are obvious echoes of Nietzsche in this advocacy, as Camus acknowledges, but without any longing for an overman or new myth of eternal recurrence. And unlike Nietzsche in most of his writings, Camus is a strong proponent of the creative power of art, particularly visual and literary art. As he concludes in his penultimate chapter, entitled "Absurd Creation": "Outside of [the] single fatality of death, everything, joy or happiness, is liberty. A world remains of which man is the sole master" (Camus 1942a: 87). So it is that, in the very brief recounting of the ancient myth of Sisyphus – condemned by the gods for all eternity to roll a stone up a hill only to have it go tumbling down once again – with which the book ends, Camus says that we must imagine Sisyphus happy. And so it is, likewise, that Meursault, the "Stranger" and narrator of the novel of that name, concludes, just prior to his execution for murder, by finally laying his "heart open to the benign indifference of the universe" and realizing that he had been happy, and "was happy still" (Camus 1942b: 154).

It is important to reiterate, if only for the sake of historical accuracy, that Camus in *The Myth of Sisyphus* distinguished his own "absurdist" thought from that of the existentialists, as he then conceived of them. However, as the post-war wave of enthusiasm for existentialism took shape and grew, Camus came to be regarded as one of the existentialists, along with Jean-Paul Sartre, Simone de Beauvoir, and the philosopher who had first invented the term, Gabriel Marcel. This identification has stuck, more or less, ever since. (Sartre himself was, at one early point, moved to say that he was not sure what "existentialism" meant, while Marcel tried to dissociate himself from the label as it came increasingly to be connected with Sartre, whom he had begun to despise.) There was in fact considerable overlap in Camus' and Sartre's thinking during that period, and Sartre had published an appreciative review of *The Stranger* in February 1943. That was the year in which they first met, at the initial performance, in June, of Sartre's play, *The Flies*, which was then promptly banned by the German occupation authorities because it could be viewed (as Sartre intended) as an allegory of that occupation. It was also during that same year that Camus began working assiduously on *The Plague*, although, in large measure because of difficulties that he encountered while writing it, it was not published until 1947. As Camus wrote to Grenier in December 1946: "I had all the trouble in the world finishing my book *La Peste*. It's finished now but I am full of doubts about it (and about myself)" (Camus, in Camus and Grenier 1932–60: 92). *The Plague* was *also* intended to serve, among other things, as an allegory of the German occupation.

There is, in the conclusion of *The Plague*, a curious and interesting reversal of tone from the theme of happiness overcoming seemingly hopeless adversity that I have cited from the closing paragraphs of *The Stranger* and *The Myth of Sisyphus*. The plague having finally ended, the port of Oran being reopened to the loud applause of the surviving citizens, Doctor Rieux makes the decision to write his chronicle of the events. He appreciates the celebration; but he knows in his heart, on the basis of past history, that someday, decades later, the plague bacillus will reappear and once again disgorge dying rats on a happy city. There was, in fact, much unhappiness in the later years of Camus' relatively short life, as I have already begun to indicate. Besides his periodic physical relapses, there was the threat of nuclear annihilation, there was the Cold War with its personal ramifications for him resulting from the publication of his book, *The Rebel*, and there was the vicious actual war in his beloved birthplace, Algeria.

The nuclear threat weighed heavily on people of Camus' generation: in that respect he was certainly not alone. He had already lived through the period of the Spanish Civil War, then the rise of Nazism and the German occupation of France, and then, as he lamented in his Nobel Prize acceptance speech, two years before his death, the new madness of the nuclear threat. If anything, he suggested, humanity was descending further into insanity, and he realized that there was no basis for optimism. Yes, he had achieved the height of fame (and, at least for a writer, of fortune), and he felt that he was fulfilling an ongoing mission through his writing, but he apparently felt very little sense of joy at this moment. (It should be noted – echoes of Sisyphus! – that this award was given to him on the eleventh occasion of his having been nominated for it.)

The Rebel (*L'Homme révolté* – "man in revolt," part of the subtitle of the English translation, is more accurate) was published in 1951; it is Camus' other more strictly philosophical book, along with *The Myth of Sisyphus*. Much longer than the latter, *The Rebel* traverses much literary and historical ground, including some fairly intensive discussions of terrorism, but central to its message is a sharp distinction between (individual) rebellion, which in effect Camus endorses, and (political) revolution, which according to him always, in the long run, ends badly. It features a strong condemnation of Communism, that product of "the prophet of justice without mercy" (Camus 1951: 306) whose body lies in Highgate Cemetery, and hence it was bound, probably even more than its author had anticipated, to draw condemnation during a period when Cold War tensions were at a height. Camus himself had briefly joined the Communist Party as a young man in Algeria (with Grenier's approval, interestingly enough, although Grenier himself was never a member), but he had long since distanced himself from the Left, at least in its French version as he observed it among Paris intellectuals. Sartre, meanwhile, was at this time going through a period of intense disgust with attitudes of anti-Communism and, although he never joined the Communist Party himself, he was attempting to collaborate with it at the international level in its commitment, as he saw it, to peace. The staff of the journal of which Sartre was editor, *Les Temps Modernes*, felt that it had to publish a review of a book as important and as oppositional to its political commitments as *The Rebel* was, and Francis Jeanson volunteered for what was viewed as a rather thankless task. Camus' reaction to this unfavorable review was one of pain and anger, expressed in a "Letter to the Director of *Temps Modernes*" which never mentioned Jeanson by name but attacked Sartre as, so to speak, Jeanson's puppeteer. Sartre responded with an equally vitriolic letter that began by regretting that his friendship with Camus was finished and included an expression of disappointment that the author of *The Myth of Sisyphus* had, in Sartre's view, so changed. It was a very public scandal.

Then there was Algeria. It may be somewhat difficult now to recreate, in imagination, the socio-political conditions of Camus' youth. Algeria, a huge territory, was technically treated as a part of "metropolitan France," not a colony like so many other political entities in northern and western Africa at the time. Algeria had been occupied, especially in its coastal cities, by large numbers of French immigrants, called *"colons,"* who as a group enjoyed privileges denied to the Arab and Berber natives. (It was also home, incidentally, to a sizeable Jewish community, which had coexisted with the Algerian Arabs for many generations, but which in 1870 was accorded French citizenship en masse, as a means of expanding the "French" population and reinforcing the subordination of the Arabs and Berbers; some well-known members of the generation of French intellectuals after Camus', such as Jacques Derrida, came from this group.) Camus' impoverished mother was of Spanish descent, his father died in France of World War I battle wounds when Camus was an infant, but as a young man he certainly thought of Algeria as his home. By the mid-1950s, however, the struggle for Algerian independence was raging, with the French military engaged in trying to suppress it, often with considerable brutality. Camus continued to advocate peace talks and compromise even after it had become clear to most observers that this was no longer possible. He himself admitted privately, in a letter to Grenier in August 1958, that it was hopeless, but still defended his public stance on the (rather shaky) ground that the worst outcome is not always certain (Camus, in Camus and Grenier 1932–60: 187). Today, of course, there are virtually no permanent French residents remaining in Algeria, while France is home to many citizens of Algerian descent.

Despite his misfortunes and his shortcomings – for example, his very public womanizing, which played a part in his wife's psychological stress, or the fact, widely noted by critics, that the Arabs in his writings seem, in general, relatively featureless – Camus can be said to have embraced life with gusto. Indeed, he might well have said about life, in a paraphrase of Tertullian's declaration of faith mentioned above, *"amo quia absurdum,"* I love it in that it is absurd. One of his strongest convictions, in line with this thinking, was his opposition to capital punishment. Meursault, the Stranger, received the death sentence not so much because he killed an Arab, as Camus tells the story, but because the prosecutor placed heavy stress on Meursault's apparent lack of feeling, as recounted by witnesses, at the funeral of his mother, with whose death that book begins. (In fact, this part of Camus' story was based on the proceedings of an actual trial that he had covered when he briefly served as a young reporter in Algeria.) In the immediate aftermath of World War II, the trial for treason of Robert Brasillach, who had edited a deeply anti-Semitic, pro-Nazi newspaper under the German occupation, occasioned the circulation of a petition to spare his life, despite the deep and widespread hostility towards him: Simone de Beauvoir, who wrote an essay about this and other trials of Nazi collaborators ("An Eye for an Eye"), refused to sign that petition, but Camus (along with Marcel, incidentally) signed it out of his deep conviction concerning capital punishment and despite his contempt, as a former Resistance fighter, for Brasillach. (Brasillach was executed.)

In short, to recall the text from *The Myth of Sisyphus* that I cited earlier, Albert Camus was master of his world, giving his own meaning to his life without any obvious external, much less transcendental, assistance, at his best moments joyful, happy, and free – until the singular fatality of death arrived in its usual, absurd way.

33 Murdoch and the meaning of life

BRIDGET CLARKE

For Iris Murdoch, moral value is a real and radiant part of the world, but human beings must exercise loving attention to apprehend it. Murdoch's bold and brilliant development of this view in the second half of the twentieth century does not purport to clarify or answer questions to do with life's meaning, but it bears on them in a number of ways. I shall examine how it leads to the idea that *moral endeavor* constitutes the prime source of meaning in a world without God.

I

There are no easy roads from Murdoch's philosophical writings to any specific views about the meaning of life. I shall begin with some preliminary points and then proceed to reconstruct the most relevant parts of her moral philosophy in order to trace some links.

In speaking of "meaning," I shall focus on meaning *in* life, and I shall take my bearings from Susan Wolf's account of it as a matter of "fitting fulfillment." This is the idea, very roughly, that meaning in life arises when one finds fulfillment in objectively worthwhile – "fitting" – activities or relationships (Wolf 2010). Wolf's view enables me to structure the discussion around some very common intuitions and ultimately to query one of them.

Murdoch's writings concern ethical or moral value as this is demarcated (chiefly) by the virtues.[1] In keeping with the ancient philosophers, she does not distinguish sharply between moral, aesthetic, meaning-bearing, and prudential dimensions of value within the regions so delimited.[2] It is not always clear, then, how much one can extrapolate from her remarks about "the moral" or value generally to anything concerning meaning in life specifically. This difficulty shall both guide and shadow the investigation.

II

Murdoch is a naturalist about value, but her notion of what counts as "natural" is decidedly expansive.[3] In an important preamble to a discussion of the good, she notes:

There are properly many patterns and purposes within life, but there is no general and as it were externally guaranteed pattern or purpose for which philosophers and theologians used to search. We are what we seem to be, transient mortal creatures subject to necessity and chance. This is to say that there is, in my view, no God in the traditional sense of that term .... Equally the various metaphysical substitutions for God – Reason, Science, History – are false deities. Our destiny can be examined but it cannot be justified or totally explained. We are simply here. And if there is any kind of sense or unity in human life ... it is of some other kind and must be sought within a human experience which has nothing outside it.

(Murdoch 1967: 77)

This passage makes clear that Murdoch rejects what has traditionally been conceived of as the supernatural as a basis for meaning in life or for value generally. At the same time, it is important to note, Murdoch allows for a "transcendent reality" *within* the realm of the natural; she takes such a reality to be at the heart of moral life.[4] In Murdoch's view, encounters with value presuppose a reality that is *transcendent* but not supernatural or metaphysical in the traditional sense (and certainly not a projection of the agent's mental states). Her vision of the moral life is one in which "the individual is seen as moving tentatively *vis-à-vis* a reality which transcends him. To discover what is morally good is to discover that reality, and to become good is to integrate himself with it" (Murdoch 1957: 70).

So what *is* the transcendent reality that Murdoch takes to figure so importantly in the experience of value? Not all of Murdoch's writings point in the same direction on this matter, but there is much to suggest that the transcendent reality Murdoch has in mind just is, or belongs to, the ordinary world in which (if we are fortunate) we go to work, raise children, pass strangers on the street, mourn loss, celebrate good things, age, develop new interests, and so on. In what sense could such a mundane world constitute, or encompass, a transcendent reality? An exceedingly compressed version of Murdoch's answer is this: because it is impossible ever to fully understand the other human beings with whom one shares this world.[5] Other people transcend – are not fully captured by – one's grasp of them at any given moment. In this sense, ordinary life involves commerce with something transcendent, but not supernatural or metaphysical; I shall refer to it as "the ordinary transcendent." Murdoch notes: "The area of morals, and ergo of moral philosophy, can now be seen, not as a hole-and-corner matter of debts and promises, but as covering the whole of our mode of living and the quality of our relations with the world" (Murdoch 1967: 95).

Since the claims others make on us are not haphazard and since there seem to be interconnections between the virtues and the multifarious cases of good action more generally, Murdoch thinks the concept of the good (or "Good") is critical if we are properly to conceive and negotiate the ordinary transcendent. For Murdoch, the concept of the good is implicit in our experience of qualitative distinctions; it testifies to *hierarchy* and *patterns* in what is valuable. It therefore hints at how, on Murdoch's account, a life organized around responsiveness to value – a morally exemplary life – could provide something in the way of meaning.

Summing up: for Murdoch value is a part of the ordinary natural world, yet it refers us to something above and beyond our present grasp. It would seem then that meaning in life would have to be found somewhere in the agent's efforts to discover and "integrate himself with" the ordinary transcendent as fully as possible. To see how this might work, we must consider more closely the idea that others inevitably elude our full comprehension, and Murdoch's conception of the proper response to this fact.

III

Murdoch writes: "[t]o understand other people is a task that does not come to an end" (Murdoch 1959a: 283). It is, in Murdoch's view, the most difficult and important task in life and it centers on appreciating that others have a substantial – extensive, intricate, and unique – inner life. (One of her main criticisms of rival theories was that they were ill-equipped to register just this.) Murdoch's conception of the inner life is itself quite intricate and it will be helpful simply to note here what I take to be some of its central features. Virtually all of them are topics in their own right and some will be given further attention in what follows.

Murdoch associates the inner life with a process of conceptual development – meaning something quite different by this than most philosophers – and she ties the inner life so characterized to the concept of the *individual* or *person*. Part of what it is to be an individual, on Murdoch's account, is to develop (within certain parameters) a unique interpretation of the available moral concepts, a distinctive conceptual "vision."[6] She takes this process of conceptual ramification to be ongoing or "historical" in that one's understandings change under pressure of experience. So individuals' visions necessarily differ from one another, and change over time. Ideally this change is for the better, i.e. in the direction of truthfulness. But it must be stressed that for Murdoch, a more truthful vision is not a less individual one. These complex ideas work together in Murdoch's writings to support a notion of individuals as essentially independent and unsurveyable centers of reality. And this notion, which is central to Murdoch's own vision, puts intrinsic limits on how completely an individual can be known by another. It also makes it conceptually true that it is difficult to come to know others in any depth.

This difficulty is amplified, on Murdoch's account, by the fact that humans are naturally egoists. It is human nature, she thinks, to adopt conceptions of ourselves that are both self-aggrandizing or self-protecting and resistant to counter-evidence. These conceptions partner with spurious internal narratives and the like, all of which Murdoch calls "fantasy," to corrupt one's perceptions of others and one's individual vision quite generally. Murdoch believes fantasy to be a deep source of gratification and consolation and therefore a constant temptation for any person (Murdoch 1992: ch. 11, esp. 316–24). The central practical question of ethics, for Murdoch, is what to do about it. This leads to the most famous part of Murdoch's theory.

IV

Following Simone Weil, Murdoch links the refinement and clarification of one's vision to the exercise of "attention."[7] Generally speaking, attention is a form of contemplation. It involves "looking carefully at something and *holding* it before the mind" in a way that respects its particularity, its separateness from other things (Murdoch 1992: 3). Given human nature, Murdoch takes this to involve both love and justice: attention is precisely "a just and loving gaze directed upon an individual reality outside the self" (Murdoch 1964: 33). While many things can be the object of such a gaze ("individual realities" is a broad category), it is other persons who most require it because they are the most natural objects of fantasy. In Murdoch's most famous example, it is by *attending* to her daughter-in-law that a mother-in-law overcomes a prejudiced view of her (ibid.: 16–23).

Some of Murdoch's language (such as "unselfing," "suppression of self"; Murdoch 1967: 82; 1969: 64) suggests that attention culminates in a loss of subjectivity. If this were correct, it would present special obstacles to the idea that it could furnish the agent with a sense of meaning in life, particularly where that meaning entails fulfillment. So it is important to register that attention leads not to a loss of subjectivity but to a purification of it, a nourishing of the parts of it that enlarge one's vision. By attending to the world around him, the agent refines the set of concepts at his disposal. As noted, this refinement is not, for Murdoch, a matter of trading a highly personal ramification of concepts for a more general impersonal one. She considers moral concepts "concrete universals"; they are the kind of thing to be understood in ever increasing *depth* by each individual (see Merritt 2017). This deepening occurs by directing "a patient, loving regard" upon "a person, a thing, a situation" (Murdoch 1964: 39).

Summarizing: the agent is surrounded by a transcendent reality in the form, paradigmatically, of other persons with inner lives as vital as her own. Because of a natural proclivity toward egoism, the agent must practice attention – a willed form of love – if she is to come to appreciate other persons, their "separateness and differentness," the fact that they have needs and wishes "as demanding as one's own" (Murdoch 1969: 64). This activity is at once richly subjective and "infinitely perfectible" (Murdoch 1964: 23).

V

We are now in a position to consider whether attention can be a source of meaning in life. To consider this aright, it is important to note that efforts of attention (and related activity) look to be, for Murdoch, the *only* possible source of meaning in life. "[N]othing in life is of any value except the attempt to be virtuous"; "The only thing which is of real importance is the ability to see it all clearly and respond to it justly ..." (Murdoch 1967: 85).[8] Such claims are not as extreme as they may appear given that the endeavor to see clearly and respond justly, on Murdoch's picture, reaches into almost all areas of life, including those typically considered outside the domain of the moral.[9] But it does imply that if efforts to apprehend the world around one in all its inexhaustible complexity are not a source of meaning in life, nothing is.[10]

Our question, specifically, is whether these efforts look to be a source of fitting fulfillment. At first glance, they certainly do. They look, that is, to be both objectively worthwhile ("fitting") as well as fulfilling to the agent whose efforts they are – in virtue of what makes them worthwhile.[11] Through efforts of attention, as noted, one develops a vision of life that is intimately one's own and that links one intimately to the world outside oneself. One comes to see more clearly the world around one in a way that entails being appropriately *moved* by what one sees. One transcends one's cognitive and motivational limitations *in perpetuum* (see Nozick 1981a: ch. 6). Accordingly, Murdoch's language is often positively stirring. She speaks of "the realisation of a vast and varied reality outside ourselves" as a source of "exhilaration and spiritual power" akin to the sublime; she describes the moral life as a "pilgrimage" from lower to higher, akin to the ascent from Plato's cave; she associates it with Platonic eros understood as "the continual operation of spiritual *energy*, desire, intellect, love, as it moves among and responds to particular objects of attention ..." (Murdoch 1959a: 282; 1992: 496). Not only do such descriptions (which abound in her works) make Murdochian morality sound like a rich source of fitting fulfillment, they also make it sound like an *archetypal* source of meaning in life, one that furnishes a spiritual "quest" for each and every person without, however, appealing to the supernatural or the esoteric. But here it is important to register a complication.

VI

The fact that moral reality transcends the agent properly leads not only to uplift and inspiration on Murdoch's picture, but also to distress, frustration, even anguish. In essence, one can be exhilarated by what one cannot encompass with one's mind or one can feel powerless and defeated by this distance.[12] Murdoch takes both types of response, not merely the former, to be intrinsic to moral life. The realm of the practical, as she once puts it, is "haunted by ... incompleteness and lack of form" (Murdoch 1959b: 220; see also 1992: ch. 4).

For Murdoch this means inter alia, that humans are destined to suffer a kind of discursive defeat. She believes that works of art may "attempt to overcome the defeat which humans suffer in the practical world," but that in everyday life "there may be only mourning and the final acceptance of the incomplete" (Murdoch 1959b: 220). This suggests that it might be inapt to characterize Murdochian morality in terms of *fulfillment*; but this is what we must do if we are to see it as a source of fitting fulfillment and hence meaning in life.

The difficulty of the agent's situation can be elucidated by considering Murdoch's notion of the "indefinability of good." I noted earlier that Murdoch thinks the concept of good requisite if one is to account properly for the ostensible *order* one finds in moral matters. She steadfastly defends the reality of such an order, but stresses that it does not admit of capture in a system (let alone a decision procedure). "It lies always beyond, and it is from this beyond that it exercises its *authority*" (Murdoch 1969: 61). The "beyondness" in question is, for Murdoch, a function of our inevitable cognitive limitations and of "the unsystematic and inexhaustible variety of the world" – particularly, but not only, in the form of individuals or persons (Murdoch 1967: 96). Murdoch further links the indefinability of the good to its "pointlessness" in the absence of a creator to ensure that good deeds are rewarded on earth or in the after-life (ibid.).[13] Necessity and chance, on her account, take the place of God and purpose. In such a context, good is very real but it cannot be *defined*. "The scene," as she puts it, "remains disparate and complex beyond the hopes of any system, yet at the same time the concept Good stretches through the whole of it and gives it the only kind of *shadowy unachieved unity* which it can possess" (ibid.: 94–95, emphasis added).

The indefinability of good ensures that one will not be able to see "how it all hangs together," morally speaking, any more than one will be able fully to comprehend another person. These things (which are of course interconnected) will poignantly elude the capture of even the most refined vision. Indeed it is precisely, for Murdoch, the exercise of loving attention that *issues in* an awareness of the incompleteness of one's understanding. The "easy patterns" of fantasy deny just this; they are *consoling* (ibid.: 84). One must add to this that loving attention inevitably confronts the agent with the more frightful aspects of reality, such things as death, brutality, and absurdity – again without giving the agent any way finally to make sense of them. (This may be why experiences of "the void" are a standing possibility for Murdochian agents; Murdoch 1992: ch. 18.) In this context, to experience the incompleteness of one's understanding is to suffer a *lack*.

None of this forecloses the possibility that efforts of attention are rewarded on Murdoch's picture or that they may be fulfilling. But it does mean that the place of fulfillment in Murdoch's picture of morality is thorny. Simply put, to view efforts of attention as a source of fulfillment (fitting or otherwise) risks slighting the importance Murdoch accords to the experience of incompleteness in the moral life. Are we then to conclude that Murdochian morality is not a possible source of meaning in life? This seems problematic in light of its edifying aspects noted in Section V. One must give the positive and negative possibilities their due in considering the potential of "a just and loving gaze" to supply meaning in life. The obvious way to do this without relinquishing that potential is to suppose that, for Murdoch, it is the *endeavor* to apprehend reality in its endless complexity that supplies meaning in life (if anything does). Not only does this fit Murdoch's picture readily, it is an attractive idea in its own right. I shall put it in broader perspective by way of conclusion.

VII

"There is meaning in struggle," Ta-Nehisi Coates tells his son as he reflects on the persistence of virulent racism in the US in the face of generations of concerted resistance. He continues, "[t]he fact of history is that black people have not – probably no people have ever – liberated themselves strictly through their own efforts .... still you are called to struggle, not because it assures you victory but because it assures you an honorable and sane life" (Coates 2015: 96–97). This seems unassailable, and it implies that lives can be meaningful even when they lack the ordinary means of fulfillment.[14] At a more general level, this is to see meaning in life as a matter of "fitting devotion" or "fitting endeavor" rather than fitting fulfillment. This agrees with the spirit and the details of Murdoch's vision as I have presented it.

Needless to say, one can be mistaken about whether one's cause is worthwhile or "fitting." Murdoch well recognizes our susceptibility to wishful thinking and other forms of fantasy when making such judgments. And she acknowledges what she views as the inevitable incompleteness of her own moral vision (see Mulhall 1997). This gives her account an achieved tentativeness which only adds to the difficulty of drawing precise links between her moral vision and the question of meaning in life. Yet the essence of Murdoch's view is quite clear, namely that anything fit to provide meaning in life comes out of the struggle to be present to the world in its inexhaustible variety and complexity. For Murdoch, this struggle *just is* morality, and it awakens one to startling depths "within a human experience which has nothing outside it" (Murdoch 1967: 77).[15]

Notes

1 How to conceptualize the region of the moral accurately and without begging substantive questions is a major theme in Murdoch's work, beginning notably with: Murdoch 1956.

2 E.g. "Goodness and beauty are not to be contrasted but are largely part of the same structure" (Murdoch 1964: 40).

3 In brief, Murdoch does not take *the natural* to be exhausted by *what is studied by the natural sciences*.

4 The failure to make such an allowance was the chief failing, as she saw it, of a "post-Kantian" approach that included both existentialism and non-cognitivism. "The centre of this type of

post-Kantian moral philosophy is the notion of the will as the creator of value. Values which were previously in some sense inscribed in the heavens and guaranteed by God collapse into the human will. *There is no transcendent reality*" (Murdoch 1967: 78; emphasis added).

5 Justin Broackes crystallizes the case for this line of interpretation in his careful analysis of "On 'God' and 'Good'" (Broakes 2012: 55–69) and in a forthcoming commentary on *Sovereignty*.

6 See in particular Murdoch 1956 and 1964. For discussion, see Bagnoli 2012.

7 I compare their conceptions in Clarke 2013.

8 Similarly: "A genuine sense of mortality enables us to see virtue as the only thing of worth..." (ibid.: 96).

9 "All just vision, even in the strictest problems of the intellect, ... is a moral matter. The same virtues, in the end the same virtue (love), are required throughout, and fantasy (self) can prevent us from seeing a blade of grass just as it can prevent us from seeing another person" (Murdoch 1969: 68).

10 In what follows I move freely, as Murdoch herself does, between the idea that value originates in the attempt to attend and the idea that it comes from attempts that succeed. As I understand her, all genuine efforts to attend are valuable and none of them are fully successful.

11 Wolf discusses and defends the idea of objective value in Wolf 2010: 34–48, 62–63 and 119–32. She discusses the concept of fulfillment on pp. 13–18 and 109–14. In both cases, she keeps within the ordinary understandings of these terms, as I mean to do.

12 My wording here is indebted to Diamond 2003.

13 "The Good has nothing to do with purpose, indeed it excludes the idea of purpose. 'All is vanity' is the beginning and end of ethics" (Murdoch 1969: 69).

14 Robert Adams presses this point in his commentary on Susan Wolf's view; see Adams 2010: 76–79.

15 I'm grateful to the editors of the collection. Thanks also to Paul Muench for incisive comments on earlier drafts and to the students in my Murdoch seminar at the University of Montana in 2017.

34 Fanon and the meaning of life

SAMUEL IMBO

Philosophy at its best is a search for ultimate truth, but must begin with reflection about mundane human experiences. The philosophy of liberation shares the concerns of the wider discipline, while specifically grappling with the implications for truth and freedom in an environment of power relations structured by imperialism and colonialism. Borrowing from Wittgenstein's comparison of philosophy to a toolbox, Frantz Fanon (1925–1961) emerges as an original theoretician whose work contains the tools necessary for untangling the complexities of the deeply unequal ordering system responsible for intellectual, political, cultural, and economic relations under globalization. Fanon gives first-hand accounts of his days at Lycée Schoelcher in Fort-de-France, Martinique; the quiet countryside in the south of France when he was a medical student; and battlefields in Morocco, Algeria, Mali, and Tunisia. In the telling of his everyday experiences, he draws out lessons about the corrosive effects of hierarchical subordination structures designed to simultaneously accomplish and mask their task. Fanon's prophetic vision remains relevant as a corrective to the persisting blind spots in the practice of academic philosophy: racism, sexism, and homophobia. Linking theory and practice, his ideas resonated in the university and on the street in a manner which the academic philosophy of today should envy.

In this chapter, what Fanon has to say about the meaning of life will be discussed under four headings – his biography and its implications for questions of identity, the influence of negritude on his conception of humanism, his views on violence and revolution, and his continuing relevance.

Biography

Frantz Fanon was born in Martinique, led the life of a medical professional and revolutionary in Africa, died in the United States, and was buried in Algeria. His biography prompts the question about the narrow and broad boundaries of where his identity belongs. He lived as if he was from Martinique, and France, and Algeria. Concepts such as hybridity and creolization had not yet become fashionable, but Fanon was transgressing boundaries and actualizing the foundations of solidarity. Moreover, he was shining a light on the intellectual elite gatekeepers who create categories of thought, for example "History" and "Reason," that in reality foreclose possibilities for thought and human development in the search for meaning. His whole existence can be seen as an extended argument for openness to a plurality of conceptions about what it means to be human, and for letting knowledge flourish by crossing disciplinary, racial, gender, and national boundaries.

There is wide agreement on the broad outlines of his life story. Fanon was born on the island of Martinique on 20 July 1925. He died 6 December 1961, of bronchial pneumonia stemming from leukemia, in Bethesda, Maryland. Fanon was a writer, theorist, psychologist, psychiatrist, political philosopher, and revolutionary. The fifth of eight children, he was born into a middle class (his father, Felix, a customs inspector and his mother, Eléanoro, a shop-keeper), in a society with a rigid, racialized, class structure. The small upper middle class was comprised of local and transplanted whites, the middle class mostly interracial or black, and the majority being a black working class. These realities would shape Fanon's class consciousness. In Martinique, he studied at Lycée Schoelcher; for a time under Aimé Césaire, whose negritude philosophy was an early influence. It is significant that the Lycée was named after Victor Schoelcher, a French abolitionist who helped end slavery in Martinique in the mid-1800s. By the time Fanon left Martinique to study medicine in France in 1947, he was already struggling with tension between the racial essentialism he saw as a pillar of negritude, and the broader black and human identity embedded in the French ideals he had grown up with.

Like the French Antilles and Guadeloupe, Martinique is an overseas department and region of France. Throughout the seventeenth and eighteenth centuries, Britain and France battled for control of the island until the French gained permanent control in 1814. In March 1946, the people of Martinique voted to transform their colonial status by becoming a regular department of France. Since then, Martinique has been represented in the French Parliament. These developments had an impact on Fanon's political consciousness.

Negritude or humanism?

The three founding fathers of the negritude literary and philosophical movement are: the poet and politician from French Guiana, Leon Damas; Leopold Sedar Senghor from Senegal; and Aimé Césaire. Césaire's influence politicized Fanon, heightening the tension between the assimilationist instincts of the middle class in Martinique and what he came to conclude was the pre-occupation with a narrow racial identity that negritude promoted. Fanon remained sympathetic to the negritude project of Césaire, which shaped his view of human nature and connected him to the negritude movement in the diaspora, from Martinique, French Guiana, and Trinidad, to the United States, Tunisia, and Algeria. The seeds of this movement may be traced to the double consciousness concept that W.E.B. Du Bois developed in *The Souls of*

Black Folk, the New Negro Movement and the Harlem Renaissance of the 1920s. Fanon expanded and exported the black consciousness to Africa, especially in regard to understanding the struggle of African people against colonial domination and global capitalism.

Philosophers see their task as the search for truth. Fanon was consumed with the task of unmasking the true structure of the colonial enterprise, exposing its contradictions, and proposing more human alternatives. In his work, we see a thinker embedded in the struggle. To put this in perspective, as a key figure in the Algerian National Liberation Front (Front de Liberation Nationale – FLN) Fanon theorized about liberation to a depth that is far removed from the average contemporary philosopher writing for an academic journal; whose primary concern may just be publishing to gain tenure. If Fanon is unrecognizable to philosophers today as one of their own because of his delving into the struggle, rather than dispassionately seeking objective truths, then this is a reflection of how far the discipline has fallen into irrelevance. His legacy rests not on his numerous articles for academic journals, his public essays in the FLN's *El Moudjahid*, or his plays. It is in living out the truth of his convictions in the very real struggle for Algerian independence, engaging with the contradictions of the anti-imperialist struggle, and searching for liberating alternatives. *Praxis* was for him theory *and* practice, both united in seeking humanity – and thus the opposite of a verbal struggle. Reality trumps rhetoric, though rhetoric rightly deployed and received uncovers and illuminates reality.

Throughout his life, Fanon highlighted this tension between two strands of his worldview. After his death, some critics and separatist groups adopted interpretations of his thought that downplay Fanon's universalism. This is a misreading. In *Toward the African Revolution*, Fanon concludes chapter 2, on racism and culture, thus:

> The end of race prejudice begins with a sudden incomprehension. The occupant's spasmed and rigid culture, now liberated, opens at last to the culture of people who have really become brothers. The two cultures can affront each other, enrich each other. In conclusion, universality resides in this decision to recognize and accept the reciprocal relativism of different cultures, once the colonial status is irreversibly excluded.
>
> (Fanon 1964: 44)

Fanon rejected both French culture and negritude insofar as they had proved unable to counter the presuppositions around the ordering of knowledge production and thereby free the colonized from their chains. Black intellectuals need to engage intellectual history, broadly construed. Affirming black identity is important, but should always be open to affronting and enriching the human race as a whole. Nevertheless, a false universalism predictably leads to epistemic dependency.

On violence and revolution

Fanon was prolific in his relatively short life. His major works get to the roots from which the pain of the colonized emanates. His method also digs behind the narrative of the colonizer to unmask the self-deception that allows the inclusivist illusion of incorporating other worldviews while distorting them. His first book, *Black Skins, White Masks* (1952), started out as his doctoral thesis, entitled "The Disalienation of the Black." As a student of medicine and psychiatry in Lyon, Fanon had to come to terms with black identity in a way Martinique had not allowed. His family background and education in Martinique had socialized him to identity primarily with white French culture. But the concrete reality of living in France confronted him with the everyday racism that until then he had thought only "real" Africans experienced. His doctoral thesis was rejected, but the patronizing compliments, vague hostility, and outright rudeness which he experienced in daily life propelled him to complement his personal experience with research on "the lived experience of the black man" and thereby flesh out the work. The reworked thesis explores the psychological effects of racism. He finds that to be black in a white world is to be dependent on the goodwill of the colonizer and thus to be saddled with feelings of inadequacy. Fanon's insight is that the colonizer and the colonized have fates that are intertwined.

In many ways Fanon and Africa are treated, within popular scholarship, in strikingly similar ways: misunderstood, marginalized, and misquoted.

Fanon does not equate revolution with armed struggle. After revolution, there is no topic on which Fanon has been more misunderstood than violence. In *The Wretched of the Earth*, his assessment is that colonialism itself is a violence that only yields to a greater violence:

> ... decolonization is always a violent phenomenon. At whatever level we study it – relationships between individuals, new names for sports clubs, the human admixture at cocktail parties, in the police, on the directing boards of national or private banks – decolonization is quite simply the replacing of a certain "species" of men by another "species" of men. Without any period of transition, there is a total, complete, and absolute substitution.
>
> (Fanon 1961: 35)

Critics who accuse Fanon of advocating violence seem to rely solely on this first paragraph of the first chapter, titled "Concerning Violence." However, as Lewis Gordon aptly argues, in *What Fanon Said: A Philosophical Introduction to his Life and Thought* (2015), understanding a thinker as complex as Fanon calls for careful acts of interpretation and presentation of what his words mean, within a framework that does not obscure their contextual meaning. It should therefore be pointed out that after his analysis of colonial violence, Fanon rounds off *The Wretched of the Earth* by discussing the strengths and weaknesses of spontaneity, the pitfalls of national consciousness, national culture, and the relationship between colonial war and mental disorders.

He was indeed outraged by the everyday racism of the French army that he joined in 1943. He was outraged, too, by the racism visited on his patients at Blida-Joinville Hospital in Algeria in 1953. Fanon distinguishes between four varieties of violence in these experiences – arbitrary force, physical or psychological injury, aggression, and coercion. Each kind calls for a dedicated measure of counter-violence. The militancy and radicalism of the colonized is thus properly seen as counter-violence. His statement, that decolonization is always a violent phenomenon, has two meanings. Firstly, that there will inevitably be counter-violence involved in physically taking back individual bodies and territories from the colonizer. Secondly, that the psychological acts of self-articulation, and decentralizing the colonizer, are a program of complete disorder that is inevitably experienced as violence.

A careful reading of *The Wretched of the Earth* reveals that Fanon does not in fact endorse violence. His point is that the colonized have all their options choked off and are reduced to violence. The colonial enterprise must be understood as a violent psychological, intellectual, cultural, political, and economic invasion. Decolonization is a counter-violence that aims to restore social structure and destroy the colonizer's capacity for continued aggression. As a way of restoring personhood to the colonized "non-persons," counter-violence is cathartic in bringing down the colonial structure and paving the way for building solidarity in the liberation struggle.

Fanon's legacy and relevance

One way to gauge Fanon's legacy as a theorist of anti-imperialism is through the international cast of thinkers he influenced. Political leaders like António Agostinho Neto and Amilcar Cabral saw culture at the heart of their liberation concerns in much the same way as Fanon did. Fanon was also an influence on activist-scholar Paolo Freire, whose pedagogy of the oppressed proceeds organically from local knowledge. Fanon's influence is also visible in the work of thinkers as diverse as Jean-Paul Sartre, Simone de Beauvoir, Edward Said, Homi Bhabha, film director Gillo Pontecorvo, and the Black Panther Party. While uncharitable critics may characterize him as an incendiary and Europhobic provocateur, his thought embodied philosophies of liberation capable of being molded to address various manifestations of colonial and neo-colonial hegemony.

Fanon can be called prophetic without hyperbole. To read "The Pitfalls of National Consciousness" chapter in *The Wretched of the Earth* is to see a prediction of the era of African dictators: Yoweri Museveni, Mobutu Sese Seko, Robert Mugabe, and Muammar Gaddafi. The valiant efforts of Kwame Nkrumah, Abdel Nasser, Amilcar Cabral, Julius Nyerere, Patrice Lumumba, Steve Biko, and Nelson Mandela to liberate the continent are noteworthy; yet the odds were stacked against them from the start. African nationalisms, with varying forms of folkloric "black culture," could not really break free from the forces of colonialism. While pretending to concede power, the same oppressive forces responsible for colonialism flourished in the neo-colonial states – only this time undergirded by home-grown political parties and nationalist bourgeoisie. Just as before, in the independent countries there are still categories of privileged human beings, marked sometimes by skin color, ethnicity, or class. They enjoy their privileged existence at the expense of the wretched of the earth, whose lives have no meaning and do not matter. The atmosphere of violence remains because the national bourgeoisie see their mission as mediating between the neo-colonial state and the Western metropolis. The leaders grow more distant from the masses as they perpetuate and sustain neo-colonial hegemony. Only revolution can transform and renew society.

Fanon's vision is that a revolution of thought, an inner revolution, is necessary in our time. In the United States, the Black Lives Matter movement is a demand to overthrow a humanism whose abstract universal principles nevertheless remain incapable of honestly addressing police brutality, mass incarceration, and second-class citizenship attributed to black lives. Fanon spoke unapologetically of violence. For him, certain forms of pacifism simply preserved colonial violence by not bringing about real change. Similarly, the Black Lives Matter protests are a critique of any humanism that mystifies. As Fanon showed, such a demand from the marginalized strikes fear in the privileged class – and must always expect a backlash when the empire strikes back.

He died in 1961, and hence did not live to see the Algerian independence, for which he sacrificed his life, come to realization the following year in 1962; but his work helped shatter the foundations of French colonialism. Fanon's life must prompt in our troubled times an honest foregrounding of our intellectual commitments, so leading us to ask the question: "What Would Fanon Do?" Words matter, but the meaning of life is in *action*.

35 Rorty and the meaning of life

ALAN MALACHOWSKI

In his introduction to *Life, Death, and Meaning*, David Benatar claims "the question of whether life has meaning is arguably the biggest of the big questions" (Benatar 2010, 6). In his book *On the Meaning of Life*, John Cottingham also suggests that the question as to whether life has meaning is one that "does not go away" (Cottingham 2003: 1). At first sight, Richard Rorty's approach to the question fails to recognize this, and is liable to appear evasive or superficial. It can look deficient in these ways from a number of angles: Rorty does not take the question seriously, he fails to acknowledge the significance of deeper problems it can raise, he does not generally engage with philosophical literature that has grown up around it,[1] and most disappointingly for those who feel this question is profoundly important, he does not approach it at all.

However, a closer, more open-minded, inspection reveals that Rorty espouses a nuanced, human-centered account of *meaning in general*, based on an interesting form of what we might call social naturalism. And, this account takes the existential edge off the traditional "biggest question," while rendering it philosophically obsolete. The charge of evasiveness then gains little traction, while complaints about superficiality seem better directed at those who hope to elevate a notion of meaning, applicable to life itself, above and beyond the realms of such naturalism, or despair of ever doing so.

Rorty does not use the phrase "social naturalism," and probably would not want to. But in this compressed context, it is a useful enough explanatory blanket to throw over his wide-ranging work when discussing how some of its components relate to issues concerning the meaning of life. This naturalism is not anchored in purely physical reality as such, so it is not a brand of *scientific* naturalism, or materialism as philosophers generally understand it. The anchor, as the first term of the phrase suggests, is the human behavior found in social life. It involves, of course, the customs and practices people create and participate in. Now surprisingly, perhaps, Rorty's approach to the question of whether life has meaning ends there. For him, there is no meaning beyond that which is conjured up by, and recognized within, such customs and practices. Moreover, the jurisdiction of social life over meaning is ubiquitous in this instance: there is no higher court of appeal in which such meaning can be invalidated or undermined in favor of a version which completely transcends its authority.

Certainly, without further elaboration and justification, this terminus will no doubt still seem unsatisfactory, especially for those who are initially inclined to find Rorty's approach evasive or superficial in the face of a recalcitrant large question. Rooting meaning *in* social life when it is the meaning *of* life that is supposed to be in question appears to be plainly misguided.

Rorty does provide elaboration and justification, but not directly, and not in a form that might normally be expected of a philosopher. He produces no battery of detailed arguments designed to refute those who claim:

1   life has a meaning independently of that conferred socially

and/or

1   life requires an independent dimension of meaning, otherwise it is fatally deficient.[2]

Instead, he offers a picture of the historical development of the realms of meaning *within* human life, a picture according to which, dependence on, or desire for, the kind of external[3] meaning referred to in such claims has been outgrown. And, he suggests that to the extent philosophy influences this picture, it does so by showing why the notion of an independent dimension of meaning has no genuine authority and is therefore dispensable.

Clearly, it matters how this picture is constructed, and what it contains: it is insufficient just to envisage social circumstances in which questions about the meaning of life happen not to arise, or are prevented from doing so. In the latter case, for instance, Stalinist repression, at its peak, created just such circumstances throughout the former Soviet Union and, to a large extent, its satellites. Seriously questioning, perhaps not even in public, whether the life promoted and sanctioned by the state lacked meaning, and hence purpose and value, was a very risky endeavor, one that was likely to lead to the Gulag. For, as Herbert Marcuse points out in his classically incisive analysis of Soviet Marxism, "society defined as socialist in terms of Marxian theory becomes the sole standard of truth and falsehood; there can be no transcendence in thought and action, *no individual autonomy* because the Nomos of the whole is the true Nomos" (1971, emphasis added). The importance of this example will resonate later.

In Rorty's picture, history and philosophy feed into one another, and then into a narrative which carries a significant stage further the maturity Kant referred to in his famous answer to the question "What is Enlightenment?," taking it much closer to complete autonomy or, in Rorty's own terms, "self-reliance." Kantian enlightenment involves the maturity to rely on one's own powers of reason rather than the guidance of authorities:

> Enlightenment is man's emergence from his self-incurred immaturity. Immaturity is the inability to use one's own understanding without the guidance of another.
>
> (Kant 1784: 54)

But for Rorty, this is maturity in name only, even though it puts such a premium on the autonomous deployment of reason. He doesn't buy it because Kant still recognizes and accepts the existence of external authority, most notably that of the Moral Law and God.[4] By contrast, the maturity Rorty endorses and expounds is *completely* anti-authoritarian.[5] It holds that there is nothing super-authoritative looming behind social practices, nothing sufficiently "remote and august" (Rorty 1989: 23) which they should be beholden to.

Historically, or so Rorty maintains, modern developed societies in the West have, at their intellectual heights at least, jettisoned not just the authorities lurking behind Kant's version of maturity as the exercise of autonomous reason, but *all* external authorities. This is how things have turned out factually speaking, as it were. At their best, humans are now, or can be, more self-reliant. Meanwhile, Rorty informs us, philosophers have developed the basis for a conception of meaning in general, a "social practice conception," which shows this is how things *ought* to have turned out.[6]

Rorty tells a number of different versions of his historical story. But, it is only the details of emphasis that tend to vary. The two main common threads are the modern trends of secularization and democratization. Both involve ordinary people getting out from under the dominance of overarching authority: divine dominion as rationalized by theology, and political supremacy as practiced and enjoyed by tyrants. Rorty offers Darwinism as a prime stimulus for liberation from the former and the French revolution for liberation from the latter. These trends made it more difficult to believe the meaning and purpose of life could only be derived from above, as it were, and never freely constructed from the ground up by human hand.

When belief in the meaningfulness of life based on external authority crumbles, it can look as if life itself has been destabilized. Hence, some major thinkers have been gravely concerned that the historical outcome of such crumbling has to be a loss of faith in the meaning, purpose and value of life, the kind of loss that signals the emergence of nihilism: the view that *nothing* has any meaning, purpose or value. Friedrich Nietzsche is the key figure here (see Nietzsche 1901), and under his influence nihilism has been taken very seriously indeed by a succession of philosophers in the so-called continental tradition running from Martin Heidegger, through Jacques Derrida, to Gianni Vattimo in the present day.[7] This is one of the reasons that the question as to whether life has meaning has been kept in *philosophical* circulation. Rorty does not pay nihilism the compliment of engaging with it; indeed, he hardly ever refers to it.[8] He seems to regard it as a form of over-intellectualized disquietude of little genuine social consequence, one that can be suitably remedied by a dose of historicism.

According to Rorty, historicist thinkers "insist that socialization, and thus historical circumstance, goes all the way down – that there is nothing 'beneath' socialization or prior to history which is definatory of the human" (Rorty 1989: xiii). Taking this on board, it is a small step to further insist that *social* identity is all that matters here; that there is no other, trans-social authority which humans are answerable to when they want to determine who they are, who they might want to be, and how they should live their life. If we put the "historicist turn" which Rorty regards as having occurred since the time of Georg Hegel (ibid.: xiii), together with the social practice account of meaning which we have been alluding to throughout, then the result provides philosophical support for Rorty's interpretation of socio-historical trends.

If it is accepted that humans are only answerable to social demands, there may still be a temptation to ask whether such answerability alone exhausts all the important meaning life can have. Then it seems another version of the biggest question might remain open. But, Rorty closes that possibility down, or rather doesn't allow it to appear feasible in the first place, by suggesting that meaning itself is a social consideration through and through and cannot be separated out far enough from life to cause problems for his own approach. He does this by blurring the distinction between linguistic meaning, or the meaning of words, and the notion of meaningfulness that has connotations of value and purpose; for when the latter remains isolated from linguistic meaning, it cannot be invoked to indicate whether or not life is worthwhile. Rorty takes his inspiration for a social practice account of linguistic meaning straight from Ludwig Wittgenstein's later philosophy (Wittgenstein 1953), where understanding the meaning of words involves acquiring the ability to use them in conformity with the way that other speakers use them. Meaning is manifested and discoverable – *only* discoverable in many cases – within practical contexts of use. By extending this sort of explanation to cover the kind of meaning which the biggest question invokes, Rorty intends to show that just as a word obtains meaning when uses are found for it on a regular basis, life acquires meaning when there are social contexts created which confer meaning upon it.[9]

Suppose we run with all this. Are there likely to be lingering concerns if we reflect back on why the biggest question could seem so compelling to so many for so long? Should there be such concerns? Leaving aside detailed objections to Rorty's interpretations of history, or his omnivorous, distinction-blurring, social practice account of meaning, there are three possibilities which come to mind.

One worry might be that Rorty's picture is far too optimistic, since it ignores the danger of making meaningfulness entirely subject to social control – mob control, so to speak – or perhaps even worse: control by a mob that runs the state, as in the case of the Soviet Union under Stalin. A second source of anxiety could be that regardless of the dangers of mob rule, Rorty's approach depicts situations in which human ambition will surely be curtailed, while drab conservatism prevails, as people self-consciously seek only to satisfy *existing* social requirements for meaningfulness, forgoing the chance to transcend them. Finally, social practices themselves seem to contain no resources to cope with the inevitable tensions between an individual's conception of a meaningful life and society's conception, and hence between individual fulfillment and social justice.

What makes Rorty's approach so interesting, and still relevant to ongoing discussion of whether life has meaning, is how he addresses such worries. He attempts to show that in his anti-authoritarian scheme of things, there should be no great cause for great concern. Indeed, he regards his scheme as prophylactic in this respect.

The problems of mob rule and drab conservatism are less likely to arise because of the dynamic nature of social contexts of meaning and the innovative part that individuals are naturally inclined to play in their creation. Once people realize meaning can be created and is not just discovered, they will be less inclined to cower down to attempts to impose meaning on their lives, politically or otherwise. They should also be less keen to merely settle for existing contexts of meaning without probing for something better. Artists, in every field, are always extending the boundaries of meaning. That offers mitigation against complacency. But, artists need not be relied upon as some sort of vanguard for creating contexts of meaning. *Every* person, in Rorty's view, has the capacity to create a meaningful life, and can do so effortlessly, without possessing special artistic skills.[10] Elitism falls by the wayside, but decidedly not as a concession to "drabness." Following Freud, Rorty contends that *each* life can best be viewed as an endlessly interesting poem when the idiosyncrasies and chance events that go into making it up are given their due. He agrees with the literary critic Lionel Trilling's assessment that Freud:

> showed us that poetry is indigenous to the very constitution of the mind; he saw the mind as being, in the greater part of its tendency, exactly a poetry-making facility.
>
> (Trilling 1967: 89)

Rorty devotes a lot of space to developing ideas about the possibility and value of self-creation (Rorty 1989: ch. 2). He valorizes what he sees as Freud's attempt to demonstrate that dullness and mediocrity are only worktop features of character:

> Freud shows that if we look inside the *bien-pensant* conformist, if we get him on the couch, we will find that he was only dull on the surface. For Freud, nobody is dull through and through, for there is no such thing as a dull unconscious ... Freud's account of unconscious fantasy show us how to see every human life as a poem.
>
> (Rorty 1989: 35)

In a society where individuals have absorbed Rorty's lessons about self-reliance and no longer feel they are constrained by "an order beyond time and change which both determines the point of human existence and establishes a hierarchy of responsibilities" (ibid.: xv), there is likely to be more energy for channeling into the construction of a meaningful personal life, spiced up with constellations of chance events and eccentric whims that may be immediately significant only to the person concerned.

But, the more opportunities there are for the sort of self-creation that embraces such idiosyncrasies, or gains momentum by moving beyond them, the more likely there are to be mismatches between an individual's conception of how *their* life should be meaningfully pursued, and the demands and expectations of society at large. In short, the normal division between private and public life is bound to erupt into a dichotomy. Rorty does not regard this as problematic. As long as neither side of this split gains too much of the upper hand for too long (leading to either anarchy, or else social repression that thwarts imaginative self-creation[11]), the dynamic involved is liable to stimulate still further contexts of meaning. Rorty urges that the desire to somehow bridge this dichotomy, or think up a theory to smooth it out, should be resisted. We should instead regard it as useful and:

> see the aim of a just and free society as letting its citizens be privatistic, "irrationalist," and aestheticist as they please so long as they do it on their own time – causing no harm to others and using no resources needed by those less advantaged. There are practical measures to be taken to accomplish this practical goal. But there is no way to bring self-creation together with justice at the level of theory.
>
> (Ibid.: xiv)

Granting that these responses are at least worth considering and that generally speaking, Rorty's approach to the biggest question is far from evasive or superficial, what are we to make of it? We should certainly be able to see that it offers a fresh perspective and floats ideas that are worth exploring. But, do we have to conclude that the task of questioning whether life has meaning has to end exactly where Rorty seems to think it should?

One strategy for getting clear about something is to step back from it. Rorty's approach involves appreciating the meaning of life from the inside of both the self and society. There is nowhere else it can be found. But, he cannot avoid offering an external perspective in order to describe why human self-reliance is important and how meaning is socially generated. But, what if we want to step back from life in order to question the kind of meaningfulness thus created?

The idea of stepping back from life is no more than a metaphor, enforceable only in the imagination. But even as such, it can be problematic. There are difficulties with what we leave behind when we attempt to step outside life, even in pretense. On Rorty's understanding, this is especially problematic because to step outside life is to step outside whom and what we are. There are also problems about what we will find even if we succeed.

Nevertheless, the idea captures something we can, and should, try to do, if only to a certain degree and with a distinct, cautionary awareness of the necessary limitations. Our ability to put *some* distance between ourselves and, for example, certain of our entrenched beliefs is an ability we should certainly treasure. In exercising this distancing ability, we can sometimes set aside anomalies caused by our history, locality and prejudices so that we can at least try to compensate for observer bias. However, by leaving too much of ourselves behind or travelling too far, we run into trouble. The immense general difficulty in leaving too much behind is summarized succinctly and with characteristic clarity by Bernard Williams:

> There is simply no conceivable exercise that consists in stepping completely outside myself, and from that point of view evaluating *in toto* the dispositions, projects and affections that constitute the substance of my own life.
>
> (Williams 1995: 169–70)

Just by saying this, Williams helps us to see more clearly that when we depart from the things that constitute what he calls "the substance" of our life, we are left with very few means of making useful and accurate assessments of that life, its value and its meaning. Consider how woefully thin, in this sense, a creature must be when it emerges from a journey that has taken it far from its normal self, with all its related beliefs, commitments and ways of behaving. What resources of assessment does it now possess, with which to compensate for the gulf this journey has created? How can it acquire a sane perspective on aspects of itself and its way of living with what little now remains of its sensibility? How can it make any informed judgments about the meaning, or otherwise, of the life it has left behind but might wish to lead in future?

So much for problems connected with what we leave behind. What we find after departure is also going to be problematic. The resources on the other side of life and the self, in the place we reach when we step away from both, are, as we said, scant. That is already a problem. But, the common, and perhaps only, solution to this difficulty makes things worse. For the solution involves reaching out to what Rorty thinks can be of no use to us: non-human, or, as we might reasonably prefer to say, "inhuman," sources of meaning. There are two disturbing features of such sources. They must operate from a region where a diminished assessment of human autonomy is taken for granted; we will have accepted this by reaching so far beyond ourselves to locate meaning. Moreover, the guidance these sources provide has to be authoritarian and dogmatic – it's difficult to see how things could be otherwise. External meaning operates, and is called upon to so operate, on the assumption that we are incapable of creating meaning by ourselves. But, it also operates at an appreciable distance from who we normally think we are and what kind of creatures we take ourselves to be. Disconnected in this way, how can it engage us and do justice to the content of our lives without *imposing* demands, demands that are categorical because, in having no other options, we are bereft of the capacity for dissent?

Suppose we agree that unrestrained, out-of-the-self, imaginary travel distorts our view of life so that it cannot provide an adequate vantage point from which to assess whether life has meaning, and may well make us vulnerable to dogmatic and authoritarian infatuations and interventions? Where does that leave us? Perhaps we could do worse than follow the advice Rorty would be likely to offer: "plunge back into life and start to exercise the meaning-detecting and meaning-creating capacities that history has fortunately endowed you with."

Notes

1 Comprehensive surveys can be found in Benatar 2010 and Seachris 2013. To be fair to Rorty, his neglect of the literature can be at least partly excused because revival of philosophical interest in the biggest question only gained momentum after his death in 2007.
2 Rorty's approach can mostly be recast in the form of such arguments on the basis of his own ideas and the work of the many thinkers he has been influenced by, but such a project is well beyond the scope of this chapter.
3 It is probably a good idea to explain what "external" means here. External authority is, quite simply, external to authority manifested in, and entirely dependent on, social practices.
4 This might seem like a mistaken reading of Kant, given that Kant held that each person has to legislate morality under the power of their own reason. But, the categorical force of morality can be seen as operating from a position outside of the legislating person, *taken as a whole* (e.g. not divided up into reasoning and emoting parts) – so it should still be viewed as an "external authority" or a "quasi divinity" (Rorty 2007b: 154).
5 For his most direct explication of his anti-authoritarianism, see Rorty 2009.
6 This "ought" is not a moral ought, but it is normative in the following sense: "it is a good thing, practically speaking, that things have turned out this way."
7 See especially Heidegger 1936–40a and 1936–40b, and Vattimo 2007.
8 For insightful discussion of Rorty's relationship to nihilism, see Llanera forthcoming.
9 His clearest exposition of the social practice account of meaning is given in Rorty 2007a.
10 Rorty allows some qualifications here: those enduring very grim circumstances may not be able to do this.
11 Rorty also has a high regard for the imagination's ability to add dimensions of meaning to life, but there is insufficient space to discuss this here.

Postscript
The blue flower

The phrase, 'the meaning of life', seems problematic to many contemporary philosophers; standard labels for other areas of philosophical interest, such as 'free will', 'the mind/body problem' or 'personal identity', have not generated similarly sustained disquiet. Nevertheless, it is emblematic of philosophy in the public domain. It provided a focal point for some classic British comedy in Douglas Adams' Hitchhiker's Guide to the Galaxy novels and Monty Python's film, The Meaning of Life, and the theme continues to the present day with Karl Pilkington's documentary series, The Moaning of Life. But the public interest is not always detached and amused: invitations to 'explore the meaning of life' have attracted over 1 million Britons (out of a total of 65) to attend the Anglican Church's 'Alpha Course'.[1] This kind of attention is part of what makes the issue unsettling to some philosophers, who think of their discipline as an essentially technical one, akin to a science or branch of mathematics, and who consequently worry that the question of the meaning of life is not only hopelessly imprecise, but also essentially religious – or at least of 'spiritual' intent. But even among the increasing number of contemporary philosophers who do try to address 'meaning of life' issues, there remains considerable unease about the world-famous formula which inevitably packages them.

This unease is neatly encapsulated in the following passage from Susan Wolf,

> What is so wrong with the question? One answer is that it is extremely obscure, if not downright unintelligible. It is unclear what exactly the question is supposed to be asking. Talk of meaning in other contexts does not offer ready analogies for understanding the phrase 'the meaning of life.' When we ask the meaning of a word, for example, we want to know what the word stands for, what it represents. But life is not part of a language, or of any other sort of symbolic system. It is not clear how it could 'stand for' anything, nor to whom. We sometimes use 'meaning' in nonlinguistic contexts: 'Those dots mean measles.' 'Those footprints mean that someone was here since it rained.' In these cases, talk of meaning seems to be equivalent to talk of evidence, but the contexts in which such claims are made tend to specify what hypotheses are in question within relatively fixed bounds. To ask what life means without a similarly specified context, leaves us at sea.[2]

So Wolf's concern – and we think it is the standard one – is that since meaning is a paradigmatically linguistic notion, and there is no obvious similarity between life and language, it is consequently very odd, and perhaps even nonsensical, to ask about the meaning of life; as opposed to, say, the meaning of a sentence in an unfamiliar language. Wolf goes on to grant that we do, in addition, speak of meaning in the Gricean sense of 'natural meaning' – we say that the clouds mean rain, for instance.[3] But in such cases, she thinks the context makes it clear what we are talking about, whereas in the case of life, no such context is apparent.

All this is readily disputable. For a start, you might think we have other rich and legitimate notions of meaning apart from linguistic and natural meaning.[4] But even if we stick with just these two, it does not seem too hard to make sense of the question. Perhaps, for instance, it invites us to compare human life – with all its comings and goings, strivings, successes and failures – to a linguistic code in need of deciphering. Thus we wonder what the whole thing means: what wider significance we should read into the 'book of life'. For although we can understand the individual episodes of life within the social settings which contextualize them for us – thereby allowing us to 'read' them with ease – it is nevertheless far from clear what theme, if any, can be discerned in life as a whole. We might ask the same question of a particularly convoluted modernist novel, and be similarly open to the possibility that there simply is no overall theme. So on the face of it, the question can readily be made sense of by analogy to linguistic meaning. The same might be said of natural meaning. If I point upwards, and ask what those clouds mean, I will typically be presupposing the context of weather. And similarly, it seems that to ask what life means, in the natural meaning sense, would also be to pre-suppose a context: one in which the existence and nature of human life indi-cates something of cosmic significance. Perhaps we know little of this context, or even whether there is one; but then, the person who asks what storm clouds indicate cannot know much about the weather either. A typical inquiry into the meaning of the clouds would indeed presuppose the context of weather, but it would also amount to an inquiry into the nature of that context.

Wolf does not linger over her phraseological reservations, as some philoso-phers do, since she knows perfectly well what is intended; as she goes on to say, to ask about the meaning of life is to ask 'why we are here (that is, why we exist at all), with the hope that an answer to this question will also tell us something about what we should be doing with our lives'.[5] Given that this seems to be common knowledge, then, the fact that philosophers do so often question, puzzle over and criticize the stock phrase, strikes us as a curious state of affairs.[6] It is as if the question had been delivered to the world's phi-losophers in a magical envelope that fell from the sky, and, knowing before-hand what the question would be about, they were baffled by the choice of words. Since the phrase must rather have been developed by people for reasons, we thought we would look into the question of how this transpired. The answer turned out to be considerably more interesting and philosophically substantive than we were expecting.

The phrase originated in German ('Der Sinn des Lebens') among Fichte and his students during the final few years of the eighteenth century. Most of the 'Jena Romantics' were Fichte's students at some point: Novalis, the Schlegel brothers (Friedrich and August), Schleiermacher, Tieck, Schelling and Hölderlin. Of these, it seems we owe the phrase specifically to Novalis and Friedrich Schlegel; given that they formed part of an exceptionally close-knit intellectual circle, it might have been coined by either – or indeed, one of the others. Nevertheless, it was Novalis – the philosopher, poet and mystic who died at just 28 – who seems to have been the first to write it down. This was in a manuscript composed between late-1797 and mid-1798, in which he wrote that: 'Only an artist can divine the meaning of life'.[7] The manuscript was not published, but in 1799, the phrase featured prominently at the end of Schlegel's *Lucinde* – a strange and melodramatic book, oozing with romantic love, which Isaiah Berlin memorably described as 'a pornographic novel of the fourth order'.[8] The passage reads as follows:

> Now the soul understands the lament of the nightingale and the smile of the newly born babe, understands the deep significance of the mysterious hieroglyphs on flowers and stars, understands the holy meaning of life as well as the beautiful language of nature. All things speak to the soul and everywhere the soul sees the loving spirit through the delicate veil.[9]

Although *Lucinde* went on to be influential, it was comprehensively slated when it first appeared in print; its public reception was so dire, in fact, that Schleiermacher was moved to publish a book of *Confidential Letters on Schlegel's Lucinde*, in which he set about refuting the most common criticisms.[10] Schleiermacher, who is represented in the novel as the character Antonio, was not its only admirer, however: Fichte absolutely loved it. By September 1799 he was already reading it a third time, and declaring it one of the greatest products of genius he had ever encountered.[11]

It was during 1799, the year of Fichte's infatuation with *Lucinde*, that he composed one of his most influential works, *The Vocation of Man*. He wrote it in a non-academic style, with the intention of making his ideas more easily accessible; especially in comparison to his foreboding *Science of Knowledge*, which was the founding philosophical text for the Jena Romantics – originally completed in 1794, it remained under revision until 1801 due to Fichte's ongoing dissatisfaction with the presentation.[12] However, although the tumultuous Romantic stylings of *The Vocation of Man* certainly do show Fichte making a concerted effort to be engaging and accessible, the philosophy itself is no stroll in the park. So despite his best efforts, readers still complained; Schleiermacher was particularly scathing.[13]

Fichte did not use the phrase within this highly stylized presentation of his conceptually challenging philosophy – or anywhere else, for that matter; although many years down the line, he did come close, in lectures of 1812, by speaking of the meaning of mankind's existence ('Sinn seines [man's] Daseins').[14] Nevertheless, *The Vocation of Man* thematically turns on the connection between meaning and life (Fichte uses 'Bedeutung', the other German word for 'meaning'). Thus he tells us that the sceptical reflections he relates disconcerted him so much that he 'cursed the appearance of day which called me to a life, the truth and meaning of which had become doubtful to me'. He ultimately regains his confidence in the meaning of life through faith in an infinite and benevolent will, and, contrasting the spiritual and sensible domains, says that, 'the former alone gives meaning, purpose, and value to the latter'.[15] As Schlegel wrote, in a similar vein (this time using 'Gehalt' – content), 'Only in relation to the infinite is there meaning and purpose; whatever lacks such a relation is absolutely meaningless and pointless'.[16]

'The meaning of life' made its first appearance in English in Thomas Carlyle's novel *Sartor Resartus*; Carlyle was influenced by Schlegel and knew *Lucinde* well.[17] It tells the tale of a fictional German philosopher (whose name, Diogenes Teufelsdröckh, means 'Zeus-born devil's dung'), and was intended, in part, as a parody of German idealism. The British always found it funny, it seems. Nevertheless, Carlyle was a great admirer of Fichte, saying of him that, 'so robust an intellect, a soul so calm, so lofty, massive and immovable, has not mingled in philosophical discussion since the time of Luther'.[18] Carlyle had previously written an influential essay on Novalis, which commends German romanticism to the British as a source of much-needed cultural enrichment, and portrays Novalis as the advocate of a 'clothes philosophy', according to which 'Nature is no longer dead, hostile Matter, but the veil and mysterious Garment of the Unseen'.[19] Teufelsdröckh, in *Sartor Resartus*, is the author of a ponderous tome entitled, 'Clothes, Their Origin and Influence'. Carlyle's novel exerted great influence on many eminent writers, such as Emerson and Walt Whitman.[20]

A final element to the historical tale concerns the symbiotic partner of 'the meaning of life', namely: 'nihilism'. Fichte started work on the *Vocation of Man* after moving to Berlin in 1799, which he did at the invitation of Schlegel, who rented him some rooms; Novalis and Schleiermacher were also living there at the time.[21] Fichte was ready for a move because he had just been dismissed from his professorship at Jena on the charge of teaching atheism. In the public controversy surrounding this affair, Friedrich Jacobi had published, also in 1799, an open letter to Fichte in which he accuses his idealist philosophy of 'nihilism' (and for being 'the most horrible of horrors', for that matter).[22] So it seems that within the space of about one year, the familiar terminologies of 'the meaning of life' and 'nihilism' had both made their debuts: the former courtesy of the original Romantics and the latter courtesy of their discontents.

As far as we are able to ascertain, then, Novalis probably coined the phrase, Schlegel placed it in the public domain with *Lucinde*, Carlyle took it from *Lucinde*, and it thereafter spread far and wide. So much for the question of provenance. But why did 'the meaning of life' suggest itself within that particular intellectual milieu? Questions about why we are here, what value there is to us being here, and whether our existence serves any purpose, have been asked for at least as long as philosophical questioning has been written down; this present volume should make that plain enough. Moreover, the Jena Romantics clearly had a particular interest in such issues; Schleiermacher completed a book called *Über den Wert des Lebens* (On the value of life) in 1792, for instance.[23] But why start to talk about the *meaning* of life? Why did 'meaning' suddenly seem like the right word?

The groundwork had been laid long before by the notion of reading the 'book of life', which as mooted earlier, remains a natural way to connect the phrase 'meaning of life' with the philosophical issues it has come to stand for. This traditional notion has been traced back as far as Bonaventure in 1273 – for if God is the 'author' of reality, it makes sense to try to 'read' his handicraft – and it is a notion which would have been perfectly familiar to the early Romantics; Kant, for instance, had written of how God 'gives meaning [*Sinn*] to the letter of his creation'.[24] Perhaps the most famous use it has ever been put to, however, is in Macbeth's nihilist speech about life being, 'a tale told by an idiot, signifying nothing'; and it is noteworthy that an influential translation of Shakespeare into German appeared in 1765 in which this was translated using 'Sinn': a life 'signifying nothing' was a life 'without meaning'.[25] August Schlegel was an important Shakespearian scholar. A more direct link is to be found in a letter from Goethe to Schiller, dated 9 July 1796, in which Goethe responds to Schiller's suggestion that he ought to have been more explicit about the philosophical ideas in his novel, *Wilhelm Meister's Apprenticeship*, by saying that he had intended to say more about 'Leben und Lebenssinn': about life and life's meaning. Then on 22 July, we find Schiller writing to thank Goethe for sending the fish which provided the centrepiece of a meal he had with the Schlegel brothers; they were spending much time together at the time.[26]

The key to understanding why the meaning/life connection particularly resonated at this time, however, is Fichte's philosophy – which Novalis and Friedrich Schlegel were both deeply immersed in. Novalis considered Fichte 'the inventor of an entirely new way of thinking'; Schlegel considered his philosophy one of the three 'greatest tendencies of the age' (along with the French Revolution and Goethe's *Wilhelm Meister's Apprenticeship*); and Isaiah Berlin, who had an enduring fascination with the Romantic movement, its roots and consequences, was always clear that Fichte was 'the true father of romanticism'.[27] The philosophical issue of the day which most concerned Fichte was that of how to undermine the deterministic materialism which had flourished in the French Enlightenment, alongside the universalist, utopian social agendas of the *philosophes*. This materialism had gained impetus in the modern era both from Spinoza's metaphysics and the successes of the new mathematical sciences; Fichte's deep disquiet with it, on the grounds that it degraded the drama and value of human life, is readily apparent from the outset of *The Vocation of Man*. Fichte's original attraction to Kant's transcendental idealism, in fact, was that he saw it as a sceptical defence against materialism – sceptical, because it said that the things-in-themselves, true reality, could not be known. However, Fichte wanted to move beyond this scepticism; like the other great German idealists who developed their ideas from Fichte's initial inspiration, he thought Kant had stopped short at the threshold of metaphysical insight. This motivation inspired Fichte's strikingly original conclusion that true reality was, in a sense, his own will – understood as a limited manifestation of the infinite will. As Novalis put it, 'We live in a colossal novel (writ *large* and *small*)'.[28]

The solipsistic resonances of this position have not been missed. Bertrand Russell called Fichte's conclusion 'a kind of insanity', and Louis Sass, in his book, *Madness and Modernism: Insanity in the Light of Modern Art, Literature, and Thought*, suggests that it quite literally was.[29] Sass, a clinical psychologist, thinks the ideas expressed in Fichte's metaphysical idealism are symptomatic of schizophrenia; or, at least, schizoid personality disorder. Hölderlin, the great poet of the Jena Romantics, did indeed suffer from schizophrenia for the last forty years of his life.[30] Certainly, Novalis sounds perfectly mad when he writes of a future time in which, 'the human being will be truly independent of nature, perhaps even in a position to restore lost limbs, to kill himself merely by his will', and when he will 'compel his senses *to produce* for him the shape he demands – and he will be able to live in *his* world in the truest sense'. But Novalis also says that, 'Communal madness ceases to be madness and becomes magic'; and you might think that suitably aided by technology, the quest for human will to acquire the kind of magical powers Novalis envisaged is a defining feature of our own world; this is a point we shall return to at the end.[31]

A radically different, but similarly reductive explanation of Fichte's position, is provided by Berlin. He thought Fichte's metaphysic was ultimately an institutional manifestation of a wider social disquiet felt among Germans at the time, as a result of the economic, cultural, intellectual and military dominance of France over the German-speaking peoples. The Germans felt belittled, and in philosophy and art, they kicked back with romanticism: they poured scorn on the shallow conformity of the French Enlightenment's belief in universally valid values from which we must seek guidance in constructing the perfect society, artwork or scientific understanding. For values, according to the Romantics, are not inherited or discovered, but rather created by an act of will; as such, what really matters in life is originality, self-expression, creativity, being authentic to our own autonomously generated visions, and ultimately, freedom. Thus 'the concept of a stable, intelligible structure of reality which calm observers describe, classify, dissect, predict' – a concept embodied by materialism, as well as by the progressive, utopian politics of the *philosophes* – was 'a sham and a delusion, a mere curtain of appearances designed to protect those not sensitive or brave enough to face the truth from the terrifying chaos beneath the false order of bourgeois existence'.[32]

A third, and this time, non-reductive kind of explanation for Fichte's radical position – which might even be compatible with the previous two – could be sought in his complex chains of metaphysical reasoning. But however we seek to explain it, Fichte's conclusion that the appearance of an independent nature which is able to exercise restraint over our wills, is itself the result of will, had some extremely far-reaching implications. The implication Jacobi saw early on was 'nihilism'; the word had been used before, but Jacobi's usage was the first to squarely relate to our contemporary notion of nihilism as a position on the meaning of life.[33] Jacobi used this word because in his view, Fichte's metaphysic entailed that *nothing* exists beyond human will – neither nature nor God. Will had been allowed to annihilate everything else. Michael Gillespie has argued that it was this Fichtean idea at the root of romanticism which led to 'the death of God and the deification of man', and that as such, Nietzsche misdiagnosed the roots of nihilism.[34] Nihilism resulted not from religion's unsustainable projection of all value into an illusory transcendent world, such that a faltering of belief in higher realities was destined to pre-cipitate a collapse of value itself; but rather from the essentially Romantic notion of our ability to will value into reality – a notion which Nietzsche himself endorsed, mistaking it for an antidote to nihilism when it was actually its source. For human will operating in the absence of any non-human restraint on what it should will, is ultimately what nihilism amounts to.

Fichte, however, had *faith*; this is made abundantly clear in *The Vocation of Man*, which was written during the atheism controversy that scarred his life. The book argues that all human understanding is ultimately rooted in the practical and moral imperatives of will; in acts of conscience guided by a faith that our endless individual strivings are in accordance with an infinite and benevolent will. So Fichte did not think he was abandoning human will to the void, since he had faith that human will is an expression of something greater; 'faith', in the sense of a free, ultimately unjustifiable positing of something greater.

In Novalis, this essentially Fichtean notion of will reaching outwards in faith is identified with *love*. We should not seek to discover the design of the world, says Novalis, since 'we are this design ourselves' – we are 'Personified *all-powerful points*'. Love, however, 'popularises the personality', making 'individual things *communicable* and *understandable*', such that beginning with the will's self-love ('Who would not like a philosophy whose germ is a first kiss?'), we can move outwards towards 'the one true and eternal love'.[35] This was the thinking behind the symbol of the blue flower which Novalis bequeathed romanticism through his unfinished novel, *Henry of Ofterdingen*;

it was most likely inspired by Schlegel's fascination with Buddhism, in which the blue lotus, often shown only partially open, symbolizes expanding wisdom.[36] The novel concerns the eponymous Henry's quest for the flower he first dreams, then ultimately plucks; a quest to merge dream with reality. The blue flower subsequently came to be the Romantics' symbol of yearning for eternal love; but given that love was 'the key to the world and to life' for Novalis, it is perhaps not too much of a stretch to say that it symbolizes a yearning for the meaning of life.[37]

Now until the middle of the nineteenth century, there were two main senses of 'Sinn'. The first was the psychological meaning of a faculty of awareness or receptivity, such that in English we might speak of a 'sense of beauty', for example. The second was linguistic meaning.[38] Both naturally suggest the phrase 'the meaning of life' in the context of Fichte's philosophy. In the first, psychological sense, the phrase suggests a receptivity and natural attunement within the practical willing that is constitutive of human life; a receptivity to the greater will of which the individual is but a limited expression. And in the second, it suggests – equally – the ideas of *reading* the outward appearance of life for the infinite, holy will it ultimately expresses, and of *writing* our own meaning into reality. The former was already well-established, as we have seen. It was the notion of *writing* the book of life which was the distinctively Romantic contribution.

The importance Fichte placed in the conjunction of both the individual creativity needed to narrate your own life, and a sensitivity to the wider holy plot in which it has its place, is in evidence in Novalis's statement that 'Only an artist can divine the meaning of life'. We must become creative artists, but with the sensitivity, or receptivity, required to 'divine' the infinite will. Emphasizing the need for creativity, Novalis tells us in the same manuscript that '[l]ife must not be a novel that is given to us, but one that is made by us'.[39] And emphasizing the need for receptivity, Schlegel writes of the soul coming to understand, 'the deep significance of the mysterious hieroglyphs on flowers and stars ... the holy meaning of life as well as the beautiful language of nature'.

So it seems 'the meaning of life' appealed to the Romantics because the phrase suggested the idea of creating our own life stories in accordance with the divine will. The meaning of 'Sinn' later expanded, in the course of the nineteenth century, to take in the notions of value and purpose, and as the phrase caught on, it became distanced from its idealist origins, to become the conventional placeholder we now use to ask, as Wolf puts it, 'why we are here (that is, why we exist at all), with the hope that an answer to this question will also tell us something about what we should be doing with our lives'.

But even though the phrase now has a life of its own, there are still lessons to be learnt from its origins. For the humanistic notion that we must make our own meaning in life, which is the secular orthodoxy of our day, is actually not far removed from the original, Romantic idea. This is noteworthy, because it is now generally thought that we must make our own meaning *because* there is no meaning of life – or, as it might otherwise be put, that there is no meaning of life *except* what we put into it. Thus the phrase the 'meaning of life' is taken to embody a false and essentially religious belief that there is a fixed meaning, out there and waiting to be discovered. This idea was certainly a major inspiration to the original Romantic notion, as was its nihilistic counterpart; but the humanistic notion of 'making your own meaning' is more germane to the thinking that inspired the phrase. In fact, the humanistic notion is essentially the same as the original Romantic one, except without the metaphysics which made sense of the original: for life really could have its own intrinsic meaning if reality itself is a willing of its own meaning. The contemporary humanist notion, by contrast, is typically upheld without any explicit thought given to metaphysics, and against the implicit metaphysical backdrop of materialism. If materialism were true, however, it would be hard to see what 'making our own meaning' could possibly amount to, other than producing certain physical patterns that we call 'meaningful' – thereby immediately raising the question of who gets to decide which patterns are to be called 'meaningful', given the extreme unlikelihood of there being any universal, ahistorical agreement to be found in such matters.

Fichte, at the start of *Science of Knowledge*, says there are two types of human being: those who have raised themselves to consciousness of freedom and those who have not.[40] This kind of elitism, embodied in Novalis's first mention of 'the meaning of life', lingers on in the contemporary humanistic notion of meaning in life as an incremental good; which tends to suggest that ordinary people are all but precluded from living particularly meaningful lives. Moreover, Fichte was a keen advocate of acquiring ever-increasing mastery over nature by means of science and technology. He thought that matter, as a projection of will, should be infinitely malleable by will, and that as such, the resistance it puts up to our autonomously conceived goals needed to be continually broken down, by technological means, in our drive to moral freedom.[41] Again, this idea seems perfectly resonant with the contemporary humanistic notion that human beings must make their own meaning; and it is an idea which is further reinforced by the materialism that typically underlies such humanism. '*God wants there to be gods*', wrote Novalis; but fading concern with what God wants has not stopped humans from wanting exactly the same thing.[42] Perhaps the original notion of a meaning of life never really left us after all.[43]

Notes

1 Bell 2013.
2 Wolf 2007: 794.
3 Grice 1957.
4 D. Cooper 2003.
5 Wolf 2007: 794.

6 We shall not name names; we mention Wolf only because she expresses the concern so succinctly and does not proceed to make a meal out of it.

7 Novalis 1797–98: 66.

8 Berlin 1966b: 114.

9 Schlegel 1799: 129.

10 Firchow 1971: 3–4. The slating was to continue: the 'Seducer's Diary' in Kierkegaard's *Either/Or* (1843) is a parody of *Lucinde* (Robinson 2008: 278–79). The meaning of life ('Livets betydning') is a central preoccupation of *Either/Or*.

11 Firchow 1971: 14.

12 Preuss 1987: ix; Gillespie 1995: 76.

13 Preuss 1987: xii–xiii; Breazeale 2013: 1–2.

14 Fichte 1812: 23. This is cited in both Gerhardt (1995: 815) and Fehige et al. (2000: 21), where in both cases it seems to have been mixed up with Fichte's much better known 1798 work of the same title.

15 Fichte 1800: 27, 99.

16 Schlegel 1800: 241.

17 Carlyle 1833–34: 137; Vida 1993: 9–22.

18 Cited in Andrews 2012: 728.

19 Cited in Maertz 2004: 351–52.

20 Tarr 2000.

21 Preuss 1987: viii; see also Estes 2010.

22 Gillespie 1995: 66.

23 Gerhardt 1995: 815.

24 Fehige et al. 2000: 20; Kant, cited in Stückrath 2006: 72.

25 Fehige et al. 2000: 21.

26 Goethe 1794–97: 209, 220. Between 1795 and 1797 Schiller and August Schlegel were working together on a journal, *Die Horen* (Paulin 2016: 69). Given that Goethe was talking about 'Lebenssinn' in 1796, for which he may as well have substituted, 'Der Sinn des Lebens' (and might have in person), perhaps it is he who deserves the credit, rather than Novalis. It was Goethe, incidentally, who secured Fichte's professorship at Jena (Paulin 2016: 71).

27 Novalis 1797–99: 49; Schlegel 1798–1800: 190; Berlin 1983: 58.

28 Novalis 1797–99: 135.

29 Sass 1992: 81–82, 302–4, 313–17; Russell 1945: 651.

30 Sass 1992: 24–25.

31 Novalis 1797–99: 75, 61.

32 Berlin 1975; quotation from p. 232.

33 Gillespie 1995: 65–66.

34 Gillespie 1995: 99.

35 Novalis 1797–99: 58–59.

36 Novalis 1802; Germana 2017: 104–7.

37 Novalis 1797–99: 107.

38 Stückrath 2006: 72ff.

39 Novalis 1797–99: 66.

40 Fichte 1797: 15.

41 Gillespie 1995: 95–99.

42 Novalis 1797–99: 76; see also 126.

43 We would like to thank Martin Müeller for his help with some of the German sources.

Bibliography

Adams, R. (2010) 'Comments', in S. Wolf's *Meaning in Life and Why It Matters*, Princeton: Princeton University Press.

Albritton, R. (2009) *Let Them Eat Junk: How Capitalism Creates Hunger and Obesity*, New York: Pluto.

Andrews, K. (2012) 'Fichte, Carlyle and the British Literary Reception of German Idealism', *Literature Compass*, 9(11): 721–732.

Aquinas (c.1259–60/1955–57) *Summa Contra Gentiles*; trans. by A.C. Pegis, J.F. Anderson, V.J. Bourke and C.J. O'Neil as *On the Truth of the Catholic Faith*, 5 vols., New York: Hanover House.

Aquinas (1265–74/1948) *Summa Theologiae*, trans. Fathers of the English Dominican Province, New York: Benziger Bros.

Arendt, H. (1958/1998) *The Human Condition*, 2nd rev. edn, Chicago: University of Chicago Press.

Aristotle (fourth century BCE/1984) *Complete Works of Aristotle: Revised Oxford Translation*, vols. 1 and 2, ed. J. Barnes, Princeton: Princeton University Press.

Arpaly, N. (2006) *Merit, Meaning, and Human Bondage*, Princeton: Princeton University Press.

Avicenna (1000–37a/1874) *Kitab al-Hidaya*, ed. M. 'Abdu, Cairo.

Avicenna (1000–37b/1959) *Avicenna's De anima*, ed. and trans. F. Rahman, Oxford: Oxford University Press.

Avicenna (1000–37c/1960) *Kitāb al-Ishārāt wa-al-tanbīhāt* [Book of remarks and admonitions], ed. S.Dunya, Cairo: Dār al-ma'ārif.

Avicenna (1000–37d/1973) *Dānish Nāmeh: Metaphysica*, trans. P. Morewedge, New York: Columbia University Press.

Avicenna (1000–37e/1975) *Kitāb al-Shifā', al-ilāhiyyāt* [Book of healing], ed. G.C. Anawati, I. Madkour and S. Zayed, Cairo: al-Hay'a al-'āmma li'l- kitāb.

Avicenna (1000–37f/1977) *Avicenna Latinus: Liber de philosophia prima sive scientia divina I–IV*, ed. S. van Riet, Leiden: E.J. Brill.

Avicenna (1000–37g/1985) *Kitāb al-Najāt, al-ilāhiyyāt* [Book of deliverance], ed. M. Fakhry, Beirut: Dār al-āfāq al-jadīda.

Ayer, A.J. (1936/1971) *Language, Truth and Logic*, Harmondsworth: Penguin.

Ayer, A.J. (1946/1971) 'Introduction' to *Language, Truth and Logic*, Harmondsworth: Penguin.

Ayer, A.J. (1947/1990) 'The Claims of Philosophy', in his *The Meaning of Life*, New York: Macmillan.

Ayer, A.J. (1973/1976) *The Central Questions of Philosophy*, Harmondsworth: Penguin.

Ayer, A.J. (1988a/1990) 'The Meaning of Life', in his *The Meaning of Life*, New York: Macmillan.

Ayer, A.J. (1988b/1990) 'That Undiscovered Country', in his *The Meaning of Life*, New York: Macmillan.

Ayer, A.J. (1988c/1990) 'Postscript to a Postmortem', in his *The Meaning of Life*, New York: Macmillan.

Ayer, A.J. (1989/1992) 'Reply to Arne Naess', in *The Philosophy of A.J. Ayer*, ed. L.E. Hahn, La Salle, IL: Open Court.

Bacon, F. (1625/2011) 'Of Custom and Education', in *The Works of Francis Bacon*, vol. VI, ed. J. Spedding, R.L. Ellis and D.D. Heath, Cambridge: Cambridge University Press.

Bagnoli, C. (2012) 'The Exploration of Moral Life', in *Iris Murdoch, Philosopher*, ed. J. Broakes, New York: Oxford University Press, 197–225.

Beauvoir, S. de (1944/2004) *Pyrrhus and Cineas*, in her *Philosophical Writings*, trans. M. Timmerman, ed. M.A. Simons, M. Timmerman and M.B. Mader, Chicago: University of Illinois Press.

Bell, M. (2013) 'Inside the Alpha Course – British Christianity's Biggest Success Story', *The Independent*, 31 March, www.independent.co.uk/news/uk/home-news/inside-the-alpha -course-british-christianitys-biggest-success-story- 8555160.html.

Belliotti, R.A. (2001) *What Is the Meaning of Human Life?* Amsterdam: Rodopi Publishers.

Belliotti, R.A. (2013) *Jesus or Nietzsche: How Should We Live Our Lives?* Amsterdam: Rodopi Publishers.

Belliotti, R.A. (2017) *Nietzsche's Will to Power: Eagles, Lions, and Serpents*, Newcastle: Cambridge Scholars.

Benatar, D. (ed.) (2010) *Life, Death, and Meaning*, New York: Rowman & Littlefield.

Bennett, J. (1984) *A Study of Spinoza's Ethics*, Cambridge: Cambridge University Press.

Berlin, I. (1966a/1999) 'In Search of a Definition', in *The Roots of Romanticism*, ed. H. Hardy, London: Random House.

Berlin, I. (1966b/1999) 'Unbridled Romanticism', in *The Roots of Romanticism*, ed. H. Hardy, London: Random House.

Berlin, I. (1975/1991) 'The Apotheosis of the Romantic Will: The Revolt against the Myth of an Ideal World', in *The Crooked Timber of Humanity*, ed. H. Hardy, London: Fontana Press.

Berlin, I. (1983/1991) 'Giambattista Vico and Cultural History', in *The Crooked Timber of Humanity*, ed. H. Hardy, London: Fontana Press.

Bernier, M. (2015) *The Task of Hope in Kierkegaard*, Oxford: Oxford University Press.

Bett, R. (2010) 'Scepticism and Ethics', in *The Cambridge Companion to Ancient Scepticism*, ed. R. Bett, Cambridge: Cambridge University Press, 181–194.

Billerbeck, M. (1996) 'The Ideal Cynic from Epictetus to Julian', in *The Cynics: The Cynic Movement in Antiquity and its Legacy*, ed. R.B. Branham and M.-O. Goulet-Cazé, Berkeley: University of California Press.

Blackburn, S. (2007) 'Religion and Respect', in *Philosophers without Gods*, ed. L.M. Antony, Oxford: Oxford University Press.

Bodhi, B. and Nyanaponika Thera (trans.) (2000) *Aṅguttara Nikāya*; trans. as *Numerical Discourses of the Buddha*, Lanham: Altamira Press.

Branham, R.B. (2004) 'Nietzsche's Cynicism: Uppercase or Lowercase?', in *Nietzsche and Antiquity: His Reaction and Response to the Classical Tradition*, ed. P. Bishop, Rochester, NY: Camden House.

Breazeale, D. (2013) 'Introduction: The Checkered Reception of Fichte's *Vocation of Man*', in *Fichte's Vocation of Man: New Interpretative and Critical Essays*, ed. D. Breazeale and T. Rockmore, Albany: State University of New York Press.

Broakes, J. (ed.) (2012) *Iris Murdoch, Philosopher*, New York: Oxford University Press.

Cahn, S. and Vitrano, C. (2015) *Happiness and Goodness: Philosophical Reflections on Living Well*, New York: Columbia University Press.

Campbell, S.M. (2012) *The Early Heidegger's Philosophy of Life*, New York: Fordham University Press.

Camus, A. (1942a/1955) *The Myth of Sisyphus and Other Essays*, trans. J. O'Brien, New York: Random House.

Camus, A. (1942b) *The Stranger*, trans. S. Gilbert, New York: Random House.

Camus, A. (1951) *The Rebel: An Essay on Man in Revolt*, trans. A. Bower, New York: Random House.

Camus, A. and Grenier, J. (1932–60/2003) *Correspondence, 1932–1960*, trans. J. Rigaud, Lincoln: University of Nebraska Press.

Carlyle, T. (1833–34/2000) *Sartor Resartus*, ed. M. Engel and R. Tarr, Berkeley: University of California Press.

Catalano, J.S. (2010) *Reading Sartre*, Cambridge: Cambridge University Press.

Chakrabarti, A. and Bandyopadhyaya, S. (eds.) (2014) *Mahābhārata Now*, New Delhi: Routledge.

Chestov, L. (1934/1969) *Kierkegaard and the Existential Philosophy*, trans. E. Hewitt, Athens: Ohio University Press.

Cicero (45 BCE/1931) *On Ends*, trans. H. Rackham, Loeb Classical Library, Cambridge MA: Harvard University Press.

Clack, B.R. (2002) 'Wittgenstein on Magic', in *Wittgenstein and Philosophy of Religion*, ed. R.L. Arrington and M. Addis, London: Routledge.

Clark, M. (1990) *Nietzsche: On Truth and Philosophy*, Cambridge: Cambridge University Press.

Clarke, B. (2013) 'Attention, Moral', in *International Encyclopedia of Ethics*, ed. H. LaFollette, Oxford: Wiley Blackwell.

Clay, D. (1983) *Lucretius and Epicurus*, Ithaca: Cornell University Press.

Coates, Ta-Nehesi (2015) *Between the World and Me*, New York: Spiegel & Grau.

Collingwood, R.G. (1924) *Speculum Mentis*, Oxford: Oxford University Press.

Confucius (sixth–fifth centuries BCE/2003) *Analects*, ed. E. Slingerland, Indianapolis: Hackett Publishing Company.

Cooper, D. (2003) *Meaning*, Chesham: Acumen.

Cooper, J.C. (2010) *An Illustrated Introduction to Taoism*, Bloomington: World Wisdom.

Cottingham, J. (2003) *On the Meaning of Life*, London: Routledge.

Cottingham, J. (2006) *Cartesian Reflections*, Oxford: Oxford University Press.

Cottingham, J. (2010) 'Cartesian Autonomy', in *Mind, Method and Morality: Essays in Honour of Anthony Kenny*, ed. J. Cottingham and P. Hacker, Oxford: Oxford University Press.

Coutinho, S. (2004) *Zhuangzi and Early Chinese Philosophy: Vagueness, Transformation and Paradox*, Aldershot: Ashgate.

Craig, W.L. (1994/2017) 'The Absurdity of Life without God', in *The Meaning of Life: A Reader*, 4th edn, ed. E.D. Klemke and S.M. Cahn, New York: Oxford University Press.

D'Alembert (1759/1769) *Mélanges de literature, d'histoire et de philosophie*, Amsterdam: Zacherie Chatelain et Fils.

Darwin, C. (1859/2007) *On the Origin of Species*, New York: Cosimo.

Davids, C.R. (trans.) (1950–56) *Saṃyutta Nikāya*; trans. as *The Book of the Kindred Sayings (Samyutta-nikaya) or Grouped Suttas*, London: Luzac.

Davidson, H.A. (2005) *Moses Maimonides*, Oxford: Oxford University Press.

Davis, W. (1987) 'The Meaning of Life', *Metaphilosophy*, 18: 288–305.

Desan, P. (2017) *Montaigne, A Life*, trans. S. Rendall and L. Neal, Princeton: Princeton University Press.

Descartes, R. (1637/1902/1985) *Discourse on the Method*, in *Oeuvres de Descartes*, vol. VI, ed. C. Adam and P. Tannery, Paris: Vrin; and in *The Philosophical Writings of Descartes*, vol. I, ed. and trans. J. Cottingham, R. Stoothoff and D. Murdoch, Cambridge: Cambridge University Press.

Descartes, R. (1641/1904/1984) *Meditations on First Philosophy*, in *Oeuvres de Descartes*, vol. VII, ed. C. Adam and P. Tannery, Paris: Vrin; and in *The Philosophical Writings of Descartes*, vol. II, ed. and trans. J. Cottingham, R. Stoothoff and D. Murdoch, Cambridge: Cambridge University Press.

Descartes, R. (1643/1899/1991) Letter to Princess Elizabeth of Bohemia, 28 June 1643, in *Oeuvres de Descartes*, vol. III, ed. C. Adam and P. Tannery, Paris: Vrin; and in *The Philosophical Writings of Descartes*, vol. III, *The Correspondence*, ed. and trans. J. Cottingham, R. Stoothoff, D. Murdoch and A. Kenny, Cambridge: Cambridge University Press.

Descartes, R. (1644/1905/1985) *Principles of Philosophy*, in *Oeuvres de Descartes*, vol. VIII, ed. C. Adam and P. Tannery, Paris: Vrin; and in *The Philosophical Writings of Descartes*, vol. I, ed. and trans. J. Cottingham, R. Stoothoff, D. Murdoch and A. Kenny, Cambridge: Cambridge University Press.

Descartes, R. (1645a/1901/1991) Letter to Mesland, 9 February 1645, in *Oeuvres de Descartes*, vol. IV, ed. C. Adam and P. Tannery, Paris: Vrin; and in *The Philosophical Writings of Descartes*, vol. III, *The Correspondence*, ed. and trans. J. Cottingham, R. Stoothoff, D. Murdoch and A. Kenny, Cambridge: Cambridge University Press.

Descartes, R. (1645b/1901/1991) Letter to Princess Elizabeth of Bohemia, 1 September 1645, in *Oeuvres de Descartes*, vol. IV, ed. C. Adam and P. Tannery, Paris: Vrin; and in *The Philosophical Writings of Descartes*, vol. III, *The Correspondence*, ed. and trans. J. Cottingham, R. Stoothoff, D. Murdoch and A. Kenny, Cambridge: Cambridge University Press.

Descartes, R. (1646/1901/1991) Letter to Chanut of 15 June 1646, in *Oeuvres de Descartes*, vol. IV, ed. C. Adam and P. Tannery, Paris: Vrin; and in *The Philosophical Writings of Descartes*, vol. III, *The Correspondence*, ed. and trans. J. Cottingham, R. Stoothoff, D. Murdoch and A. Kenny, Cambridge: Cambridge University Press.

Descartes, R. (1647/1904/1985) Preface to the French translation of the *Principles of Philosophy*, in *Oeuvres de Descartes*, vol. IX, ed. C. Adam and P. Tannery, Paris: Vrin; and in *The Philosophical Writings of Descartes*, vol. I, ed. and trans. J. Cottingham, R. Stoothoff and D. Murdoch, Cambridge: Cambridge University Press.

Descartes, R. (1648/1903/1991) Letter to Silhon, March or April 1648, in *Oeuvres de Descartes*, vol. V, ed. C. Adam and P. Tannery, Paris: Vrin; and in *The Philosophical Writings of Descartes*, vol. III, *The Correspondence*, ed. and trans. J. Cottingham, R. Stoothoff, D. Murdoch and A. Kenny, Cambridge: Cambridge University Press.

Descartes, R. (1649/1909/1985) *Passions of the Soul*, in *Oeuvres de Descartes*, vol. XI, ed. C. Adam and P. Tannery, Paris: Vrin; and in *The Philosophical Writings of Descartes*, vol. I, ed. and trans. J. Cottingham, R. Stoothoff and D. Murdoch, Cambridge: Cambridge University Press.

Desmond, W.D. (2008) *Cynics*, Stocksfield: Acumen.

DeWitt, N.W. (1950) 'Epicurus: The Summum Bonum Fallacy', *Classical Weekly*, 44(5): 69–71.

Diamond, C. (2003) 'The Difficulty of Reality and the Difficulty of Philosophy', *Partial Answers*, 1(2): 1–26.

Diogenes Laertius (third century CE/1991) *Lives of the Eminent Philosophers*, 2 vols., trans. R.D. Hicks, Cambridge, MA: Harvard University Press.

Doniger, W. (ed.) (1200–900 BCE/1981) *Rig Veda*, London: Penguin.

Donne, J. (1624/1959) 'Meditation XVII', in *Devotions upon Emergent Occasions*, Ann Arbor: University of Michigan Press.

Dostoevsky, F. (1869/1996) *The Idiot*, trans. C. Garnett, Ware: Wordsworth Classics.

Dreyfus, H. and Kelly, S. (2011) *All Things Shining*, New York: Free Press.

Düring, I. (1961) *Aristotle's Protrepticus: An Attempt at Reconstruction*, Göteborg: Institute of Classical Studies.

Eagleton, T. (2007) *The Meaning of Life: A Very Short Introduction*, Oxford: Oxford University Press.

El-Bizri, N. (2000) *The Phenomenological Quest between Avicenna and Heidegger*, Binghamton, NY: Global Publications SUNY.

El-Bizri, N. (2001) 'Avicenna and Essentialism', *Review of Metaphysics*, 54(4): 753–778.

El-Bizri, N. (2006) 'Being and Necessity', in *Islamic Philosophy and Occidental Phenomenology on the Perennial Issue of Microcosm and Macrocosm*, ed. A.-T. Tymieniecka, Dordrecht: Springer.

El-Bizri, N. (2010) 'The Labyrinth of Philosophy in Islam', *Comparative Philosophy*, 1(2) : 3–23.

El-Bizri, N. (2011) 'Ibn Sīnā's Ontology and the Question of Being', *Ishrāq: Islamic Philosophy Yearbook of the Russian Academy of Sciences and the Iranian Institute of Philosophy*, 2: 222–237.

El-Bizri, N. (2014) 'Le renouvellement de la falsafa?' *Les Cahiers de l'Islam*, 1: 17–38.

El-Bizri, N. (2016) 'Avicenna and the Problem of Consciousness', in *Consciousness and the Great Philosophers*, ed. S. Leach and J. Tartaglia, London: Routledge.

Eliade, M. (1963) *Myth and Reality*, New York: Harper & Row.

Emerson, R.W. (1848/1983) *Essays and Lectures*, New York: Library of America.

Engels, F. (1845/1958) *The Condition of the Working Class in England*, Oxford: Basil Blackwell.

Epictetus (c. 108 CE/2014) *Discourses, Fragments, Handbook*, trans. R. Hard, Oxford: Oxford University Press.

Epicurus (fourth–third century BCE/1994) *Vatican Sayings*, in *The Epicurus Reader*, ed. and trans. B. Inwood and L.P. Gerson, Indianapolis and Cambridge: Hackett Publishing Company.

Estes, Y. (2010) 'J.G. Fichte: "From a Private Letter"', in *J.G. Fichte and the Atheism Dispute*, trans. C. Bowman, ed. C. Bowman and Y. Estes, Farnham: Ashgate.

Fanon, F. (1952/1967) *Black Skin, White Masks*, trans. C.L. Markmann, New York: Grove Press.

Fanon, F. (1961/1965) *The Wretched of the Earth*, trans. C. Farrington, New York: Grove Press.

Fanon, F. (1964/1967) *Toward the African Revolution*, trans. H. Chevalier, New York: Grove Press.

Farrington, B. (1938) 'The Gods of Epicurus and the Roman State', *Modern Quarterly*, 1(3): 214–232.

Fehige, C., Meggle, G. and Wessels, U. (2000) 'Vorab', in *Der Sinn des Lebens*, Munich: Deutscher Taschenbuch.

Feingold, L. (2010) *The Natural Desire to See God according to St Thomas Aquinas and His Interpreters*, 2nd edn, Ave Maria, FL: Sapientia Press of Ave Maria University.

Ferreira, J.M. (2013) 'Hope, Virtue, and the Postulate of God: A Reappraisal of Kant's Pure Practical Rational Belief', *Religious Studies*, 50: 1–24.

Feser, E. (2008) *The Last Superstition: A Refutation of the New Atheism*, South Bend, IN: St Augustine's Press.

Feser, E. (2009) *Aquinas*, Oxford: Oneworld Publications.

Feser, E. (2013) 'Between Aristotle and William Paley: Aquinas's Fifth Way', *Nova et Vetera*, 11(3): 707–749; repr. in *Neo-Scholastic Essays*, South Bend, IN: St Augustine's Press, 2015.

Feser, E. (2014a) 'Being, the Good, and the Guise of the Good' in *Neo-Aristotelian Perspectives in Metaphysics*, ed. D.D. Novotny and L. Novaks, London: Routledge; repr. in *Neo-Scholastic Essays*, South Bend, IN: St Augustine's Press, 2015.

Feser, E. (2014b) *Scholastic Metaphysics: A Contemporary Introduction*, Heusenstamm: Editiones Scholasticae.

Feser, E. (2017) *Five Proofs of the Existence of God*, San Francisco: Ignatius Press.

Fichte, J.G. (1797/1982) 'First Introduction to *The Science of Knowledge*', in *The Science of Knowledge*, ed. and trans. P. Heath and J. Lachs, Cambridge: Cambridge University Press.

Fichte, J.G. (1800/1987) *The Vocation of Man*, trans. P. Preuss, Indianapolis: Hackett Publishing Company.

Fichte, J.G. (1812/1835) *Das System der Sittenlehre: Vorgetragen von Ostern bis Michaelis 1812*, in *Johann Gottlieb Fichte's nachgelassene Werke*, vol. 3, ed. I.H. Fichte, Bonn: Adolph-Marcus.

Firchow, P. (1971) 'Introduction' to F. Schlegel's *Lucinde and the Fragments*, trans. P. Firchow, Minneapolis: University of Minnesota Press.

Frankfurt, H. (1970) *Demons, Dreamers and Madmen: The Defense of Reason in Descartes's Meditations*, New York: Bobbs Merrill.

Freud, S. (1920/1940–52) *Jenseits des Lustprinzips*, in *Gesammelte Werke*, vol. 13, Leipzig, Vienna, Zürich: Internationaler Psychoanalytischer Verlag.

Friedrich, H. (1991) *Montaigne*, Berkeley: University of California Press.

Frischer, B. (1982) *The Sculpted Word: Epicureanism and Philosophical Recruitment in Ancient Greece*, Berkeley and Los Angeles: University of California Press.

Galen (c. 150–90 CE-a/1985) 'An Outline of Empiricism', in *Three Treatises on the Nature of Science*, trans. R. Walzer and M. Frede, Indianapolis: Hackett Publishing Company.

Galen (c. 150–90 CE-b/1985) 'On Sects for Beginners', in *Three Treatises on the Nature of Science*, trans. R. Walzer and M. Frede, Indianapolis: Hackett Publishing Company.

Gardet, L. (1952) *La connaissance mystique chez Ibn Sīnā et ses présupposés philosophiques*, Cairo: Institut Français d'Archéologie Orientale.

Gerhardt, V. (1995) 'Sinn Des Lebens', in *Historisches Wörterbuch der Philosophie*, vol. 9, ed. J. Ritter, K. Gründer and G. Gabriel, Darmstadt: Schwabe.

Germana, N.A. (2017) *The Anxiety of Autonomy and the Aesthetics of German Orientalism*, New York: Camden House.

Gillespie, M.A. (1995) *Nihilism before Nietzsche*, Chicago: University of Chicago Press.

Goethe, J.W. (1794–97/2012) *Briefwechsel zwischen Schiller und Goethe*, vol. 1, Hamburg: tredition GmbH (Projekt Gutenberg-DE).

Gordon, L. (2015) *What Fanon Said: A Philosophical Introduction to his Life and Thought* New York: Fordham University Press.

Gordon, P. (2004) 'Remembering the Garden: The Trouble with Women in the School of Epicurus', in *Philodemus and the New Testament World*, ed. J.T. Fitzgerald, D. Obbink and G.S. Holland, Leiden: Brill.

Graham, A.C. (1995) *Disputers of the Tao: Philosophical Argument in Ancient China*, La Salle: Open Court.

Grice, H.P. (1957) 'Meaning', *Philosophical Review*, 66(3): 377–388.

Griffin, M. (1986) 'Philosophy, Cato, and Roman Suicide', *Greece & Rome*, 33(1): 64–77.

Guignon, C. and Pereboom, D. (eds.) (2001) *Existentialism: Basic Writings*, 2nd edn, Indianapolis: Hackett Publishing Company.

Haidt, J. (2010) Commentary, in S. Wolf, *Meaning in Life and Why it Matters*, Princeton: Princeton University Press.

Hampshire, S. (1956) *The Age of Reason*, New York: Mentor.

Harpham, G.G. (1987) *Ascetic Imperative in Culture and Criticism*, Chicago: University of Chicago Press.

Haught, J.F. (2006) *Is Nature Enough? Meaning and Truth in the Age of Science*, Cambridge: Cambridge University Press.

Hazlitt, W. (1819) 'On Wit and Humour', in *Lectures on the English Comic Writers*, London: Taylor & Hessey.

Heidegger, M. (1927/1962) *Being and Time*, trans. J. Macquarie and E. Robinson, Oxford: Blackwell.

Heidegger, M. (1927–64/1993) *Basic Writings*, 2nd rev. exp. edn, ed. D.F. Krell, San Francisco: HarperCollins.

Heidegger, M. (1936–40a/1991) *Nietzsche, Vols. 1 and 2*, trans. D.F. Krell, New York: HarperCollins.

Heidegger, M. (1936–40b/1991) *Nietzsche, Vols. 3 and 4*, trans. D.F. Krell, New York: HarperCollins.

Heidegger, M. (1938–55/1977) *The Question Concerning Technology and Other Essays*, trans. W. Lovitt, New York: Harper & Row.

Heidegger, M. (1954) *Vorträge und Aufsätze*, Pfullingen: Günther Neske.

Heidegger, M. (1966) *Discourse on Thinking*, New York: Harper & Row.

Heidegger, M. (1971a) *On the Way to Language*, New York: Harper & Row.

Heidegger, M. (1971b) *Poetry, Language, Thought*, trans. A. Hofstadter, New York: Harper & Row.

Hemingway, E. (1940/1966) *For Whom the Bell Tolls*, New York: Scribner.

Hogeveen, J., Inzlicht, M., Obhi, S.S. and Gauthier, I. (2014) 'Power Changes How the Brain Responds to Others', *Journal of Experimental Psychology: General*, 143(2): 755–762.

Honderich, T. (1990) 'Introduction' to A.J. Ayer, *The Meaning of Life*, New York: Macmillan.

Hopkins, G.M. (1877/1986) 'God's Grandeur', in *Gerard Manley Hopkins: The Major Works*, Oxford: Oxford University Press.

Hosseini, R. (2015) *Wittgenstein and Meaning in Life*, New York: Palgrave Macmillan.

Hudson, E. (2013) *Disorienting Dharma: Ethics and the Aesthetics of Suffering in the Mahābhārata*, Oxford: Oxford University Press.

Hume, D. (1739–40/1969) *A Treatise of Human Nature*, ed. E.C. Mossner, Harmondsworth: Penguin.

Hume, D. (1779/1980) *Dialogues Concerning Natural Religion*, ed. R.H. Popkin, Indianapolis: Hackett Publishing Company.

Hutchinson, D.S. and Johnson, M.R. (2005) 'Authenticating Aristotle's *Protrepticus*', *Oxford Studies in Ancient Philosophy*, 29: 193–294.

Inwood, M. (1997) *Heidegger: A Very Brief Introduction*, Oxford and New York: Oxford University Press.

Ivry, A.L. (2008) 'Moses Maimonides: An Averroist *avant la lettre*?', in *Maimonidean Studies*, vol. 5, ed. A. Hyman and A. Ivry, New York: Yeshiva University Press.

James, W. (1902/1982) *The Varieties of Religious Experience: A Study in Human Nature*, ed. with introd. by M.E. Marty, New York: Penguin.

Kahneman, D. and Deaton, A. (2010) 'High Income Improves Evaluation of Life but Not Emotional Well-Being', *Proceedings of the National Academy of Sciences*, 107(38): 16489–16493.

Kant, I. (1747–1802/1900–) *Gesammelte Schriften*, Berlin and Göttingen: Reimer (later de Gruyter).

Kant, I. (1784/1991) 'An Answer to the Question: "What Is Enlightenment?"', in *Kant's Political Writings*, ed. H.S. Reiss, Cambridge: Cambridge University Press.

Kant, I. (1785a/2006) *Anthropology from a Pragmatic Point of View*, ed. R.B. Louden and M. Kuehn, Cambridge: Cambridge University Press.

Kant, I. (1785b/1999) *Groundwork of the Metaphysics of Morals*, in *Practical Philosophy*, ed. and trans. M.J. Gregor, New York: Cambridge University Press; and in vol. 4 of *Gesammelte Schriften*, ed. Preussiche (Deutsche) Akademie der Wissenschaften, Berlin: Reimer.

Kant, I. (1787/1998) *Critique of Pure Reason*, in *The Cambridge Edition of the Works of Immanuel Kant*, ed. and trans. P. Guyer and A.W. Wood, Cambridge: Cambridge University Press.

Kant, I. (1788/1997) *Critique of Practical Reason*, trans. M. Reath, with introd. by A. Gregor, Cambridge: Cambridge University Press; and in vol. 5 of *Gesammelte Schriften*, ed. Preussiche (Deutsche) Akademie der Wissenschaften, Berlin: Reimer.

Kant, I. (1790/1987) *Critique of Judgment*, ed. and trans. W.S. Pluhar, Indianapolis: Hackett Publishing Company.

Kant, I. (1793/1996) *Religion within the Boundaries of Mere Reason*, in *Religion and Rational Theology*, ed. and trans. A.W. Wood and G. Di Giovanni, New York: Cambridge University Press; and in vol. 6 of *Gesammelte Schriften*, ed. Preussiche (Deutsche) Akademie der Wissenschaften, Berlin: Reimer.

Kant, I. (1795–1804/1993) *Opus Postumum*, ed. E. Förster, trans. E. Förster and M. Rosen, New York: Cambridge University Press; and in vol. 21 of *Gesammelte Schriften*, ed. Preussiche (Deutsche) Akademie der Wissenschaften, Berlin: Reimer.

Kant, I. (1797/1999) *The Metaphysics of Morals* in *Practical Philosophy*, ed. and trans. M.J. Gregor, New York: Cambridge University Press; and in vol. 6 of *Gesammelte Schriften*, ed. Preussiche (Deutsche) Akademie der Wissenschaften, Berlin: Reimer.

Kaufmann, W. (1974) *Nietzsche: Philosopher, Psychologist, Antichrist*, 4th edn, Princeton: Princeton University Press.

Kekes, J. (1985) 'Moral Tradition', *Philosophical Investigations*, 8(4): 252–268.

Kekes, J. (1998) *A Case for Conservatism*, New York: Cornell University Press.

Keltner, D. (2016) *The Power Paradox*, New York: Penguin.

Kierkegaard, S. (1835–55/1967) *Søren Kierkegaard's Journals and Papers*, Bloomington, IN: Indiana University Press.

Kierkegaard, S. (1843/2006) *Fear and Trembling*, trans. S. Walsh, New York: Cambridge University Press.

Kierkegaard, S. (1844/1992) *Concluding Unscientific Postscript to Philosophical Fragments*, trans. H.V. Hong and E.H. Hong, Princeton: Princeton University Press.

Kierkegaard, S. (1849/1980) *The Sickness Unto Death*, trans. H.V. Hong and E.H. Hong, Princeton: Princeton University Press.

Klemke, E.D. and Cahn, S.M. (eds.) (2017) *The Meaning of Life: A Reader*, 4th edn, New York: Oxford University Press.

Koheleth (c. 450?–180 BCE/1985) *Ecclesiastes*, in the *Tanakh: The Holy Scriptures*, Philadelphia: Jewish Publication Society, 1441–1456.

Korab-Karpowicz, W.J. (2017) *Tractatus Politico-Philosophicus: New Directions for the Future Development of Humankind*, New York: Routledge.

Kraemer, J.L. (2008) *Maimonides*, New York: Doubleday.

Lacey, A. (1995) 'Life, the Meaning of', in *The Oxford Companion to Philosophy*, ed. T. Honderich, Oxford: Oxford University Press.

Lagrée, J. (1994) 'Spinoza, athée et épicurien', *Archiv de Philosophie*, 57: 541–558.

Lao Tzu (sixth century BCE/2002) *The Daodejing of Laozi*, trans. P.J. Ivanhoe, Indianapolis: Hackett Publishing Company.

Lao Tzu (sixth century BCE/2007) *Daodejing*, trans. H.-G. Moeller, Chicago: Open Court.

Levinas, E. (1979/1991) *Le temps et l'autre*, Paris: Presses Universitaires de France.

Levinas, E. (1982/1985) *Ethique et infini*; trans. R.A. Cohen as *Ethics and Infinity*, Pittsburgh: Duquesne University Press.

Levy, N. (2005) 'Downshifting and Meaning in Life', *Ratio*, 18(2): 176–189.

Linder, M. (1998) *Void Where Prohibited: Rest Breaks and the Right to Urinate on Company Time*, Ithaca: Cornell University Press.

Llanera, T. (forthcoming) 'Rorty and Nihilism', in *A Companion to Rorty*, ed. A. Malachowski, Oxford: Wiley-Blackwell.

Long, A.A. (2002) *Epictetus: A Stoic and Socratic Guide to Life*, Oxford: Oxford University Press.

Lucretius (c. 55 BCE/2001) *On the Nature of Things*, trans. M.F. Smith, Indianapolis: Hackett Publishing Company.

Luper, S. (2014) *The Cambridge Companion to Life and Death*, Cambridge: Cambridge University Press.

Luper-Foy, S. (1987) 'Annihilation', *Philosophical Quarterly*, 37(148): 233–252.

McCullough, L. (2014) *The Religious Philosophy of Simone Weil: An Introduction*, London: I.B. Tauris.

McCullough, L. (2017) 'The Death of God', in *Edinburgh Critical History of Nineteenth-Century Theology*, ed. D. Whistler, Edinburgh: Edinburgh University Press.

MacIntyre, A. (2016) *Ethics and the Conflicts of Modernity*, Cambridge: Cambridge University Press.

Maertz, G. (2004) 'Novalis', in *The Carlyle Encyclopaedia*, ed. M. Cumming, Madison: Fairleigh Dickinson University Press.

Maimonides (1168/1975) *Eight Chapters*, in *Ethical Writings of Maimonides*, trans. R.L. Weiss and C.E. Butterworth, New York: New York University Press.

Maimonides (1170–80/1972) *Mishneh Torah* [selections], trans. M. Hyamson, in *A Maimonides Reader*, ed. I. Twersky, New York: Behrman House.

Maimonides (c. 1190/1963) *A Guide of the Perplexed*, 2 vols., trans. S. Pines, Chicago: University of Chicago Press.

Maimonides (c. 1194–1204/2004–17) *Medical Aphorisms*, ed. and trans. G. Bos, Provo, UT: Brigham Young University Press. (Treatises 1–5, 2004; 6–9, 2007; 10–15, 2010; 16–21, 2015; 22–25, 2017.)

Malamoud, C. (1996) *Cooking the World: Ritual and Thought in Ancient India*, Delhi: Oxford University Press.

Marcuse, H. (1971) *Soviet Marxism: A Critical Analysis*, Harmondsworth: Penguin.

Marx, K. (1844/1972) 'Economic and Philosophical Manuscripts of 1844', in *The Marx–Engels Reader*, ed. R.C. Tucker, New York: Norton.

Marx, K. and Engels, F. (1846/1972) *The German Ideology*, in *The Marx–Engels Reader*, ed. R.C. Tucker, New York: Norton.

Mawson, T.J. (2016) *God and the Meanings of Life*, London: Bloomsbury.

Mengzi (fourth–third centuries BCE/2008) *Mengzi, with Selections from Traditional Commentaries*, ed. B.W. van Norden, Indianapolis: Hackett Publishing Company.

Merritt, M.M. (2017) 'Love, Respect, and Individuals: Murdoch as a Guide to Kantian Ethics', *European Journal of Philosophy*, 25(2): 1844–63.

Metz, T. (2012) *Meaning in Life: An Analytic Study*, Oxford: Oxford University Press.

Metz, T. (2013) 'The Concept of a Meaningful Life', in *Exploring the Meaning of Life*, ed. J. Seachris, Chichester: Wiley-Blackwell.

Michot, J.R. (1986) *La destinée de l'homme selon Avicenne*, Leuven: Aedibus Peeters.

Miles, S. (1986/2005) 'Introduction' to *Simone Weil: An Anthology*, ed. S. Miles, London: Penguin.

Mill, J.S. (1859/1977) *On Liberty*, in *Collected Works of John Stuart Mill*, vol. 18, ed. J.M. Robson, Toronto and Buffalo: University of Toronto Press.

Mill, J.S. (1865/1985) *Auguste Comte and Positivism*, in *Collected Works of John Stuart Mill*, vol. 10, ed. J.M. Robson, Toronto and Buffalo: University of Toronto Press.

Mill, J.S. (1873/1981) *Autobiography*, in *Collected Works of John Stuart Mill*, vol. 1, ed. J. M. Robson and J. Stillinger, Toronto and Buffalo: University of Toronto Press.

Mill, J.S. (1874/1985) *Utility of Religion* in *Collected Works of John Stuart Mill*, vol. 10, ed. J.M. Robson. Toronto and Buffalo: University of Toronto Press.

Møllgaard, E. (2011) *An Introduction to Daoist Thought: Action, Language and Ethics in Zhuangzi*, London: Routledge.

Montaigne, M. (1580–92/2003) *The Complete Works*, trans. D.M. Frame, London: Everyman.

Montano, A. (1994) *Il Disincanto della Modernità*, Naples: La Città del Sole.

Morris, T. (1992) *Making Sense of It All: Pascal and the Meaning of Life*, Grand Rapids, MI: William B. Eerdmans.

Mulhall, S. (1997) 'Constructing a Hall of Reflection: Perfectionist Edification in Murdoch's *Metaphysics as a Guide to Morals*', *Philosophy*, 72(280): 219–239.

Murdoch, I. (1956) 'Vision and Choice in Morality', *Proceedings of the Aristotelian Society, Supplementary Volume*, 30, 32–58.

Murdoch, I. (1957/1998) 'Metaphysics and Ethics', in *Existentialists and Mystics: Writings on Philosophy and Literature*, New York: Allen Lane/Penguin.

Murdoch, I. (1959a/1998) 'The Sublime and the Beautiful Revisited', in *Existentialists and Mystics: Writings on Philosophy and Literature*, New York: Allen Lane/Penguin.

Murdoch, I. (1959b/1998) 'The Sublime and the Good', in *Existentialists and Mystics: Writings on Philosophy and Literature*, New York: Allen Lane/Penguin.

Murdoch, I. (1964/2001) 'The Idea of Perfection', in *The Sovereignty of Good*, New York and London: Routledge.

Murdoch, I. (1967/2001) 'The Sovereignty of Good over Other Concepts', in *The Sovereignty of Good*, New York and London: Routledge.

Murdoch, I. (1969/2001) 'On "God" and "Good"', in *The Sovereignty of Good*, New York and London: Routledge.

Murdoch, I. (1992) *Metaphysics as a Guide to Morals*, London: Chatto & Windus.

Nagel, T. (1971) 'The Absurd', *Journal of Philosophy*, 68(20): 716–727.

Nagel, T. (1987) *What Does It All Mean?* New York and Oxford: Oxford University Press.

Nagel, T. (2010) 'Secular Philosophy and the Religious Temperament', in his *Secular Philosophy and the Religious Temperament*, Oxford and New York: Oxford University Press.

Ñānamoli, B. and Bodhi, B. (trans.) (1995) *Majjhima Nikāya*; trans. as *The Middle Length Discourses of the Buddha*, Boston: Wisdom Publications.

Navia, L.E. (1998) *Diogenes of Sinope: The Man in the Tub*, Westport, CT.: Greenwood Press.

Nietzsche, F. (1882/1967) *The Gay Science*, trans. W. Kaufmann, New York: Random House.

Nietzsche, F. (1883–85/1954) *Thus Spoke Zarathustra*, in *The Portable Nietzsche*, trans. W. Kaufmann, New York: Viking Press.

Nietzsche, F. (1886/1966) *Beyond Good and Evil*, trans. W. Kaufmann, New York: Random House.

Nietzsche, F. (1901/2017) *The Will to Power*, trans. W. Kaufmann and R.J. Hollingdale, ed. W. Kaufmann, London: Penguin.

Nietzsche, F. (1908/1967) *Ecce Homo* (1967), in *Werke: Kritische Gesamtausgabe*, vol. 3, ed. G. Colli and M. Montinari, Berlin: De Gruyter.

Novalis (1797–99/1997) *Philosophical Writings*, ed. and trans. M.M. Stoljar, Albany: State University of New York Press.

Novalis (1802/1964) *Henry of Ofterdingen*, trans. P. Hilty, Long Grove, IL: Waveland Press.

Nozick, R. (1974) *Anarchy, State and Utopia*, New York: Basic Books.

Nozick, R. (1981a) *Philosophical Explanations*, Oxford: Oxford University Press.

Nozick, R. (1981b/2013) 'Philosophy and the Meaning of Life', in *Exploring the Meaning of Life: An Anthology and Guide*, ed. J.W. Seachris, Chichester and Malden, MA: Wiley-Blackwell, 62–78.

Nussbaum, M.C. (1990) *Love's Knowledge: Essays on Philosophy and Literature*, Oxford: Oxford University Press.

Ortega y Gasset, J. (1914/1961) *Meditations on Quixote*, trans. E. Rugg and D. Marin, New York: W.W. Norton.

Ortega y Gasset, J. (1930/1993) *The Revolt of the Masses*, New York: W.W. Norton.

Ortega y Gasset, J. (1932/1968) 'In Search of Goethe from Within', in *The Dehumanisation of Art and Other Essays on Art, Culture and Literature*, Princeton: Princeton University Press.

Ortega y Gasset, J. (1939/1968) 'The Self and the Other', in *The Dehumanisation of Art and Other Essays on Art, Culture and Literature*, Princeton: Princeton University Press.

Ortega y Gasset, J. (1943/1985) *Meditations on Hunting*, trans. H.B. Wescott, New York: Charles Scribner's Sons.

Parfit, D. (1984) *Reasons and Persons*, New York: Oxford University Press.

Paulin, R. (2016) *The Life of August Wilhelm Schlegel: Cosmopolitan of Art and Poetry*, Cambridge: Open Book Publishers.

Pereboom, D. (2002–3) 'Meaning in Life without Free Will', *Philosophic Exchange*, 33: 18–34.

Perkins, F. (2010) 'Of Fish and Men: Species Difference and the Strangeness of Being Human in *Zhuangzi*', *Harvard Review of Philosophy*, 16: 117–136.

Pindar (fifth century BCE/1995) 'The Nomos-Basileus Fragment', in *Early Greek Political Thought from Homer to the Sophists*, ed. M. Gargarin and P. Woodruf, Cambridge: Cambridge University Press.

Pisciotta, T. (2013) 'Determinism and Meaningfulness in Lives', PhD diss., University of Melbourne, https://minerva-access.unimelb.edu.au/handle/11343/38249.

Plato (fifth–fourth century BCE/1997) *Plato: Complete Works*, ed. J. Cooper, Indianapolis: Hackett Publishing Company.

Polt, R. (1999) *Heidegger: An Introduction*, Ithaca: Cornell University Press.

Popkin, R. (2003) *The History of Scepticism: From Savonarola to Bayle*, Oxford: Oxford University Press.

Preuss, P. (1987) 'Introduction' to J.G. Fichte's *The Vocation of Man*, trans. P. Preuss, Indianapolis: Hackett Publishing Company.

Putnam, H. (1986) 'Levinas and Judaism', in *The Cambridge Companion to Levinas*, ed. S. Critchley and R. Bernasconi, Cambridge: Cambridge University Press.

Quinn, P. (2000) 'How Christianity Secures Life's Meanings', in *The Meaning of Life in the World Religions*, ed. J. Runzo and N. Martin, Oxford: Oneworld Publications.

Rancière, J. (1995/1999) *Disagreement: Politics and Philosophy*, trans. J. Rose, Minneapolis: University of Minnesota Press.

Reginster, B. (2006) *The Affirmation of Life*, Cambridge, MA: Harvard University Press.

Rhys Davids, T.W. (trans.) (1890–94/1965) *Milindapañho*; trans. as *The Questions of King Milinda*, repr. edn, Oxford: Oxford University Press.

Robinson, M. (2008) 'Tieck: Kierkegaard's "Guadalquivir" of Open Critique and Hidden Appreciation', in *Kierkegaard and His German Contemporaries*, vol. 3: *Literature and Aesthetics*, ed. J. Stewart, Aldershot: Ashgate.

Rogers, B. (1999) *A.J. Ayer: A Life*, New York: Grove.

Rorty, R. (1989) *Contingency, Irony, and Solidarity*, Cambridge: Cambridge University Press.

Rorty, R. (2007a) 'Wittgenstein and the Linguistic Turn', in his *Philosophy as Cultural Politics*, Cambridge: Cambridge University Press.

Rorty, R. (2007b) 'Heideggerianism and Leftist Politics', in *Weakening Philosophy: Essays in Honour of Gianni Vattimo*, ed. S. Zabalo, Montreal: McGill-Queen's University Press.

Rorty, R. (2009) 'Pragmatism as Anti-authoritarianism' in *A Companion to Pragmatism*, ed. J. Shook and J. Margolis, Chichester: Wiley-Blackwell.

Rosenbaum, S.E. (1986) 'How to be Dead and Not Care: A Defense of Epicurus', *American Philosophical Quarterly*, 23(2): 217–225.

Rosenberg, A. (2011) *The Atheist's Guide to Reality*, New York: W.W. Norton.

Russell, B. (1922) *The Problem of China*, London: George Allen & Unwin.

Russell, B. (1945/2004) *History of Western Philosophy*, London: Routledge.

Russell, B. (1968) *The Autobiography of Bertrand Russell, Volume II: 1914–44*, London: George Allen & Unwin.

Ryle, G. (1949/2009) *The Concept of Mind*, Abingdon: Routledge.

Sartre, J.-P. (1938/1963) *Nausea*, trans. R. Baldick, London: Penguin.

Sartre, J.-P. (1943/2010) *Being and Nothingness*, in *Reading Sartre*, ed. J.S. Catalano, Cambridge: Cambridge University Press.

Sartre, J.-P. (1946/1958) 'Existentialism Is a Humanism', in *Existentialism from Dostoyevsky to Sartre*, ed. W. Kaufman, New York: Meridian Books.

Sartre, J.-P. (1952/2012) *Saint Genet: Actor and Martyr*, trans. B. Frechtman, Minneapolis: University of Minnesota Press.

Sartre, J.-P. (1960/2004) *Critique of Dialectical Reason, Volume One*, trans. A. Sheridan-Smith, London and New York: Verso.

Sartre, J.-P. (1971–72/1981–87) *The Family Idiot*, trans. C. Cosman, 5 vols., Chicago: Chicago University Press.

Sartre, J.-P. (1983/1993) *Notebooks for an Ethics*, trans. D. Pellauer, Chicago: Chicago University Press.

Sass, L. (1992) *Madness and Modernism: Insanity in the Light of Modern Art, Literature, and Thought*, Cambridge, MA: Harvard University Press.

Schipper, K. (1993) *The Taoist Body*, Berkeley: University of California Press.

Schlegel, F. (1798–1800/1971) 'Athenaeum Fragments', in *Lucinde and the Fragments*, trans. P. Firchow, Minneapolis: University of Minnesota Press.

Schlegel, F. (1799/1971) *Lucinde*, in *Lucinde and the Fragments*, trans. P. Firchow, Minneapolis: University of Minnesota Press.

Schlegel, F. (1800/1971) 'Ideen', in *Lucinde and the Fragments*, trans. P. Firchow, Minneapolis: University of Minnesota Press.

Schopenhauer, A. (1818/1966) *The World as Will and Representation, Volume I*, trans. E.F. J. Payne, New York: Dover.

Schopenhauer, A. (1844/1966) *The World as Will and Representation, Volume II*, trans. E.F. J. Payne, New York: Dover.

Schopenhauer, A. (1851a/1974) *Parerga and Paralipomena, Volume II*, trans. E.F.J. Payne, Oxford: Oxford University Press.

Schopenhauer, A. (1851b/1996) 'Additional Remarks on the Doctrine of the Vanity of Existence', in *Arthur Schopenhauer: Philosophical Writings*, ed. W. Schirmacher, trans. E. F.J. Payne, New York: Continuum.

Schwartz, B. (1985) *The World of Thought in Ancient China*, Cambridge, MA: Harvard University Press.

Seachris, J.W. (ed.) (2013) *Exploring the Meaning of Life*, Chichester: Wiley-Blackwell.

Searle, J. (1964) 'How to Derive "Ought" from "Is"', *Philosophical Review*, 73(1): 43–58.

Seneca (62–65 CE/2015) *Letters on Ethics*, ed. and trans. M. Graver and A.A. Long, Chicago: University of Chicago Press.

Sextus Empiricus (150–200 CE/2000) *Outlines of Scepticism*, ed. J. Annas and J. Barnes, Cambridge: Cambridge University Press.

Shakespeare, W. (1606/1997) *King Lear*, ed. G.K. Hunter, London: Methuen (Arden).

Shea, L. (2010) *The Cynic Enlightenment: Diogenes in the Salon*, Baltimore: Johns Hopkins University Press.

Singer, P. (1995) *How Are We to Live?* Amherst, NY: Prometheus Books.

Skempton, S. (2010) *Alienation After Derrida*, London: Continuum.

Sloterdijk, P. (1983/1987) *Critique of Cynical Reason*, trans. M. Eldred, Minneapolis: University of Minnesota Press.

Smuts, A. (2011) 'Immortality and Significance', *Philosophy and Literature*, 35: 134–149.

Soll, I. (2012) 'Nietzsche's Will to Power as a Psychological Thesis', *Journal of Nietzsche Studies*, 43(1): 118–129.

Spinoza, B. (1665/2016) *Letter to Oldenberg*, c. 1 October 1665 (Letter 30), in *A Spinoza Reader: The Collected Works of Spinoza, Volume II*, ed. and trans. E. Curley, Princeton: Princeton University Press.

Spinoza, B. (1670/2016) *Theological-Political-Treatise*, in *A Spinoza Reader: The Collected Works of Spinoza, Volume II*, ed. and trans. E. Curley, Princeton: Princeton University Press.

Spinoza, B. (1677/1985) 'Ethics', in *A Spinoza Reader: The Collected Works of Spinoza, Volume I*, ed. and trans. E. Curley, Princeton: Princeton University Press.

Stephens, W.O. (2007) *Stoic Ethics. Epictetus and Happiness as Freedom*, London: Continuum.

Strawbridge, D. and Strawbridge, J. (2010) *Self Sufficiency for the 21st Century*, London: Dorley Kindersley.

Strawson, G. (2017) 'Free Will and the Sense of Self', in *Buddhist Perspectives on Free Will*, ed. R. Repetti, London: Routledge.

Striker, G. (2010) 'Academics versus Pyrrhonists, Reconsidered', in *The Cambridge Companion to Ancient Scepticism*, ed. R. Bett, Cambridge: Cambridge University Press.

Stückrath, J. (2006) '"The Meaning of History": A Modern Construction and Notion', in *Meaning and Representation in History*, ed. J. Rüsen, New York andOxford: Berghahn Books.

Svolos, T. (2017) *Twenty-First Century Psychoanalysis*, London: Karnac,

Tarr, R. (2000) 'Introduction' to T. Carlyle's *Sartor Resartus*, ed. M. Engel and R. Tarr, Berkeley: University of California Press.

Tartaglia, J. (2016a) *Philosophy in a Meaningless Life*, London: Bloomsbury.

Tartaglia, J. (2016b) 'Is Philosophy All about the Meaning of Life?', *Metaphilosophy*, 47(2): 283–303.

Taylor, R. (1970) *Good and Evil*, Amherst, NY: Prometheus Books.

Thomas, L. (2005) 'Morality and a Meaningful Life', *Philosophical Papers*, 34(3): 405–427.

Tolstoy, L. (1882/2017) *My Confession* in *The Meaning of Life: A Reader*, 4th edn, trans. L. Wiener, ed. E.D. Klemke and S.M. Cahn, New York: Oxford University Press.

Trilling, L. (1967) *Beyond Culture*, Harmondsworth: Penguin.

Trisel, B.A. (2017) 'How Human Life Could Be Unintended but Meaningful: A Reply to Tartaglia', *Journal of Philosophy of Life*, 7(1): 160–179.

Useem, J. (2017) 'Power Causes Brain Damage', *The Atlantic*, July/August, www.theatlantic.com/magazine/archive/2017/07/power-causes-brain-damage/528711/.

Vattimo, G. (2007) *Nihilism and Emancipation: Ethics, Politics, and Law*, New York: Columbia University Press.

Velleman, J.D. (2005) 'Family History', *Philosophical Papers*, 34(3): 357–378.

Vida, E. (1993) *Romantic Affinities: German Authors and Carlyle*, Toronto: University of Toronto Press.

Vyāsa (c. fifth century BCE/1883–96) *The Maharabata of Krishna-Dwaipayana Vyasa*, trans. K.M. Ganguli, Calcutta: Bharata Press.

Wagner, N.-F. (forthcoming) 'Letting Go of One's Life Story', *Think*.

Walshe, M. (trans.) (1995) *Dīgha Nikāya*; trans. as *The Long Discourses of the Buddha*, Boston: Wisdom Publications.

Warren, J. (ed.) (2009) *The Cambridge Companion to Epicureanism*, Cambridge: Cambridge University Press.

Webber, J. (2018) *Rethinking Existentialism*, Oxford: Oxford University Press.

Weil, S. (1949/1971) *The Need for Roots*, trans. A. Wills, New York: Harper & Row.

Weil, S. (1951/1973) *Waiting for God*, trans. E. Craufurd, with introd. by L.A. Fiedler, New York: Harper & Row.

Weil, S. (1956) *The Notebooks of Simone Weil*, trans. A. Wills, London: Routledge & Kegan Paul.

Weil, S. (1957) *Intimations of Christianity among the Ancient Greeks*, trans. E.C. Geissbühler, London: Routledge & Kegan Paul.

Weil, S. (1968) *On Science, Necessity, and the Love of God*, trans. R. Rees, London: Oxford University Press.

Weil, S. (1970) *First and Last Notebooks*, trans. R. Rees, Oxford: Oxford University Press.

Weil, S. (1989–2006) *Oeuvres complètes*, 6 vols., ed. A.A. Devaux and F. de Lussy, Paris: Gallimard.

White, M.P. and Dolan, P. (2009) 'Accounting for the Richness of Daily Activities', *Psychological Science*, 20(8): 1000–1008.

Williams, B. (1973) 'The Makropulos Case: Reflections on the Tedium of Immortality', in his *Problems of the Self*, Cambridge: Cambridge University Press.

Williams, B. (1995) 'The Point of View of the Universe: Sidgwick and the Ambitions of Ethics', in his *Making Sense of Humanity*, Cambridge: Cambridge University Press.

Wilson, C. (2008) *Epicureanism at the Origins of Modernity*, Oxford: Oxford University Press.

Wilson, C. (2015) *A Very Short Introduction to Epicureanism*, Oxford: Oxford University Press.

Wittgenstein, L. (1914–51/1980) *Culture and Value*, ed. G.H. Nyman, trans. P. Winch, Oxford: Basil Blackwell.

Wittgenstein, L. (1922/1966) *Tractatus Logico-Philosophicus*, ed. D.F. Pears, trans. B.F. McGuiness, London: Routledge.

Wittgenstein, L. (1929/2014) *Lecture on Ethics*, ed. E. Zamuner, E.V. Di Lascio and D.K. Levy, Chichester: Wiley & Sons.

Wittgenstein, L. (1930/1979) *Ludwig Wittgenstein and the Vienna Circle: Conversations Recorded by Friedrich Waismann*, ed. B.F. McGuiness, Oxford: Blackwell.

Wittgenstein, L. (1930–37/2003) 'Diaries', in *Public and Private Occasions*, ed. J.C. Klagge and A. Nordmann, Lanham, MA: Rowman & Littlefield.

Wittgenstein, L. (1931/1996) 'Remarks on Frazer's Golden Bough', in *Wittgenstein: Sources and Perspectives*, ed. C.G. Luckhardt, trans. J. Beversluis, Bristol: Thoemmes Press.

Wittgenstein, L. (1933–35/1969) *The Blue and Brown Books: Preliminary Studies for the 'Philosophical Investigations'*, Oxford: Basil Blackwell.

Wittgenstein, L. (1938/1967) *Lectures and Conversations on Aesthetics, Psychology and Religious Belief*, ed. C. Barrett, Berkeley: University of California Press.

Wittgenstein, L. (1946–49/1980) *Remarks on the Philosophy of Psychology: Volume II*, ed. G.H. von Wright and H. Nymann, trans. C.G. Luckhardt and M.A. Aue, Oxford: Basil Blackwell.

Wittgenstein, L. (1953/1958) *Philosophical Investigations*, trans. G.E. Anscombe, Oxford: Basil Blackwell.

Wittgenstein, L. (1969/1975) *On Certainty*, ed. G.E. Anscombe and G.H. von Wright, trans. D. Paul and G.M. Anscombe, Oxford: Basil Blackwell.

Wolf, S. (1997a) 'Happiness and Meaning: Two Aspects of the Good Life', *Social Philosophy and Policy*, 14 (December): 207–225.

Wolf, S. (1997b/2017) 'Meaning in Life', in *The Meaning of Life: A Reader*, 4th edn, ed. E. D. Klemke and S.M. Cahn, New York: Oxford University Press.

Wolf, S. (2007/2010) 'The Meanings of Lives', in *Introduction to Philosophy: Classical and Contemporary Readings*, ed. J. Perry, M. Bratman and J. Fischer, 5th edn, Oxford: Oxford University Press.

Wolf, S. (2010) *Meaning in Life and Why It Matters*, Princeton: Princeton University Press.

Xunzi (third century BCE/2014) *Discourse on Ritual*, in *Xunzi: The Complete Text*, ed. and trans. E.L. Hutton, Princeton andOxford: Princeton University Press.

Young, J. (2002) *Heidegger's Later Philosophy*, Cambridge: Cambridge University Press.

Young, J. (2014) *The Death of God and the Meaning of Life*, 2nd edn, London: Routledge.

Zhuangzi (fourth–third century BCE-a/2001) *Chuang-Tzu: The Inner Chapters*, trans. A.C. Graham, Indianapolis: Hackett Publishing Company.

Zhuangzi (fourth–third century BCE-b/2009) *Zhuangzi: The Essential Writings*, trans. B. Ziporyn, Indianapolis: Hackett Publishing Company.

Index

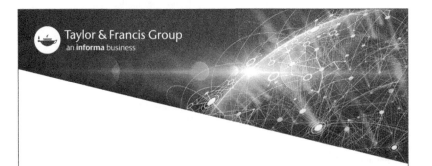